The Bilingual Child

How does a child become bilingual? The answer to this intriguing question remains largely a mystery, not least because it has been far less extensively researched than the process of mastering a single first language.

Drawing on new studies of children exposed to two languages from birth (English and Cantonese), this book demonstrates how childhood bilingualism develops naturally in response to the two languages in the children's environment. While each bilingual child's profile is unique, the children studied are shown to develop quite differently from monolingual children. The authors demonstrate significant interactions between the children's developing grammars, as well as the important role played by language dominance in their bilingual development.

Based on original research and using findings from the largest available multimedia bilingual corpus, the book will be welcomed by students and scholars working in child language acquisition, bilingualism and language contact.

VIRGINIA YIP is Professor in Linguistics and Modern Languages at the Chinese University of Hong Kong.

STEPHEN MATTHEWS is Associate Professor in Linguistics at the University of Hong Kong.

This book is supplemented by material available on the web at http://www.cuhk.edu.hk/lin/book/bilingualchild/

Cambridge Approaches to Language Contact

General Editors:
SALIKOKO S. MUFWENE,
University of Chicago

Editorial Board:
ROBERT CHAUDENSON, *Université d 'Aix-en-Provence*
BRAJ KACHRU, *University of Ilinois at Urbana*
LESLEY MILROY, *University of Michigan*
SHANA POPLACK, *University of Ottawa*
MICHAEL SILVERSTEIN, *University of Chicago*

Cambridge Approaches to Language Contact is an interdisciplinary series bringing together work on language contact from a diverse range of research areas. The series focuses on key topics in the study of contact between languages or dialects, including the development of pidgins and creoles, language evolution and change, world Englishes, code-switching and code-mixing, bilingualism and second language acquisition, borrowing, interference, and convergence phenomena.

Published titles
Salikoko Mufwene, *The Ecology of Language Evolution*
Michael Clyne, *The Dynamics of Language Contact*
Bernd Heine and Tania Kuteva, *Language Contact and Grammatical Change*
Edgar W. Schneider, *Postcolonial English*
Virginia Yip and Stephen Matthews, *The Bilingual Child*

Further titles planned for the series
Guy Bailey and Patricia Cukor-Avila, *The Development of African-American English*
Maarten Mous, *Controlling Language*
Clancy Clements, *The Linguistic Legacy of Spanish and Portuguese*

The Bilingual Child

Early Development and Language Contact

Virginia Yip

Chinese University of Hong Kong

Stephen Matthews

University of Hong Kong

CAMBRIDGE
UNIVERSITY PRESS

KH

CAMBRIDGE UNIVERSITY PRESS
Cambridge, New York, Melbourne, Madrid, Cape Town, Singapore, São Paulo

Cambridge University Press
The Edinburgh Building, Cambridge CB2 8RU, UK

Published in the United States of America by Cambridge University Press, New York

www.cambridge.org
Information on this title: www.cambridge.org/9780521544764

© Virginia Yip and Stephen Matthews 2007

First published 2007

Printed in the United Kingdom at the University Press, Cambridge

A catalogue record for this publication is available from the British Library

Library of Congress Cataloguing in Publication data
Yip, Virginia, 1962–
    The bilingual child: early development and language contact / Virginia Yip and
Stephen Matthews.
      p.   cm. – (Cambridge approaches to language contact)
Includes bibliographical references and index.
ISBN-13: 978-0-521-83617-3 (hardback)   .
ISBN-10: 0-521-83617-4 (hardback)
ISBN-13: 978-0-521-54476-4 (pbk.)
ISBN-10: 0-521-54476-9 (pbk.)
1. Bilingualism in children.   2. Language acquisition.   3. Languages in contact.
I. Matthews, Stephen, 1963–   II. Title.   III. Series.

P115.2.Y55   2007
404'.2083 – dc22   2007006787

ISBN 978-0-521-83617-3 hardback

ISBN 978-0-521-54476-4 paperback

10 / 13 / 09

For our children:

Out of the mouth of babes and sucklings hast thou ordained strength . . .

Psalm 8:2

「…從嬰孩和吃奶的口中建立了能力…」

詩篇第八章第二節

Contents

List of tables and figures   *page* ix
Series editor's foreword   xii
Preface   xiv
Acknowledgments   xvii
List of abbreviations   xxi

1   Introduction   1
   1.1   Introduction   1
   1.2   Research questions   5
   1.3   The ecology of bilingual development   7
   1.4   The Hong Kong speech community   9
   1.5   Bilingual development and language contact   12
   1.6   Mechanisms of language contact   14
   1.7   Summary   19
   1.8   Overview of the book   20

2   Theoretical framework   22
   2.1   Epistemological status of bilingual acquisition   22
   2.2   The logical problem of bilingual acquisition and the poverty of the dual stimulus   30
   2.3   Language differentiation in bilingual acquisition   33
   2.4   Language dominance in early bilingual development   35
   2.5   Cross-linguistic influence in bilingual development   37
   2.6   Input ambiguity and learnability   44
   2.7   Vulnerable domains in bilingual development   49
   2.8   Bilingual development and language contact   50
   2.9   Summary   54

3   Methodology   56
   3.1   Methodologies in the study of bilingual acquisition   56
   3.2   The Hong Kong Bilingual Child Language Corpus and other data for this study   63
   3.3   Quantitative measures of bilingual development: language dominance and MLU differentials   72
   3.4   Other indicators of language dominance   81
   3.5   Conclusions   84

4   *Wh*-interrogatives: to move or not to move?   87
   4.1   *Wh*-interrogatives in English and Cantonese   88
   4.2   *Wh*-interrogatives in bilingual children   93
   4.3   Emergence and order of acquisition of *wh*-phrases in English and
        Cantonese: bilingual and monolingual children compared   104
   4.4   Discussion: language dominance, input ambiguity and asymmetry 119
   4.5   *Wh*-in-situ in contact languages   123
   4.6   Conclusions   126

5   Null objects: dual input and learnability   133
   5.1   Null objects in adult Cantonese   134
   5.2   Null objects in English: cross-linguistic influence and learnability 136
   5.3   Input ambiguity and language dominance   147
   5.4   Null objects in Singapore Colloquial English   152
   5.5   Conclusions   152

6   Relative clauses: transfer and universals   155
   6.1   Introduction   155
   6.2   Development of pronominal relative clauses in the bilingual
        children   162
   6.3   The emergence of postnominal relatives in English   170
   6.4   Accounting for transfer   174
   6.5   Relative clauses in Singapore Colloquial English   181
   6.6   Conclusions   184

7   Vulnerable domains in Cantonese and the directionality
     of transfer   189
   7.1   Placement of prepositional phrases in bilingual children's
        Cantonese   190
   7.2   Dative constructions with *bei2* 'give' in bilingual children's
        Cantonese   200
   7.3   Bidirectional transfer in verb-particle constructions in bilingual
        development   216
   7.4   Conclusions   223

8   Bilingual development and contact-induced
     grammaticalization   227
   8.1   Contact-induced grammaticalization   228
   8.2   *Already* as marker of perfective aspect   235
   8.3   *Give*-passives and replica grammaticalization   239
   8.4   *One* as nominalizer   248
   8.5   Discussion   251

9   Conclusions and implications   255
   9.1   Theoretical issues   256
   9.2   Methodological issues   260
   9.3   Implications for first and second language acquisition   260
   9.4   Implications for language contact   261
   9.5   Prospects for future research   262

   References   265
   Index   287
   Author index   292

Tables and figures

Tables

1.1 English grammar in contact with Chinese at societal and individual levels *page* 13

1.2 Language contact phenomena at individual and societal levels 17

2.1 Syllable-final consonants in Cantonese and English 35

3.1 Background of six bilingual children 64

3.2 Number of files and number of child utterances produced by six children in the Hong Kong Bilingual Child Language Corpus 67

3.3 Mean MLU and MLU differentials in six bilingual children 80

4.1 Distribution of English *wh*-in-situ questions in Timmy, a bilingual child and Eve, a monolingual child 97

4.2 English in-situ *what* and *where* questions in six bilingual children 102

4.3 Developmental order for English *wh*-words in monolingual children 105

4.4 Developmental order for Cantonese *wh*-words in eight monolingual children in Cancorp 105

4.5 Age of first emergence of English *wh*-words in four Cantonese-dominant bilingual children 106

4.6 Age of first emergence of Cantonese *wh*-words in four Cantonese-dominant bilingual children 106

5.1 Frequency of null objects in the English of a monolingual child, Adam 139

5.2 Frequency of null objects with seven transitive verbs in the English of a monolingual child, Adam 139

5.3 Frequency of null objects with five transitive verbs in the English of six bilingual children 142

5.4   Frequency of null objects in the Cantonese of two
      bilingual children, Timmy and Sophie   143
5.5   Distribution of null objects in English verb-particle
      constructions in six bilingual children   144
5.6   Distribution of null objects in English verb-particle
      constructions in two monolingual children, Peter and
      Allison   145
6.1   Age of first emergence of subject and object relative
      clauses in Cantonese and English diary and corpus data in
      three bilingual children   162
7.1   Placement of Cantonese locative PPs with *hai2* 'at' in six
      bilingual children   194
7.2   Placement of Cantonese locative PPs with *hai2* 'at' in
      eight monolingual children in Cancorp   195
7.3   Placement of Cantonese locative PPs with *hai2* 'at' in six
      bilingual and six monolingual children   195
7.4   Non-target placement of Cantonese locative PPs with *hai2*
      'at' in six bilingual children   196
7.5   Distribution of locative PPs with *hai2* 'at' in two adult
      Cantonese corpora and the Hong Kong Bilingual Child
      Language Corpus   198
7.6   Frequency of Cantonese full *bei2* 'give' datives in six
      bilingual children   206
7.7   Frequency of Cantonese full *bei2* 'give' datives in eight
      monolingual children in Cancorp   207
7.8   Age of first emergence of Cantonese full *bei2* 'give'
      datives in six bilingual children   209
7.9   Age of first emergence of Cantonese full *bei2* 'give'
      datives in eight monolingual children in Cancorp   209
7.10 Distribution of lexical NPs and pronouns in four
      Cantonese-dominant bilingual children's English
      verb-particle constructions   221
7.11 Distribution of lexical NPs and pronouns in two
      non-Cantonese-dominant bilingual children's English
      verb-particle constructions   221
7.12 Distribution of lexical NPs and pronouns in the English
      verb-particle constructions in two monolingual children,
      Peter and Allison   222

Figures

2.1 Relationship between cross-linguistic influence and
     transfer   *page* 38
2.2 Structural overlap between two grammatical systems   47
2.3 Input ambiguity within a grammar   47
2.4 Input ambiguity with two languages in contact   47
3.1 Sample English transcript at age 2;10;15   69
3.2 Sample Cantonese transcript at age 1;10;16   70
3.3 Timmy's MLU (2;01;22–3;06;25)   76
3.4 Sophie's MLU (1;06;00–3;00;09)   77
3.5 Alicia's MLU (1;03;10–3;00;24)   78
3.6 Llywelyn's MLU (2;00;12–3;04;17)   78
3.7 Charlotte's MLU (1;08;28–3;00;03)   79
4.1 Longitudinal development of Timmy's English
     what-in-situ questions (2;01–3;06)   98
4.2 Frequency of English in-situ *what* and *where* questions in
     six bilingual children   99
5.1 Percentage of null objects in the English of a bilingual
     child, Timmy   140

Series editor's foreword

The series *Cambridge Approaches to Language Contact* was set up to publish outstanding monographs on language contact, especially by authors who approach their specific subject matter from a diachronic or developmental perspective. Our goal is to integrate the ever-growing scholarship on language diversification (including the development of creoles, pidgins and indigenized varieties of colonial European languages), bilingual language development, code-switching and language endangerment. We hope to provide a select forum to scholars who contribute insightfully to understanding language evolution from an interdisciplinary perspective. We favour approaches that highlight the role of ecology and draw inspiration both from the authors' own fields of specialization and from related research areas in linguistics or other disciplines. Eclecticism is one of our mottoes, as we endeavour to comprehend the complexity of evolutionary processes associated with contact.

We are very proud to add to our list *The Bilingual Child: Early Development and Language Contact* by Virginia Yip and Stephen Matthews, a most authoritative book that combines the latest scholarship on language contact and child language development in a multilingual setting. It has the distinction of being based on the most extensive longitudinal database on the subject matter to date, involving a relatively large population of children studied over a long period of time, and contributing to the relevant research areas insights from an examination of typologically and genetically quite unrelated languages: Cantonese and English. Three of the protagonists are the authors' own children, whose speech constitutes the core and largest part of the database. These data are compared with those obtained from children in similar bilingual families, in inter-peer interaction settings which generated the most naturalistic and reliable data an investigator can collect. This book presents findings from this unique gold mine.

Students of various aspects of language contact must be asking any subset of the following questions and others: Are children really perfect language learners? If they are, do they manage to keep separate the systems of the different languages to which they are concurrently exposed? If they are not, to what extent do their transfer phenomena differ from those of adult L2 learners? What particular insights can the study of such a population contribute to scholarship on community-based language contact phenomena, such as the emergence of creoles and indigenized Englishes? Can the labels 'L1' and 'L2' apply to situations of bilingual child development, or is it more appropriate to speak of 'dominant' and 'subordinate' languages? Are these situations inherently different from those in which the child is exposed to different dialects of the same language? Will having a dominant language affect the direction of transfer from one language to the other? Is there some sort of division of labour in the way one language influences the other, for instance, morphology in one case but syntax in the other, one particular aspect of syntax in one language but another in the other language? What is the role of the social ecology in determining language dominance in bilingual children? In such populations, to what extent does one child replicate another, and under what particular conditions?

These are among the many questions that Virginia Yip and Stephen Matthews address in this exciting book. Even if some readers disagree (on some details) with the authors, they will find substantive information and theoretical challenges prompting them to rethink their own positions. In my own personal case, with my own bias that 'language acquisition' is a misnomer for what is otherwise a 'system-construction' process by the learner, I have enjoyed learning more about how competition and selection operate in a multilingual feature pool and what ecological factors influence the young learner's selections. I am more convinced now that language boundaries are more real to the linguist than they are to the speaker, although the latter aims at speaking one rather than the other language on a particular occasion. There must also be some constraints on how elements from separate languages can be combined into a new system (not necessarily along the lines sought by students of code-switching), and *The Bilingual Child* addresses this kind of issue. By the same token it seems necessary to distinguish between, on the one hand, features imported intact from the other language into the one intended to be spoken and, on the other, those modifications that are taking place in a particular language because the structures of the languages in contact are partly congruent.

This book, to which I do more justice by enumerating some of the questions it addresses than by attempting to summarize, is a rich addition, with new sets and kinds of data, to the literature on language contact. I am sure most scholars tired of repetitions of the same kinds of data that do not question established positions will be happy with *The Bilingual Child*, especially because its tenor is also non-polemical. I feel especially privileged that the authors chose Cambridge Approaches to Language Contact as the venue to disseminate their findings.

Salikoko S. Mufwene, *University of Chicago*

Preface

Compared to mastering a single language, the process of becoming bilingual in the child's first few years of life has been much less comprehensively studied, and therefore remains all the more enigmatic and intriguing. The title of this book, *The Bilingual Child*, is intended to refer generically to a child who learns two languages in early childhood. The book tells the stories of how six children became bilingual in Cantonese and English given exposure to both languages from birth. We provide a detailed account of how childhood bilingualism develops naturally in response to the two languages in their environment. This intimate account is presented through our dual perspectives as parent-researchers continuously observing and participating in our own three children's bilingual experience.

Parents and researchers alike often raise basic questions such as the following about children's bilingual development:

- Are two languages too many for a child?
- Do children confuse the two languages?
- Can they be equally proficient in both?
- If children have a 'language instinct' as has often been suggested, how does this instinct cope with two languages at the same time?

While the book reports an abundance of research findings, we also hope to alleviate some typical concerns of parents and demonstrate that two languages are not a burden for a child, and that children have the ability to differentiate the two languages from early on. They can develop high proficiency in both, though one language may develop ahead of the other. To account for this ability we appeal to a *bilingual instinct* which enables the child to develop two languages in response to dual input in the environment. With developing knowledge of two languages, young bilingual children are able to produce language forms and functions of stunning complexity as a result of integrating features from two grammars. We shall show that the product often comes about through the interaction of two language systems, reflecting language-specific properties and universal factors.

Though the children studied grow up bilingually in Hong Kong, their experience should in many ways transcend the specificities of this particular context and speak to the bigger picture of how children become bilingual. The findings reported here are based on a large-scale multimedia corpus which documents the bilingual development of the six children from age one to four and a half and is now in the public domain. Many of the examples discussed in the book come to life when heard or seen on digitized audio and video files, demonstrating the interactions of the bilingual children in real-life contexts. We have also made use of diary data collected by ourselves in the case of our own children. The combination of corpus and diary data yields a rich database from which the strength of our arguments is derived.

Though each bilingual child's linguistic and cultural background as well as developmental profile is unique, the process they go through shows some common features that set them apart from monolinguals in interesting ways. In children with one language developing ahead of the other, features of the stronger language often find their way into the grammar of the other language. But the interaction is by no means a one-way street: features of the weaker language also influence the grammar of the stronger language in certain respects. Thus transfer in both directions is found in bilingual development.

Our sub-title, *Early Development and Language Contact*, represents an interdisciplinary effort to integrate insights from two fields. The two languages to be learned may be said to be in contact in the bilingual child's environment as well as in the mind of the child. Throughout the bilingual child's development, there are clear and systematic signs that the two language systems interact with each other, shaping the child's overall development. Looking beyond bilingualism at the individual level, we draw parallels between bilingual development in children with bilingual and multilingual communities. In cases such as those of Singapore Colloquial English, Hawaiian Creole English and other creole languages, contact between languages gives rise to new languages with similar features to those we observe in children's bilingual development. A second theme of this book is therefore that of languages in contact. We know that languages influence each other. But how does this actually happen? What does the development of bilingual children tell us about the interaction of the languages in contact? Do bilingual children themselves play a role in spreading features from one language to another? To illustrate these possibilities, we shall see that the English our bilingual children produced bears striking similarity to the English spoken in Singapore, known as Singapore Colloquial English, which is born of a multilingual situation in which several varieties of Chinese are prevalent in the environment. This suggests that the way Chinese and English interact in the mind of the child may shed light on the way the same two languages have interacted in multilingual societies such as Singapore.

In the age of globalization, contact between individuals and between communities has become intensified and the bilingual experience will become the norm in many children's early development. In writing this book we hope to raise the awareness of the assets of being bilingual and help bilingual children to affirm and appreciate their dual heritage – especially those born of parents from two different languages and cultures.

The process of language development has often been described as an odyssey, suggesting a journey full of mystery and excitement. We invite the reader to share the highlights of our discovery in the bilingual child's journey toward active bilingualism in the following chapters.

Acknowledgments

The research findings reported in this book come from a series of projects that have spanned over a decade of work, beginning serendipitously when our first bilingual child was born. The gestation period for this book has necessarily been a long one, as it took some seven years to produce three bilingual children and another few years to put our ideas together and write up the book. It has taken three 'co-authored' bilingual children to witness the process of bilingual development in a close and intimate manner. When we see the structures appear in the first, then the second, and followed by the third child, it is immensely gratifying to confirm the pathway taken by these children on their way to bilingualism. We feel compelled to share what we have observed with interested readers.

We thank Salikoko Mufwene for welcoming this book to the CALC series. Sali has been a source of immense inspiration and support as editor and scholar in many interdisciplinary fields. His meticulous comments have rendered our book much more readable and coherent. Brian MacWhinney has been indefatigable in his pursuit of excellence: we thank him for being the architect behind our multimedia bilingual corpus, his interest in bilingual acquisition and his constructive comments on our manuscript.

Thanks are due to many leading scholars working in different frameworks ranging from emergentism to generative grammar for discussing our work with us, notably Joan Bybee, Stephen Crain, Fred Genesee, François Grosjean, Usha Lakshmanan, Jürgen Meisel, Johanne Paradis, Bonnie Schwartz, Carmen Silva-Corvalán, Rosalind Thornton and Marilyn Vihman. William O'Grady, whose unusually wide spectrum of scholarly expertise spans these frameworks has generously offered insightful comments and suggestions on the entire manuscript. We would like to pay special tribute to the late Rudolf de Rijk, who together with Virginia de Rijk-Chan, produced the definitive Basque Grammar, and whose interest in Cantonese grammar and appreciation of our work has been most inspiring.

We are grateful for the opportunity to present our work at the Max Planck Institute for Evolutionary Anthropology in Leipzig, where we thank Mike Tomasello for his kind invitation and Angel Chan, Peter Cole, Bernard Comrie,

Stefan Gries, David Gil, Martin Haspelmath, Gabriella Hermon, Elena Lieven and Daniel Stahl for stimulating discussion. At the Research Centre for Linguistic Typology at La Trobe University in Melbourne we thank Bob Dixon and Sasha Aikhenvald, Randy LaPolla, Dory Poa and Peter Bakker for their hospitality and helpful feedback. At the Society for Pidgin and Creole Linguistics, we have benefited from discussion with Dany Adone, Bao Zhiming, Adrienne Bruyn, Clancy Clements, Genevieve Escure, Claire Lefebvre, Sarah Roberts and Armin Schwegler. We had the privilege of presenting different chapters at various institutions and international conferences at which we have benefitted from discussion and feedback: Beijing Foreign Studies University, Cornell University, Guangdong University of Foreign Studies, Max Planck Institute of Evolutionary Anthropology, University of British Columbia, University of Hawaii, University of Oregon, University of Southern California, the International Symposium on Contemporary Linguistics, International Symposium on Bilingualism, Second Language Research Forum, and the Language Acquisition and Bilingualism Conference in Toronto.

We thank our former Research Assistants and graduate students who have contributed to our projects. It has been our pleasure working with these young talents at both of our universities. At the Chinese University of Hong Kong: Angel Chan, Winnie Chan, Lawrence Cheung, Gene Chu, Chloe Gu, Simon Huang, Victoria Lam and Linda Peng Ling Ling. Uta Lam has been tremendously resourceful and reliable in her technical support. Graduate students at the University of Hong Kong have included Betty Chan, Chen Ee San, Stella Kwan, Regine Lai, Bella Leung, Ingrid Leung, Michelle Li, Richard Wong and Emily Yiu. Further contributions have come from students from the Cognitive Science Programme at the University of Hong Kong: especially Antonio Cheung, Helen Ching, Samantha Ho, Elaine Lau and Fiona Leung.

We thank our mentors William Rutherford, Jacqueline Schachter, Bernard Comrie and John Hawkins, who have nurtured our interest in grammar, language typology, processing, language acquisition and learnability. Over the years we have enjoyed the friendship and fruitful collaboration of many colleagues, especially Umberto Ansaldo, Lisa Cheng, Samuel Cheung Hung-Nin, Mary Erbaugh, Huang Yue Yuan, Shin Kataoka, Cream Lee, Li Ping, Li Wei, Lisa Lim, Yasuhiro Shirai, Siok Wai Ting, Rint Sybesma, Tan Li Hai, Tang Sze-Wing, and the phenomenal team at CUHK: Gu Yang, Jiang Ping, Thomas Hun-Tak Lee, Gladys Tang and Yap Foong Ha.

This book could not have been written without the unwitting support of our children Timmy, Sophie and Alicia. We thank Kathryn, Llywelyn and Charlotte, their parents and caregivers who participated in our longitudinal study. We thank the Almighty God for the gift of all these wonderful bilingual children. Members of the extended Yip family have been backing us up every step of the way with their powerful prayers and unlimited support. We express our deepest gratitude to each of them, the children's grandmother Liu Yuk Chun, grandparents Jan and Alan Matthews, their uncles and aunts: Patrick Yip and Linda Lee, Peggy Yip, Dan Yip and Kennis Lam, their cousins: Lulu, Kasen and Darren for providing the best possible nurturing environment for the children to grow up in. We would like to take the opportunity to congratulate Timmy on being awarded first prize by the HKSAR government as 'Hong Kong Budding Poet 2005–06' and 'Poet of King George V School'. We feel blessed and privileged to have combined our research with family life, spending quality time with our children, participating in the recording sessions and keeping a precious diary record of their language development. The vivid images and cheerful laughter that come with the documentation of their childhood bilingualism will be preserved as an indelible testament for posterity. It is difficult to think of a more rewarding research topic than to study one's own children.

Finally we have been fortunate to enjoy the support of our institutions and their funding organizations. The research reported in this book is fully supported by a series of grants from the Research Grants Council of the Hong Kong Special Administrative Region, China (Project Nos. HKU336/94H, CUHK4002/97H, CUHK4014/02H and CUHK 4692/05H) and direct grants from the Chinese University of Hong Kong (2001/02, 2003/04).

July 2006, Hong Kong

Parts of chapters 1 and 2 were first published as 'Early bilingual acquisition in the Chinese context', in the *Handbook of East Asian Psycholinguistics* Vol. I, ed. Ping Li, Li-Hai Tan, Elizabeth Bates and Ovid Tzeng, Cambridge University Press (Yip 2006, pp. 148–162). Some materials in chapter 3 were published as 'Assessing language dominance in bilingual acquisition: a case for Mean Length Utterance differentials', in *Language Assessment Quarterly* (Yip & Matthews 2006, 3: 97–116). An earlier version of chapter 5 was published as 'Dual input and learnability: null objects in Cantonese-English bilingual children', in *Proceedings of the 4th International Symposium on Bilingualism*, eds. James Cohen, Kara McAlister, Kellie Rolstad and Jeff MacSwan, Cascadilla Press (Yip & Matthews 2005, pp. 2421–2431). Parts of chapter 6 were published as 'Relative clauses in early bilingual development: transfer and universals', in *Typology and Second Language Acquisition*, ed. Anna Giacalone Ramat, Mouton de Gruyter (Matthews & Yip 2002, pp. 39–81) and 'Relative clauses in Cantonese-English bilingual children: typological challenges and processing motivations', in *Studies in Second Language Acquisition* (Yip & Matthews 2007, 29: 277–300).

All of the above chapters are reprinted here in substantially revised versions with the kind permission of Cambridge University Press, Lawrence Erlbaum Associates, Cascadilla Press and Mouton de Gruyter. The picture of Sophie Matthews, Alicia Matthews and Virginia Yip on the book cover appeared in the 30 September 2003 issue of East Week magazine, published in Hong Kong and is reproduced with the kind permission of the publishers.

Abbreviations

APS	Argument from the Poverty of the Stimulus
ASP	aspect marker
BFLA	Bilingual First Language Acquisition
BSLA	Bilingual Second Language Acquisition
Cancorp	The Hong Kong Cantonese Child Language Corpus
CHAT	Codes for the Human Analysis of Transcripts
CHI	child
CHILDES	Child Language Data Exchange System
CL	classifier
CLAN	Computerized Language Analysis
COP	copula verb
CP	complementizer phrase
CPE	Chinese Pidgin English
CRD	Constituent Recognition Domain
DEM	demonstrative
DO	direct object
DOC	double object construction
DP	determiner phrase
DUR	durative marker
EC	empty category
HCE	Hawaiian Creole English
HKCAC	The Hong Kong Cantonese Adult Language Corpus
IL	interlanguage
INT	interjection
INV	investigator
IO	indirect object
IP	inflectional phrase
LF	Logical Form
L1	first language
L2	second language
MLU	Mean Length of Utterance

MLUw	Mean Length of Utterance in words
Mx	grammatical category x in a model language M
N	noun
NOM	nominalizer
NP	noun phrase
NPAH	Noun Phrase Accessibility Hierarchy
OV	object verb
PASS	passive
PFV	perfective
POSS	possessive
PP	prepositional phrase
PRED	predication marker
PRT	particle
PTCP	participle
R	recipient
RC	relative clause
RVC	resultative verb complement
Rx	grammatical category x in a replica language R
S	subject
SAI	subject – auxiliary inversion
SCE	Singapore Colloquial English
SFP	sentence-final particle
SLA	second language acquisition
SLI	Specific Language Impairment
SVC	serial verb construction
SVO	subject verb object
T	theme
TRS	transitive verb
UG	Universal Grammar
V	verb
VAC	verb-adverb construction
VO	verb object
VP	verb phrase
VPC	verb-particle construction
2sg	second person singular
3sg	third person singular

Conventions used in the examples taken from the transcripts

| [>] | overlap follows |
| # | pause between words |

< >	repetition of words in the utterance
[//]	retracing with correction
[/]	a speaker begins speaking, stops and then repeats the earlier material
xxx	unintelligible string of words

1   Introduction

Mother: Daddy hai6 me1 jan4 aa3? 'What's Daddy's nationality?'
Child: Ing1gok3jan4 'English person.'
Mother: Jing1gok3jan4 'English person.'
Child: Ing1gok3jan4 'English person.'
        Maa1mi4 hai6 zung1gok3jan4 'Mummy is Chinese.'
Mother: Timmy hai6 me1 jan4 aa3? 'What about Timmy?'
Child: Bilingual!   (Timmy 2;00;14)

1.1   Introduction

Talking to a young bilingual child can be both entertaining and eye-opening.
Even at the tender age of two, the bilingual child is capable of expressing
complex ideas, having two languages at his disposal as seen in the above
exchange between Timmy and his mother (the first author). Timmy refers to his
father as *ing1gok3jan4* 'English person', his mother as *zung1gok3jan4* 'Chinese
person' and he surprises everyone, not least his mother, by referring to himself as *bilingual*.[2] Apart from raising deep issues of awareness of identity, this
exchange epitomises an important phenomenon typical of a bilingual child,
namely that he is in contact with two languages on a daily basis.

What is it like being a bilingual child? How do children cope with learning
two languages simultaneously in the first years of life? Many children, like
those of cross-cultural marriages, grow up in families where more than one
language is spoken on a regular basis. Their parents may each speak a different
language natively, thus exposing these children to two languages from birth.
The principal protagonists of this book are three siblings born in such a family
where the mother is a native speaker of Cantonese (the first author) and the
father of British English (the second author). As the parents of the children, we
have the advantage of observing their language development on a daily basis,
making a first-hand eye-witness account possible. As linguists specializing in
language acquisition and language contact respectively, we have followed our
bilingual children's emerging language from their first forms of vocalization to

mastery of complex syntax. Following their linguistic odyssey in these golden years of language acquisition, one can only wonder at the inexorable process of acquisition gradually unfolding before our eyes and ears. With the help of modern technology, their language development over time has been captured and recorded in the form of audio and video-recordings. The corpus containing these three siblings' transcriptions of longitudinal recordings from the age of 1;03 and 3;06 forms the primary empirical basis for the present study. Known as the *Hong Kong Bilingual Child Language Corpus*, it documents the longitudinal development of a total of six bilingual children growing up in Hong Kong and is available via the *Child Language Data Exchange System* (CHILDES).[3] At the time of writing, it was the largest multimedia bilingual corpus and also 'the largest corpus of linked video data on child language development available in any language (in CHILDES)' (Brian MacWhinney p.c.).[4] In addition, we have kept our own diary of our observations of their progress. Taken together, we have assembled not only an endless repertoire of anecdotes, but also a wealth of data which provide compelling evidence for a set of propositions about these children's bilingual development, including the following:

* While the two languages are differentiated from early on, there is strong evidence for syntactic transfer and interaction between the two linguistic systems developing in the mind of the bilingual child.
* There are principles determining the direction of transfer and mechanisms which account for how it takes place: these include *language dominance*, *developmental asynchrony* and *input ambiguity*. The cross-linguistic influence evidenced in the bilingual development is bidirectional, going primarily from the *dominant language* to the *non-dominant language* but in certain domains also from the non-dominant to the dominant language. We shall refer to the non-dominant language as weaker language interchangeably throughout the book.
* The developmental patterns in bilingual individuals parallel and reflect prominent features of contact varieties, such as *Singapore Colloquial English*, spoken by a community of adult bilingual speakers at the societal level. This comparison in turn sheds light on processes and mechanisms of language contact at large.

This book presents a series of case studies in early bilingual development involving a so far largely unstudied and divergent pair of languages, Cantonese and English, focusing on some features which shed light on the nature and processes of bilingual development. This is the first systematic longitudinal study of Cantonese-English bilingualism in childhood covering the children's language development in the first three years, extending to five and beyond in some cases. Just as bringing a wider range of languages into consideration changes our view of what is possible in human languages, so it promises to change our view of what is possible in language development. The bulk of previous research on bilingual development in the period from zero to three years has been focused on European languages. The languages in both classic and recent longitudinal studies include Indo-European language pairs such as English – German (Leopold 1939–1949, Döpke 1992), English – Dutch (De Houwer 1990), English – Norwegian (Lanza 2004), English – Spanish (Deuchar & Quay 2000), French – German (Ronjat 1913, Meisel 1990, 1994), French – Serbian (Pavlovitch 1920) and German – Italian (Taeschner 1983).[5] Of the thirty-odd longitudinal studies listed by Hoffman (1991), from Ronjat (1913) to De Houwer (1990), all but four involved Indo-European language pairs; notable exceptions include Smith (1931; 1935),[6] the first case study involving Chinese and English, and Vihman (1985) on English-Estonian bilingual development. Chang-Smith (2005) compares the development of a Mandarin-English bilingual child with that of a monolingual Mandarin-speaking child in a study of nominal expressions in Mandarin. These studies have been revealing in many respects, but in terms of global linguistic diversity, they have investigated only a tiny fraction of the possible language combinations a child might be faced with. The ways in which a typologically divergent language pair such as Cantonese and English differ open up possibilities for interaction which would not exist with other language pairs. The numerous fundamental contrasts between the two languages provide potential for cross-linguistic influence and transfer in various grammatical domains of acquisition which form the focus of our case study. The study of bilingual development involving a Chinese language will contribute to diversification of language pairs in the study of childhood bilingualism, providing a new window for viewing developmental processes and pathways and enriching both the theoretical investigation and empirical coverage of early bilingual acquisition.

1.1.1 Practical and cognitive implications

The study of this particular language pair is also of growing practical importance, since the number of bilingual families with children speaking English and Cantonese, Mandarin or another Chinese language is on the rise in the twenty-first century. They represent a significant population of children around the world who share similar bilingual experiences as our children in this study. At a more general level, the study of Cantonese-English bilingual development can be seen as an instantiation of bilingual development in a broader sense: what is observed here should be to some extent generalizable to other cases of bilingual development.

Another category of children who are drawing increasing attention from the international academic community is that of adopted children whose language development before and after adoption has become an intriguing domain of inquiry. Recent years have seen the rising number of international adoptions around the world, with China being the number one source of children adopted into the United States. Many of the adoptees from China into American families leave their home at infancy before age two or three and have to acquire a 'second first language' (Pollock, Price & Fulmer 2003; Roberts et al. 2005). In monolingual English-speaking homes, it is likely that these children's first language, Chinese, will gradually be lost while English takes the place of Chinese as their first language (Nicoladis & Grabois 2002). For those adopted into homes with Chinese spoken regularly and English in the community, some form of bilingualism is likely to develop, with both Chinese and English acquired together. Questions arise as to whether these constitute cases of bilingual or child second language acquisition (as discussed in chapter 2). Similarly, preschool immigrant children who move from Chinese-speaking communities to an English-speaking country or vice versa will have the opportunity to develop childhood bilingualism. Li and Lee (2002) investigate the development of Cantonese in British-born Chinese-English bilinguals and report delayed and stagnated development of Cantonese due to incomplete learning of their L1 Cantonese and influence of English, a dominant language in the environment. The present study may shed light on language acquisition by these populations given that a Chinese language and English are involved across these acquisition contexts. A recent study of childhood bilingualism in Korean immigrant children in America by Shin (2004) shows that the children 'follow similar but delayed patterns of first language acquisition of Korean and second language acquisition of English' (Shin 2004: 12), while bidirectional influence is found, with L1 Korean influencing the development of L2 English which in turn influences the development of Korean.

At the general level, childhood bilingualism offers many cognitive advantages for the developing bilingual child. From the perspective of cognitive development and language processing, Bialystok (2001) examines various linguistic and cognitive consequences of developing two languages in childhood, discussing the potential contribution of childhood bilingualism in illuminating the nature of linguistic knowledge, organization of cognitive processes and the functional structure of the brain. Among the issues covered are developmental issues in language acquisition, metalinguistic awareness, literacy and problem solving. She explores and highlights the complexities and intricacies that make the empirical study of bilingual development so challenging, arguing that bilingual children are different from monolinguals in the way they acquire language and concluding that 'The vast majority of cognitive differences were advantageous to the bilingual children' (Bialystok 2001: 232). Her views also echo Grosjean's (1989) insight that 'bilinguals are not two monolinguals in one'. According to Grosjean's holistic view of bilingualism, the bilingual is not the sum of two complete or incomplete monolinguals but an integrated whole with a unique linguistic profile.

1.2 Research questions

Acquiring two languages in childhood holds endless fascination for lay people and specialists alike. As the leading American structuralist Leonard Bloomfield (1933: 29) remarked, the acquisition of language 'is doubtless the greatest intellectual feat any one of us is ever required to perform'. If a child's acquisition of a language is a miracle, then acquiring two at the same time is doubly so. Given that our children have become fluent speakers of two languages in the space of a few years, one cannot help but wonder how they accomplish this feat. Language acquisition by children has been compared to natural and effortless activities like walking and recognizing faces which in fact involve complex mental processes and mechanisms. The naturalness and inevitability of the outcome is compared to the perception of solid objects and attention to line and angle by Chomsky (1965: 59). The ability of the child to acquire language is what Pinker (1994) calls the 'language instinct': knowledge of language is not acquired as a result of teaching, but is to a large extent attributable to the human innate capacity for language acquisition. The field of first language acquisition has been far from unanimous regarding what exactly is attributed to nature vs. nurture, which will continue to be one of the central themes of debate in the years to come. We remain open as to how to characterize this language instinct. While Chomsky and Pinker see the language instinct as specific to the language faculty, an alternative possibility is that articulated by Bates and MacWhinney (1989: 10):

The human capacity for language could be both innate and species-specific, and yet involve no mechanisms that evolved specifically and uniquely for language itself. Language could be viewed as a new machine constructed entirely out of old parts.

This alternative view espouses explanations that are not domain-specific, but encompass general cognition, processing and neuro-cognitive functions as new research findings continue to challenge much of our received wisdom. We do not venture to take a definitive position on which aspects of knowledge of language are derived from domain-specific innate Universal Grammar and which from domain-general mechanisms. The issue of how to characterize the nature of linguistic knowledge will be further discussed in chapter 2.

In the present context of bilingual development, we shall refer to the *bilingual instinct*, the language instinct given full expression in the simultaneous acquisition of two languages by children. It is simply human, and totally natural, for the bilingual child to acquire both languages in response to the dual input in the environment. Compared with acquiring one language in monolingual contexts, the acquisition of two languages in bilingual or multilingual contexts poses even more challenges to the child on many grounds, beginning with the fact that the quantity of input in each language is necessarily reduced by around one half (cf. Paradis & Genesee 1996). We shall show that the processes involved in the simultaneous construction of two grammars in the child's mind are inherently different from that of constructing one grammar only. Bilingual children often take a different path from the monolingual counterparts to reach the target, as is clearly instantiated in the case studies discussed in the following chapters.

The questions we address in this work include the following:

- How does bilingual development differ from acquisition of the same two languages by monolingual children?
- Do the two languages develop independently or do they interact systematically? Is there evidence for transfer or cross-linguistic influence? What factors determine the direction of transfer?
- What can the linguistic features of bilingual children's developing languages reveal about more general processes in language acquisition and language contact?

In studying our own children we are following a time-honoured tradition beginning with the classic studies of Ronjat (1913) and Leopold (1939–49). Ronjat (1913) inaugurated Grammont's principle, *une personne, une langue*, i.e. the one parent – one language approach in addressing the bilingual child.[7] Ronjat's longitudinal study of his own son Louis' development in French and German is generally considered the earliest bilingual study in the twentieth century (see Hoffmann 1991: 50–53). Werner Leopold, a professor of German with the combined passion of a father and a developmental psychologist, recorded the bilingual development of his daughters Hildegard and Karla in German and English, culminating in the monumental work *Speech Development of a Bilingual Child: A Linguist's Record* published in four volumes between 1939 and 1949 and containing over eight hundred pages of intense and close observation of bilingual development in early childhood. Without the help of a tape recorder, Leopold recorded his daughters' speech data in the form of a diary with extensive commentaries on specific linguistic features. Leopold's linguistic study of early bilingual development remains unparalleled in terms of the comprehensive coverage of the details of a child's simultaneous acquisition of two languages. Even today, Leopold is held in high esteem as one of the founding fathers of the study of bilingualism as well as of child language at large. Leopold felt that the study of child language would reveal much about general principles of language and language change: 'every pattern of grammar, every process of language shows up in child language in a nascent state, in coarser, more tangible shapes, compressed into a much shorter time and therefore more accessible to observation'. Leopold's legacy will always remain a source of inspiration and serve as an important reference for case studies in bilingual development.

Building on the foundations established by our predecessors and inspired by their vision, we have conducted a longitudinal study of our own children using the recording techniques and apparatus available and feasible at the time. The case-study approach continues to be fruitful: contemporary studies in the field of bilingual development include De Houwer's (1990) study of a Dutch-English bilingual child, Lanza's (2004) case study of two bilingual children from Norwegian-American families and Deuchar and Quay's (2000) study of Deuchar's English-Spanish bilingual daughter, all of which fall squarely in this tradition of longitudinal case studies.

We are convinced that the advantages of studying one's own children outweigh the disadvantages. The advantages include:
- privileged access to the children throughout, and beyond, the period of study;
- first-hand knowledge of the children's environment and experiences;
- the unique dual status of linguists and parents (doubled in the case of both parents being linguists);

Among these advantages, it is only thanks to the diary data that we are able to document the emergence of English prenominal relative clauses, which are scarcely found in the regular longitudinal recordings. We shall see, in the case study of relative clauses (chapter 6), how shared knowledge between parent and child is a prerequisite for the felicitous use of this construction. We also take responsibility for ethical issues such as privacy (and trust that our children will understand). The drawbacks include:
- potential for subjectivity (for example, in selection and transcription of diary data);
- enhanced potential for rich interpretation of the data (for example, in attributing more advanced knowledge to the children than they have actually demonstrated);
- the Observer's Paradox, whereby the very presence of the observer changes the situation being observed (Labov 1972).

A poignant example of the Observer's Paradox is the case of the parent-researcher going away to record in the diary what the child has just said, thereby interrupting the conversation and changing the course of events. There is inevitably a trade-off here since one needs to record the utterances while they are still fresh in the mind, within seconds or minutes of the utterances being produced.

1.3   The ecology of bilingual development

The social context in which acquisition takes place to a large extent determines the input to the child and the outcome. This is especially important in bilingual and multilingual contexts where the nature and quantity of input in each language, and the prevailing attitudes to each, all contribute to determining processes and outcomes of development. For example, the prevalence of code-mixing in children's language depends on both its occurrence in the adult input, and adult attitudes to it (Lanza 2004).

The notion of ecology, applied by Mufwene (2001) primarily to the evolution of languages in contact, is equally applicable to the development of individual bilingualism.[8] Ecology here begins as a metaphor from biology: the environment in which languages are spoken determines the course of development of languages, much as habitats determine the evolution and fate of species in competition with each other. This point is undoubtedly applicable even to monolingual contexts:[9] for example, social factors such as prestige may determine the selection of variant forms leading to sound change (Nettle 1999). It is still more salient and important, however, in determining the outcomes of language contact situations such as those discussed by Mufwene (2001), and the cases of bilingual development at issue here. This is because the range of variants from which linguistic options may be selected (the 'feature pool' in Mufwene's terms, see chapter 2) is so much wider compared to monolingual contexts. In the case of a bilingual environment, the feature pool is in principle doubled, or even (to the extent that code-mixing and intermediate options exist) more than doubled. In the case of creoles:

> The ethnographic ecology . . . affected the role of the external structural ecology toward more, or less, influence, as it determined the particular conditions under which it was possible for a language to influence the restructuring of the target language. (Mufwene 2001: 161)

Ecology in this sense refers to the social environment in which a language is spoken. The external ecology of a language encompasses all other languages with which its speakers come into contact, the number of speakers of each language and their social status. Mufwene (2001: 21–24) further extends the notion of ecology to internal factors affecting the evolution of language. Within languages, 'Linguistic features in a system also constitute part of the ecology for one another' (Mufwene 2001: 22). Internal ecology in this sense is again analogous to a related concept in biology where ecology can be taken as internal to a species. For example, dialectal variation and co-existent systems within a language all impact the evolutionary trajectory of a language.

In the context of bilingual development, internal ecology involves the competition between, and selection of, variants available in language systems (with some variants being made available through transfer from another language system). Consider, for example, the acquisition of *wh*-interrogatives as discussed in chapter 4. Between ages two and three, the child has two forms of *wh*-question competing with each other (Yip & Matthews 2000a: 199):

(i) The target *wh*-movement represented in the input, as in *What is this for?*
(ii) The *wh*-in-situ form transferred from Cantonese, as in *This is for what?*
With the external ecology (input from adult speakers of English) supporting option (i), our bilingual children eventually select option (i) over (ii). Given a community of bilingual speakers using option (ii), however, the child might select the *wh*-in-situ form (ii) instead, or allow both forms to co-exist. Just such a community of bilingual speakers exists in the case of contact varieties such as Singapore Colloquial English, as discussed in chapter 4.

1.4　　The Hong Kong speech community

The children of the present study were born and raised in Hong Kong. Cantonese is the community language of Hong Kong spoken by around 90% of its residents.[10] According to figures given in the entry [Chinese, Yue] in the *Ethnologue* (Gordon 2005: 331), native speakers of Yue dialects (the dialect group to which Cantonese belongs) in all countries amount to some 55 million, ranking 16th in the top 100 languages by population. A former British colony for over 150 years, Hong Kong continued to recognize English as an official language, along with Cantonese and Mandarin, after the handover of sovereignty to China in 1997. The official language policy of Hong Kong is for its citizens to be 'biliterate and trilingual', speaking Cantonese, Putonghua and English and being literate in both English and standard written Chinese.

Among Hong Kong people who are ethnic Chinese, Cantonese is the lingua franca. In the Hong Kong Chinese community, many children like our own grow up in an extended family situation (as they do in Singapore, cf. Gupta 1994). Since the relatives speak primarily Cantonese, the children's everyday environment provides more input in this community language than in English.

It should be noted that Cantonese is essentially a spoken language. To the extent that Cantonese is written down at all, it is heavily affected by standard written Chinese, which is based on Mandarin. A tradition of vernacular literature exists using Chinese characters to represent Cantonese as it is spoken, but such writing has low status (Snow 2004). Many colloquial morphemes in Cantonese do not have a corresponding character in the written language, though attempts have been made to standardize usage and fill the gaps (Cheung & Bauer 2002). Reference works on Cantonese grammar include Cheung (1972), Matthews and Yip (1994) and Yip and Matthews (2000b, 2001).

In this book, we are solely concerned with the acquisition of the spoken language, leaving aside the acquisition of literacy in bilingual development.[11] Many aspects of Cantonese and Mandarin child language development, including both spoken language and literacy, are covered in Li et al. (2006).

Like individual speakers, bilingual communities including Hong Kong are best characterized along a continuum of bilingualism. In a multilingual community such as Hong Kong, it is common to speak of bilingualism as a matter of degree. Parents, for example, may discuss children's bilingualism using code-mixing:

(1)   Keoi5 go3 zai2 zan1hai6 hou2 *bilingual* gaa3
       she   CL son really   very bilingual SFP
       'Her son is really very bilingual.'

A commercial radio station advertised its bilingualism in similar terms:

(2)   Disc jockey 1: Next, we have bilingual news.
       Disc jockey 2: Hai6 aa3, hou2 *bilingual* aa3
                      is   PRT very bilingual SFP
                      'Yes, very bilingual.'

Compared to Singapore, for example, the use of English in the Hong Kong speech community is relatively restricted: it is used widely in secondary and higher education, the higher courts and international companies, but rarely on the street, or even in markets or shopping malls, outside typical tourist haunts. Much more widely used than pure English is code-mixing, in which English terms (such as *bilingual* in the above examples) appear within a Cantonese sentence structure (Li 1996; B. Chan 1998; 2003). With a long history of contact between English and Cantonese, code-mixing has been a ubiquitous phenomenon in educated Hong Kong speech (Li & Lee 2004).

In Hong Kong, as in Singapore, Chinese dialects other than Cantonese form part of the picture, typically being spoken by older relatives as well as recent immigrants from mainland China. In the case of our own children, the Chaozhou dialect is spoken by their grandmother and relatives of her generation and above; the children had some passive knowledge of it, but produced it rarely, usually for jocular effect. For example, inserting a Chaozhou phrase produces a trilingual utterance:

(3)   Gong2 Ciu4zau1 waa2 is *puah lok k'u*, fall down. [laughs]
       'Speaking in Chiu Chow, *puah lok k'u* means "fall down".'
                                                      (Timmy 2;02;10)

For the most part, influence of other southern Chinese dialects on English will be similar to that deriving from Cantonese: all Chinese dialects exhibit certain broad typological traits such as *wh*-in-situ, null arguments and prenominal relative clauses, all of which will be central to our analyses of the bilingual children's syntactic development. In certain domains, however, the roles of different dialects can and should be differentiated. Min dialects of Chinese such as Hokkien and Chaozhou (known as *Teochew* in Singapore) are particularly divergent, and may account for specific features of Singapore Colloquial English (SCE). For example, questions of the form 'X or not?' produced by Singaporean children were recorded by Kwan-Terry (1986) and Gupta (1994: 127):

(4)   You got automatic or not?   (EG 5;08)

Questions of this form [*X or not?*] are limited in Mandarin and in Hong Kong Cantonese, but in southern Min dialects such as Hokkien and Chaozhou constitute the dominant form of yes/no question:

(5)   U   tsi   a   bo?   (Chaozhou)
        have money or   not
        'Do you have money?'

Questions of the form *X or not?* as in (4) therefore specifically reflect influence from the Min dialects as in (5) which are the predominant substrate languages in Singapore. They are not found in our own children's Cantonese or English, despite their passive exposure to Chaozhou, presumably because this interrogative structure is not 'ecologically nurtured' in Mufwene's terms: that is, it is instantiated only in a minority dialect which lacks prestige and of which the children have at best passive knowledge.

Another part of the language ecology involves domestic helpers. In Hong Kong, professional couples typically employ live-in helpers, who play an important role in the children's upbringing. At the time of the study most domestic helpers came from the Philippines, speaking English with varying degrees of proficiency; increasingly they have been joined by Thai and Indonesian helpers who often speak Cantonese rather than English, thus changing the ecological balance. The children pick up a few words and phrases of Tagalog and other Philippine languages, often from overhearing domestic helpers' conversations, and may produce them as a kind of language game (our daughter Sophie, for example, liked to use the Tagalog word *maganda* 'beautiful'). The Filipina helpers speak to the children in some form of English interlanguage, however, and their English is thus a potentially important ecological factor. In households where the parents speak Cantonese and the Filipina helper provides the sole source of English input, the English acquired by the children may bear some Tagalog characteristics. In families such as those of our children where a native speaker of English provides input, the domestic helpers' English seems to have rather less effect than might be expected given their major role as caregivers. A number of factors may be relevant here which could limit their role as speech models:

1. The repertoire of exchanges between children and helpers tends to be limited, typically focused on daily routines;
2. The children may be conscious that the helpers are not fully proficient English speakers;
3. Children may be conscious of the low socio-economic status of the helpers.

A final point on the children's environment is that Mandarin or Putonghua plays almost no role as far as children's language input is concerned. Although use of Mandarin has increased since the resumption of Chinese sovereignty over Hong Kong in 1997, it is still rarely heard in the majority of homes. Mandarin lessons are given in primary school, but these begin later than the crucial period of language acquisition (up to around age five) with which we are concerned.

1.5   Bilingual development and language contact

A central theme of the book is the relationship between bilingual development and language contact, mirroring a growing trend in recent studies drawing together the fields of bilingualism and second language acquisition on the one hand and the field of contact linguistics on the other hand (Montrul 2004, Sánchez 2004, Toribio 2004).

Languages may be said to be in contact at two levels:

(a) In the individual speaker/hearer,

(b) In a bilingual speech community.

The term 'language contact' today generally refers to (b), whereby languages spoken in close proximity in the speech community are the focus of inquiry. Weinreich (1953) however also considered language contact at the individual level. His seminal work foreshadows many important theoretical concepts central to current studies of second language acquisition and bilingualism, such as transferability and permeability. He also recognized that these individual-level phenomena are mechanisms of cross-language influence in contact situations. Whether at the individual level or at the community level, languages influence each other in interesting ways.

Having developed into distinct fields, language acquisition research and the study of language contact have proceeded largely in isolation from each other, though there have been some noteworthy attempts to link the two fields, such as Schumann (1978), Bickerton (1981), Andersen (1983a) and most recently DeGraff (1999). In the context of pidgin and creole linguistics, Arends, Muysken and Smith (1994) suggest that some cross-fertilization may be overdue here:

Assumptions are often made about second language learning, interference, relexification, etc, which are not based on what has come to be known about these processes. In the areas of acquisition, code-switching and mixing, borrowing, and bilingual processing tremendous progress has been made, which has not had sufficient effect on the scenarios around, it seems. (Arends, Muysken & Smith 1994: 330)

From the perspective of individual bilingualism, Romaine (1996) makes a similar point, leading to an insight which motivates situating our case study in the wider context of language contact:

Table 1.1. *English grammar in contact with Chinese at societal and individual levels*

	Singapore Colloquial English (Gupta 1994)	Hong Kong bilingual children (diary data, this study)
Interrogatives: is it . . . ?	Is it come? (EB 7;08)	Is it works? (Sophie 3;08)
Wh-in-situ	And I go where? (YB 4;06)	Put in where? (Sophie 3;08)
Relatives: [RC . . .] one	My this can change one ah (EB 5;11)	The . . . blow the flute that one? (Sophie 5;03)
Conditionals: X then Y	Mummy, you didn't-you didn't buy Care Bear, then ah, then you don't have ticket. (EG 4;03)	Eat so much this, then got sore throat. (Sophie 3;03)
Passives: give NP verb	John give his boss scold. (Bao & Wee 1999: 5)	Here is give Timmy scratch. (Sophie 3;06)

EB, YB, EG and MP are initials of (anonymous) individual children in Gupta's study.

Linguists who study language contact often seek to describe changes at the level of linguistic systems in isolation and abstraction from speakers. Sometimes they tend to treat the outcome of bilingual interaction in static rather than dynamic terms, and lose sight of the fact that *the bilingual individual is the ultimate locus of language contact.* (Romaine 1996: 573, our emphasis)

Lightfoot (1999) adopts a relevant position of 'methodological individualism' which he attributes to Jon Elster (1993: 8): one should 'study the individual human action as the basic building block of aggregate social phenomena'. Just as Lightfoot argues that language change is best understood as an aggregate of changes in individual grammars, we take a similar view that the processes and effects of language contact are best revealed by detailed study of developing individual grammars. To accomplish this, we shall compare the data from our Hong Kong bilingual children with data from contact languages such as Singapore Colloquial English. We begin with the observation that the *effects* of interaction in the two cases can be strikingly similar. Table 1.1 shows how a number of features of Singapore Colloquial English are paralleled in our Hong Kong bilingual children.

While Singapore Colloquial English represents the contact language most closely parallel to our study of bilingual development, another case is offered by Hawaiian Creole English (HCE) which is relevant in at least two respects:
(i) Cantonese, the dominant language for the children of our case study was (together with the structurally similar Hakka dialect) one of the major substrate languages spoken by immigrants to Hawaii in the nineteenth century (Reinecke 1969);

(ii) It has been shown that children of immigrants were typically bilingual, speaking their parents' languages as well as the locally developing form of English (Roberts 1998, 2000).

More specifically, a number of grammatical features in HCE have been attributed to Cantonese influence. Siegel (2000: 212) notes that *get* is used in existential as well as possessive senses both in SCE and in HCE:

(6)   Get wan wahine shi get wan data.
        'There is a woman who has a daughter.'

Here the first *get* has the existential sense 'there is' while the second has possessive sense 'has', like the Cantonese verb *jau5*, which has both the existential and possessive senses. The same goes for serial verbs with 'come/go' (Roberts 1999):

(7)   Bring the book come.
        'Bring the book here.'

The point is not merely that HCE has serial verbs (many creoles do) but that it uses a specific type of serial verb with a directional function as in the Cantonese equivalent (Matthews 2003: 5):

(8)   Daai3 bun2 syu1 lai4
        bring CL   book come
        'Bring the book here.'

To the extent that we find parallels or overlap between bilingual development and the putative cases of substrate influence, Siegel's argument is strengthened. Substrate influence, which has often been considered mysterious and controversial, can be seen in progress as in the case of SCE and HCE. Conversely, we have evidence that the kind of interaction we observed in bilingual development can, given a favourable ecology, result in a contact language in which those features are retained.

1.6   Mechanisms of language contact

The deeper interest of comparisons such as those drawn above between bilingual development and language contact lies in what individual bilingualism may reveal about the *mechanisms* by which language contact phenomena come about. In a recent review, Thomason (2001: 148) mentions bilingual first language acquisition as one of seven mechanisms of contact-induced change. She notes that in situations of widespread bilingualism, any combination of the following factors could be operating:
1. Code-switching
2. Code alternation

3. Passive familiarity
4. 'Negotiation' (approximation)
5. Second language acquisition strategies (interference/transfer)
6. Bilingual first language acquisition
7. Deliberate decision (language planning/engineering)

Noting that the question has been relatively little studied to date, Thomason cites a number of examples to suggest that bilingual first language acquisition may play a role as a mechanism of change. In French-German bilingual children, for example, the frequency of certain French word orders (also found in monolinguals) is increased as a result of German influence. Such individual-level effects could be one mechanism by which structural influence takes place on a community level. Elaborating on this possibility, Thomason notes that it depends on whether there is interaction between the child's developing grammatical systems:

Bilingual L1 acquisition, by its nature, can lead to contact-induced change only where there are deviations from adult norms in one language as a result of interference from the other language. (Thomason 2003: 32)

To expand on Thomason's observations, let us consider a parallel case involving contact between French and Dutch. In a case study of French-Dutch bilingual development, Hulk and van der Linden (1996) argue that the child's Dutch influences her French quantitatively, raising the frequency of object fronting. The following French examples from Hulk and van der Linden (1996: 98) illustrate object fronting:

(9)   La carte de mami tu vois
        'the card of granny you see'   (Anouk 2;11;27)

(10)   Une maison et une tour Eiffel je fais
        'a house and an Eiffel tower I make'   (Anouk 3;01;04)

In these examples the object of the verb, such as in *la carte de mami* 'the card of granny' in (9) and *une maison et une tour Eiffel* 'a house and an Eiffel tower' in (10), is 'fronted' so that it appears before the subject. Although monolingual children also produce such object fronting, the bilingual children do so more frequently and in a wider range of contexts, which may be attributed to the occurrence of object verb (OV) as a basic order in Dutch. The authors go on to note that fronting of objects is also observed in the varieties of French spoken in Brussels and Strasbourg, under Germanic influence:

We might argue that . . . just as in the variety of French spoken by the French/Dutch bilingual girl Anouk, it is the contact with superficially similar OV patterns in the 'other' language – Dutch in Brussels and German in Strasbourg – that has an influence on the acceptability and the frequency of the non-standard object fronting in these varieties of French. (Hulk & van der Linden 1996: 99)

We shall observe comparable quantitative influences on word order in our bilingual children. While the more salient, qualitative influence is from Cantonese syntax to English (see chapters 4–6), there is also evidence of quantitative effects from English to Cantonese, notably in the case of prepositional phrases, and dative constructions (chapter 7). In these cases structural precedents exist in Cantonese, but the bilingual children make more extensive and protracted use of them under English influence.

These findings in bilingual development suggest an individual-level mechanism for language contact phenomena which have often been described in terms of *convergence*. The term 'convergence' describes the phenomenon whereby languages which are in contact with each other tend to become similar and to share particular properties. Appeals to convergence have often been seen as mysterious and thus questionable: with regard to language areas, for example, 'the term "convergence" is used as a kind of shorthand for "there is no evidence about how this areal feature arose"' (Thomason 2001: 90). Silva-Corvalán (1994: 4–5), examining processes involved in language change by analysing the Spanish spoken by Mexican-American bilinguals in Los Angeles, argues that convergence results from language transfer interacting with internally motivated language change.

Mufwene (2001: 22) also raises problems concerning the notion and instead invokes the notion of *congruence*, denoting degrees of matching or isomorphism between language systems as a synchronic factor favouring retention or expansion of a given structural feature. In the context of creole development, those features of the substrate language(s) which have (at least partially) matching counterparts in the lexifier are especially likely to be incorporated into the developing creole. In ecological terms, if the option is already available in the lexifier, then the substrate language provides a favourable ecology for the selection of that particular option.

In our study, a number of mechanisms invoked to account for several quantitative and qualitative effects of bilingualism will also be possible mechanisms of contact-induced change. These mechanisms include Bilingual Bootstrapping (Gawlitzek-Maiwald & Tracy 1996) and input ambiguity (Müller 1998; Hulk & Müller 2000) as outlined in chapter 2. Input ambiguity arises where 'two different grammatical hypotheses are compatible with the same surface string' (Müller 1998: 153) and the hypothesis adopted by the learner is one provided by the other language being acquired. Unlike language dominance which exerts a unidirectional influence, effects of input ambiguity are observable in both directions: from Cantonese to English in the domain of null objects (chapter 5), and from English to Cantonese in the placement of *hai2* 'at' prepositional phrases and order of the two objects in dative constructions with *bei2* 'give' (chapter 7).

Other processes we observe at work in bilingual development have counterparts in language contact and change. Table 1.2 suggests some of these parallels.

Table 1.2. *Language contact phenomena at individual and societal levels*

	Micro-processes in bilingual individuals	Macro-processes in bilingual communities
Lexical	code-mixing	borrowing
Grammatical	transfer	substrate influence
	bilingual bootstrapping	grammaticalization
		convergence
Developmental	language acquisition	pidginization
		creolization
	language attrition	language shift

The lexicon provides a clear example of this relationship between micro- and macro-processes, though not one with which we will be concerned directly. English words enter Cantonese in the speech of code-mixing bilingual speakers, as in *ni1 go3 case* 'this case . . .' Eventually code-mixed words become assimilated to Cantonese and are described as instances of lexical borrowing (thus *case* gives rise to the loan word *kei1si2*, with lexical tones assigned).

At the grammatical level, with which we are primarily concerned, we observe syntactic transfer in individual speakers, as in the relatively straightforward case of *wh*-in-situ (see section 1.2 above and chapter 4). At the societal level, families or groups shifting from a Chinese dialect to English may 'assimilate' the same transferred structures, which are then observable as substrate features. Like convergence as discussed above, substrate influence has often been seen as mysterious or epistemologically dubious (Lass (1997) associates it with 'Contact Romantics' who see effects of contact wherever they look). It may be mysterious in cases where nothing is known about the putative substrate languages, but hardly so when it can be observed directly in generations of families undergoing language shift. In Singapore Colloquial English (SCE) a typical substrate feature is seen in conditional sentences marked with *then* such as *you didn't buy Care Bear, then ah, then you don't have ticket* produced by a Singapore child (see table 1.1) and *You put up there, then how to go up?* produced by an adult Singaporean (Gupta 1994: 11). The role of bilingual children in the evolution of conditional constructions in SCE is discussed by Chen (2002, 2003).

1.6.1   Contact-induced grammaticalization

Another area in which individual processes underlie those taking place in a speech community is grammaticalization, as it is observed in creole languages and other language contact situations. Several creolists have noted that while grammaticalization is conventionally viewed as a language-internal process, it often appears to involve contact: 'what at first sight looks like internal grammaticalization may well be due to influence from other languages as well' (Arends, Muysken & Smith 1994: 120). That is, grammaticalization of a lexical item may proceed by calquing based on a structure already grammaticalized in another language. Bruyn (1996) suggests a mechanism for essentially this process, which she terms 'apparent grammaticalization', in contact situations:

I. Grammaticalization of item X has already occurred in language A;
II. Item Y in language B is identified with item X (on the basis of its lexical meaning);
III. The range of functions of item X (some being lexical and others grammatical) is transferred to item Y.

Stages II and III of this mechanism invoke processes which have been widely studied at the individual level in the field of Second Language Acquisition, namely interlingual identification (as in II) and language transfer (III) as discussed for example by Selinker (1992). This overlap would again suggest that studying the phenomenon at the level of individual development should shed light on larger scale developments in contact languages.

These points are instantiated in our study of ontogenetic grammaticalization of 'give' in bilingual children (chapter 8). From being the verb 'give' as in (11) and (12) it develops via the permissive (13) and (14). Sophie further extends give to the passive as in (15) and (16).

I. Lexical 'give'

(11)   I give you. I want to watch this one. [holding video]   (Sophie 2;05)

(12)   You give me that one, one only. [pointing to after-shave]

(Sophie 2;06)

II. Permissive 'give'

(13)   Daddy I give you see. [appearing in swimsuit]
        [i.e. I let you see]   (Sophie 3;04)

(14)   If Timmy don't give me to play this one, then I not be her brother.
        [i.e. 'If Timmy doesn't let me play this one I won't be her sister.']
        (Sophie 3;07)

III. Give-passives

(15)   Here is give Timmy scratch. [points to scratched leg]
        [i.e. Here I was scratched by Timmy]   (Sophie 3;06)

(16)   Daddy, I already give the mosquito to bite. [shows bite on tummy]
        [i.e. I've been bitten by a mosquito]   (Sophie 4;09)

The outcome here is parallel to the *give*-passive in SCE (Bao & Wee 1999: 5) as in (17).

(17)   John give his boss scold.
         [i.e. John was scolded by his boss]

This is one of a number of competing passive constructions in SCE and clearly calqued on the *give*-passive of southern Chinese dialects such as Hokkien as in (18), see Bao and Wee (1999: 7):

(18)   Ah Hock Tapai   hor   lang   me
         Ah Hock always give   people scold
         'Ah Hock always gets scolded by people.'

Thus the development of *give*-passives in the case of the individual child parallels that at the level of the speech community. Naturally, the cases again differ in the subsequent course of development: as we shall see in chapter 8, Sophie, lacking a community of speakers to nurture the *give*-passive, moves beyond this stage to acquire the target English passives.

1.7   Summary

In this introductory chapter we have laid out the overall background to the present study of Cantonese-English bilingual development, posing the major research questions and raising the important theoretical issues that are addressed in this book. To recapitulate:

1. How and why does the development of grammar in bilingual children differ from that observed in their monolingual counterparts?
2. What light does bilingual development shed on language contact phenomena such as substrate influence and contact-induced grammaticalization?

The case studies of our bilingual children serve to illuminate the nature and general processes underlying bilingual development and illustrate how mechanisms of transfer at the individual level find their expression at the societal level. The study of bilingual development is thus linked up with the study of language contact, and ontogeny with language evolution.

In discussing language change and language contact, Sebba (1997: 34) remarks that creoles 'compress "the centuries of slow evolution" into just one or two decades, as they originate from pidgins and go through rapid changes to become fully-fledged languages complete with native speakers'. As we shall argue, what takes decades to develop as a distinct variety of English in a community actually can develop naturally in the bilingual children in a matter of a few years. Alongside the 'vanishing voices' of endangered languages (Nettle & Romaine 2000), the 'emerging voices' of new languages are arising through language contact. Both processes are results of the ecology of language evolution, as Mufwene (2001) makes clear.

1.8   Overview of the book

The theoretical framework that embeds the empirical findings in our case studies is presented in chapter 2, drawing together the fields of bilingual development and language contact. The methods of data collection, corpus construction and subject information are discussed in chapter 3 followed by an investigation of a number of transfer phenomena with Cantonese as the dominant language influencing English, the non-dominant language: *wh*-interrogatives in chapter 4, null objects in chapter 5 and relative clauses in chapter 6. The question of direction of influence is investigated in chapter 7 in three areas which are shown to involve 'vulnerable' domains: influence from English to Cantonese is seen in the placement of prepositional phrases with *hai2* 'at' and the order of objects in dative constructions with *bei2* 'give', while in the case of verb-particle constructions bidirectional influence is evidenced. Chapter 8 discusses the ontogenetic developments that parallel contact-induced grammaticalization, focusing on the analysis of *already*, *give* and *one* in the bilingual children's English. The development of these transfer-based phenomena in English will be examined and shown to reflect mechanisms of language contact. The highlights of our findings are presented in chapter 9 together with some implications for future research in bilingual acquisition.

NOTES

1. The age specification 'a;bb;cc' represents the age of the child in years, months and days. Thus (Timmy 2;00;14) indicates that Timmy was at age 2 years, zero months and 14 days when this dialogue was recorded. The formula is sometimes abbreviated to 'a;bb' (years and months), such as when generalizing about a developmental period.
2. The child repeats the non-target form *ing1gok3jan4* with the first syllable *ing1* lacking the initial glide [*j*] as in *jing1gok3jan4* despite the mother's use of target form immediately after the first appearance of the child's non-target form. The non-target syllable *ing1* could be attributed to influence from English, or from the Chaozhou dialect as spoken by the child's maternal grandmother. The word *gok* 'country' shows a sound change from [kw] to [k].
3. The Hong Kong Bilingual Child Language Corpus can be accessed at http://childes. psy.cmu.edu/
4. As Director of CHILDES, Professor Brian MacWhinney highlighted 'the qualitative jump afforded by full linked digitization' in our corpus, noting that it is 'currently the most complete and state-of-the-art corpus in the field of childhood bilingualism' (letter dated October 20, 2004).

5. Only book-length studies are included here, inevitably leaving out many important studies in bilingual acquisition covering the first three years.
6. Smith's (1935) study of eight bilingual children from the same family, based on diary data, concerned factors including sentence length, grammatical errors, English inflection and language mixing. The children had English-speaking missionary parents and acquired Chinese when growing up in China with Chinese-speaking servants and children. See also Section 3.1.3.
7. Grammont was a linguist who advised Ronjat that separating the two languages from infancy would help the child to learn both without confusion (see Lanza 2004).
8. Ecology as a factor in child second language acquisition is also invoked by Pallotti (1996) in a longitudinal ethnographic study of a 5-year-old Moroccan child acquiring Italian in an Italian nursery. Her study investigates the process of language socialization in its ethnographic context.
9. Roeper's notion of 'universal bilingualism' refers to the fact that since monolingual speakers have tacit knowledge of some range of lects and variants, their linguistic competence includes distinct 'mini-grammars' which constitute a form of bilingualism. For example, informal registers of English allow null subjects as in *sounds good to me*, which implies a different parameter setting from formal English (Roeper 1999: 173).
10. Cantonese is spoken by 89% of the people aged five or above according to the Population Census conducted by the Census and Statistics Department, HKSAR in 2001 (see http://www.info.gov.hk/censtatd/).
11. Different aspects of literacy development in Chinese children and the effects of bilingualism on the acquisition of literacy are discussed in McBride-Chang (2004). Processes underlying the reading of Chinese and English are compared in Tan and Perfetti (1998) while neurolinguistic aspects of Chinese bilingual children's reading abilities are investigated in Tan et al. (to appear).

2 Theoretical framework

Father: Why doesn't Alicia speak English?
Child: He's bigger first. Then he know already.[1]
['Once she's bigger, then she'll know how.']
M4hou2 gaau3 keoi5, keoi5 daai6 go3-zo2 zau6 sik1-zo2
['Don't teach her, when she's bigger she'll just know how.']
(Sophie 5;03;02)

At the time of the above dialogue, Alicia at age one understands English but does not produce it, while already producing recognizable words in Cantonese. Such a 'silent period' is a common situation in bilingual children, as discussed in chapter 3, and one indication that one of the child's languages is dominant. As her elder sister Sophie has worked out by age five, somehow Alicia will grow up to be bilingual just like her, without actually being taught. Sophie even has a 'theory' of how this happens, which she elaborated on another occasion: children who hear each parent speaking a different language reply in the same language, becoming bilingual as a matter of course.

This chapter presents a theoretical framework within which we embed the central issues discussed in the book. We first raise and discuss theoretical issues concerning the epistemology of bilingual first language acquisition in relation to child second language acquisition (section 2.1) and the logical problem of bilingual acquisition (section 2.2). We then discuss central research issues in bilingual acquisition including language differentiation (section 2.3), language dominance (section 2.4), cross-linguistic influence (section 2.5), input ambiguity and learnability (section 2.6) and vulnerable domains (section 2.7). The synergistic relationship of bilingual development and language contact is addressed in section 2.8, and a summary is presented in section 2.9.

2.1 Epistemological status of bilingual acquisition

Does the bilingual child have two first languages, or one first language plus one second language? If the bilingual child acquires another language in addition to the two original languages, is that language a second language or third language? These are some of the challenging issues that the field of bilingual acquisition is confronted with. The list of questions goes on: do the two languages develop at the same rate and in similar ways as in monolingual children? Are they two fully or partially differentiated systems from the beginning? Do they develop independently or do they interact with each other? To what extent is the development of a bilingual child's two languages similar to that of a child learning a second language?

2.1.1 Bilingual acquisition and second language acquisition

To term one of the bilingual child's languages a second language would imply that it has the same nature and status as the second language of a child/adult L2 learner who has already acquired at least one language. However, this is still very much an open question: as Thomason (2001: 51) puts it, do young children learn a second language as if it were a first language? By extension, do young children learn two languages as if they were both first languages learned individually? As implied by the above questions, the relationship between bilingual acquisition and second language acquisition (SLA), and the distinction between them, have been recurrent points of controversy. We consider this as a question of epistemology: what is the nature of the knowledge of each language being acquired and represented by the learner? Schwartz (1986) has raised this fundamental question that has important consequences for theory and research in second language acquisition: what is the content of the notions 'first' and 'second' language, in terms of processes of development and representation of knowledge? Similarly, a coherent theory of bilingual acquisition hinges on one's assumptions about the nature and status of the bilingual child's developing language systems. As a null hypothesis, Schwartz (1986) proposes that knowledge of a second language has the same status as that of a first language: unless proven otherwise, it should be seen as a modular, domain-specific system based on an innate endowment. While Schwartz makes this point for child and adult second language acquisition, independent of age, in the case of early bilingual development there are even stronger grounds for the assumption that the child's two languages have the same epistemological status, since the language instinct (or whatever mechanisms are responsible for acquiring a first language) must still be operating while the knowledge of the 'L2' (or the bilingual's weaker language) is developing – if only in order to continue and complete the acquisition of the 'L1' (or dominant language) which is still in progress.

These questions of epistemology are by no means pegged to one particular theoretical position. While Schwartz (1986) assumes a generative model and a modular language faculty with innate linguistic knowledge, similar questions arise under different theoretical assumptions. Bates (1998: 462) remarked that the generative paradigm's 'epistemological baggage' carries with it 'radical claims about the innateness and autonomy of grammar'. These claims are not palatable to many researchers in psychology who seek other alternatives:

many developmental psycholinguists have abandoned linguistic theory altogether, basing their explanations on more general principles of representation and learning taken from developmental psychology and cognitive science. Although these fields also have a lot to offer, they do not provide the detail or the rigour that we once derived from a fruitful relationship with linguistics. (Bates 1998: 462)

The value of a rigorous linguistic model is that acquisition issues can be framed in precise terms. Bates suggests construction grammar as a linguistic model that would be compatible with an interactionist/emergentist epistemology (Elman et al. 1996; MacWhinney 1999) which directly challenges nativist views of language acquisition. Under a usage-based view of language acquisition and a construction-based view of grammar (Tomasello 1998) it equally makes sense to pursue the null hypothesis that the same learning mechanisms are involved in first, bilingual and second language acquisition. A theory of bilingual acquisition and its epistemology needs to be grounded in the more general context of grammatical theory and to achieve compatibility and coherence with theories of language and representation of linguistic knowledge. Without a theory of what is acquired one cannot address the question of acquisition:

the form taken by linguistic theory has an enormous effect on the question of learnability. Without a precise characterization of what is to be learned, the question of whether it can be learned is virtually meaningless. (Wexler & Culicover 1980: 486)

The form of linguistic theory changes over time as a natural consequence of progress, and varies depending on particular theoretical orientations. The diversity of approaches to the study of language acquisition reflects the diverse range of formal and functional approaches to the study of language itself. We cannot do justice to this diversity here, but would like to draw attention to alternative approaches to the nativist/generative paradigm such as emergentism (MacWhinney 1999; 2000b; O'Grady 2005b). A host of theories falling under the general rubric of emergentism include connectionism (Plunkett 1998) and the Competition Model (Bates & MacWhinney 1989) which are open to general cognitive explanations for linguistic phenomena. For example, they seek to investigate how domain-general learning processes such as sentence processing and neuro-cognitive functions interact with domain-specific abilities:

by studying the interaction between domain-specific landscapes and domain-general processes, emergentism opens up paths for detailed empirical investigations. (MacWhinney 2000b: 728)

A recent formulation of the emergentist theory of syntax is articulated in O'Grady (2005b), who proposes a single efficiency-driven computational system that offers a novel solution to classic problems in core areas of grammatical

analysis by subsuming syntactic theory as part of a theory of sentence processing, obviating the need for an autonomous domain of grammar altogether. In
this work we underscore the close affinity between linguistic phenomena and
processing, showing that in a number of constructions, the bilingual child produces structures as a response to processing contingencies (such as null objects
in English transitive constructions and verb-particle constructions in chapter 5,
relative clauses in chapter 6). Regardless of one's theory of language, formal
or functional, generative, typological, cognitive, constructionist, connectionist
or some combination of the above, the need to specify the content of what is
acquired in early bilingual acquisition is no different from acquisition in other
contexts. How one formulates and represents knowledge of language as the end
point of acquisition will have a great impact on how one accounts for language
acquisition.

Our work is inspired by both the generative and typological paradigms. While
each framework gives priority to different issues, we see them as providing
complementary views on the analysis of linguistic phenomena and acquisition
issues with special reference to bilingual acquisition. Yip (1995) argues that
the two approaches can be of mutual benefit to each other in different areas of
grammatical analysis, pointing toward their convergence in shedding light on
the study of interlanguage syntax. Just as Yip demonstrates that 'SLA research
could certainly exploit the complementary strengths of the two paradigms in the
analysis of IL (interlanguage) syntax' (Yip 1995: 29–30), our investigation of
bilingual development and language contact will adopt insights from research
in both these paradigms in the treatment of *wh*-questions (see chapter 4), null
objects (see chapter 5), relative clauses (see chapter 6), placement of PPs, word
order of *bei2* 'give' datives and verb-particle constructions (see chapter 7).

2.1.2   Forms of early bilingualism

An influential distinction made by McLaughlin (1978) somewhat arbitrarily set
age three as a cut-off point, whereby a child who receives regular exposure to
two languages before three is considered a case of *simultaneous acquisition*,
while a child who does not receive input in a second language until after age
three will be a case of *successive acquisition*. Even within the 'simultaneous
bilingual' category, when input from both languages is available to the child
before three, there is variation as to whether the exposure starts right from
birth or is delayed by up to three years. Such variation could have far-reaching
consequences for the course of acquisition and the relationship between the
developing language systems. Factors such as age of first exposure, degree of
balance, interruption and deprivation of input are all variables whose effect
remains to be investigated systematically. Consider a hypothetical case where
a child's exposure to two languages does not start until after two to six months

of birth: can this be considered a case of bilingual first language acquisition (BFLA)? For De Houwer (1995: 223), who defines BFLA as applying to cases where the age of first regular exposure to both languages happens within the first month of birth, the delay of exposure for up to six months after birth would make this a case not of BFLA but rather of 'bilingual second language acquisition' (BSLA). Or to make the case more complex, if the exposure to one language lags behind the other one by anywhere from six to ten months within the first year of life but both languages are then available to the child from that point onwards, will this be considered BSLA or BFLA?

To subsume these cases under second language acquisition would be premature, in particular because the 'first' language is still being acquired when acquisition of the 'second' language begins. This fact has several consequences, including the following:

(i) the 'L1' knowledge acquired, and hence the repertoire of L1 structures potentially available for transfer to the 'L2', is more limited than in adult SLA. In terms of the Full Access/Full Transfer hypothesis (Schwartz & Sprouse 1996), at most a subset of the cases of transfer attested in adult SLA would be expected in BFLA. In the case of adult SLA, one can safely assume that the complete grammar of the L1 is well in place and therefore constitutes the totality of transferable domains. In the case of bilingual acquisition, however, the 'L1' or dominant language, being a developing system with many structures and properties still to be acquired, will necessarily form a subset of the target full competence at any given point on the developmental path.

(ii) as long as the acquisition of neither language is complete, there is the possibility for the two simultaneously developing linguistic systems in contact to interact bidirectionally. We use the term *bidirectional influence* to refer to the two-way interaction between two linguistic systems of the bilingual child where either language may influence the other. As we argue in chapters 4 to 7, the direction and degree of influence are determined in part by language dominance but also by language-specific factors such as developmental asynchrony (see section 2.5.3) and input ambiguity (see section 2.6). In 'vulnerable domains' which are acquired relatively late and/or with difficulty due to ambiguous input, we may find the child's 'second' or weaker language influencing the first or dominant language (see section 2.7).

When the first language has already been fully acquired (as in adult SLA) the influence is often reported as largely one-way, from first to second. Recent studies of language acquisition by post-puberty second language learners, however, draw attention to the heretofore understudied phenomenon of bidirectional transfer (Pavlenko 2000). In the case of bilingual children, such bidirectional influence is argued to be an intrinsic part of their competence rather than an epiphenomenon (Pavlenko & Jarvis 2002: 209–210). Beyond the influence of the first (or previously learned) language on the second, as studied in the field of second language acquisition, researchers have yet to examine in detail the reverse directionality of influence of the second on the first language, as seen in cases of first language attrition and loss (Seliger & Vago 1991; Major 1992; Waas 1996; Schmitt 2000).

For Deuchar and Quay (2000), the term 'bilingual acquisition' refers to situations where the child's exposure to both languages begins in the first year of life, a more relaxed definition than that of De Houwer (1995) discussed above. Either definition will cover the children of the present study as bona fide cases of bilingual acquisition and bilingual first language acquisition. While Deuchar and Quay (2000) recorded the child's speech data from Spanish and English from before 0;04 to 3;02 over almost three years addressing issues relating to the onset of phonology, lexicon and syntax and language choice focusing on 0;10 to 2;03, De Houwer (1990) studied the morphosyntactic development of a Dutch-English bilingual child over a period of eight months from 2;07 to 3;04. The present study starts with children as young as age 1;03 and focuses on the first three years of the bilingual children's development, extending in some cases to five years of age and beyond.

While all of our children began their exposure to both Cantonese and English from birth, variables involving the input soon intervene. Within Timmy's first year, for example, exposure to native English was interrupted for four months (between ages 0;03 and 0;07) due to his father's sabbatical in the United States. Timmy subsequently spent half a year in the USA and resumed regular exposure to English as well as Cantonese. With Sophie there was no such interruption, yet her Cantonese was even more dominant than Timmy's in the first three years (see chapter 3).

The occurrence of transfer in our bilingual children often resembles familiar transfer effects in SLA. The interaction of Chinese and English grammatical systems gives rise to similar phenomena in the two cases. For example, the bilingual children produce sentences with the object in initial position, serving as topic of the sentence:

(1)   Schoolbag put here, put at the door.   (Timmy 2;07;13)

(2)   Shoes put in a shoes place. And bag put in a bag place.   (Sophie 5;01;25)

These are clear counterparts of the 'pseudo-passive' construction analysed in Yip (1995) in adult second language learners. The examples in (3) and (4) are from the interlanguage of intermediate Chinese learners of English (Yip 1995: 97):

(3)   New cars must keep inside.

(4)   Erhu (Chinese violin) can play like this.

The non-target structures in each case are clearly transferred from the Chinese as in (5), the Cantonese counterpart of (1):

(5)   [TOPIC syu1-baau1]ᵢ *pro* baai2 eᵢ hai2 ni1dou6, baai2 eᵢ hai2
       book-bag   put   at   here   put   at
       mun4hau2 dou6
       doorway   there
       '(Let's) put the school bag here, put (it) by the door.'

Here the object 'school bag' is made the topic of the sentence, but is understood as the object of the verb *baai* 'put' (indicated by the empty category *e*), while the subject is left implicit (indicated by *pro* representing an empty subject pronoun). The relationship between topicalization and null objects is discussed further in chapter 5.

The results of transfer, then, can be similar or even identical in children and adult learners. This finding will be important in evaluating bilingual first language acquisition by children and second language acquisition by child and adult learners as mechanisms of contact-induced language change (see section 2.8). However, this is not sufficient grounds to consider our case studies as belonging epistemologically to the field of second language acquisition (SLA). One cannot straightforwardly assume that they are of the same type of phenomenon solely on the basis that similar transfer phenomena occur in both. The logical and practical problems facing the adult learner are quite different from those facing the bilingual child. While the adult has fully acquired one of the two languages involved, in bilingual development the 'first' or dominant language has not been fully acquired but is still developing at the time when transfer occurs. The epistemological status of the two languages simultaneously developing in the mind of the bilingual child is thus necessarily different from that of two languages acquired successively. However this debate raises some challenging questions:

• To what extent is the difference between the bilingual child's dominant and non-dominant languages of a similar magnitude to that between a first and second language in child second language acquisition?
• How far apart do the two simultaneously developing languages have to be (in terms of age of first exposure) before one can consider them first and second languages?

Two relevant hypotheses are discussed by Bernardini (2003: 43): (1) simultaneous bilingual acquisition = 2 L1 acquisition (Meisel 1990, 1994, 2004; Genesee, Nicoladis & Paradis 1995) and (2) 'weaker language = L2' (Schlyter 1993, Schlyter & Håkansson 1994). The first hypothesis predicts that the developmental profile of the bilingual child should be more like that of the monolingual counterparts, hence two first languages. The second hypothesis highlights the similarity of bilingual acquisition and second language acquisition whereby the weaker language of a bilingual child develops like a second language which is subject to the influence of the first language, the stronger language. Each hypothesis may be correct for a particular type of child.

Schlyter (1993) investigates six Swedish-French bilingual children, three of whom have Swedish and three French as the weaker language. The findings suggest that when either Swedish or French is the weaker language, it exhibits variable or incomplete acquisition in core grammatical domains such as finiteness, word order and placement of negation, much like the development of a second language. In contrast, the stronger language shows all characteristics of typical monolingual L1 development in these same domains. There seems to be a split in the developmental profile of the bilingual child's two languages: the stronger language patterns like monolingual L1 children while the weaker language develops like a second language.

Bernardini (2003) takes up the issue of language dominance in the acquisition of word order in the Italian DP, comparing three different learner groups including (a) two Italian-Swedish bilingual children, one with Italian as the weaker language and the other with Italian as the stronger language, (b) monolingual L1 Italian children and (c) adult Swedish learners of Italian as L2. In the case of the placement of possessives and attributive adjectives in Italian, the findings suggest that the bilingual child with Italian as the stronger language was more similar to monolingual children in that they acquire the target order of adjectives from early on, while the bilingual child with Italian as the weaker language patterned more like adult second language learners of Italian: in particular, variable adjectives (those which may appear either before or after the noun) proved to be problematic, consistent with predictions based on input ambiguity (section 2.6). As one of the possible word orders, namely the prenominal placement of adjectives, is shared with Swedish, transfer of this order from Swedish to Italian is found. The alignment is again between the bilingual child's stronger language and the monolingual counterpart on the one hand, and the child's weaker language and the adult learner's L2 on the other hand. To complete the picture, testing relatively balanced Italian-Swedish bilingual children in future studies would provide additional crucial evidence on how the children's two languages are similar to and different from their monolingual counterparts.

The relationship between early bilingual acquisition and child second language acquisition is likely to continue to generate abiding controversies and fruitful research addressing issues such as whether there is a dichotomy between bilingualism and SLA, or even a clear distinction between bilingual acquisition and second language acquisition (Grosjean 1995; Foster-Cohen 2001). Based on current evidence, we assume that there is a continuum whereby one merges seamlessly into the other.

Whether children or adults, bilinguals have a distinct profile that defies a simple characterization of the bilingual individual as a composite of two monolinguals housed in the same mind. In the holistic view advocated by Grosjean (1989), 'bilinguals are not two monolinguals in one', nor 'two monolinguals joined at the neck' like the mythical bilingual characterized by Zentella (1997: 270): the bilingual is not the sum of two complete or incomplete monolinguals, but an integrated whole with a unique linguistic profile. Grosjean argues against the monolingual or fractional view of bilingualism which holds that contact between the two languages should be minimal, or accidental with the assumption that the two monolingual systems should be autonomous and remain so throughout development. We shall show that contact between the bilingual child's two languages can result in a high degree of interaction.

2.2   The logical problem of bilingual acquisition and the poverty of the dual stimulus

In the fields of first and second language acquisition, the logical problem of language acquisition has been widely discussed in association with generative approaches espousing Universal Grammar (UG: Baker & McCarthy 1981; White 1989, 2003). The 'logical problem of language acquisition' (Hornstein & Lightfoot 1981), or alternatively the 'projection problem' (Peters 1972; Baker 1979) refers to the gap between the input available to the learner and the endpoint of acquisition, a highly complex grammar that goes far beyond the input: the learner ends up with complex knowledge of grammaticality, ungrammaticality and ambiguity despite the degenerate nature of the input (Lightfoot 1982). Such considerations motivate the theory of UG which bridges the gap by constraining grammatical development, responsible for the rapid and uniform success of first language acquisition.

Although the logical problem of language acquisition is often linked to UG, it is important to note that the problem exists independent of whether UG is the solution to it (Yip 1995). Children are known to overgeneralize both aspects of grammar which are constrained by UG and those which are not including idiosyncratic, lexical rules (Bowerman 1988). To this extent, the logical problem arises regardless of the role attributed to UG. We now consider the logical problem of language acquisition that the bilingual child is confronted with vis-à-vis the monolingual child. We shall discuss the similarities and differences that make up *the logical problem of bilingual acquisition*.

Given exposure to two languages, the bilingual child will acquire knowledge of two grammars that is underdetermined by the input, in essentially the same time span within which the monolingual child acquires knowledge of a single grammar. Though the attained grammars may differ from those of monolingual children, as long as the bilingual child attains some knowledge of two languages that goes beyond the input, the gap will have to be accounted for.

We may distinguish two sides of the logical problem of bilingual acquisition:

1. To account for the successful, or even accelerated acquisition of aspects of one or both languages by the bilingual child. An example of acceleration in our bilingual children's acquisition of English *why* questions is discussed in section 4.3.

2. To account for the incomplete acquisition, delay or partial outcome with respect to aspects of one or both languages, especially in bilingual children with uneven development. Various examples of delay in English and Cantonese are discussed in chapters 4 to 8.

Accounting for successful acquisition (and hence resolving the logical problem) is the goal of *learnability* theory. In the context of first language acquisition, learnability arguments are typically based on the *'poverty of the stimulus' argument* (Chomsky 1980; Lightfoot 1982). The input is considered impoverished in that it is finite: the child hears only a finite number of sentences which under-determine the target grammar that is able to generate an infinite number of sentences. The problem of under-determination faced by the child is characterized as follows:

Learning a language involves going beyond the data . . . The trouble that the child faces is thus a problem of under-determination: any finite set of example sentences is compatible with an infinite number of grammars. The child's task is to pick among those grammars. (Marcus 1999: 660)

Moreover, the input available to children crucially lacks negative evidence that would inform them of the ungrammaticality of their non-target sentences. Despite the finite nature of the input and the lack of negative evidence, children succeed in converging on the target grammar rapidly and uniformly, prompting nativists to argue that the child is constrained by innately given knowledge (we leave aside the issue of whether the constraints are specific to language or not). In particular, the 'no negative evidence' problem has been the cornerstone of nativist argumentation. The empirical validity of the poverty of stimulus argument is critically assessed in a recent debate (see Crain & Pietroski 2002; Fodor & Crowther 2002; Pullum & Scholz 2002; Sampson 2002; Scholz & Pullum 2002).

To the extent that such deficiencies exist and impact first language acquisition, a parallel argument based on impoverished input can be made in the case of bilingual first language acquisition. Paradis and Genesee (1996: 9) note that 'it seems reasonable to conjecture that bilingual children have their input space divided, so their frequency of exposure to each language at any given time is smaller than that of monolinguals acquiring each language'. If one considers the input to be impoverished in the case of monolingual children who are exposed to one language at a time, then this poverty must be considered even more acute in the case of bilingual children since the input is more limited in terms of both quantity and quality of input: quantitatively, the frequency of structures in the dual input may be reduced to varying degrees in each language compared to the monolingual child's input, while qualitatively, code-mixing in the adult input may further make the acquisition of each target language more challenging. Paradis and Genesee use this poverty of input argument to support acquisition by UG-governed triggering as opposed to learning by induction in bilingual children: 'if bilingual children demonstrate the same rate of syntactic development as monolinguals, this could argue for a process of development through selection or triggering, as opposed to learning' (Paradis & Genesee 1996: 9). While in this work we set aside the issue of triggering vs. learning, we agree with Paradis and Genesee that the dual input is necessarily more limited at least in terms of frequency of input, an aspect of the triple deficiency of input as discussed in Lightfoot (1982). The impoverished nature of the input also finds parallels in the conditions under which pidgins and creoles arise.

The *Argument from the Poverty of the Stimulus* (APS) has been a major driving force in the construction of theories of first and second language acquisition. Fodor (1981: 258) even saw the APS as 'the proof for the existence of Cognitive Science'. In the context of bilingual acquisition it is useful to review the main arguments, especially since some points are different. In fact, several aspects of the logical problem of language acquisition are more severe for the bilingual child than for the monolingual child:

(i) Quantity of input: even in an 'ideal' environment where the input is divided on a 50–50 basis, an idealized balanced bilingual child can expect to receive only 50% of the input available to a monolingual child. In a more realistic case where the input is less than balanced (say 60:40 or 70:30), the amount of input from one of languages will be less than 50% to varying degrees depending on the prevailing ecology. In an attempt to ensure that the bilingual infants participating in their experiments have about equal exposure to both languages, some researchers impose a requirement such that the infants have a minimum of 30% and a maximum of 70% input in each language as determined by a parental report scale (Bosch and Sebastián-Gallés 1997, Werker, Weikum & Yoshida 2006: 2). Faced with a reduced quantity of input in each language compared with the monolinguals, the challenge for the bilingual child is to project a target grammar solely based on the available input without the benefit of negative evidence.

(ii) Indeterminacy of input: such data as are available in the input are compatible with numerous hypotheses, from which the child somehow selects the correct one. The grammar eventually attained by the child is underdetermined by the input data. The fact that both target grammars are underdetermined by the input data in this sense is exacerbated in bilingual acquisition to the extent that the two (or more) languages provide conflicting evidence. This problem of indeterminacy is the basis of the input ambiguity account for cross-linguistic influence to be discussed in section 2.6.2.

To the extent that the bilingual child succeeds in acquiring full competence in two languages within the same time span as the monolingual counterparts on the basis of impoverished dual input that underdetermines the attained knowledge of two languages, the argument for innate knowledge (domain-specific or otherwise) that bridges the gap between *poverty of the dual stimulus* and the end state grammar is at least twice as strong. The logic is somewhat different, however, because in fact the course and developmental patterns of bilingual acquisition can be different from those of monolingual acquisition, as we show in the case studies in this book. For example, in our bilingual children's English, there are protracted periods of *wh*-in-situ, null objects and prenominal object relatives. These non-target structures contrast with monolingual development where the acquisition of *wh*-movement, obligatoriness of overt objects and postnominal relatives occurs more rapidly and uniformly. For example, we show in chapter 5 that the unlearning of null objects in English may take years in some bilingual children, and the rates of ungrammatical null objects in English vary among the six bilingual children depending on their patterns of language dominance. Thus the acquisition of the obligatoriness of overt objects of English transitive verbs is neither as rapid nor as uniform as in monolingual acquisition.

Finally we should note that even an 'ideal' 50-50 distribution does not necessarily lead us to predict balanced bilingualism as an outcome. It could be that some languages are acquired with more difficulty and/or over a longer period than others. For example, if there is any truth in McWhorter's (2001) argument that the simplest grammars are creole grammars, a child learning a creole (or creole-like) language together with a non-creole language will acquire the creole grammar earlier and with less difficulty (showing fewer developmental errors) than the other language. We are not aware of any studies of bilingual development which test this prediction directly. However, Adone (1994) found that the grammar of Mauritian Creole was indeed acquired in a relatively error-free manner.

2.3   Language differentiation in bilingual acquisition

For a long time, much of the research in the field of bilingual first language acquisition has been centred on the question of whether bilingual children begin with a unitary undifferentiated system, as proposed by Volterra and Taeschner (1978). The issue of grammatical differentiation assumes critical theoretical significance, since our understanding of the human capacity for language can be enriched once the question of how humans are cognitively equipped to become bilingual is addressed. Thus far, the collective weight of the empirical evidence suggests that bilingual children are able to differentiate two language systems from early on (De Houwer 1990; Genesee, Nicoladis & Paradis 1995; Paradis 2000, Meisel 2001 among others). The more interesting question now is how early the differentiation is evident in terms of perception and production. Evidence for early language differentiation includes the following:

- Experimental evidence shows that 4–5-month-old bilingual infants have the perceptual abilities to distinguish two rhythmically close languages (Spanish and Catalan), for which discrimination is considered especially challenging (Bosch & Sebastián-Gallés 2001).[2] Bilingual infants, like monolinguals show clear and early auditory discrimination between languages without any delay. Such evidence for early perceptual differentiation during infancy makes it 'strange to imagine that languages would be undifferentiated at age 3' (MacWhinney 2001: 257). What remains to be fully specified are the underlying perceptual mechanisms that make differentiation possible.
- In terms of production, there is evidence that bilingual infants develop differentiated systems during the babbling stage before they begin to produce their first words (Poulin-Dubois & Goodz 2001). Thirteen French-English infants with average age at 12.6 months were found to babble in a dominant language, i.e. French-type babbling is seen in the majority of bilinguals with French mothers. The dominance of French in the babbling was attributed to the prosodic salience of maternal speech and the 'bilingual-to-be infants' going for a syllable-timed structure with more regular suprasegmental properties as a model for early babbling.
- Another major type of evidence for differentiation comes from word order and morphosyntax observed in the speech of a wide variety of bilingual children acquiring different language pairs which reflect structural properties and constraints on grammatical operations specific to each of the two languages, e.g. language-specific headedness of syntactic categories (VP and IP), finiteness and its syntactic consequences such as verb raising are acquired early in French-German bilingual children (Meisel 2001).[3]

We have evidence from our daughter Alicia that her English phonology is differentiated from the Cantonese system from around one year old. One important contrast in the phonological systems of Cantonese and English is that Cantonese has unreleased final stops while English final stops are released, as shown in table 2.1 (see Matthews & Yip 1994; Bauer & Benedict 1997). At the beginning of Alicia's one-word stage, she already distinguished between these two kinds of final stops. In fact, she often produced English words ending in voiceless stops such as *rabbit* and voiced stops such as *bird*, with an exaggerated release of air, striking the listener as an over-released final stop. Meanwhile, her Cantonese checked syllables were produced in a native-like manner, i.e. appropriately unreleased as the adult would pronounce them. We take this as evidence that she is actively differentiating between two phonological systems – indeed, her hyper-released finals can be construed as the result of *over*-differentiating

Table 2.1. *Syllable-final consonants in Cantonese and English.*

Cantonese	English
sap1[sɐp˥]	sap [sæp]
sat1 [sɐt˥]	sat [sæt]
sak1[sɐk˥]	sack [sæk]

these systems. Yip and Matthews (2003) argue for early phonological differentiation based on video-recordings of our bilingual children's early production. The data show that syllable-final stops in each language are subject to different language-specific features, i.e. syllable-final stops are unreleased in Cantonese but optionally released or even over-released in English, putatively exhibiting a form of *hyper-differentiation*.

Do bilingual children begin with an undifferentiated phonological system which gradually becomes differentiated? There are divergent views regarding the question of whether and when differentiation is achieved in phonological systems, ranging from total undifferentiation at two years old to partial or total differentiation by age two (see review in Paradis 2001, papers in the special issue edited by Lleó & Kehoe 2002).

In terms of lexical differentiation, evidence is sought in the degree of overlap in the vocabularies in each language. If the child has a sufficient number of translation equivalents of the same word such as two words for *car*, one in German and one in English, then this is taken as evidence for two separate lexicons (Pearson, Fernandez & Oller 1995, Lanvers 1999). Lam (2006) found that as early as 1;06, Sophie had numerous translation equivalents among her English and Cantonese nouns.

2.4   Language dominance in early bilingual development

In the bilingual acquisition literature, the notion of language dominance is widely used in a pre-theoretical sense to describe a situation where one of a child's languages is more advanced or developing faster than the other.[4] Dominance is argued to be important in identifying types and degrees of bilingualism (Romaine 1995: 15). Dominance may also have a role in predicting and explaining outcomes: for example, certain non-target features such as null objects in a bilingual child's non-dominant language, English, tend to persist or are unlearned slowly over a protracted period (cf. Yip & Matthews 2005) or aspects of the non-dominant language may fail to develop fully, or be lost (Romaine 1995: 224). The importance of dominance extends into later childhood and adulthood, where it is acknowledged that an individual child's pattern of dominance can change with shifting home and school environments. Thus Baker and Prys Jones (1998: 12) observe that 'in the majority of bilinguals one language is more dominant than the other'. One point which is uncontroversial is that dominance is by no means static: dominance patterns may change over time depending on individual experiences (Romaine 1995: 84, 191). Such changes in dominance will be illustrated with our bilingual children's corpus data in chapter 3.

2.4.1   Defining language dominance

The term *dominance* is often defined in terms of *proficiency*: the dominant language is that 'in which the bilingual is informally considered to be most proficient' (Petersen 1988: 487; see also Genesee, Nicoladis & Paradis 1995; Deuchar & Muntz 2003 among others). De Houwer (1998a) points out that 'proficiency' is scarcely used in monolingual child language research, yet it is readily used in a relative sense when two or more languages are involved, as in bilingual first language acquisition. Such invocation of proficiency is 'quite at odds with the general thinking in monolingual child language research today', according to De Houwer (1998a: 259), leading her to question whether the notion of dominance is needed at all in connection with young bilingual children.

We adopt the view that language acquisition research should be concerned with investigating a learner's knowledge that underlies language use and proficiency (Lakshmanan 1995). Knowledge of language is taken to involve a mentally represented grammar (Chomsky 1986). For example, when we claim that bilingual children use null objects (see chapter 5), we do not merely mean that learners 'omit' objects. Rather, a null object is part of the structure assigned to sentences in the children's grammar. This point may be illustrated with a typical example from diary data (6):

(6)   You get, I eat.   [father takes chocolates off shelf]   (Timmy 2;02;03)

The child's hypothetical representation for this sentence includes a null topic ('chocolate' being the focus of his attention) and two null objects whose reference is determined by the null topic, as formalized in (7):[5]

(7) $[\text{TOPIC}]_i$ you get $[e]_i$, I eat $[e]_i$

Given such a view, in order to be of theoretical interest (e.g. in accounting for how knowledge of language is acquired on the basis of dual input, how two linguistic systems interact in transfer, code-mixing etc.), dominance must be related to underlying competence and not merely a measure of performance or language use. We assume that syntactic transfer, for example, takes place at the level of competence. If dominance is taken to be merely a property of performance, then it cannot explain the occurrence of transfer, unless one resorts to a surface-oriented and performance-driven concept of transfer. To the extent that the theory of transfer is competence-based, the conceptualization of language dominance should be correspondingly competence-based in order for the two notions to be theoretically compatible and coherent (Yip & Matthews 2006).

A view of dominance compatible with these assumptions is that 'Language dominance is essentially a psycholinguistic phenomenon closely intermeshed with sociolinguistic parameters' (Lanza 2004: 172–173). As a psycholinguistic phenomenon, language dominance should be characterized as a property of the mind, albeit influenced by sociolinguistic parameters such as quantity of input and influencing aspects of performance such as fluency. Like Lanza (2004: 330), we believe that the problems that arise in defining dominance do not invalidate the pre-theoretical notion. In chapter 3 we discuss how dominance can be measured.

2.5 Cross-linguistic influence in bilingual development

As discussed above, a major theme of research in bilingual acquisition has been the question of one unitary system versus two differentiated systems in children exposed simultaneously to two languages. Recent studies agree that bilingual children are able to differentiate between the two languages from early on (Genesee 1989; Meisel 1989; De Houwer 1990; Genesee, Nicoladis & Paradis 1995) but the picture with regard to transfer remains more mixed. Some studies have suggested that separation of two grammars also implies autonomous development without interaction, and hence developing grammars much like those of monolinguals (e.g. De Houwer 1990, Meisel 1994); others have found various forms of interaction and cross-linguistic influence between the languages (Döpke 2000, Hulk & Müller 2000 among others). Thus the development of separate grammars in bilingual children does not preclude cross-linguistic influence; what is at issue is the nature of the influence and whether it constitutes transfer.

2.5.1 Defining transfer and cross-linguistic influence

While the terms *transfer* and *cross-linguistic influence* are sometimes used interchangeably, we adopt the usage whereby transfer is a particular form of the more general notion of cross-linguistic influence. We see the relationship between transfer and cross-linguistic influence as falling into a subset–superset as in figure 2.1.

We assume a working definition of transfer as 'incorporation of a grammatical property into one language from the other' (Paradis & Genesee 1996: 3). If transfer is defined in this way, the clearest cases of transfer will be those that

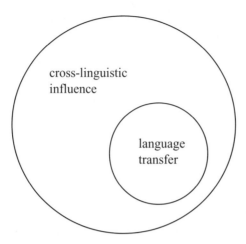

Figure 2.1 Relationship between cross-linguistic influence and transfer

involve grammatical properties not already present in the recipient language, so that these properties can be directly and unambiguously attributed to the source language. Moreover, these properties should not be found in monolingual development, since the putative source language is not available.

Cross-linguistic influence can also take more subtle forms, such as quantitative differences between monolingual and bilingual development. For example, null objects are found in early monolingual child English with a frequency of around 2.8% to 9%. As we show in chapter 5, the frequency of null objects in five out of six of our bilingual children ranging from 19% to 34% is much higher than the monolingual counterparts. While it is difficult to show that the property of null object is 'transferred' from Cantonese, since monolingual English children also show this property to some extent, the quantitative difference in the occurrences of null objects between the two groups of children can reasonably be attributed to cross-linguistic influence.

We also assume that in order to constitute transfer, cross-linguistic influence must be systemic, in the sense of Paradis and Genesee (1996: 3): 'By systemic, we mean influence at the level of representation or competence, sustained over a period of time.' An example that does *not* constitute systemic influence would be episodic code-mixing where two languages interact in performance, but not necessarily at the level of competence. Systemic influence also rules out one-off performance errors: De Houwer (1990) acknowledges such occasional 'slips' while arguing that in her case study there is no systemic transfer. In order to be considered systemic, a putative instance of transfer must be recurrent: we take this to mean at least three attestations in the same individual at the same stage of development. It is *not* necessary that similar instances of transfer be found in more than one child: individual differences between individual children are too great, given the variation in input conditions and other variables. To the extent that transfer does recur in different children, however, this represents a further degree of regularity. A case in point is the transfer of prenominal relative clauses from Cantonese to English: as discussed in chapter 6, this recurs independently in our three siblings, recapitulating essentially the same patterns.

Even in children for whom transfer is highly systematic, as in the case of our three siblings, it is not the case that all aspects of the dominant language undergo transfer. Furthermore, transfer in the other direction, affecting the dominant language, is even more restricted. We therefore need to constrain transfer. Concerning the conditions under which transfer takes place, several principles have been discussed in the field of second language acquisition:

- Interlingual identification (Weinreich 1953): learners perceive an equivalence between items (sounds, words, constructions, etc.) in the L1 and L2. This is a prerequisite for applying the grammar of L1.
- Transfer to somewhere (Andersen 1983b): in order for a property of the L1 to be transferred, the L2 must be 'receptive' to the property: there must be a domain or slot into which the L1 property can be fitted. Andersen's original principle reads: 'A grammatical form or structure will occur consistently and to a significant extent in the interlanguage as a result of transfer *if and only if* there already exists within the L2 input the potential for (mis)-generalization from the input to produce the same form or structure' (1983b: 178).

Instead of adapting these principles, recent research in bilingual acquisition has tended to propose new principles specific to the bilingual context, at some danger of reinventing the wheel: the notion of input ambiguity as a condition for transfer, for example, can be seen as a reformulation of Andersen's hypothesis for SLA as cited above. A number of proposals have been put forward which have yet to be fully evaluated. These proposals include language dominance (see section 2.5.2), developmental asynchrony (see section 2.5.3), input ambiguity (see section 2.6) and structural overlap between the two target grammars. Hulk and Müller (2000) propose two 'sufficient but not necessary' conditions for cross-linguistic influence to occur:

(a) the domain involves an interface level, such as the interface between syntax and pragmatics as in the C (Complementizer)-domain;
(b) the domain in which cross-linguistic influence takes place is one where the two languages overlap: 'there has to be a certain overlap of the two systems at the surface level' (Hulk & Müller 2000: 228).

While Hulk and Müller's (2000) proposal points to plausible factors in cross-linguistic influence, it is far from established that these apply to all contexts, or that they represent the only conditions. The authors argue that the instances of cross-linguistic influence (object drop and root infinitives) they identify are not predicted by language dominance. Unsworth (2003) tests their proposal by investigating cross-linguistic influence in the domain of root infinitives in a bilingual German-English child under a reanalysis of root infinitives as fulfilling both of the conditions in (a) and (b), rather than just condition (a) involving the interface of two modules (syntax and pragmatics) but not condition (b) structural overlap as assumed by Hulk and Müller (2000). The findings show no quantitative or qualitative cross-linguistic influence though the conditions are met, raising some questions regarding Hulk and Müller's conditions. In particular, it needs to be clarified that the 'overlap' in their condition (b) refers to *partial* overlap, since given complete overlap it would not be possible to identify cross-linguistic influence (Unsworth 2003: 155). What this means for the bilingual child is that certain overlapping forms have to be perceived as equivalent as a result of interlingual identification.

Another question is whether the two conditions are sufficient for transfer to occur. Kupisch (2003: 34) points out that 'an interface status alone is not sufficient to account for the vulnerability of a grammatical domain'. Examining the French DP domain, she invokes language-specific factors such as transparency of the target system.

2.5.2   Language dominance and transfer

Language dominance is widely considered to be one of the important factors in accounting for the direction of transfer in bilingual acquisition. A number of studies report incorporation of elements from a dominant to a non-dominant language (Gawlitzek-Maiwald & Tracy 1996; Hulk & van der Linden 1996; Döpke 1997). As discussed in chapter 3, language dominance can be measured most objectively by computing Mean Length of Utterance (MLU) for each language at different stages: the dominant language is expected to have a higher MLU value than the less dominant one. Less direct indications of dominance come from children's language preferences (Saunders 1988). The amount of input from each language is thought to play a major role in determining language dominance (Döpke 1992).

Yip and Matthews (2000a) discussed aspects of syntactic transfer in Timmy, including *wh*-in-situ (8) and null objects, as in (9):

(8)   It is for what?   (Timmy 2;05;03)

(9)   Adult: Where shall we stick it?
       CHI: Put here.   (Timmy 2;05;05)

The occurrence of these structures was shown to be qualitatively and quantitatively distinct from that found in monolingual development. The occurrence of *wh*-in-situ and null objects peaks during the period when Timmy's MLUw for Cantonese is most clearly ahead of that for English, suggesting a close relationship between direction of transfer and language dominance.

Recent work has questioned whether dominance is necessary in accounting for transfer. Müller (2004: 276) even sets the 'main goal of discarding language dominance as an explanation for cross-linguistic influence'. Comparing two French-German bilingual children, one being a balanced bilingual child and the other with German as dominant language, with monolingual French children, she found the rate of object drop in the two bilingual children's French to be much higher than in monolingual French children, as a result of German influence, regardless of whether German is the dominant language. Dominance in German is thus taken to be irrelevant in accounting for German influence on French grammar. Müller's analysis of subject realization in the two bilingual children's French shows that this domain of grammar patterns like monolingual French children, not subject to influence from German, showing developmental phenomena independent of language dominance. Whether a domain of grammar is susceptible to cross-linguistic influence or not, she reasons that language dominance does not provide a plausible account. Instead the focus should be on factors internal to the grammatical phenomenon in order to explain cross-linguistic influence.

Müller's argument against dominance focuses on one particular grammatical domain (involving object drop and subject realization) with a particular language pair (French and German), and is initially based on two children. In these particular cases it may well be that dominance plays little or no role, and cross-linguistic influence is determined by other factors. This is not, however, sufficient grounds to rule out dominance as a relevant factor in other cases. In order to demonstrate convincingly that dominance is irrelevant to cross-linguistic influence, many more domains and language pairs need to be investigated, preferably with bilingual children showing different patterns and degrees of dominance. Until and unless robust evidence is available to support such a position, we maintain that dominance is not only relevant but an important factor in accounting for early bilingual development. Excluding dominance from the picture would leave other factors such as input ambiguity and other language-internal factors as the only ones worth pursuing. While we accept that language-internal factors are important, notably input ambiguity as discussed in section 2.6 below, we incorporate dominance as an indispensable factor interacting with other factors, showing that different patterns of dominance produce differential cross-linguistic effects in our children. If input ambiguity were solely responsible for the effects observed, we would expect similar effects to show up in all of our bilingual children, regardless of their dominance patterns. But the extent of cross-linguistic influence is clearly different across individual children, commensurate with their degree of dominance. This pattern is demonstrated in the case of wh-in-situ questions in chapter 4 and null objects in chapter 5.

To characterize the role of language dominance in bilingual acquisition, we formulate the language dominance hypothesis as follows:

Language Dominance Hypothesis: for a child exposed to two or more languages simultaneously, if one of the languages develops faster than the other in terms of measurable differences such as mean length of utterance (MLU) differentials, there will be cross-linguistic influence from the dominant language to the weaker language.

In our Cantonese-English bilingual children, transfer is asymmetrical in a way which is predicted by dominance: as noted by Yip and Matthews (2000a: 206), transfer from Cantonese to English is clearly visible in many areas of grammar (see chapters 4, 5, 6 and 8), whereas influence of English on Cantonese, if any, is subtle and much more difficult to demonstrate (see chapter 7). Furthermore, degrees of language dominance may also play a role in determining the extent of transfer effects in certain domains of grammar. In chapter 5, we show that MLU differentials predict differential rates of cross-linguistic influence in the domain of null objects.

2.5.3   Bilingual bootstrapping and developmental asynchrony

Paradis and Genesee (1996: 3) suggest an important qualification to the view of transfer as determined by language dominance:

> Transfer is most likely to occur if the child has reached a more advanced level of syntactic complexity in one language than the other. Such a discrepancy could occur either *because it is typical in the monolingual acquisition of the two languages*, or because the child is more dominant in one of his or her languages [emphasis added].

The first possibility, highlighted in the quotation above, involves a discrepancy in development between the bilingual child's two languages which is in accordance with the normal acquisition schedules for monolingual children in each language. For example, if relative clauses normally develop in Chinese at age 2;06 and in English at age three, there should be a period of development in which even balanced bilingual children will be able to construct relative clauses in Chinese but not in English, and will thus have reason to transfer the Chinese structure to their English. On this account, a discrepancy in syntactic complexity between the bilingual child's languages is not necessarily due to dominance. This is recognized in the notion of *developmental asynchrony* which forms part of the Bilingual Bootstrapping Hypothesis proposed by Gawlitzek-Maiwald and Tracy (1996: 902).

The idea of 'bootstrapping' is built on the insight that one type of information leads to another type of information, much as in tying bootstraps tightening one lace enables the other to be tightened further. A host of hypotheses fall under the general rubric of bootstrapping theories. For example, semantic bootstrapping (Pinker 1989) – using semantics to get to syntax (the argument structure of the verb), while syntactic bootstrapping (Gleitman 1990) involves using argument structure and order of the arguments to get to meaning. Different approaches to bootstrapping are discussed in Chiat (2000) and Weissenborn and Höhle (2001).

In the bilingual context, bootstrapping means using knowledge of one language to deal with another. In bilingual bootstrapping as defined by Gawlitzek-Maiwald and Tracy (1996: 903), 'something that has been acquired in language A fulfills a booster function for language B'. The authors also entertain a weaker version of the hypothesis, in which there is 'a temporary pooling of resources' from both languages.

The precondition for bilingual bootstrapping to work is a situation where one of the languages develops ahead of the other with respect to a certain property or grammatical domain. The more developed language performs a facilitative function in boosting the development of the less developed language. In their study of an English-German bilingual child whose German is ahead of English, tense and agreement was absent in the child's English but were marked productively in his German. In mixed utterances, 'left-periphery items of main clauses are taken from German' (Gawlitzek-Maiwald & Tracy 1996: 915). Typical mixed utterances consist of an English verb phrase (VP) embedded within a German clause structure (IP):

(10)   Ich hab   ge-climbed up
        I   have   PTCP-climbed up
        'I have climbed up'

(11)   ⌐ Kannst du   move a bit?
        can   you   move a bit
        'Can you move a bit?'

The reverse pattern (an English IP together with a German VP) was not found. Gawlitzek-Maiwald and Tracy (1996) attribute this to developmental asynchrony: the children's German is more advanced than their English, at least in this domain.

While considering bilingual bootstrapping as 'a plausible account of certain types of cross-linguistic influences in bilingual language use', Meisel (2001: 31) raises some questions with the account. One problem involves whether 'one can really claim that something is missing if she appears to know very well what it is and how to fill the gap' (2001: 31). The child seems to know more than just the need for a functional projection above VP. The use of an English-type left-headed IP instead of the German right-headed IP casts doubt on German syntax as the source of this knowledge. Meisel (2001: 32) concludes that 'it is therefore of crucial importance to define those factors which favor cross-linguistic influences in general, and bilingual bootstrapping in particular'. Another issue involves whether 'temporary pooling of resources', as posited in the weaker form of the bootstrapping hypothesis, constitutes systemic influence as defined by Paradis and Genesee (1996) and discussed in section 2.5.1 above. To make the insight of asynchrony as precise as possible, we formulate this possibility as the *developmental asynchrony hypothesis*, which we define as follows (Matthews & Yip 2002: 42):

Developmental Asynchrony Hypothesis: given a property P_a which develops at an earlier stage in monolingual children acquiring language A than a corresponding property P_b in monolingual children acquiring language B, in a bilingual child acquiring languages A and B simultaneously, property P_a is expected to develop in language A before P_b in language B. This creates a *developmental asynchrony* between the two languages, allowing property P_a to be transferred to language B.

We shall discuss how the developmental asynchrony hypothesis accounts for the acceleration of acquisition of English *why* questions in the bilingual children compared to the monolingual counterparts (section 4.3). A comparison of the two monolingual developmental schedules shows that Cantonese *dim2gaai2* 'why' questions are acquired 3.7 months earlier than English *why* questions (cf. tables 4.3 and 4.4). If the bilingual children develop in accordance with the monolingual schedule, Cantonese 'why' questions are expected to emerge first. Our findings show that our bilingual children's Cantonese *dim2gaai2* 'why' questions indeed emerge early at 27.8 months, setting the stage for the transfer of knowledge of such questions to English at 30.8 months. Thus our bilingual children an advantage here over monolingual English-speaking children, and this is not because of language dominance since the four bilingual children in question are not dominant in English; rather, their development in accordance with the typical monolingual Cantonese schedule enables them to acquire 'why' questions earlier in Cantonese, which in turn facilitates their acquisition of these questions in English at an earlier age compared to the monolingual English schedule. Another possible case of developmental asynchrony, and its relationship to language dominance, arises in the development of relative clauses in our bilingual children (section 6.4).

2.6   Input ambiguity and learnability

The factors of language dominance, developmental asynchrony and bilingual bootstrapping all concern the relative development of the two languages concerned. Another set of factors involves the input available to children in each language, and what hypotheses the child might entertain about the target language given such input. The nature and properties of the input form an important part of classical learnability arguments which have tended to be focused on first language acquisition (though extended to SLA in studies such as Rutherford 1989 and Yip 1995). Yip (2002, 2004) argues for framing a number of issues

in bilingual acquisition, such as input ambiguity, as questions of learnability. In first language acquisition, the basic questions are:
  (i) What can a child learn from a particular sample of input?
  (ii) What kinds of evidence are necessary for the acquisition of a given property?
In the bilingual context, a further question arises:
  (iii) How are questions (i) and (ii) affected by the child's exposure to another language?

2.6.1   Ambiguous data and unambiguous triggers in first language acquisition

Gibson and Wexler (1994) and Fodor (1998) pointed out that for a learner who has yet to acquire English, a string as simple as (12) is structurally ambiguous:

(12)   Mary saw me.

Although apparently straightforward, sentence (12) is compatible with both English and German word order parameter settings, as shown in (13) and (14) respectively:

(13)   English settings include SV, VO and –V2.

(14)   German settings include SV, OV and +V2.

That is, the verb is in second position in the sentence, consistent with the verb-second (V2) rule of German as well as the SVO clause structure of English. Meisel (2001: 18) discusses similar ambiguities with respect to French-German bilingual acquisition, pointing out that 'surface word-order patterns do not easily reveal the kind of information needed' in order for the bilingual child to determine the difference between underlying OV and VO orders and between V2 and non-V2 languages. In generative terms, the SVO string as in (12) is ambiguous as to whether the V appears in the head of CP (as in Germanic V2 languages) or in the head of IP position (as in French-type languages). This is a nice illustration of how a piece of ambiguous input can be analysed in radically different ways. The learner has to make use of other, unambiguous input to determine the correct combination of parameter settings of a particular target language. For example, in (15) the verb is no longer in second position and the evidence it provides is thus incompatible with a verb-second rule:

(15)   Just now Mary saw me.

For cases of monolingual acquisition such as those considered by Fodor (1998), it is a matter of logical necessity that the input be unambiguous, hence the term 'unambiguous triggers' in models assuming parameter-setting: for each parameter, a set of unambiguous 'triggering data' must be identified. The logical problem still holds, however, whether or not one assumes that developing a grammar involves setting parameters. Moreover, the logical problem identified by Fodor is exacerbated in the case of bilingual children. For monolingual children acquiring English, the evidence will overwhelmingly favour SVO as opposed to V2 as the basic order. A bilingual child acquiring both English and German, however, has additional reason to consider the V2 hypothesis for English: namely, his or her developing German grammar in which V2 is a major element.

2.6.2   Input ambiguity in bilingual development

The case with which Fodor (1998) is concerned involves the logical problem facing the child, and therefore also facing theories of typical first language acquisition which have to guarantee uniform success. A parallel problem, but a practical as well as a logical one, arises in accounting for non-target structures produced by bilingual children. Müller (1998) proposes that ambiguous input is in fact a major source of cross-linguistic influence in bilingual development. Specifically, transfer from language A to language B can result from ambiguity in the input in language B, when 'two different grammatical hypotheses are compatible with the same surface string' (Müller 1998: 153). A strong hypothesis based on this proposal states that transfer can occur when surface structures overlap:

> Syntactic cross-linguistic influence occurs only if language A has a syntactic construction which may seem to allow more than one syntactic analysis and, at the same time, language B contains evidence for one of these two analyses. In other words, there has to be a certain overlap of the two systems at the surface level. (Hulk & Müller 2000: 228–229)

There are two factors here which, although related in practice, are in principle independent of each other:
(i) overlap in surface structures between the two target languages. As depicted in figure 2.2, this is a property of the *language pair* being acquired, which can only arise where two languages are in contact.
(ii) ambiguity in the input in a particular language. This is a property of the *specific language* being acquired as represented in figure 2.3. It therefore potentially poses problems in monolingual, as well as bilingual development.

For a bilingual child, where there is overlap between the two languages, a particular piece of input data from language A may be consistent with both the grammar of A and that of language B. Such ambiguous data in a language A opens the door to transfer of a property from a language B, as schematized in figure 2.4.

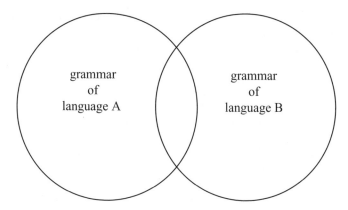

Figure 2.2 Structural overlap between two grammatical systems

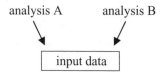

Figure 2.3 Input ambiguity within a grammar

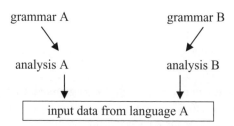

Figure 2.4 Input ambiguity with two languages in contact

Ambiguities of this kind will be invoked in Cantonese-English development as a factor in transfer in both directions. In the transfer of the null objects from Cantonese to English, discussed in chapter 5, ambiguous input is invoked as a factor in addition to language dominance. Input ambiguity is also invoked to account for cases of influence from English to Cantonese as the dominant language. In chapter 7, vulnerable domains in the acquisition of Cantonese are attributed to ambiguous input, as in the case of the placement of prepositional phrases with *hai2* 'at': in the children's Cantonese, variable placement of PPs instantiated in the input leads bilingual children to follow the order of English which is invariant. A similar, but more complex explanation is available for the order of the two objects in Cantonese dative constructions with *bei2* 'give', as discussed in section 7.2.

2.6.3   Forms of input ambiguity

Apart from distinguishing structural overlap between languages from ambiguity within a language, it proves necessary to distinguish different types of ambiguity in the input. Importantly, we distinguish:

(a) ambiguity of analysis as identified by Fodor (1998) and illustrated in (12) above, or structural ambiguity as defined by Müller (1998: 153), i.e. a single string can be assigned different structural analyses. For example, as we discuss in chapter 5, (16) is compatible with an English-based analysis (in which *eat* is an intransitive verb) as well as a Chinese-based analysis (in which *eat* is a transitive verb with a null object):

(16)   Let's eat.

(b) ambiguity of evidence, whereby the input data do not provide unambiguous evidence about the target language. For example, in French adjectives can precede or follow the noun, in some cases even with the same adjective (see Nicoladis 2006):

(17)   a. un pauvre homme
            a   poor   man
            'a poor man (to be pitied)'

        b. un homme pauvre
            a   man   poor
            'a poor man (lacking wealth)'

In such cases, the evidence is ambiguous as to the target grammar (in this case, where adjectives are to be placed). If a language A showing such ambiguity is in contact with a language B where the evidence is unambiguous, the grammar of B may be hypothesized to influence the developing grammar for language A. For example, the unambiguously prenominal adjectives of English would be expected to favour prenominal placement of adjectives in French. In chapter 7, we discuss cases of ambiguous evidence in Cantonese including placement of PPs with *hai2* 'at', word order of double object constructions with *bei2* 'give' and verb-particle constructions, showing how these areas open the door to influence from English which presents unambiguous evidence in the input data. Interestingly, verb-particle constructions in both Cantonese and English present ambiguous evidence to the bilingual child. Not only are non-target word orders based on English found in children's Cantonese, certain Cantonese verb-particle constructions prove to be transferable to English, resulting in ungrammatical structures in English. The domain of verb-particle constructions thus provides a window into bidirectional influence in bilingual development (section 7.3).

In principle, both these types of ambiguity pose a challenge to monolingual as well as to bilingual children. The particular relevance to bilingual children lies in the way the ambiguity interacts with the other grammar: ambiguity in language A favours the option which matches language B, i.e. structural overlap combines with input ambiguity in leading to influence of language B on language A.

2.7 Vulnerable domains in bilingual development

Some of the hypotheses discussed above involve the child's two languages as a whole: thus a dominant language is usually considered to be dominant across the board. Most of the other hypotheses, however, involve specific areas or 'domains' of grammar. Thus developmental asynchrony (section 2.5.3) and input ambiguity (section 2.6.2) apply only to specific areas of grammar, such as relative clauses or null objects. The notion of vulnerable domains has been invoked to refer to particular phenomena that are acquired late and often produced in a non-target manner (Müller 2003). Vulnerable domains are contrasted with invulnerable (or less vulnerable) ones which are acquired early and relatively free of errors. Which grammatical domains are vulnerable can be identified on the basis of the relevant acquisition data. While the vulnerable domains for each language call for detailed description, the problem of explaining vulnerability remains challenging. For whatever reasons, the vulnerability of certain domains seems to be equally applicable to different groups of language learners including monolingual and bilingual children, as well as those with language disorders.

Some vulnerable domains such as word order in the DP in the case of Swedish-Italian bilingual children (Bernardini 2003) have been attributed to input ambiguity: possessives and attributive adjectives in Italian are both pre- and post-nominal, but with invariant order in Swedish, i.e. only pre-nominal. A child with Italian as the weaker language showed a preference for prenominal possessive and attributive adjectives in Italian, which in turn coincides with the order found in Swedish. Ambiguous input (in our terms, ambiguity of evidence, as defined in 2.6.3 above) as well as language dominance are considered as factors that cause difficulties in the domain under investigation.

Beyond typical bilingual and monolingual acquisition, the notion of vulnerable domain is also applicable to atypical populations. For example, children with Specific Language Impairment (SLI) and speakers suffering from aphasia show difficulty with particular grammatical domains such as that of CP (complementizer phrase) (Platzack 2001). There is scope for interdisciplinary studies here.

2.8 Bilingual development and language contact

An old insight recognizes the child as a microcosm of language history, and the bilingual child in particular as a microcosm of language contact:

Toutes les modifications phonétiques, morphologiques et syntaxiques qui caractérisent la vie des langues apparaîssent dans le parler des enfants. ('All phonetic, morphological, and syntactic changes that are characteristic of the lives of languages occur in children's language.') (Grammont 1902: 61)

Previous works that draw together language acquisition and language contact include book-length treatments such as Andersen (1983a), Adone and Plag (1994) and Wekker (1996). DeGraff's comprehensive edited volume addresses the convergence of 'conditions that constrain the changes that grammatical systems undergo, both within individual speakers and across generations of speakers' (1999: 1). Thus Mufwene's (1999) study compares his daughter's language development to the universal claims of the Language Bioprogram Hypothesis of Bickerton (1981). The interdisciplinary combination of language acquisition, language change and creolization 'attempts to triangulate the cognitive roots of language development' (DeGraff 1999: 1). Continuing the spirit of this line of inquiry, we extend the empirical domain to include bilingual language acquisition in children.

2.8.1 Creoles and other contact languages

For a variety of reasons, many scholars no longer see a clear distinction between creoles and other languages resulting from situations of language contact (Corne 1999, Mufwene 2001). Empirically, this results from the recognition of a continuum between typical creoles and other varieties showing effects of contact (Ansaldo & Matthews 2001). For example, is Singapore Colloquial English a variety of English, a 'creoloid' or 'almost a creole' (Gupta 1994)? Is Baba Malay a creole, or a dialect of Malay with influence from Hokkien (Ansaldo & Matthews 1999)? While McWhorter (2005) reiterates the case that creoles form a typologically distinct class of languages, the assumption of 'creole exceptionalism' is argued to be inconsistent with current assumptions about the language faculty, Universal Grammar and language acquisition (DeGraff 2003a). To sidestep this controversy, we adopt the general term *contact language*, defined as 'a language that arises as a direct result of language contact and that comprises linguistic material which cannot be traced back primarily to a single source language' (Thomason 1996: 3). Under this definition, Baba Malay and Singapore Colloquial English are clearly contact languages: while their vocabulary is primarily from Malay and English respectively, they incorporate substantial material not deriving from these languages, including grammatical structures as well as lexical items from Chinese dialects. Whether they should be considered 'creoles' is not a substantive linguistic question, though it may have some sociological import.

2.8.2   Children versus adults in the development of contact languages

Approaches to creole formation differ with regard to whether children or adults are seen as primarily responsible (DeGraff 1999: 12). In the case of adults, it is a matter of second language acquisition, with transfer from the first language to the second as a mechanism of substrate influence. In the case of children, the structure of the creole is attributed to Chomskyan Universal Grammar (UG) or Bickerton's Language Bioprogram which leaves little scope for substrate influence. A third possibility considered by DeGraff (1999: 13) is that 'children and adults both participate (perhaps via different mechanisms . . .)'. This possibility is elaborated in the 'L2A-L1A cascade' model, in which adult second language acquisition is the conduit for substrate influence in the developing creole (DeGraff 2003b). The creole as spoken by adults is part of the input to children, who adopt features of the adult variety while developing their own language in accordance with UG.

Previous work has typically assumed adult second language acquisition as the route by which substrate features enter a contact language:

Creolists generally accept that creole formation was primarily a process of second language acquisition in rather unusual circumstances. Moreover, children may have played a role in regularizing the developing grammar. The processes of restructuring that created creoles are in principle the same as those found in SLA and to a lesser extent first language acquisition. (Winford 2003: 356)

This assumption is spelt out explicitly in Lefebvre's Relexification model:

substratal features are transferred into the creole by means of relexification . . . this mental process applies in a situation which involves second language acquisition. (Lefebvre 1998: 34–35)

the creators of a creole, *adult native speakers* of substratum languages, use the properties of their native lexicons, the parametric values and the semantic interpretation rules of their native grammars in creating the creole. (Lefebvre 2001:186–187, emphasis added)

In the case of Haitian Creole, the focus of Lefebvre's research, this assumption is justified by her argument that very few children were present: few children were born to slaves in the early plantation period, and slaves were replenished by adults newly imported from Africa. In cases such as Singapore Colloquial English and Hawaiian Creole English, however, no such assumption is justified.

Curiously absent from this discussion has been the possibility of bilingual (or multilingual) children as agents of transfer and thus of contact-induced change. A dichotomy is assumed between adults (who are acknowledged to transfer features of substrate languages) and children (who are assumed not to do so). While a similar assumption is implicit in the discussion of substrate influence in Mufwene (2001: 131), his ecological model does not rule out a role for bilingual children: both adults and children can contribute features, such as grammatical usages derived by replication, to the feature pool from which features are selected based on ecological factors.[6]

2.8.3   Child bilingualism in the formation of contact languages

Studies of grammatical interaction in bilingual children, including those presented in the following chapters, suggest that child bilingualism is a potential mechanism for contact-induced change and substrate influence in particular. Whether bilingual acquisition has actually been a causal factor in particular cases of formation of creoles and other contact languages is then an empirical question.

Bakker (2002: 70) argues that creoles could not have developed in mixed households where the parents are native speakers of different languages, one reason being that in such situations a mixed language rather than a creole develops. As we shall see, our Cantonese-dominant bilingual children growing up in such mixed households develop something very much like a creole: in particular, transfer in bilingual development is closely parallel to substrate influence as seen in Singapore Colloquial English, as in the case of *wh*-in-situ (see section 4.5), null objects (section 5.4), relative clauses (section 6.5) and contact-induced grammaticalization (chapter 8). However, the assumption of mixed households is not necessary to our argument. While our own data do come from mixed households, there are many other ways in which children may grow up bilingual (cf. Romaine 1995). As long as bilingual children are present, interactive development of the kind discussed in this study provides a potential mechanism for phenomena observable in creoles, such as substrate influence.

The historical question then involves whether there is evidence that children grew up bilingual in the societies in which particular contact languages have evolved. The answer to this question appears to vary from one environment to another. In the case of Haiti, it has been argued that too few children were present at the time Haitian Creole was developing in the late seventeenth century: in 1681, twenty-two years after colonization, only 14.9% of Africans in Haiti were children (Lefebvre 1998: 53). Even if children were effectively absent from some situations of creole formation, this does not preclude the possibility that they have played a role in others. As discussed in section 2.1 above, similar transfer effects can and do occur in child bilingualism and adult second language acquisition. Thus adults may have been the primary agents of substrate influence in the case of Haitian Creole, as argued by Lefebvre (1998), and children or adolescents in the case of Hawaiian Creole English as argued by Roberts (2000).

A case for the role of bilingual acquisition in the formation of creoles is made by Satterfield (2005). Computer simulations, supported in the case of Sranan Tongo by historical records, suggest that 'Locally born bilingual children appear to be the primary contributors to the emerging creole' (Satterfield (2005: 2075). Regardless of how accurately the computer simulations model the environments and processes of creole formation, the logic of her argument leads to a rethinking of the Language Bioprogram Hypothesis of Bickerton (1981):[7]

If indeed a bioprogram exists, it may well be in the form of an expansive blueprint toward bilingualism, instead of its present conceptualization as a reduction to a default monolingual grammar. (Satterfield 2005: 2091)

Returning to Hawaii, the birthplace of the Language Bioprogram Hypothesis, Roberts (2000) argues that bilingual children and adolescents were primarily responsible for developing HCE. The ancestral languages spoken by immigrants (including Japanese, Chinese and Philippine languages) did not disappear as quickly as Bickerton (1981) had assumed. A survey conducted in 1926, covering children born between 1902 and 1913, showed that ancestral languages were spoken in the majority of households, reaching 100% in Japanese and 94.7% in Chinese households (Roberts 2000: 280). The children surveyed had varying degrees of competence in the ancestral languages of their parents, who in many cases did not speak 'Pidgin'. This bilingual, locally-born generation (Roberts' 'G2') provides a population in whom interactive development could have introduced substrate features. There is evidence that they did so: Roberts (2000: 287) examines characteristic creole grammatical features such as the progressive aspect marker *stei*. Of eleven grammatical features examined, seven prove to be exclusive to locally born speakers, as opposed to adult immigrants. Thus the grammatical features found exclusively in locally born speakers would not appear to be a result of adult second language acquisition, but rather that of bilingual and/or child second language acquisition.

If bilingual children contributed to the structure of the emerging creole in Hawaii, where the historical records are relatively rich, it may be that they also did so in other cases where the records are less informative. Mufwene (2004, 2005) argues that the social circumstances in Hawaii were different from those in the Caribbean and Indian Ocean creoles in ways which are directly relevant to this question. In particular, ethnic groups such as the Chinese and Japanese lived in separate communities, speaking their ancestral languages at home and the developing creole for interaction with other groups. Children thus grew up bilingual, and were responsible for introducing many of the distinctive features of the creole.

2.9   Summary

We have outlined a theoretical framework for the analysis of grammatical development in childhood bilingualism and its role in language contact at large. A number of theoretical issues have been raised and discussed. Fundamental epistemological issues of bilingual and second language acquisition have led us to examine important differences in the two acquisition contexts, while viewing them as constituting a continuum rather than a dichotomy. We have also raised the logical problem of bilingual acquisition and discussed the poverty of the dual stimulus, showing how the acquisition task poses a more severe challenge to the bilingual than the monolingual child. Two sides of the logical problem are distinguished: on the one hand, the successful acquisition of knowledge of two languages that goes beyond the dual input strengthens the argument from the poverty of stimulus, since the deficiency of input is more acute and the success all the more remarkable; on the other hand, cases of uneven development where the course of development of one or both languages may be less rapid and uniform than the monolingual counterparts with delay in some grammatical domains, also call for explanation.

While we assume that the child's developing grammars constitute separate systems, interaction between them is commonly found at the grammatical level, and is increasingly well understood. Cross-linguistic influence is bidirectional and in many cases asymmetrical. These patterns of interaction may be explained by a number of factors including language dominance, developmental asynchrony and input ambiguity, each of which we have formulated as hypotheses for the purpose of the present study.

Finally, interaction between developing grammatical systems in childhood bilingualism provides a possible route for substrate influence as seen in contact languages. While we focus in this study on early bilingualism, we assume that these effects occur alongside classical second language acquisition: for example, Chinese substrate features are incorporated into Singapore Colloquial English in the course of both bilingual first language acquisition and second language acquisition (whether by children or adults).

NOTES

1. In the dialogue, Sophie refers to Alicia using the pronoun *he* instead of *she*, which illustrates one feature of our bilingual children's English, i.e. the lack of gender distinction whereby they do not distinguish between *he* and *she* or *him* and *her* in the early stages, and even at age five as in the case of Sophie. This is also a prominent feature in adult Chinese second language speakers especially in their spoken English, and of Singapore Colloquial English where gender agreement is sporadic. Chinese influence plays a role here, since no such gender distinction is made in the spoken language.

2. Bosch and Sebastián-Gallés (2003: 238) remark that 'even though Catalan and Spanish languages can be distinguished rather early in development (at least from 4.5 months of age), phonetic information would not be initially differentiated in language-specific files'. They hypothesize that lexical knowledge may trigger the reorganization of the phonetic categories into language-specific ones. A number of recent papers in McCardle and Hoff (2006) discuss the findings of bilingual infants' speech processing experiments (Fernald 2006; Vihman et al. 2006; Werker, Weikum & Yoshida 2006).

3. See Deuchar and Quay (1998) for a different interpretation of the question of early syntactic differentiation.

4. It may be significant that there is no established term for the child's 'other' language(s). The term 'recessive' as used in genetics does not seem appropriate in bilingual development, since recessive genes are typically unexpressed (rather than under-expressed). Bernardini and Schlyter (2004) use the term 'non-dominant' before introducing their own distinction between 'stronger' and 'weaker' languages.

5. In particular models of grammar, technical distinctions are made between various null elements: thus the null pronominal element might be treated as a variable (x) or a null pronoun *pro*. Such distinctions are highly theory-dependent, whereas the observations we wish to make transcend such distinctions: in particular, the null pronominal element, however represented, is essential to the interpretation of the sentence. The subscript *i* indicates that the null objects *e* refer to the same entity as the sentence topic.

6. We thank Salikoko Mufwene for clarifying this point.

7. In reviewing the vicissitudes of the Language Bioprogram Hypothesis, Bickerton (2003) remarked that some scholars apparently believe that the structure of another language can somehow be 'smuggled' into a developing creole. Rethinking the bioprogram hypothesis along bilingual lines, as suggested by Satterfield (2005), removes much of the mystery (or illegal activity) here.

3 Methodology

Child: You write that down.
Father: What shall I write down?
Child: Just now I say that one. [i.e. 'What I said just now.']
Daddy, you write that down, you tell me all that I say.

(Sophie 5;05;00)

At age five, Sophie begins to appreciate the purpose of the notebooks in which her parents have been writing down utterances produced by herself and her siblings. In expressing her new-found interest in her own language, Sophie reveals that her English is in a period of transition between the Cantonese form of relative clause (preceding the noun, as in [*just now I say*] *that one*) and the English one (as in *all that I say*). During this transitional period she also produces hybrid forms such as *that I write that one* (section 6.3.2). As discussed in chapter 6, it is only thanks to the diary data that we are able to document this transition.

In this chapter we first survey some methodological issues in the field of early bilingual acquisition at large (section 3.1). We then discuss the methods of data collection, background of the bilingual children, and types of data that form the basis for our investigation of the bilingual child (section 3.2). Finally, we discuss measures of language dominance: we motivate the measurement of dominance using MLU differentials (section 3.3) and discuss the relationship of language preferences, silent periods and code-mixing to language dominance (section 3.4).

3.1   Methodologies in the study of bilingual acquisition

A variety of methods have been used to collect data from bilingual children for analysis. Two methods are most commonly used in current bilingual acquisition research:
(1)   case studies using a longitudinal design over an extended period of time during which the child is audio- and/or video-taped regularly in a natural-istic setting, usually in the home interacting with the parents, caregivers or

research assistants. The recordings are then transcribed and the resulting transcripts form a corpus for systematic analysis. Sometimes the corpus data are supplemented by diary records kept by the parent and/or researcher (as in the case of Deuchar & Quay 2000);

(2) cross-sectional experimental studies that compare children at different ages testing their perception, production or comprehension of language in a controlled setting (cf. papers in Cenoz & Genesee 2001; Paradis 2001; Nicoladis 2003, 2006 among others).

Whatever methods are used, studies of bilingual development call for systematic comparison with monolingual data for the acquisition of the same target languages. When bilingual acquisition data are compared with monolingual data, factors such as comparability of ages, size of corpus, and levels of language development need to be taken into consideration so that valid quantitative and qualitative comparisons can be made (De Houwer 1998b).

Some general methodological issues in the study of bilingual development will be raised and discussed. We shall consider the nature of data produced by sampling spontaneous speech production in creating corpora for case studies, as well as data collected using the diary method. We discuss the advantages and disadvantages of each of these methods in our study of bilingual acquisition, drawing attention to the limitations of both corpus and diary data.

3.1.1 The case study

Following Platt (1988: 18), the value of case studies in the field of bilingual acquisition is argued for by Deuchar and Quay (2000: 2), Lanza (2004: 81–82) and others on a number of grounds:

(a) case studies reveal what features and patterns of development are possible, and hence need to be taken account of in any generalization that applies to all bilingual children;

(b) a case may be used to refute a generalization, since even a single counterexample suffices for this purpose;

(c) a case study may provide a source of hypotheses that inform the overall theory of bilingual acquisition. Such hypotheses can be tested and refined in cross-sectional or experimental studies. In practice, most recent contributions to bilingual first language acquisition have come from detailed case studies of a few children rather than experimental studies of a large number of children. For example:

- Gawlitzek-Maiwald and Tracy's (1996) Bilingual Bootstrapping Hypothesis is based largely on a single child, Hannah;
- Lanza's (2004) hypotheses for language mixing are derived from two children, Siri and Tomas;

- Bernardini and Schlyter's (2004) Ivy Hypothesis for uneven development is based largely on three children (Lukas, Paul and Léo);
- Müller's (2004) argument against language dominance is based on two children, Ivar and Céline.

A practical consideration underlying the prevalence of case studies is that a longitudinal study over one or more years is a major undertaking which limits most researchers to a small number of children. A more substantive factor involves the multitude of variables that may impinge on bilingual development, from different language pairs and age of exposure to personality factors and idiosyncratic language preferences. Given so many potentially relevant variables, group data involving a number of disparate bilingual children will show greater heterogeneity compared to a group of monolingual children, which calls into question their validity. For example, if (as we argue in section 3.3) language dominance is a matter of degree, to assign a particular child to an 'English-dominant' group would be an arbitrary step which could obscure the true pattern of variation.

The major limitation of the case study is that generalization to a wider population may not be justified. Some studies make rather broad claims on the basis of a comparison of two children. For example, in attempting to 'eliminate dominance' as an explanation for cross-linguistic influence, Müller (2004: 276) uses a comparison between Céline (who shows a clear pattern of dominance) and Ivar (who does not). This point may be valid for the particular grammatical domain and language pair being investigated, but the case study of two children is far from sufficient for dominance to be eliminated as a factor in general (see section 2.5.2).

3.1.2   Advantages and limitations of studying spontaneous speech

Spontaneous speech data for analysis are typically collected by recording interaction between the child and adult interlocutors in naturalistic settings. Studying such production data has the advantage of avoiding the artificiality induced by experimental methods such as elicited production tasks. For example, in their experiments on long-distance *wh*-movement, Thornton and Crain (1994: 220) found that some children produced examples of 'partial *wh*-movement' as in (1):

(1)   Who do you think who is in the box?

One may wonder whether such questions are representative of the child's knowledge, or whether they are only produced in response to an experimental situation. In chapter 4 we show that the bilingual children do produce examples of partial movement in spontaneous speech, as recorded in the diary data.

A major limitation of spontaneous speech data is that the child may not produce everything that has been acquired. It may well be that the child does not have the opportunity to use a certain structure in certain contexts and therefore fails to produce it, even though the structure is already part of the child's grammar. This is especially likely when the structure in question is rare and complex (Stromswold 1996: 24–26).

Another weakness of spontaneous production data is that 'A restricted sample of the learner's production cannot unambiguously determine hypothesis type' (Bley-Vroman 1986: 367). That is, even when the children produce utterances relevant to the domain under investigation, they may be consistent with any number of hypotheses. Even large, dense corpora do not solve this problem. The following example from Timmy, for example, is ambiguous:

(2)   Bei2   shark   sik6   laa1
         give   shark   eat   SFP   (Timmy 2;03;17)

Given the polysemy of Cantonese *bei2*, this utterance could be interpreted in at least three ways (Wong 2004):
  (i) lexical: 'Give [it] to the shark to eat'
  (ii) permissive: 'Let the shark eat (it)'
  (iii) passive: '[it] gets eaten by the shark'
These various interpretations of *bei2* and *give* are further explored in chapter 8.

3.1.3   The diary method

In the earliest child language studies, before the advent of audio- and video-recording technology, the diary method was invariably used. Clara and William Stern's (1907) classic volume *Die Kindersprache* 'Children's Language', contains details of their own three German-speaking children Hilde, Günther and Eva's language development. This was followed by Werner Leopold's (1939–1949) bilingual diary studies of his two daughters Hildegard and Karla. The diary method was the principal method used in the classic studies of child language, and has continued to be a valuable source of data in recent times. The advantages of having the parent keeping a diary of the child's development include the parent's close observation on a daily basis, and in many cases the overall period of observation yields an extended developmental trajectory from birth into the school years. Through the eyes of the parent-researcher across a much wider range of real-life situations than is possible for researchers who make weekly visits, the spontaneous data produced by the child outside of recording sessions can be captured, partially if not exhaustively. Despite the inevitable bias in selecting data for recording and description, the diary method can be updated to become more systematic, minimizing problems such as the selectivity in data collection (Braunwald & Brislin 1979; Mervis et al. 1992).

The earliest studies of Chinese-English bilingual development date back to Madorah Smith (1931, 1935). Her study was based on diary records of eight bilingual children from the same family kept by their mother from the time of the birth of the eldest child in China until their return to America. The children were exposed to two languages from birth: English from their missionary parents, and Mandarin Chinese from their servants. This was during the 'period of detrimental effects' (Baker 2001: 136) when it was assumed that bilinguals were linguistically confused and mentally disadvantaged. Sure enough, Smith found evidence that the English vocabulary of the bilingual children was significantly less rich than that of a monolingual child of the same age. Language mixing was found to be frequent and treated as a sign of confusion, while bilingualism was seen as a handicap especially at the age of eighteen months. The modern view which has replaced this anachronistic view points instead to many cognitive advantages of childhood bilingualism (Bialystok 2001; see also section 1.1.1).

The renowned Chinese linguist Chao Yuen Ren sketched a snapshot of his grandchild Canta's Mandarin, which he termed 'the Cantian idiolect' at twenty-eight months including phonology, grammar and vocabulary (Chao 1976). Canta was born and raised in the USA and spoke Mandarin with a few English words occasionally due to some contact with English in her language environment.

Timothy Light (1977) was the first linguist to describe a case of Cantonese-English bilingual development. His daughter Claire grew up in a Cantonese-dominant household and arrived in the United States at sixteen months. Light made interesting observations regarding *Clairetalk*, discussing some striking features of her 'increasingly Anglicized' Cantonese that were argued to reflect the influence of English in her new linguistic environment. The shift from Cantonese dominance to English dominance produced anomalies including what Light called 'disintegration' of the Cantonese tonal system and there was cross-linguistic influence in syntax too.

Notable diary records of child language development include Junya Noji's (1973–1977) comprehensive diary corpus documenting the development of his Japanese-speaking child Sumi from birth to age seven during 1948–55 and the entire diary corpus has since been romanized and is available via CHILDES.[1] The number of child utterances amount to 40,000 and about 22,000 utterances by other family members with a specially detailed record of Sumi's third year. This represents by far the densest sampling of a single child's speech data and most extensive coverage well into school age. This density permits investigation of infrequent structures such as relative clauses, of which some 290 are produced by Sumi in 1,331 files from 0;00–3;11 (Ozeki & Shirai 2005).

Recent studies such as Deuchar and Quay (2000) also use the diary method alongside video and audio-recording data to investigate a bilingual child's simultaneous acquisition of English and Spanish from six months to seven years old. A remarkable feature is that from the age of 1;02 until 2;10, daily records of the child's utterances were kept. A sample page of diary entry in

CHAT format is given in Deuchar and Quay (2000: 16). Turning diary records into computerized corpora further enhances the database, yielding a more complete documentation of a child's development. The combination of the updated diary method and multimedia recording makes a great leap forward over previous studies which predate modern technology: the two-pronged data collection method yields a much more comprehensive and reliable empirical basis for the systematic study of bilingual development. With the world-wide accessibility of such databases, anyone can make use of the data and verify factual claims, thanks to the ever-expanding CHILDES archive.

3.1.4 Longitudinal corpus data

Today the diary method has been largely superceded by the use of computerized corpora. By sampling children's speech at regular intervals, the selection bias of diary studies is avoided, making quantitative analysis more reliable.

A limitation of corpus data involves the limited duration of each recording session and the frequency of recording. Tomasello and Stahl (2004) raise a number of substantive issues regarding quantitative aspects of child language sampling, such as how much to sample, at what intervals and for how long and for how many children. They estimate that the majority of databases in CHILDES represent around 1% of all the language produced and heard by the child. If the structure of interest is highly frequent, these databases may already serve the purpose, but structures which are less frequent cannot easily be captured during brief recording sessions which are typically conducted once or twice a week. Rare constructions may not appear in such data, even in many hours of recording. The issue of how frequent sampling of spontaneous speech data should be and how much data is sufficient becomes important especially when arguments are built on quantitative analysis and the precise point of emergence of particular structures. In the case of our corpus data, half an hour of interaction in each language may not be sufficient to fully capture what the child is capable of producing outside of the recording sessions. In some sessions, the child needs to take time to warm up in the non-dominant language before productive language use is recorded.

Several solutions to these problems can be pursued. One method, pioneered by Michael Tomasello and his colleagues, is to expand the duration and frequency of recording to create a 'dense' corpus. In one such corpus, the data consist of 330 hour-long recordings of one child from 2;00 to 3;11 (Maslen et al. 2004). The child was recorded on a dense schedule, '5 days on and 2 days off'. For every five sessions, one video- and four audio-recordings were made. The 'talk week' of a child of this age is estimated to be around 40 hours (Maratsos 2000). Based on this estimate, the sample density would be around 8–10% of the child's total production. From 3;03 to 3;11, recordings were made on 4 or

5 consecutive days out of each month, thus retaining the earlier density of data for each week's sample. The production of such a dense corpus offers many advantages especially when the argumentation and statistical analyses hinge on frequency of child utterances and input structures.

3.1.5   Experimental methods

An alternative response to the limitations of spontaneous speech data is to conduct experiments tapping particular domains of linguistic knowledge. A variety of experimental methods in production and comprehension have been pioneered and developed in first language acquisition by monolingual children (McDaniel, McKee & Cairns 1996, Crain & Thornton 1998, Menn & Ratner 2000) but such sophisticated experiments on bilingual children's grammatical development are still few and far between.

One methodological challenge posed to researchers in bilingual acquisition is the relative complexity of experimental design and control of variables, since any experiment calls for monolingual controls for each language, matched to the bilingual children. Thus, whereas a monolingual study could minimally be carried out with one experimental group, at least three are called for in a well-controlled experiment in bilingual acquisition: a bilingual group, and a monolingual group for each language (assuming that the development of both languages is under investigation). For example, an experiment conducted by Yip, Matthews and Huang (1996) investigating the interpretation of reflexives and pronouns by Cantonese-English bilingual children involved six groups of participants: bilingual children as experimental groups, monolingual Cantonese-speaking and monolingual English-speaking children as control groups, all divided into two age groups. As the field of bilingual acquisition develops, we anticipate that rigorous experimental verification of hypotheses will become the norm, as it is in studies of monolingual acquisition.

3.1.6   Studying and sampling input

Much research proceeds by comparing a child's production with target forms produced by native speakers of the languages involved. Such comparison is not strictly relevant to the acquisition process, however: what is relevant is the input actually available to the children. Corpora, including ours, often contain adult speech produced by researchers, but without necessarily involving the parents and regular caregivers. The language produced by researchers in the recording contexts is indeed part of the input to the child, but only a relatively small part thereof. Caution is therefore required in using such data as a proxy for the input available to the children. The study of input properties is given a higher priority in usage-based approaches to language acquisition (see Tomasello 2003) than in other approaches such as the generative paradigm. Lightfoot (1991: 20) notes a 'pathological lack of interest among generativists in the triggering experience', that is, a failure to consider how the input data 'trigger' parameter setting and other changes in the learner's grammar. We underscore the importance of investigating input properties in acquisition studies regardless of one's theoretical framework.

3.2 The Hong Kong Bilingual Child Language Corpus and other data for this study

Our own longitudinal data are derived from a series of projects conducted in Hong Kong between 1994 and 2005, funded by the Hong Kong Research Grants Council. The objectives of the projects included the creation of the Hong Kong Bilingual Child Language Corpus as well as case studies of developing grammatical competence in bilingual children. The creation of a large-scale longitudinal corpus allows us to systematically investigate many aspects of childhood bilingualism.[2] From the six Hong Kong bilingual children studied in the course of these projects we focus primarily on our own three children in this book, for reasons that will become clear. In particular, the diary data for the three siblings enable all grammatical topics to be investigated more thoroughly, while for some topics (such as relative clauses, discussed in chapter 6) the diary data play a crucial role in filling the gaps left by the corpus data. Since our diary entries primarily record the noteworthy examples while leaving out many other relevant details, the frequency of a certain construction can at most indicate the relative productivity but does not lend itself to statistical analysis in the absence of information regarding the quantity of obligatory contexts.

In addition to our corpus of bilingual development, we make use of Lee et al.'s (1996) corpus of Cantonese monolingual development (see section 3.2.5), alongside child English corpora including the classic longitudinal studies such as Brown (1973) and Bloom (1973) in the CHILDES database (see MacWhinney 2000a). These monolingual corpora make it possible for us to conduct systematic comparison of our bilingual children and their monolingual counterparts' longitudinal development (see chapters 4, 5 and 7).

3.2.1 Children for our case study

The longitudinal data in this study come from the Hong Kong Bilingual Child Language Corpus, which is available through the Child Language Data Exchange System (CHILDES) based in Carnegie Mellon University. The Corpus documents the longitudinal development of six children growing up in Hong Kong exposed to Cantonese and English from birth. These children grew up in a one parent – one language environment where each parent is a

Table 3.1. *Background of six bilingual children*

Child	native language of mother	native language of father	age span of corpus study (years; months; days)
Timmy	Cantonese	English	2;01;22–3;06;25
Sophie	Cantonese	English	1;06;00–3;00;09
Alicia	Cantonese	English	1;03;10–3;00;24
Llywelyn	Cantonese	English	2;00;12–3;04;17
Charlotte	Cantonese	English	1;08;28–3;00;03
Kathryn	English	Cantonese	3;01;05–4;06;07

native speaker of the respective language (see table 3.1).[3] All the children in our study are offspring of cross-cultural marriages, known as *wan6hyut3ji4* 'mixed blood children' in Cantonese. Although the focus of our inquiry is on the three siblings, reference will be made to the other three bilingual children whenever relevant.

The principal protagonists of the present case study are the three children of the co-authors, the mother being a native speaker of Hong Kong Cantonese and the father of British English. Timmy is the first-born son, Sophie the daughter born two years and nine months later and Alicia the second daughter born seven years later. The family lives in Hong Kong and adopted the one parent – one language principle when addressing the children. In the case of the third child, Alicia, the policy was relaxed in order to provide more English input as the balance of input was clearly in favour of Cantonese, and English was occasionally used by the mother. The language between the parents is mainly Cantonese, with frequent code-mixing, as is characteristic of the speech of Hong Kong middle-class families. Despite the one parent – one language principle, the quantity of input from the two languages is by no means balanced: the language of the community is Cantonese, while the children's extended family (maternal relatives) also speak Cantonese. Consequently, the children received more Cantonese than English input in their first five years.

In addition to Cantonese, the maternal grandmother also speaks the Chiu Chow dialect (often mixed with Cantonese). Chiu Chow (also known as Chaozhou or Teochew), the ancestral language of a sizeable minority in Hong Kong, is spoken in eastern Guangdong province and belongs to the southern Min dialect group. Although diverging from Cantonese in many respects, it shares the same broad typological characteristics which are at issue in this study, such as *wh*-in-situ, null objects and prenominal relative clauses. The children have some passive knowledge of Chiu Chow but seldom produce it.

At home, regular input in English came solely from the father and the family's Filipina domestic helper, while other English-speaking relatives visited only occasionally. Like most middle-class families in Hong Kong, all the families in our study employed domestic helpers at some point. They are native speakers of Philippine languages such as Tagalog and Cebuano. The question of what role the non-native English spoken by the domestic helpers has in the children's language development is a pertinent one. As far as the features discussed in this book are concerned, we observe that the English of the helpers conforms to standard English: they do not, for example, use *wh*-in-situ or prenominal relative clauses.

The three siblings attended two kindergartens each day, one with Cantonese and the other with English as medium of instruction. Timmy began by attending a bilingual kindergarten from age 2;04 for three hours a day, with approximately equal amounts of input from each language; from 3;04, he attended a Cantonese-medium kindergarten in the morning and an English-medium kindergarten in the afternoon. Sophie attended a Cantonese-medium kindergarten from 2;06, and from 3;02 also attended the English kindergarten in the morning. Alicia attended a Cantonese-medium kindergarten from 2;03 and the English-medium kindergarten as well from 3;03. From age 5;03 (5;01 in Sophie's case), all three siblings entered the same full-time English-medium primary school.

Despite these similar histories, the three siblings have somewhat different sources of input, primarily due to birth-order effects. Since Timmy is the first-born son, during the first three years of language development, there was no other sibling to talk to him, which precludes siblings as a source of input. But for his two younger sisters, input comes from their elder siblings as well as parents and other caregivers. As the preferred language among the siblings is Cantonese, at least up to age five, the balance of the input increasingly favours Cantonese throughout the preschool years.

Differences in personality are also reflected in the corpus data. Timmy and Alicia were by nature reserved, which is reflected in some of their transcripts. In contrast, Sophie is more sociable and talkative, the self-styled 'talking girl' of the family. Her extrovert personality makes her a fruitful source of data and insights: under normal circumstances, it takes only minimal prompting to get her to speak in either language.

The three additional bilingual children, Llywelyn, Charlotte and Kathryn are from similar family backgrounds (see table 3.1) with the exception that in Kathryn's case it is the mother who speaks English, and the father Cantonese. These three children show different patterns which are used for comparison with those of the three siblings. Llywelyn's development resembles Timmy's but is less strongly Cantonese-dominant. Charlotte's English was ahead of her Cantonese, resulting in very different patterns. Kathryn is of particular interest as the most balanced child represented in the corpus.

Kathryn's father, a neuro-surgeon at a university hospital, is a native speaker of Cantonese and her mother of British English.[4] The mother, a housewife at the time of study, was the principal caregiver. The family employed a Filipina domestic helper for a brief period until Kathryn was around age three, and subsequently a part-time Cantonese cleaner who also spoke fluent English. Kathryn attended the Cantonese section of an international kindergarten from 2;07. According to her mother's observations this set her subsequent pattern of language use, with Cantonese as the language of social interaction, and English used in academic settings. Of the six Cantonese-English bilingual children studied, Kathryn shows the most balanced pattern of development, with relatively little evidence of language dominance or concomitant transfer compared to the three siblings who show dominance in Cantonese over English.

Llywelyn (a name of Welsh origin) is the second of two children. His father is a native speaker of British English and a professional linguist. He was occasionally away from home during Llywelyn's early years during 1;06–2;00, including six months' sabbatical leave in Australia. Llywelyn's mother is a native Cantonese speaker and an accountant by profession. The family employed two Filipina domestic helpers. Another important role in Llywelyn's language ecology was played by his brother, three years and eight months older, who was very advanced in terms of language and cognitive development. Llywelyn's English shows some of the same features observed in the Cantonese-dominant siblings, such as *wh*-in-situ questions (see chapter 4) and null objects (see chapter 5).

Charlotte is the second of two children. Charlotte's elder sister is two years and nine months older.[5] Charlotte's mother, a teacher, is a native speaker of Cantonese. Her father is a professor from the UK, who was on sabbatical leave in New Zealand when Charlotte was born. At four and a half months she moved to Hong Kong where she was cared for by a Filipina domestic helper. Throughout the period of study, Charlotte was more dominant in English, making an interesting contrast with Cantonese-dominant children. Charlotte's Cantonese shows strong English influence such as producing Cantonese words with non-target tones and sentences with English prosody, sounding very much like a non-native speaker of Cantonese.

3.2.2   Recording

Spontaneous speech data were recorded at the child's home where the routines included activities such as playing with toys and telling stories. The interactions consisted of conversations between the child and the investigator and whichever adult caregiver was present. In the case of Alicia, the father, i.e. the second author, served as the English-speaking interlocutor in almost every recording session. The details of the period of corpus study for each child are given in table 3.1.

The researchers sought to reproduce the one person – one language approach in the elicitation environment by having one of the two research assistants

Table 3.2. *Number of files and number of child utterances produced by six children in the Hong Kong Bilingual Child Language Corpus*

Child	Timmy	Sophie	Alicia	Llywelyn	Kathryn	Charlotte	Total
Age	2;01.22–	1;06;00–	1;03;10–	2;00;12–	3;01;05–	1;08.28–	
	3;06;25	3;00;09	3;00;24	3;04;17	4;06;07	3;00;03	
No. of Cantonese files	35	40	40	17	17	19	168
No. of utterances in Cantonese files	10,631	12,574	6,217	3,831	4,281	4,012	41,546
No. of English files	38	40	40	17	17	19	171
No. of utterances in English files	6,241	6,717	5,109	4,121	4,202	4,621	31,011

involved in each recording session responsible for speaking each language, though English was a second language for all the assistants. In practice, this one person – one language strategy did not always work as intended for elicitation purposes. As a result one or more adults present at the recording session may be speaking both English and Cantonese to the child who in turn code-mixes from time to time. Hence some files, especially the early ones under the category Cantonese, for example, actually contain a considerable amount of English and language mixing. As the child's languages develop, the division into Cantonese and English files can be made more easily.

The children's development in both languages was observed and recorded at weekly or bi-weekly intervals for periods of one to two and a half years. On average, each recording session consisted of an hour of audio and in some cases video-recordings of the children engaged in their daily activities such as playing, reading and role playing. The children were encouraged to speak in Cantonese for half an hour and in English for half an hour.

The entire database contains 352 files in two languages coded in CHAT (Codes for the Human Analysis of Transcripts) format and tagged with a set of 33 word-class labels. The age range covered by the corpus starts at 1;03 and ends at 4;06. The creation of the tagged corpus in electronic format allows world-wide access via the internet and enables systematic search of data to be conducted efficiently and rapidly. Table 3.2 shows the individual child's number of files and number of utterances in these files.

The total number of child utterances is 41,546 and 31,011 in the Cantonese and English files respectively. There is a total of 339 files, 168 in Cantonese and 171 in English, excluding Timmy's 13 mixed files from 1;06–2;01. Unlike in monolingual transcripts, a number of utterances in these files in our bilingual corpus contain code-mixed utterances in the respective language contexts. For example, a number of utterances in the English files of our Cantonese-dominant children Timmy, Sophie, Alicia and Llywelyn contain Cantonese utterances and code-mixed Cantonese words in their English utterances. The reverse pattern is observed in the English-dominant child Charlotte whose Cantonese files contain many English utterances as well as code-mixing with English words (see further discussion of language dominance in section 3.3).

The availability of computerized transcripts provides researchers with a useful source of data, enabling them to easily cull lines that contain the features of interest as well as lines from the surrounding context, before and after the target utterances. This can be done by using a search program such as the CLAN command "kwal" (keyword and line) to extract a specified number of lines immediately preceding and following a target utterance. The prior utterances preceding the child's utterances are important in interpreting the data in context so that irrelevant factors such as imitations, repetitions and transcription errors can be excluded and prevented from influencing the analysis of the target structure and biasing the hypothesis being tested.

The bilingual corpus was created by regular audio-recording of Timmy, Llywelyn and Kathryn and, in the case of Sophie, Alicia and Charlotte, video-recording over a period of one to two years. The digitized audio and video files together with the transcripts make it possible for the researcher to obtain information about the nonlinguistic context and interpret the data more accurately by eliminating some ambiguities. The actual sounds produced by the child can also be heard, bringing the corpus to life and opening up the phonological aspects of bilingual development to systematic study. Sample transcripts for each subject are linked to audio and video files so that the children's speech can be heard while reading the transcripts, and the action viewed on screen. The full set of video data for Alicia from 1;03–3;00 is available for access via CHILDES.

3.2.3   Transcription

The speech data were transcribed by the research assistants and then checked by members of the research team. The transcript for English files has the format as in figure 3.1 while the Cantonese transcript is exemplified in figure 3.2. In figure 3.1, the sample English transcript shows that a postcode @sl is attached to the child's first utterance *sap6zi6gaa3* 'cross', which is in Cantonese. The postcode is attached to all the Cantonese words in an English file and all the English words in a Cantonese file in order to exclude them from calculations of Mean Length of Utterance (MLU), see note 11. In figure 3.2, the child's Cantonese as shown on the main tier was initially transcribed using romanized Cantonese instead of Chinese characters. Cantonese was transcribed using the *Jyut6Ping3* romanization system, developed by the Linguistic Society of Hong Kong (Tang et al. 2002). The %can tier in Chinese characters was generated at

@Begin
@Languages: en, zh-yue
@Participants: CHI Alicia Target_Child , MIC Michelle Investigator , FAT
        Father , SIS Sophie Sister , HOU Belma Housekeeper
@ID: zh-yue, en|yipmatthews|CHI|2;10.15||||Target_Child||
@ID: zh-yue, en|yipmatthews|MIC|||||Investigator||
@ID: en, zh-yue|yipmatthews|FAT|||||Father||
@ID: en, zh-yue|yipmatthews|HOU|||||Housekeeper||
@ID: zh-yue, en|yipmatthews|SIS|||||Sister||
@Birth of CHI: 28-MAY-2000
@Date: 12-APR-2003
@Coder: Michelle Li, Uta Lam
@Comment: 30 minutes recording

*CHI: sap6zi6gaa3@sl .
%mor: nn|sap6zi6gaa3 .
%ort: 十字架
*FAT: what's that , Alicia ?
%mor: pro:wh|what~v|be&3S pro:dem|that n:prop|Alicia ?
*CHI: &craise .
*FAT: +" &craise ?
*CHI: yeh .
%mor: co|yeh .
*FAT: cross .
%mor: n|cross .
*FAT: it's a cross, isn't it ?
%mor: pro|it~v|be&3S det|a n|cross v:aux|be&3S~neg|not pro|it ?
*FAT: a cross .
%mor: det|a n|cross .
*CHI: www [= "cross" in Chaozhou dialect] .
*FAT: hey , we could draw that .
%mor: co|hey pro|we v:aux|could v|draw pro:dem|that .
*FAT: can you draw that ?
%mor: v:aux|can pro|you v|draw pro:dem|that ?
*CHI: www [= " cross" in Chaozhou dialect] .
*FAT: you know how to draw that ?
%mor: pro|you v|know adv:wh|how inf|to v|draw pro:dem|that ?
*CHI: < yeh > [>] .
%mor: co|yeh .
*FAT: < oh , > [<] the other way round .
%mor: co|oh det|the qn|other n|way adv|round .
*FAT: what colour it's going to be ?
%mor: pro:wh|what n|colour pro|it~v:aux|be&3S v|go-PROG inf|to v|be ?
*FAT: it's going to be < blue > [/] blue or green ?
%mor: pro|it~v:aux|be&3S v|go-PROG v|be adj|blue conj:coo|or
        adj|green ?
*CHI: green # this one xx .
%mor: adj|green det|this pro:indef|one.
*FAT: it's going to be green .
%mor: pro|it~v:aux|be&3S v|go-PROG inf|to v|be adj|green .
*CHI: yah .
%mor: co|yah .
*CHI: green this < one > [>] .
%mor: adj|green det|this pro:indef|one .
@End

Figure 3.1 Sample English transcript at age 2;10;15

@Begin
@Languages: zh-yue, en
@Participants: CHI Alicia Target_Child, MOT Mother, FAT Father, BRO Timmy
Brother, SIS Sophie Sister, GRA Grandmother
@ID: zh-yue, en|yipmatthews|CHI|1;10;16||||Target_Child||
@ID: zh-yue, en|yipmatthews|MOT|||||Mother||
@ID: zh-yue, en|yipmatthews|FAT|||||Father||
@ID: zh-yue, en|yipmatthews|BRO|||||Brother||
@ID: zh-yue, en|yipmatthews|SIS|||||Sister||
@ID: zh-yue, en|yipmatthews|GRA|||||Grandmother||
@Birth of CHI: 28-MAY-2000
@Date: 13-APR-2002
@Tape Location: A087
@Coder: Michelle Li, Uta Lam
@Comment: 30 minutes recording
*MOT: okay .
%mor: co|okay .
*MOT: Alicia, li1dou6 zou6 mat1je5 aa3, lei5 tai2 haa5 .
%mor: n:prop|Alicia loc|li1dou6 vt|zou6 wh|mat1je5 sfp|aa3 nnpr|lei5 vt|tai2 asp|haa5 .
%ort: Alicia 呢度 做 乜嘢 呀 你 睇 吓.
*CHI: xx goi2 xx go2 go3 aa3 li1 hai2 dou6 zong6 ce1 go2 go3 .
%mor: vt|goi2 det|go2 cl|go3 sfp|aa3 det|li1 prep|hai2 loc|dou6 vt|zong6 nn|ce1 det|go2
cl|go3 .
%ort: 改 嗰 個 呀 呢 喺 度 撞 車 嗰 個.
*MOT: lei5 daai6 seng1 gong2 laa1 .
%mor: nnpr|lei5 adj|daai6 nn|seng1 vt|gong2 sfp|laa1 .
%ort: 你 大 聲 講 啦.
*MOT: lei5 gong2 .
%mor: nnpr|lei5 vt|gong2 .
%ort: 你 講.
*CHI: xx .
*MOT: <go3 bou3zi2> [>] +/.
%mor: cl|go3 nn|bou3zi2 +/.
%ort: 個 報紙.
*CHI: <&=yells> [<] .
*MOT: lei5 tai2 haa5 go3 bou3zi2 .
%mor: nnpr|lei5 vt|tai2 asp|haa5 cl|go3 nn|bou3zi2 .
%ort: 你 睇 吓 個 報紙.
*MOT: tai2 haa5 zoeng1 bou3zi2 .
%mor: vt|tai2 asp|haa5 cl|zoeng1 nn|bou3zi2 .
%ort: 睇 吓 張 報紙.
*MOT: go2dou6 jau5 gaa3 mat1je5 ce1 aa3 ?
%mor: loc|go2dou6 vf|jau5 cl|gaa3 wh|mat1je5 nn|ce1 sfp|aa3 ?
%ort: 嗰度 有 架 乜嘢 車 呀.
*CHI: jat1, ji6, saam1, sei3, m5, luk6, cat1 .
%mor: q|jat1 q|ji6 q|saam1 q|sei3 q|m5 q|luk6 q|cat1 .
%ort: 一 二 三 四 五 六 七.
@End

Figure 3.2 Sample Cantonese transcript at age 1;10;16

a later stage to provide researchers who can read Chinese with easier access to the speakers' utterances. It also enables searches to be carried out for particular characters or strings of characters.[6]

The same characters are used for allophonic representations of the same morpheme. Due to ongoing sound changes in Cantonese, there is variation especially between the initial consonants *n/l*, *ng/0* and *gw/g* (Matthews & Yip 1994: 29–30). For example, the second person pronoun is represented as *lei5* although the prescribed form is *nei5*. For the demonstrative 'this' there are several variant forms, including *li1/ni1/ji1/* and *nei1/lei1*. The first person pronoun is represented as *ngo5* in the corpus but is often pronounced *o5*, while the experiential aspect marker may appear as *gwo3* or *go3*. Additional alternative forms result from contraction, for example *mat1je5* 'what' becomes *me1* and *hou2 m4 hou2* 'is it okay?' becomes *hou2 mou2*.

3.2.4 Tagging

For the purpose of grammatical analysis, words are 'tagged' with category labels. These labels are shown on a line under the transcript itself, termed the morphological tier and marked by '%mor'. The grammatical category labels for the English corpus are based on the MOR grammars for English in the CHILDES Windows Tools, while those for the Cantonese corpus are based on those of the monolingual Cantonese corpus (see section 3.2.5 below) which distinguishes thirty-three categories, with some modifications (details are given in the documentation in the CHILDES online database manual). The %mor tier was generated using a tagging program. Since Cantonese has many homophonous morphemes, it was necessary to carry out disambiguation with respect to word class. For example, the syllable *saai3* represents both the verb 'to be exposed to the sun' and a verbal particle meaning 'all, completely'. Disambiguation and checking were then conducted by hand for both Cantonese and English files.

3.2.5 The Hong Kong Cantonese Child Language Corpus (Cancorp)

For comparison with monolingual Cantonese development, we make use of the Hong Kong Cantonese Child Language Corpus (Cancorp) created by Lee et al. (1996), see also Lee and Wong (1998).[7] Cancorp includes eight Cantonese-speaking children's longitudinal developmental speech data covering the age range from one year five months to three years eight months, with each child recorded for an hour over a year on a bi-weekly basis. For our bilingual corpus to achieve comparability with Cancorp in terms of the transcription and tagging of parts of speech, both corpora use the same *Jyut6Ping3* system of romanization for Cantonese (Tang et al. 2002), and a similar classification system of grammatical categories in child Cantonese. The availability of Cancorp provides a baseline for our bilingual corpus, facilitating the comparison of Cantonese bilingual and monolingual data. Our comparison of bilingual children's Cantonese with that of their monolingual counterparts will make use of Cancorp, especially in analysing the influence of English on Cantonese in chapter 7.

3.2.6   Diary data

Following a time-honoured tradition in bilingual acquisition research, we as parent-researchers have kept our own record of our three children's language development in the form of diary entries. The availability of diary data enables us to address the development of phenomena such as relative clauses which appear rarely, if at all, in our longitudinal corpus data. The diary was kept from 1;03–6;00 for Timmy, 1;06–5;06 for Sophie, and 1;00–5;04 for Alicia. The diaries include several entries per week and were intended to complement the audio- and video-recording data. Both parents were involved in recording the data in the two languages, although the coverage of English data was more extensive than for Cantonese. The contexts of these data were mostly interaction between the child and parents at home or occasionally away from home. Relevant contextual information was given as far as possible in the diary entries. We believe that the diary data are reliable to the extent that they are systematic: all the patterns described here are instantiated at least three times, and frequently more. Such recurrent patterns imply developing competence rather than performance alone.

How representative the diary data are presents a more serious problem: there is inevitably selection bias, whereby unusual and non-native-like utterances are more likely to be recorded than unremarkable and well-formed ones. For this reason, we use the diary data essentially for qualitative analysis, and do not base any quantitative claims on them. For example, recurrent diary entries allow us to show that non-target-like structures such as prenominal relative clauses are used productively in the three siblings' English; they do not allow us to quantify the frequency of these structures relative to monolingual children.

3.3   Quantitative measures of bilingual development: language dominance and MLU differentials

Yip and Matthews (2006) discuss issues in the assessment of child bilingualism, focusing on measures of language dominance. Here we review the methodological aspects of this discussion; theoretical issues regarding dominance are discussed in chapter 2.

Objective measures of early bilingual development include several measures adopted from research on first language acquisition (Brown 1973). Those used by Genesee, Nicoladis and Paradis (1995) and Deuchar and Muntz (2003) are:

- Mean Length of Utterance (MLU), measured in words (MLUw) or morphemes (MLUm);
- Upper Bound (length of the longest utterance in a given sample);
- Multi-word (or Multi-morpheme) Utterances (percentage of utterances containing more than one word/morpheme);
- Word types (or verb types): number of different lexical items used in a sample.

To apply these measures to dominance in bilingual children, the measures must be comparable across the two (or more) languages being acquired: 'One must have a baseline for cross-linguistic comparison that works equally well for both languages. This is a fundamental problem that has so far not been solved' (De Houwer 1998b: 258). These problems are discussed in section 3.3.1 below in relation to MLU.

Another set of criteria is specific to bilingual first language acquisition:
- Language preference: in some situations (including recording sessions) children prove reluctant to use a certain language. If this behaviour is systematic over a period of development, the language that the child is more willing to speak is considered to be dominant (Saunders 1988).
- Direction of language mixing: here the proposal is that when speaking his or her weaker language, a child is more likely to resort to words from the stronger language, resulting in code-mixing or switching. Swain and Wesche (1975) found French functional morphemes mixed with English in their bilingual children, attributing this to French being the stronger language. A recent formulation of this idea is the Ivy Hypothesis of Bernardini and Schlyter (2004), according to which functional elements of the stronger language are retained when speaking the weaker language. Lanza (2004: 175) also invokes directionality of mixing as evidence of language dominance.

The relationship between these phenomena and dominance is discussed in section 3.4.

3.3.1   Measuring dominance: MLUw

We take MLU to be the most objective indicator of a child's linguistic development in each language, and hence of language dominance. The calculation of MLUw depends on decisions regarding what constitutes a word – a problem which has not been resolved, either in general (see Dixon & Aikhenvald 2002) or specifically with regard to Chinese (see Packard 2000): in particular, the phonological, morphological and syntactic criteria for wordhood do not always coincide.

It is recognized that while MLUw is useful for within-language comparisons, it may not be directly comparable across languages, especially those of different morphological types (cf. Döpke 1998: 564). If a child is acquiring an agglutinating language such as Turkish together with an isolating language such as Cantonese, for example, MLU measured in words will not be comparable because of the greater complexity of individual words in Turkish. In an agglutinating language, numerous affixes may be attached to a word stem: consequently, at the same stage of development, we can expect a higher MLU in Cantonese than in Turkish. In such cases, a possible solution is to measure MLU in terms of morphemes (MLUm) rather than words (MLUw): if the corpus is transcribed in such as way as to mark morpheme divisions, MLU (as computed automatically by CLAN software) can be counted in terms of morphemes per utterance and the resulting figures (MLUm) will provide a more comparable measure of complexity. This option, however, is only feasible if (a) both languages allow segmentation of morphemes (which is often not the case in fusional languages such as Russian) and (b) this segmentation is fully coded in the available corpus.

These issues of comparability arise in a study of Swedish-French and Swedish-Italian bilingual children by Bernardini and Schlyter (2004: 58) who use MLU measured in words (MLUw) to demonstrate that the children have 'stronger' and 'weaker' languages. The authors note that Swedish is expected to show lower MLUw values than French or Italian, as it has additional bound morphemes: for example, Swedish has a suffixed definite article, as in *stad-en* 'the city' where Italian has a separate word (*la città* 'the city'). The same expression 'the city' will therefore be counted as one word in Swedish and two words in Italian. Despite such 'deflationary' factors, the children in fact show a *higher* MLU in Swedish than in Italian. The discrepancy between the MLUw measures for the children's two languages is therefore not an artifact of morphological differences between the languages being acquired; indeed, the true discrepancy is even stronger than it appears in the MLU charts (Bernardini & Schlyter 2004: 58).

Our MLU calculations are based on the word divisions as made in the transcripts in the Corpus. The transcription and word divisions are modelled on the description of Cantonese grammar by Matthews and Yip (1994) except that (for consistency with the format of CHAT (Codes for the Human Analysis of Transcripts)) the hyphen notation is not used to show word-internal divisions (see section 3.2.3 above).[8]

Yip and Matthews (2000a: 198) suggest two lines of response to the question of comparability. Firstly, Cantonese and child English can both be treated as predominantly isolating languages, especially since in the children's English inflectional morphology is not yet in place. In an ideal isolating language, by definition, each morpheme is a separate word.[9] Cantonese is not a perfect isolating language in this sense as it has compound words composed of two or more morphemes as in (3), and a small number of bound affixes, some of which are frequent in child language, such as the perfective aspect marker *zo2* in (4):

(3)   fan3-gaau3
        lie-asleep
        'sleep'

(4)   sik6-zo2
        eat-PFV
        'have eaten'

Klee et al. (2004: 1401) treat compounds such as (3) as single words but aspect markers like *zo2* in (4) separately.[10] It is arguable that by transcribing all these items as separate words, our transcripts inflate the MLU for Cantonese. Another relevant feature of Cantonese is sentence-final particles: while these are generally regarded as separate words, it is arguable that their inclusion inflates MLU, since even at what is essentially the one-word stage the children often add a particle, as seen in (5):

(5)   Child: tung3-tung3 aa3
                hurt-hurt   SFP
                'It hurts.'

        Mother: Lei5 tung3 aa4?
                you hurt SFP
                'You're hurting?'

        Child: Ni1dou6 aa3
                here   SFP
                'Here.'   (Alicia 1;04;12)

Other factors may compensate for these 'inflationary' factors, however. One such factor is the presence of null subjects and objects in Cantonese, as noted by Klee et al. (2004). As discussed in chapters 2 and 5, we consider these null elements to be part of the structure of the sentence, but they are disregarded in the computation of MLU, while the corresponding English sentences would be more likely to contain overt subjects and objects. MLU will therefore *under*-estimate the complexity of Cantonese utterances containing null subjects and objects.

A potential solution to this problem involves establishing baseline MLUs as a function of age for monolingual children acquiring the two languages concerned. In establishing such a baseline for monolingual children, Klee et al. (2004: 1403) show that MLU rises more sharply with age in English monolingual children (partly as a result of acquisition of inflectional morphology) than in Cantonese monolingual children. However, between thirty and thirty-six months the MLU curves for the two languages intersect. It is therefore at this stage of development that the MLU values are most closely comparable. This period (2;06–3;00) corresponds to a crucial period of development in

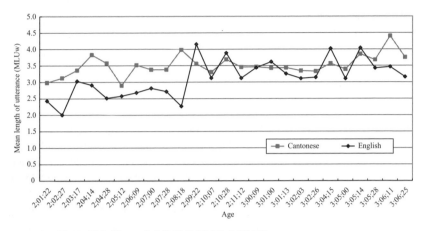

Figure 3.3 Timmy's MLU (2;01;22–3;06;25)

our case studies, during which we observe transfer of a number of constructions such as *wh*-in-situ questions (chapter 4) and prenominal relative clauses
(chapter 6).

A further methodological issue concerns how to measure MLU when code-
mixing occurs in the corpus. This could be another 'inflationary' factor: English
words occurring in 'Cantonese' data files would arguably inflate the MLU
figures for Cantonese. Lai (2006) found that Charlotte's MLU was in fact higher
in mixed utterances than in either of her two languages, suggesting that she was
pooling resources to express more complex content. Bernardini and Schlyter
(2004) count only 'pure' utterances, excluding those containing code-mixing
for the purpose of MLU calculation. We use a postcode to mark code-mixed
words, which are then ignored by CLAN in calculating MLU.[11]

3.3.2   MLU differentials

Regardless of the extent to which MLU values are comparable across the two
languages, it is still possible to use MLU *differentials* between a bilingual child's
two languages to compare individual bilingual children with each other, and
to chart changes in dominance patterns over time. Consider figure 3.3 showing
the development of MLUw in Timmy's two languages.

Figure 3.3 appears to show that Timmy's Cantonese developed faster than
English in the period 2;01 to 2;08, while after age 2;09 the MLU values are
closely matched.[12] Given the uncertainty concerning comparability of MLUw
across languages, however, this pattern allows for a number of interpretations.
To the extent that the measures for the two languages concerned are comparable,
the pattern shown is one of a period of Cantonese dominance followed by a

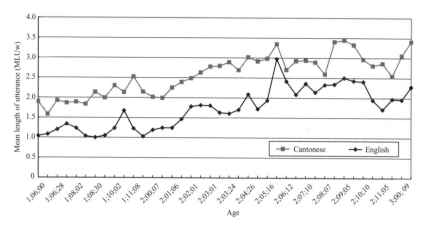

Figure 3.4 Sophie's MLU (1;06;00–3;00;09)

period of more balanced development. If the first period is an artifact of the calculation method (e.g. if the word divisions assumed for Cantonese have the effect of substantially inflating MLUw), then the Cantonese MLU should be lowered across the board: the gap between English and Cantonese would close in the initial period, followed by a period of *English* dominance after age 2;09. Alternatively, if the Cantonese MLU is somehow *under*-estimated (perhaps due to the prevalence of null subjects and objects), the evidence for dominance is even stronger than figure 3.3 suggests. Since there is no independent reason to assume English dominance (given the child's input conditions and language preferences), the first interpretation seems most plausible: in the period 2;01–2;08 Cantonese is dominant relative to the later period of development, where the two languages are more evenly balanced.

Timmy's two younger sisters, Sophie and Alicia, show a more consistent pattern: throughout the period of study, the MLU is higher for Cantonese than for English (see figures 3.4 and 3.5). Over the whole period of study, the mean Cantonese MLU values for Sophie and Alicia are above those for English. We do not believe that the difference can be merely an artifact of problems of comparability in MLUs for English and Cantonese, since (i) the differences are too high to be attributed to the 'inflationary' factors discussed above; (ii) the pattern relates clearly to the children's observed language production: between ages one and two, for example, Sophie understood English but produced only occasional words, whereas she was producing whole sentences in Cantonese (see section 3.4.1 below); and (iii) the consistent pattern contrasts with other children who, in at least some periods, show comparable MLUs for English and Cantonese. The MLU charts for Llywelyn and Charlotte are given in Figures 3.6 and 3.7 respectively.

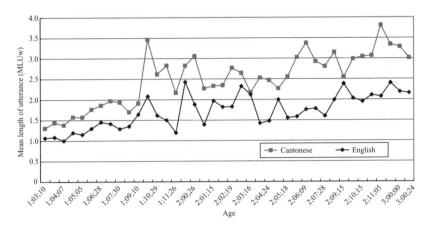

Figure 3.5 Alicia's MLU (1;03;10–3;00;24)

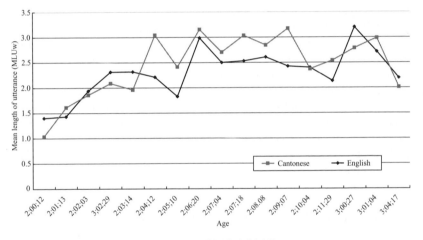

Figure 3.6 Llywelyn's MLU (2;00;12–3;04;17)

Llywelyn's MLU chart in figure 3.6 shows that Cantonese is consistently ahead of English from 2;04 to 2;11, followed by a period where the gap between the both languages gradually closes (3;00–3;04). Llywelyn's early developmental profile thus fits that of a Cantonese-dominant child. A number of structures in the Llywelyn corpus will be attributed to Cantonese dominance in addition to other language-internal factors in the following chapters.

Charlotte's MLU development in figure 3.7 shows a rather consistent pattern of English dominance emerging during the period of study from 1;08 to 3;00, with only three data points (2;00;25, 2;03;17 and 2;05;19) where Cantonese

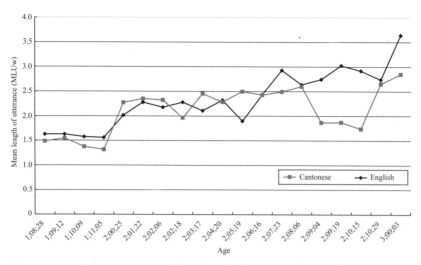

Figure 3.7 Charlotte's MLU (1;08;28–3;00;03)

MLU figures are appreciably higher than the corresponding English figures. We take this as objective evidence supporting the assessment that Charlotte is an English-dominant child. To the extent that the Cantonese MLUs are inflated for reasons of morphological typology and/or transcription, Charlotte's English dominance must be sufficiently strong as to override this factor.

Kathryn is the most balanced bilingual child among the six bilingual children. She was older than the other children when the recording started and the period represented in the corpus is from 3;01–4;06. From listening to her interactions on tape, she appears very fluent in both languages. Her MLU figures show very high values in Cantonese and English (an MLU chart is not shown because they soon reach a ceiling: see discussion below).

Yip and Matthews (2006) propose to use MLU differential, defined as follows, as a measure of language dominance.[13]

> **MLU differential**: the difference between MLU values for a child's two languages at a given sampling point, or (expressed as a mean) over a period of development.

The mean MLU differential is therefore the mean MLU for language A minus the mean MLU for language B. The differential may also be expressed in proportional terms as a percentage: the MLU for language A as a percentage of the MLU for language B. Table 3.3 shows the mean MLUw differentials for each of the six bilingual children represented in the corpus.

Applying the MLU differentials as a measure of dominance, table 3.3 suggests that Sophie and Alicia (with mean MLU differentials of 0.85 and 0.79

Table 3.3. *Mean MLU and MLU differentials in six bilingual children*

	Timmy	Sophie	Alicia	Llywelyn	Kathryn	Charlotte
Age range	2;01;22–	1;06;00–	1;03;10–	2;00;12–	3;01;05–	1;08;28–
	3;06;25	3;00;09	3;00;24	3;04;17	4;06;07	3;00;03
Cantonese MLU	3.51	2.58	2.50	2.39	4.15	1.74
English MLU	3.12	1.73	1.71	2.22	3.69	2.33
MLU differential (Cantonese MLU – English MLU)	0.39	0.85	0.79	0.17	0.46	−0.59
MLU differential (Cantonese MLU % as of English MLU)	112.5	149.0	146.0	108.0	112.5	75.0

respectively) are more strongly and consistently Cantonese-dominant than Timmy and Llywelyn, who show mean MLU differentials of 0.39 and 0.17 respectively.[14] In percentage terms, the Cantonese MLUs for Sophie and Alicia are 149% and 146% of their respective English MLUs, while Timmy and Llywelyn's Cantonese MLU values are 112.5% and 108% of their respective English MLU values. By contrast, Charlotte appears clearly English-dominant with a differential of −0.59, and her Cantonese MLU represents 75% of her English MLU.

Since dominance patterns change over time, it is also useful to measure MLU differentials for specific periods of dominance. Thus, focusing on the period of Cantonese dominance that is apparent in the MLU chart for Timmy (figure 3.3), if we only consider the period from 2;04–2;08, the MLU differential between Cantonese and English is 0.87. Similarly Llywelyn, in the period from 2;04;12–2;11;29 (a total of 18 files), shows a differential of 0.41, as against 0.17 over the whole period of study.

We shall argue that these contrasts are borne out when we examine the relationship between dominance and transfer. First, quantitative differences between the bilingual children correlate with MLU differentials: in the case of transfer of null objects discussed in chapter 5, for example, Sophie and Alicia show higher rates of null objects than Timmy and Llywelyn overall. Second, periods of dominance may correlate with periods of transfer: as we shall see in chapters 4 and 5, extensive transfer from Cantonese is observed in Timmy and Llywelyn during periods of Cantonese dominance.

Kathryn shows a differential of 0.46, apparently comparable to Timmy's 0.39 with her Cantonese MLU value being 112.5% of her English MLU value. This might suggest her Cantonese is dominant. However, the age range for Kathryn (3;01;05–4;06;07) is not comparable to that for Timmy (2;01;22–3;06;25) and the other bilingual children (1;03–3;04) in our study. Kathryn's mean MLU values of 4.15 for Cantonese and 3.69 for English are close to the ceiling above which MLU ceases to be a reliable predictor of grammatical development (at around 4.0 for English). Note also that it is most unlikely that even a balanced child would show a 'perfect' differential of zero. Kathryn is argued to be balanced based on additional measures (Upper Bound and vocabulary diversity) by Yiu (2005a).

3.4 Other indicators of language dominance

As noted in section 3.3 above, other indicators of dominance include language preferences and directionality of mixing. We now discuss how these indicators relate to the picture of dominance as measured by quantitative measures such as MLU differentials.

3.4.1 Language preferences and silent periods

Language preferences can often be observed in bilingual children's interaction with their interlocutors. In the recording sessions on which the Hong Kong Bilingual Child Language Corpus is based, it was necessary for at least one research assistant or caregiver to interact with the child in English and the other in Cantonese, each for a half-hour period. Frequently the child would be reluctant to use one language or the other. Sometimes this was part of a consistent pattern over a period, as with Charlotte (identified as English-dominant based on her MLU values) who was often reluctant to speak Cantonese in a recording session. These patterns, however, are overlaid with temporary and idiosyncratic ones, such as having spoken largely English on the day of recording. Even Kathryn, the most balanced of our bilingual children, showed such preferences in the form of periodic reluctance to speak one language or the other.[15] It is not clear how such temporary factors can be separated from longer term preferences.

A related phenomenon which appears more amenable to systematic study is that of 'silent periods' during which one of the languages is understood but not produced by the child. Silent periods are generally associated with second language acquisition (Krashen & Terrell 1983, Lakshmanan & Selinker 2001). The duration of the silent period, characterized by a time lag between comprehension and production, varies from child to child. As already observed (see section 3.3.2), Sophie went though a 'silent period' between ages one and two in which she understood English but did not respond, or responded with single words only. Alicia went through a similar period of struggling to produce English, but occasionally resorted to using Cantonese (sometimes accompanied by an apologetic expression) to respond to her father's English. In the early corpus data Sophie often responds in Cantonese to questions posed by the investigators in English, as in (6) and (7):

(6)   INV: What is in this cat's hand?
        INV: What is in his hand?
        CHI: *baak6tou3*.
               rabbit
               'a rabbit'
        INV: *baak6tou3* okay, it's a rabbit.   (Sophie 2;00;18)

(7)   INV: Sophie, what's this?
        CHI: *<jyu2 aa3> [/] jyu2 aa3.*
               fish   SFP   fish SFP
               'a fish'
        INV: It's a fish?
        INV: Where's the fish?
        CHI: Here   (Sophie 2;02;16)

These observations are consistent with the MLU differentials suggesting that the two girls' Cantonese is ahead of their English throughout the period of study (see figures 3.3 and 3.4).

It is generally assumed that despite the lack of production in the language, passive acquisition of aspects of the target language on the basis of comprehension must be in progress during the silent period. It might be argued that children showing a silent period, like Sophie and Alicia, are *de facto* cases of child second language acquisition; yet they fit most definitions of bilingual first language acquisition, given that the child is exposed to both languages from birth. We therefore conclude that silent periods can be a feature of uneven bilingual first language acquisition. It remains to be seen to what extent the development of such children is similar to or different from clear cases of child second language acquisition, where exposure to the second language only begins at age two or three.

3.4.2   Code-mixing

Another phenomenon thought to be related to language dominance is code-mixing. For example, 'a *propensity* to use a certain directionality of mixing can be an indicator of dominance' (Lanza 2004: 173; her emphasis). While rates of code-mixing can readily be quantified, we do not see this as a potential *measure* of dominance; rather, like syntactic transfer as argued in chapter 2, it would be an aspect of language production which might be partially explained by dominance. Petersen (1988) found that an English-Danish bilingual child used English morphology with Danish lexical items but not vice versa; this asymmetry was attributed to dominance of English, i.e. the inflectional morphology of the dominant language is used with lexical morphemes of the non-dominant language. A recent formulation of this idea is the Ivy Hypothesis (Bernardini

& Schlyter 2004), whereby it is proposed that children will resort to the functional elements of their stronger language when speaking the weaker language. Thus, when Swedish is the stronger language, Swedish functional items such as determiners are combined with lexical items from the weaker language.

In our bilingual children, asymmetries in the direction of code-mixing are observed: English items are mixed into Cantonese speech more frequently than vice versa. However, we doubt whether these asymmetries can in general be attributed to dominance. Even Kathryn, who shows the most balanced pattern of development among all the bilingual children studied, mixes English items in her Cantonese more frequently than vice versa (Yiu 2005a, 2005b). Charlotte, a bilingual child showing unbalanced development, is English-dominant as indicated by MLU values and language preference. She nevertheless shows bidirectional code-mixing, and her patterns of mixing do not conform to the predictions of the Ivy Hypothesis as outlined above (Lai 2005, 2006).

To account for these findings, we suggest that individual patterns of language dominance interact with code-mixing as instantiated in the input to the children. In the Hong Kong context, code-mixing is part of the adult Cantonese input, i.e. English words (especially nouns and verbs) are commonly inserted into Cantonese discourse (see for example Chan 1998). This practice is particularly widespread among middle-class speakers such as the parents of the children in our study. Much of the Cantonese-English code-mixing produced by the children is in fact adult-like, and may simply show that the child is acquiring code-mixing in response to input of this kind. In the most typical case, an English noun is inserted into a Cantonese utterance, as in example (8) where Kathryn follows the adult investigator's lead in inserting the noun *turtle* (see Yiu 2005a):

(8)   INV: Ngo5dei6 waan2-zo2 # turtle sin1 laa1, hou2 mou2 aa3
              we   play-ASP   turtle first SFP good   not   SFP
              'Let's play the turtle first, shall we?'

        CHI: Ngo5dei6 jau5 [/] jau5 loeng5 go3 turtle gaa3
              we   have   have two   CL   turtle SFP
              'We have two turtles!'   (Kathryn 3;02;19)

A subset of cases could be attributed to developmental factors, such as temporary lexical gaps in one language. In the following exchange, for example, Sophie inserts the English word *ant* into a Cantonese sentence. The adult prompts her with the Cantonese equivalent *ngai* 'ant,' which she then uses herself:

(9)   CHI: Ngo5 zek3 ant le1
              I   CL   ant SFP
              'Where's my ant?'
        INV: ant?

CHI: Ant hai6 gam2 joeng2 gaa3
      Ant is   like that   SFP
      'Ants are like that.'

INV: Ngai5 hai6 mai6   aa3
      ant   be   not-be SFP
      'You mean ants?'

CHI: Ngo5 waak6 ngai5 sin1   aa3
      I   draw   ant   first SFP
      'I'll draw an ant first.'   (Sophie 2;03;14)

The general implication of this line of work is that code-mixing is a feature of most bilingual societies which is acquired in response to the input. In such environments it will always be difficult, if not impossible, to separate the acquisition of adult-like mixing behavior from developmental processes reflecting underlying competence in each language. In speech communities where code-mixing is *not* a general feature of the input, this factor is removed and code-mixing may indeed be an essentially developmental feature which could serve as an index of dominance.

3.5   Conclusions

We have reviewed methods used in current research on bilingual development, and in this study in particular. As in many current studies, we rely principally on a corpus of transcripts of spontaneous speech data collected over a period of one to two years for each of the six bilingual children. The traditional diary method used by many parents and researchers still plays an important role in our study, supplementing the corpus data in particular where less frequent structures are concerned.

As argued in chapter 2, the notion of language dominance is applicable to many bilingual children in whom development is unbalanced. Language dominance can be measured objectively using quantitative measures such as Mean Length of Utterance (MLU) over time. There are well-known problems in comparing MLU values across particular language pairs, especially where different morphological types are involved. Nevertheless, we have shown how MLU differentials between the two languages under investigation during a specific period of development as well as over the entire period of development can be used to compare children acquiring the same language pair (see section 3.3.2). This option will be pursued in the case of null objects (chapter 5): Cantonese-dominant children with a greater MLU differential are found to use null objects more frequently than children with a lower MLU differential.

Finally, observational criteria, such as language preferences shown by the bilingual child in choosing a particular language in certain language contexts and silent periods during which production of the weaker language is lacking, can be used to corroborate quantitative measures such as MLU differentials. In the case of Cantonese-English bilingual children, code-mixing is not closely tied to dominance patterns due to the extensive use of code-mixing by educated bilingual speakers in the speech community, and hence in the adult input to our children.

NOTES

1. The Noji corpus is available at the CHILDES website under 'East Asian languages'. We thank Yasuhiro Shirai for drawing our attention to this remarkable diary corpus of Japanese child language.
2. The parental speech from the Hong Kong Bilingual Child Language Corpus was used by Li and Farkas (2002) as input to their network which was trained to learn words in Cantonese and English in a connectionist model of bilingual lexical and sentence processing (see also Li 2006).
3. The age span of study for each child shown in table 3.1 indicates the duration for which data had been released and were accessible at the time of writing. Additional tapes for some children have been transcribed but not yet released, while others await transcription.
4. Kathryn made a perhaps unintentionally funny remark about her father's profession:

(i)   Ngo5 de1di4 hai6 zing2 tau4 gaa3
          my   daddy   is   do   head SFP
          'My daddy fixes heads.'   (Kathryn 3;11;27)

   In Cantonese this phrase would normally denote a hairdresser, but here describes her father's work as a neuro-surgeon.
5. The siblings are very close to each other and often appear together in the taping session. Charlotte's sister is referred to as *gaa1gaa1* 'big sister' or (when speaking English) *gaa1gaa4* with falling intonation, a coinage based on the Cantonese kinship term *gaa1ze1* 'elder sister'.
6. Fonts for Cantonese characters are available at the Hong Kong SAR government website, http://www.5c.org/ as well as through Microsoft. The format of the on-line transcript is subject to change in line with technological advances.
7. Cancorp is available at the CHILDES website under East Asian languages.
8. The transcription format of CHAT (Codes for the Human Analysis of Transcripts) is available at http://childes.psy.cmu.edu/manuals/CHAT.pdf
9. In the isolating type, 'affixes are absent' and 'there are monosyllabic words, both lexical . . . and grammatical' (Sgall 1995: 56).
10. A potential problem arises when compounds as in (6) are treated as single words but aspect markers as in (7) are treated as separate words, as in Klee et al. (2004). The two cases in (6) and (7) are related since aspect markers come between the two parts of the compound verb, as in *fan3 zo2 gaau3* 'has gone to sleep'. Consequently, if aspect markers are treated as separate words, this implies that the parts of the compound verb will also be separated.
11. The MLU values are generated by using a CLAN command (mlu t*CHI −s'@sl'*.cha) to exclude code-mixed words, such as Cantonese words appearing

in the English files. If an utterance consists of both English and Cantonese words, only the English words are included in the calculation of MLU; if an utterance in these English files consists of entirely Cantonese words, the whole utterance will automatically be excluded from MLU calculation. The MLU values presented in Peng (1998), Huang (1999) and Yip and Matthews (2000a) are based on a previous version of the corpus without postcodes marking code-mixed words, whereas the MLU values used in this chapter are based on an updated version of the corpus with postcodes, hence there are some discrepancies in the two sets of MLU values.

12. The MLU values and differentials for Timmy are computed only for those files for which both English and Cantonese files are available from the same date, giving a total of 25 sampling points. The total corpus contains 34 Cantonese and 38 English transcripts. No such discrepancy arises in the datasets for Sophie and Alicia, where matching Cantonese and English files are available at each sampling point.

13. Bernardini and Schlyter (2004: 58) effectively use the same concept when they note that 'uneven development' in their bilingual children is characterized by a difference of about one MLU point between the child's two languages. Ideally, MLU differentials would be calibrated based on baseline data from monolingual speakers of each language.

14. The mean MLU values for both languages are higher for Timmy because the corpus covers a somewhat later period of development, extending from 2;01;22–3;06;25. Prior to age 2;01 the recordings did not separate the languages, resulting in mixed files (which are also available at the CHILDES archive).

15. For example, Kathryn refused to speak Cantonese with one of the research assistants who was assigned to speak English in the recording sessions, but also spoke Cantonese as a second language. Bilingual children seem to develop an intuitive sense of who should speak which language based on their own views of who qualifies as a native speaker of that language.

4   *Wh*-interrogatives: to move or not to move?

Child: It is for what?
Father: What is it for?
Child: What is it for what?
Child: It is for what?
Child: What is this for?   (Timmy 2;05;03)

The above dialogue illustrates a striking aspect of Timmy's early English grammar: the *wh*-word in questions such as *It is for what?* remains 'in-situ' instead of moving to the sentence-initial position. When his father reformulates Timmy's question using *wh*-movement (*what is it for?*) Timmy responds with the *wh*-word both preposed and in situ (*what is it for what?*) in the same utterance, before reverting to the *wh*-in-situ version and finally arriving at the fronted form (*what is this for?*). As we show in this chapter, all four of our bilingual Cantonese-dominant children go through such a developmental stage in which *wh*-movement is optional in their English grammar, which can be attributed to transfer based on Cantonese *wh*-in-situ questions.

The acquisition of *wh*-interrogatives is fundamental to the child's developing grammar. Syntactically, simple single clause *wh*-questions form the basis of more complex structures involving multiple *wh*-questions and embedded clauses. The movement of *wh*-phrases involved in *wh*-questions is also hypothesized to be involved in other complex structures like relative clauses.[1] Cognitively, it is important for children to learn to ask various forms of *wh*-questions to obtain information regarding objects and events (*what* questions), location (*where* questions), people around them (*who* questions), cause and effect relations (*why* and *how* questions) and time relations (*when* questions).[2]

Cantonese and English contrast with respect to *wh*-movement in *wh*-interrogatives, which is required in English but not an option in Cantonese. We focus on this typologically significant contrast between English and Cantonese and show that transfer effects are traceable to this structural difference: *wh*-in-situ interrogatives are produced to varying degrees by all six bilingual children.

87

The case study of *wh*-interrogatives has several implications. It offers:

- a clear case of systemic syntactic transfer in bilingual first language acquisition (section 4.2);
- cases of intermediate structures some of which are not attested in naturalistic data in the monolingual acquisition of English, such as partial *wh*-movement and split *what* questions (section 4.3);
- a clear case for the role of language dominance in the direction of transfer (section 4.4);
- a clear parallel with Singapore Colloquial English (SCE) and Chinese Pidgin English (CPE) where essentially the same two languages in contact lead to similar results in an emergent contact language (section 4.5).

The case of *wh*-in-situ thus prepares the ground for more complex cases of grammatical interaction such as those studied in the following chapters. Since our aim is not to present a comprehensive picture of the development of *wh*-questions in our bilingual children, many details of such a treatment will inevitably be left out here. Our focus lies on those aspects of development which set bilingual children apart from their monolingual counterparts, and in the possibilities arising due to language contact as in the case of SCE and CPE.

4.1   *Wh*-interrogatives in English and Cantonese

English is said to have '*wh*-movement' because *wh*-phrases such as *what* and *where* are displaced relative to the corresponding declarative sentences. While English *wh*-interrogative sentences involve syntactic movement, Cantonese interrogatives do not, at least in their overt syntax. *Wh*-interrogatives in English are formed by moving the *wh*-words to a sentence-initial position (1), while *wh*-words in the Cantonese counterparts remain 'in situ' (2):

(1)   *What* did you buy?

(2)   Lei5 maai5-zo2 *mat1je5*?
       you   buy-PFV   what
       'What did you buy?'

If the *wh*-phrase has the role of subject, this displacement is not visible on the surface, and the English and Cantonese interrogative sentences are superficially similar, as in (3) and (4):[3]

(3)   *Who* bought the house?

(4)   *Bin1go3* maai5-zo2 gaan1 uk1   aa3?
       who   buy-PFV   CL   house SFP
       'Who bought the house?'

The contrast between Cantonese and English thus shows up most clearly in object questions as in (1) vs. (2) where the *wh*-words occur in different positions, while no contrast is exhibited in subject questions since both languages have the *wh*-expression appearing in the sentence-initial position as in (3) and (4). The data we present below that bear on syntactic transfer therefore focus on the development of non-subject questions, in particular, questions with *what* and *where* in the bilingual children's English.

4.1.1   Wh-*in-situ* in Chinese

The Chinese type of interrogative exemplified by (2) is known as '*wh*-in-situ'. The Latin term *in situ* 'in place' indicates that the *wh*-phrase such as *mat1je5* 'what' in (5) appears in the same position as a corresponding non-interrogative phrase like *gam3 do1 je5* 'so many things' in (6):

(5)   Lei5 maai5-zo2 *mat1je5*   aa3?
       you buy-PFV   what-thing SFP
       'What did you buy?'

(6)   Lei5 maai5-zo2 *gam3 do1   je5*
       you buy-PFV   so   many things
       'You bought so many things.'

It should be noted that 'in situ' does not mean 'after the verb', although in the typical case of a direct object such as (2) the *wh*-phrase does follow the verb. More precisely, the in-situ *wh*-phrase occurs wherever the corresponding non-interrogative expression would occur. In a *where* question, for example, the questioned constituent comes immediately before the verb as in (7), just as it does in a statement such as (8):

(7)   Bi4bi1 bin1dou6 lai4   gaa3?
       baby   where   come SFP
       'Where do babies come from?'

(8)   Bi4bi1 hai2 maa1mi4 tou5   lai4 ge3
       baby   at   mummy   stomach come SFP
       'Babies come from Mummy's tummy.'

While *wh*-phrases in Chinese and other *wh*-in-situ languages (e.g. Japanese and Korean) do not move in overt syntax, theorists have debated whether *wh*-movement applies at an abstract level of representation such as Logical Form (LF: Huang 1982, Aoun & Li 2003). It is agreed, however, that overt *wh*-movement does not occur in Chinese (including Cantonese). Moreover, *wh*-in-situ also occurs in Cantonese 'echo' questions (Matthews & Yip 1994: 319):

(9)   A: Ngo5 tung4 Waa4zai2 ting1   ziu1   gau2 dim2 hai2
        I   with Wah   tomorrow morning nine hour at
        Tin1sing1 Maa5tau4 dang2 lei5
        Star   Ferry   wait you
        'Wah and I'll be waiting for you at the Star Ferry tomorrow
        morning at nine.'

        B: Lei5 tung4 bin1go3 dang2 ngo5 waa2? Hai2 bin1dou6
        you with who   wait me   SFP   at   where

        dang2 waa2?
        wait SFP
        'You'll be waiting with who? Waiting where did you say?'

The echo questions produced by interlocutor B in (9) are based on A's previous statement, with the addition of the particle *waa2* (deriving from the verb *waa6* 'say' but with rising intonation).[4] See below for more on echo questions.

4.1.2   Wh-*in-situ in English*

The straightforward contrast as shown in (1) and (2) above is complicated by the fact that English allows *wh*-in-situ in a number of cases:

(10)   A: I learnt prestidigitation.
        B: You learnt *what*?

(11)   'Ma,' he said, softly. 'Dad's gone.'
        'Gone *where*?' (Mitch Albom, *The Five People You Meet in Heaven*, 2003: 135)

(12)   A is for Alicia, and B is for *what*?

(13)   Who brought *what*?

Example (10) is an 'echo' question, where *what* is left in object position to show incredulity, lack of understanding or unfamiliarity with the word (in this case *prestidigitation*, meaning the ability to perform tricks by sleight of hand). This is a 'recapitulatory' echo question as described by Quirk et al. (1972: 408). A somewhat different type is illustrated in (11): the mother asks her son to elaborate, using *where* in situ to prompt further specification of the verb phrase *gone*. This type is described as an 'explicatory' echo question by Quirk et al. (1972: 409). Echo questions typically appear as a variant of a previous utterance with a particular intonation, and bear a close resemblance to it in form and meaning (hence the term 'echo', see Artstein 2002). Example (12) involves a 'rhetorical' use of *wh*-in-situ, where the speaker knows the answer but uses the question to prompt a response from the child. (13) is a multiple *wh*-question, in which only one *wh*-phrase can occupy the initial position and *what* is therefore left in situ.

Further examples of *wh*-in-situ interrogatives can be illustrated by a dialogue on emergentism in the Journal of Child Language which features two papers with titles involving *wh*-in-situ: MacWhinney (2000b) 'Emergence from what?' which is a response to the target article and Sabbagh and Gelman's (2000) summary article 'Emergence is what?' in response to all the commentaries on their position paper. In the context of the dialogue, one may wonder whether a regular fronted *wh*-questions would work equally well in place of the in-situ questions. The effect of *wh*-in-situ here is both to echo claims of the article (that language emerges) and to query them rhetorically. Thus the *wh*-in-situ interrogatives in the title of the papers achieve effects that are not achievable by *wh*-interrogatives with fronted *wh*-words.

In adult – child interactions, questions with *wh*-in-situ such as (10)–(13) are certainly used by mothers and caregivers, and therefore available in the input to children. Noting 'occasional' questions such as (14) used by a mother, de Villiers and de Villiers (1985: 91) suggest that by leaving *wh*-words in situ, mothers may be helping children to understand the role of *wh*-words:

(14)   You're trying to find what?

Such examples appear in our diary data:

(15)   Child: Po4po2 have 'ready. [i.e. 'Grandma has some already']
        Father: Po4po2 have *what*?
        Child: medicine.   (Alicia 2;10;00)

In (15), the father asks a *wh*-in-situ question in response to Alicia's previous utterance in which the object of the verb *have* is dropped. In this context, the question *Po4po2 have what?* is a natural way to elaborate on the child's utterance, prompting Alicia to respond by providing the missing object, *medicine*. The occurrence of such cases in the input raises a logical problem of learnability: since children occasionally hear such examples of *wh*-in-situ, what is to prevent them from assuming that *wh*-in-situ is generally a grammatical option, or that *wh*-movement is optional in English? In the context of monolingual development, de Villiers and de Villiers (1985: 91) comment that 'Interestingly, children themselves do not seem to use occasional [*wh*-in-situ] questions.' In the case of bilingual children, a parallel question arises: given that it is instantiated in both languages, why should children not assume that *wh*-in-situ is an option in English just as it is in Cantonese? We return to this question below in section 4.4.2 in relation to input ambiguity as a factor in transfer.

The existence of *wh*-in-situ constructions in English also has methodological implications. Examples such as (10)–(13) need to be acquired as part of the normal acquisition of full competence in English, whether by monolingual or bilingual children.[5] It will therefore be necessary to distinguish the acquisition of grammatical, pragmatically appropriate *wh*-in-situ questions from transfer of Cantonese-based *wh*-in-situ as a developmental stage in bilinguals. The two can often be distinguished by pragmatic aspects of the context: echo questions as in (10) are easily identified as a reaction to an unintelligible phrase or outrageous assertion in the preceding context. The type in (11) can be identified by the way the question builds on the previous utterance, as in (16):

(16)   INV: Yeah, <he's had> [/] he's had so much.
         CHI: So much what?   (Sophie 2;09;24)

The rhetorical type (12) can be identified based on the function of the question in the discourse context (typically involving a teaching activity). These pragmatic cues also suggest an answer to the logical problem just posed: children must learn that *wh*-in-situ in English is associated with specific pragmatic functions, while *wh*-movement applies to ordinary interrogatives.

Setting aside these limited cases, English and Chinese (including Cantonese) represent two types of language: those with *wh*-movement and those without overt *wh*-movement. When the grammars of two such contrasting languages are in contact, several questions arise:

1. Will *wh*-in-situ be transferred to languages of the English type?
2. Will *wh*-movement be transferred to languages of the Chinese type?
3. Is there any asymmetry which would point to a universal preference for *wh*-in-situ or *wh*-movement, or a default choice between these two options?
4. Are there intermediate options or developmental stages such as optional *wh*-movement, or partial *wh*-movement (McDaniel, Chiu & Maxfield 1995)?

These issues will be discussed first with respect to bilingual acquisition, and subsequently in relation to language contact on a community level, as instantiated in SCE and CPE.

The acquisition issues raised here are of interest to language typology since children's grammars are expected to fall within the range of possible human language types. Languages can be classified into different types with regard to *wh*-movement. At least four types are identified in Stromswold (1995: 7, footnote 4): (a) Chinese-type languages without overt *wh*-movement, (b) French-type languages with optional single overt *wh*-movement, (c) English-type languages with obligatory single overt *wh*-movement and (d) Russian-type languages with multiple overt *wh*-movement. In addition, some languages such as dialects of German and Romani also allow partial *wh*-movement (McDaniel 1989, de Villiers, Roeper & Vainikka 1990). Children's *wh*-questions might instantiate these different options as long as they fall within the variation sanctioned by Universal Grammar (UG), though not necessarily in accordance with the input the children are exposed to. Partial *wh*-movement is a case in point (see section 4.3.6). Another possibility is optional movement: while L. Cheng (1997) argues against admitting languages with optional *wh*-movement, some languages appear to have optional *wh*-movement where the *wh*-phrase may stay in situ or move to clause-initial position, such as Ancash Quechua (Cole & Hermon 1994) and the Athabaskan language Babine-Witsuwit'en (Denham 2000).

4.2   *Wh*-interrogatives in bilingual children

To establish transfer of *wh*-in-situ interrogatives, we discuss quantitative and qualitative aspects of bilingual acquisition of *wh*-questions, and pursue comparisons with monolingual development.

4.2.1   *Methodological preliminaries*

To quantify the prevalence of *wh*-in-situ interrogatives, relevant types of *wh*-interrogatives occurring in the bilingual and monolingual corpus are counted and categorized. For this purpose, various types of utterance are excluded:
* When the child's utterance is an exact repetition of all or part of the previous adult utterance;
* When the child repeats the same utterance in the same turn;
* When the *wh*-word is a single-word utterance (so that no syntactic structure can be determined);[6]
* When the utterance contains unintelligible portions (transcribed 'xxx' in the corpus) that preclude any analysis. Insofar as the unintelligible portion in an utterance does not interfere with the analysis of the construction under investigation, the utterance is included.

Similar criteria are adopted in the following chapters for the investigation of different constructions in bilingual and monolingual development.

4.2.2   Wh-*in-situ in monolingual acquisition of English*

As a representative sample of monolingual development we take the classic corpus of Eve (Brown 1973).[7] The rare examples of *wh*-in-situ in Eve's data are typically (partial) repetitions of the prior utterance produced by the adult. In (17), the mother uses an embedded *where* question (abbreviated from *do you know where he/she is hiding?*), which is followed by the child's partial repetition of the utterance.

(17)   CHI: xxx hiding.
Mother: Do you know where?
CHI: Know where?   (Eve 1;08)

In (18) the mother herself uses *wh*-in-situ *he's eating what?* in eliciting the child's response, apparently in the rhetorical sense discussed in section 4.1.2 above ('do you know what he's eating?') and the child follows suit:

(18)   Mother: He's eating what?
          CHI: Eating what?   (Eve 1;08)

These examples are modelled directly on the parental input: they clearly do not indicate a developmental stage at which Eve leaves *wh*-phrases in situ. Utterances such as (17)–(18) are therefore not counted as tokens exemplifying spontaneous *wh*-in-situ in Eve's development in table 4.1 in section 4.2.4 below).

Radford (1990), however, gives one example of *wh*-in-situ questions produced by a monolingual English-speaking child in response to an adult question using *wh*-movement:

(19)   Adult: What are they doing there?
          CHI: Doing what there?   (Claire 23 months)

For Radford, *wh*-movement is not possible at this stage because the child has not developed the CP structure which provides the landing site (Specifier of CP) for movement of the *wh*- phrase.[8] However, robust empirical evidence for such a stage is lacking. Stromswold (1995:18) reports that apart from 'echo' questions, she found no clear examples of object *wh*-phrases in situ in twelve children represented in the CHILDES database.

4.2.3   *Wh-in-situ interrogatives in the bilingual children's English*

As discussed by Yip and Matthews (2000a), Timmy passed through a developmental stage during which *wh*-phrases in his English are commonly left in situ. Examples from diary data include:

(20)   This what colour?   (Timmy 2;10;01)

(21)   The snail why live in the water?   (Timmy 3;03;08)

The placement of *what colour* in (20) and *why* as in (21) matches the corresponding adult Cantonese word order as shown in (22) and (23):[9]

(22)   Li1 go3 *mat1je5* (ngaan4)sik1 aa3?
          this CL   what   colour   SFP
          'What colour is this?'   (adult Cantonese)

(23)   Zek3 wo1ngau4 *dim2gaai2* zyu6 hai2 seoi2 dou6 aa3?
          CL   snail   why   live in   water there SFP
          'Why does the snail live in the water?'   (adult Cantonese)

The development of Timmy's Cantonese *wh*-questions exhibits a similar pattern to the monolingual counterparts in terms of acquisition order (see section 4.3). The earliest spontaneous productive use of Cantonese *wh*-in-situ questions occurred at age 1;08:

(24)   Baai2 ... hai2 bin1 ... ?
        put   at   where
        'Where (do) you put (it)?'   (Timmy 1;08;26)

A Cantonese 'why' question parallel to the English case (21) is (25):

(25)   Lei5 *dim2gaai2* jau5 li1   go3 gaa3?
        you why   have this CL SFP
        'How come you have this?'   (Timmy 3;02;26)

The English *wh*-in-situ questions were produced after the corresponding Cantonese ones were well in place (Peng 1998). These early acquired *wh*-in-situ questions in Cantonese serve as a basis for transfer to English.

In the bilingual data, crucially, the *wh*-in-situ interrogatives are non-echo object questions where English grammar calls for the *wh*-phrase to be fronted. Especially revealing of the child's developing grammar are examples where an adult prompts or poses a question formed by *wh*-movement, but the child responds with a *wh*-in-situ question as illustrated in the following examples (26) and (27):

(26)   Father: What does it say? (on the card)
        CHI: Say what?   (Timmy 2;04;15)

(27)   INV: Look, what do they want?
        CHI: It's a what?[10]   (Timmy 2;07;00)

A more elaborate example of this kind is discussed at the beginning of this chapter.

The development of the other five bilingual children will be further discussed below. Sophie and Alicia show a similar picture, as does Llywelyn: all go through a stage during which they produce non-target-like *wh*-in-situ questions.

4.2.4   *Bilingual and monolingual acquisition of* wh-*questions compared*

The earliest *wh*-questions in both bilingual and monolingual children alike have a formulaic character, taking the form of a *wh*-word followed by an optional contracted copula and an NP as in *What('s) that? Where papa?* (O'Grady 1997: 130–131). These are considered instantiations of a formula, rather than derived by movement as in adult grammar, for two reasons. Firstly, the bilingual children at this stage do not yet have agreement (Yip, Matthews & Leung 2001), but show formulaic questions with fronted *wh*-phrases, as in (28) where the absence of a copula in the second clause suggests that *where's* is formulaic:

(28)   [looking for story book] where's the wolf? I think the wolf there.

(Timmy 2;01;06)

Secondly, even monolingual children who have acquired subject – verb agreement often fail to produce the grammatical form of the copula verb in these sentences with correct agreement with the NP, as noted by Radford (1990: 126):

(29)   *What colour* is these?   (Holly 24 months)
        What's these?   (Adam 26 months, Jonathan 28 months)
        What's those?   (Jonathan 28 months)
        Where's my hankies?   (Katy 28 months)

These examples suggest that the adult syntax of *wh*-questions is not yet in place, so that these formulaic expressions do not conform to the general grammatical rules of agreement.[11]

As children's competence develops towards the complexity of adult grammar, the early formulaic patterns will not be adequate to produce complex structures such as those involving embedded questions and multiple questions. The child will need to acquire the corresponding mechanisms for producing these in adult grammar including long-distance *wh*-movement (section 4.3.6) and subject – auxiliary inversion (section 4.3.8).

Quantification of the *wh*-in-situ phenomenon in the bilingual children shows that (a) transfer in this domain is systemic in the sense outlined in chapter 2, i.e. part of the child's grammatical competence as opposed to sporadic errors in performance, and (b) the data are not comparable to occasional cases of grammatical *wh*-in-situ in monolingual children (which are to be expected, for reasons discussed above). Peng (1998) compared Timmy's bilingual data with Eve's monolingual data (Brown 1973). One file was selected from each month from the monolingual data and matched with a file of similar MLUw from the bilingual data in order to achieve comparability. Table 4.1 shows the overall number of *wh*-questions, and the number of *wh*-in-situ questions produced by Timmy and Eve in the specified period.[12]

In the six selected files for Timmy (2;01–2;11 MLU 2.236–3.12), 38 (65.5%) out of a total of 58 *wh*-questions are in-situ questions. In Eve's matching six files (1;08–2;00 MLU 1.99–2.973), only 2 (1.1%) out of a total of 176 *wh*-questions are in-situ questions. From 1;08 to 1;11, most of the *wh*-questions produced by Eve are formulaic ones such as *What's that?* and *Where Papa?* Questions with *what* and *where* account for the entire corpus of *wh*-questions in this period of development. The types of *wh*-questions are restricted to these two types in the next two files (2;00) except for two instances of *who* questions in the last file.

Table 4.1. *Distribution of English* wh-*in-situ questions in Timmy, a bilingual child and Eve, a monolingual child (based on Peng 1998: 70–71, data from Brown 1973)*

	Timmy (bilingual)			Eve (monolingual)			
Age	MLU	no. of *wh*-questions	no. of *wh*-in-situ	Age	MLU	no. of *wh*-questions	no. of *wh*-in-situ
2;01;92	2.236	8	5	1;08	1.990	7	0
2;02;27	2.000	12	1	1;09	2.268	15	1
2;04;28	2.512	13	11	1;10	2.892	14	0
2;07;28	2.813	18	16	1;11	2.854	22	1
2;10;00	3.119	5	3	2;00	3.116	84	0
2;11;12	3.120	2	2	2;00	2.973	34	0
	total	58	38		total	176	2
	% of *wh*-in-situ	65.5			% of *wh*-in-situ	1.1	

Subject *what* questions are low in frequency, mostly occurring with the verb *happen* as in:

(30)   What happen my pencil?   (Eve 1;09)

From 2;00 on, non-formulaic *wh*-questions are produced frequently by Eve: *what* and *where* questions with fronted *wh*-words become increasingly productive:

(31)   What you have?   (Eve 2;00)

(32)   Where give for Papa?   (Eve 2;00)

Only two instances of *wh*-in-situ questions are found in the Eve files selected for comparison:

(33)   CHI: Where clam chowder.
         Mother: What?
         CHI: Clam chowder what?
         Mother: What?
         CHI: Clam chowder.   (Eve 1;09)

(34)   CHI: What?
         Adult: What?
         CHI: I: t's wha: t?[13]
         Adult: It's what?   (Eve 1;11)

In (33) Eve first demonstrates *wh*-movement with *where* in clause-initial position before her mother asks '*what?*' which Eve adds to her utterance (*clam chowder what?*). In (34), Eve's in-situ question *It's what?* expands on the

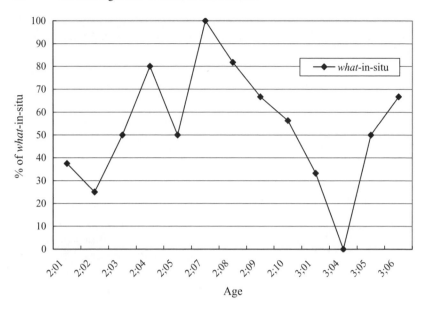

Figure 4.1 Longitudinal development of Timmy's English *what*-in-situ questions (2;01–3;06)

previous adult utterance *What?* but is not entirely spontaneous. In the data files represented in table 4.1, only 2 (1.1%) of Eve's *wh*-questions had in-situ *wh*-expressions (both in the period from 1;08–2;00), while 65.5% of Timmy's *wh*-questions were in-situ ones (between 2;01–2;11). Apart from rare occurrences of *wh*-in-situ modelled on parental utterances as already illustrated, the placement of *wh*-expressions in the whole corpus of Eve's *wh*-questions is target-like, whether formulaic or derived by *wh*-movement. Monolingual data as represented by Eve show that *wh*-expressions in *wh*-questions consistently appear in clause-initial position, in striking contrast with the bilingual data.

The longitudinal development of Timmy's questions with *what* in situ from age 2;01–3;06 is shown in figure 4.1,[14] where the data available during a month are combined into a single time interval to facilitate the representation of the overall developmental pattern.[15] A first stage from 2;01 to 2;04 shows a steady growth of *what* in situ ranging between 25%–80%, followed by a period from 2;05–2;08 where *what* in situ predominates, reaching up to 100% of object in-situ questions, and finally a period from 2;09–3;04 where *what* in situ gradually recedes but still remains optional with the percentage ranging from 33%–67% toward the end of the period under investigation at 3;05–3;06.

The peaks in *wh*-in-situ correspond to peaks in the MLU differential observed in Timmy's development (see discussion in chapter 3): between ages 2;01 and 2;08, (a) the MLU for Cantonese consistently exceeds that for English, and

In-situ *what* and *where* questions

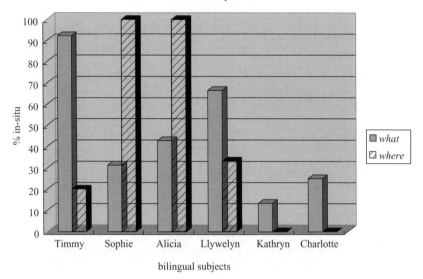

Figure 4.2 Frequency of English in-situ *what* and *where* questions in six bilingual children

(b) the proportion of *wh*-words left in situ peaks (reaching 100% at 2;07 and 81.8% at 2;08). We thus have quantitative evidence for a relationship between dominance of Cantonese and transfer of *wh*-in-situ. These *wh*-in-situ structures persist in Timmy's English grammar for a rather extended period, as shown in figure 4.1: even toward the end of recording, Timmy still produced them, though they were unlearned gradually as his English progressed, as indicated by diary records.

Timmy's diary data include a total of 43 *what* in situ and 6 *where* in situ questions. The majority of *what* in situ questions are recorded between 2;04 and 3;03, while the *where* in situ questions emerged at around 3;03. The *where* in situ questions are relatively few because the functions of *where* are taken over by *what*, as in *Move to what?* meaning 'Where (did it) move to?' (see section 4.3.2).

4.2.5   *Quantitative and qualitative analysis of* wh-*in-situ*

A noteworthy feature in Timmy's data is the coincident emergence of *wh*-in-situ questions and true echo questions. Alongside clearly ill-formed examples such as (26) and (27), we find what are essentially grammatical echo questions, such as the following:[16]

(35)   INV: Ladybug, is it a ladybug?
        CHI: Lady what what?   (Timmy 2;01;02)

(36)   INV: She had wood.
        CHI: He had . . . he had what?   (Timmy 2;09;15)

Other cases which can be interpreted as target-like echo questions include the following, which appear to represent the type in which the *wh*-phrase serves to prompt completion of an adult utterance (see example (11)):

(37)   INV: He's . . .
        CHI: He's a what?   (Timmy 2;05;05)

(38)   INV: The Lion King is . . .
        CHI: The Lion King is what?   (Timmy 2;08;18)

(39)   INV: He can bite . . .
        CHI: Bite the what?   (Timmy 2;08;18)

(40)   INV: Yeh, if you won't open the door then I have to call the police.
        CHI: to what?   (Timmy 3;05;25)

In such cases, English speakers have the option of using either *wh*-movement (*what is he?*) or *wh*-in-situ (*he's what?*). Indeed, in (41) Alicia uses *wh*-movement in exactly such a context:

(41)   Father: And God said . . .
        CHI: What did God said?[17]   (Alicia 2;01;00)

We hypothesize that bilingual children would be less likely than monolinguals to use *wh*-movement in such optional contexts.

The co-occurrence of grammatical echo questions and ungrammatical non-echo *wh*-in-situ questions in Timmy's corpus points to a potential ambiguity in the child's analysis of the target structure: if the child does not distinguish between these two types, the learnability problem will be rather acute. The problem of input ambiguity in such cases may pose a problem for the bilingual child (see chapter 2).

Timmy's first clear examples of object-fronted *what* questions appear after 2;08:

(42)   What he's doing?   (Timmy 2;08;18)

(43)   What are you writing?   (Timmy 3;01;00)

Throughout this period, Timmy continues to produce *wh*-in-situ questions. Especially revealing are the following two questions in the diary data:

(44)   What are you cutting? You want to cut the what?   (Timmy 3;02;08)

The *wh*-word is preposed in the first question while the same *wh*-word remains in situ in the next question. We take this as evidence for a stage of development where *wh*-movement has been acquired, but is applied optionally.

Building on the findings from Timmy, we expand the scope of the study to include the other five bilingual children represented in our corpus. The different types of *wh*-questions (subject vs. non-subject *what* and *where* questions) and *wh*-in-situ questions produced by six bilingual children are given in table 4.2.

Table 4.2 shows the prevalence of in-situ *what* and *where* questions in the three siblings (Timmy, Sophie and Alicia) and Llywelyn, while much lower frequencies are seen in Kathryn and Charlotte. In the category of *what* questions, many more non-subject *what* questions are produced by the bilingual children than subject *what* questions, which rarely appear in the corpus (five examples appear in Timmy's data, one each in Sophie and Llywelyn's, and none in Alicia, Kathryn or Charlotte's data). Questions where the *wh*-phrase plays the role of subject of the sentence are not of immediate interest because *wh*-in-situ cannot be distinguished from *wh*-movement. Our focus is on questions where *what* and *where* appear in non-subject roles (that is, functioning as object of a transitive verb, object of a preposition or complement of the verb *be*).

In considering the figures presented in table 4.2 and figure 4.2, we set aside utterances which are likely to be formulaic (and hence do not provide evidence for a productive rule of *wh*-movement). To compute the percentage of fronted vs. in-situ *wh*-questions, we deduct the formulaic questions from the total number of *wh*-questions as the denominator. After excluding the potentially formulaic utterances, a clearer picture emerges. The percentage of *wh*-in-situ questions is calculated by dividing the number of in-situ tokens by the total number of non-formulaic *wh*-questions in each case. For example, Timmy produced 19 formulaic [*what* (copula) X?] out of a total of 97 non-subject *what* questions. Taking away these 19 formulaic questions, the total of Timmy's non-formulaic non-subject *what* questions is 78, out of which 6 (7.7%) are fronted and 72 (92.3%) are in situ. Out of 108 *what* questions produced by Sophie, 76 are formulaic; of 32 non-formulaic *what* questions, 22 (68.8%) are fronted and 10 (31.2%) are in situ.[18] Out of 40 *what* questions produced by Alicia, some 33 are formulaic; 4 (57.1%) are fronted and 3 (42.9%) out of 7 non-formulaic *what* questions are in situ. Llywelyn's results are similar to those of the three siblings, though the overall frequency of *what* questions is not as high: out of 33 tokens, 27 are formulaic, 2 (33.3%) are fronted and 4 (66.7%) in situ. The data for Kathryn and Charlotte pattern alike, with considerably fewer tokens and smaller proportion of *wh*-in-situ questions than the other four bilingual children presented above: out of Kathryn's 29 tokens, 14 are formulaic, 13 (86.7%) are fronted and 2 (13.3%) out of 15 non-formulaic tokens are in situ, while out of Charlotte's 17 tokens, 9 are formulaic and out of 8 non-formulaic tokens, 6 (75%) are fronted and 2 (25%) in situ.

Table 4.2. *English in-situ* what *and* where *questions in six bilingual children*

Type of *wh* question	Timmy	Sophie	Alicia	Llywelyn	Kathryn	Charlotte
What (subject)	5	1	0	1	0	0
What (non-subject)						
fronted	6 (7.7%)	22 (68.8%)	4 (57.1%)	2 (33.3%)	13 (86.7%)	6 (75.0%)
in-situ	72 (92.3%)	10 (31.2%)	3 (42.9%)	4 (66.7%)	2 (13.3%)	2 (25.0%)
Total no. of non-formulaic tokens	78	32	7	6	15	8
Formulaic [*what* ('s/is/are) X?]	19	76	33	27	14	9
Total no. of *what* (non-subject) questions	97	108	40	33	29	17
Where						
fronted	8 (80.0%)	0	0	6 (66.7%)	6 (100%)	3 (100%)
in-situ	2 (20.0%)	11 (100%)	9 (100%)	3 (33.3%)	0	0
Total no. of non-formulaic tokens	10	11	9	9	6	3
Formulaic [*where* ('s/is/are) X?]	14	1	7	10	11	11
Total no. of *where* questions	24	12	15	19	17	14

Here we present some of the clearest cases of object *what* in situ:

(45)   You eat what? [sees father having breakfast]   (Sophie 2;08;03)

(46)   CHI: He want what?
        CHI: He want the what?
        Father: Ah, which one do you think she wants?   (Alicia 2;11;19)

Diary data show that Alicia still uses *what* in situ up until age five:

(47)   Daddy, Lulu birthday you give to Lulu what?[19]   (Alicia 4;04;11)

(48)   This one is what? [points to gloves in fairy castle]   (Alicia 4;10;12)

Llywelyn is recorded as producing four tokens of *what* in situ (66.7%), including:

(49)   This is what, this? [holding an empty box with animal pictures on it]
                                                        (Llywelyn 2;07;04)

(50)   This is what?   (Llywelyn 2;08;08)

Kathryn's corpus data contain two in-situ *what* questions, which are clearly non-echo questions and therefore imply Cantonese influence:

(51)   Mine is what colour?   (Kathryn 3;02;19)

(52)   I can hear what noise?   (Kathryn 4;04;29)

Charlotte produces two *what*-in-situ questions in the earlier stages (53)–(54), preceding examples of *wh*-movement such as (55)–(56):

(53)   This is what?   (Charlotte 2;01;22)

(54)   Claire has what?   (Charlotte 2;08;06)

(55)   What you need?   (Charlotte 2;09;19)

(56)   What do you want?   (Charlotte 2;09;19)

The phenomenon of *where*-in-situ questions is rather dramatic given the results of two children: 100% of the non-formulaic *where* questions produced by Sophie and Alicia are in-situ questions (11 by Sophie and 9 by Alicia). In contrast, all of the non-formulaic *where* questions produced by Kathryn and Charlotte are fronted (6 by Kathryn and 3 by Charlotte). The results for Timmy and Llywelyn are intermediate between these extremes: 8 fronted vs. 2 in situ for Timmy, and 6 fronted vs. 3 in situ in Llywelyn. Timmy seems to apply *wh*-movement to *where* productively at around 2;07, as in (57)–(58):

(57)   Where she go?   (Timmy 2;07;28)

(58)   Where are you?   (Timmy 3;01;00)

The two cases of *where*-in-situ questions produced by Timmy are as follows:

(59)   INV: Then we can go to Seven Eleven, right?
        CHI: Seven Eleven where.
        INV: Where, Seven Eleven where, where is the Seven Eleven? (laughs)
                                                            (Timmy 3;05;28)

(60)   He get it to where?   (Timmy 3;05;28)

To corroborate the corpus findings, Sophie's diary data feature 14 *what*-in-situ
and 23 *where*-in-situ questions mostly recorded from 2;05–4;01 and Alicia's
20 *what*-in-situ and 38 *where*-in-situ questions from 2;04–5;00.

Llywelyn produced 3 *where*-in-situ questions (33.3%): in (61) *where* in situ
is used in the same session as fronted *where* in (62). The in-situ example (61),
however, could be a well-formed question of the kind discussed in section 4.1.2
above:

(61)   INV: And this one is . . .
        CHI: is where?   (Llywelyn 3;00;27)

(62)   Where it come off?   (Llywelyn 3;00;27)

Llywelyn also produced one *who*-in-situ question (out of a total of seven *who*
questions), and two instances of *which one* in situ:

(63)   This is who?   (Llywelyn 2;03;14)

(64)   I just use . . . which one. [repeated again a few utterances later]
                                                            (Llywelyn 3;01;04)

Taken together, Llywelyn produced four *what*-in-situ, one *who*-in-situ and two
which-in-situ questions: the composite picture suggests a *wh*-in-situ stage in his
development. In contrast, no evidence suggests that Kathryn and Charlotte went
through a similar developmental stage. However, occasional *wh*-in-situ questions were produced by these two non-Cantonese-dominant children, suggesting
that there is some subtle cross-linguistic influence from Cantonese to English
though not as pervasive and visible as in the four Cantonese-dominant children.
To summarize, the findings on the development of *wh*-questions in a number
of Cantonese-dominant children's English evidence a stage where systemic
influence of Cantonese manifests itself in the form of *wh*-in-situ structures.

4.3   Emergence and order of acquisition of *wh*-phrases in English and Cantonese: bilingual and monolingual children compared

Transfer of *wh*-in-situ implies that the corresponding Cantonese interrogative
structures have been acquired; we shall show that this is the case. Also of interest
is whether the order of acquisition matches the typical monolingual acquisition
sequences for English and Cantonese.

Table 4.3. *Developmental order for English* wh-*words in monolingual children (cited in O'Grady 1997: 130)*

Wh-word	average age of acquisition (months)
where, what	26
who	28
how	33
why	35
which, whose, when	after 36

Table 4.4. *Developmental order for Cantonese* wh-*words in eight monolingual children in Cancorp (Lee et al. 1996, modified based on Cheung 1995: 63–64)*

wh-word	average age of acquisition (months)
mat1(je5) 'what'	26.8
bin1(dou6) 'where'	28.6
dim2gaai2 'why'	31.3
bin1go3 'who'	31.9
dim2(joeng2) 'how'	32.5
bin1 CL 'which'	33.6
bin1go3 gaa3(SFP) 'whose'	35.0
zou6mat1(je5) 'why/what for'	37.3
gei2si4 'when'	not attested

Table 4.3 presents the order of acquisition of *wh*-words by seven monolingual English-speaking children in a longitudinal study reported by Bloom, Merkin and Wootten (1982: 1086).

A number of factors conspire to determine this order (beginning with *where* and *what*), including (a) frequency effects in the input: for example, Clark and Clark (1977: 352) reported that *where* questions account for 80% of the *wh*-questions in the caregivers' input addressed to Adam, Eve and Sarah; (b) early grasp of reference of concrete objects; and (c) children's greater need to know about things, as opposed to people with whom they have more familiarity (O'Grady 2005a). These factors together account for the earlier emergence of *what* and *where* questions than *who* questions (O'Grady 1997: 130).

The order of acquisition of Cantonese *wh*-words is investigated by Cheung (1995) based on the longitudinal development of eight monolingual children in Cancorp (Lee et al. 1996). Table 4.4 presents the first emergence of Cantonese *wh*-words in direct questions produced by monolingual children.[20,21,22]

Table 4.5. *Age of first emergence of English* wh-*words in four Cantonese-dominant bilingual children*

	Timmy	Sophie	Alicia	Llywelyn	Average age (months)
what	2;01;02	2;03;20	2;01;00	2;07;04	27.2
where	2;04;21	2;05;25	2;05;05	2;06;20	29.6
who	2;04;21	1;10;02	3;00;02	2;03;14	28.1
why	2;09;15	2;11;18	1;10;16	2;07;18	30.8

Table 4.6. *Age of first emergence of Cantonese* wh-*words in four Cantonese-dominant bilingual children*

	Timmy	Sophie	Alicia	Llywelyn	Average age (months)
mat1(je5) 'what'	1;11;21	2;03;25	1;07;03	2;07;04	25.5
bin1(dou6) 'where'	1;11;00	2;03;25	2;00;13	2;03;14	26.0
bin1go3 'who'	2;01;08	2;01;06	2;00;26	2;05;10	26.2
dim2gaai2 'why'	3;01;01	1;11;08	1;09;03	2;06;20	27.8
zou6 mat1(je5) 'why/what for'	2;04;14	2;09;24	2;03;16	2;11;29	31.4

The monolingual acquisition orders in both English and Cantonese bear a strong resemblance in that *what* and *where* questions emerge at 26 months in English and 26.8 to 28.6 months in Cantonese before *who*, *how* and *why* questions which emerge at 28 to 35 months in English and 31.3 to 32.5 months in Cantonese. Other *wh*-expressions such as *which*, *whose*, *when* are acquired later. Of special interest to us is the emergence of *why* questions in the two monolingual developmental schedules: Cantonese *dim2gaai2* 'why' questions are acquired at 31.3 months while English *why* questions at 35 months. It seems that Cantonese 'why' questions have a language-specific advantage (see below) over the English ones in having a 3.7 month lead in the developmental schedule.

We now discuss the emergence of individual *wh*-phrases in our bilingual children's English and Cantonese and compare the findings with the monolingual counterparts, highlighting the ways in which bilingual development is similar to and differerent from monolingual development.

Tables 4.5 and 4.6 show the age of first emergence of non-formulaic *wh*-questions attested in the corpus and diary data for the four children identified as Cantonese-dominant in chapter 3.[23] It is notable that:

(i) English *what* and *where* questions emerge at around 27 and 29 months in the bilingual children (table 4.5) while they both emerge at 26 months in monolingual children (table 4.3). English *who* questions emerge at 28.1 months in bilingual children, closely matching the monolingual schedule at 28 months. Interestingly, English *why* questions appear 4.7 months earlier at around 30.8 months in bilinguals vs. 35 months in monolinguals, a striking finding which we will further discuss below.

(ii) The Cantonese *wh*-expressions *mat1je5* 'what' and *bin1dou6* 'where' emerge at 25 months in bilingual children (table 4.6) vs. 26.8 and 28.6 months in the monolingual children (table 4.4), while *dim1gaai2* 'why' and *zou6 mat1je5* 'why/what for' questions emerge at 27.8 and 31.4 months in bilingual children vs. 31.3 and 37.3 months in monolingual children. This suggests that the Cantonese-dominant bilingual children's developmental schedule in Cantonese closely matches that of the monolingual counterpart and in some cases is ahead of it (in particular a lead of some 6 months in acquiring *zou6 mat1je5* 'why/what for' questions). The earlier emergence of Cantonese *dim2gaai2* 'why' questions at 25 months is also evidenced in Charlotte, an English-dominant child, 3 months ahead of the emergence of her English *why* questions at 28 months.

(iii) When the *wh*-expressions in the bilingual children's two languages are compared, the findings show that they are attested earlier or at the same time in Cantonese as the English equivalents.[24]

(iv) The first attestations of 'what' and 'where' in non-formulaic utterances in both languages are in situ.

(v) Overall, the Cantonese-dominant bilingual children's Cantonese *wh*-questions are on, or even ahead of, the monolingual schedule while the emergence of their English *wh*-expressions closely matches the schedule of monolingual children according to the findings here (with an apparent advantage in the acquisition of *why* questions).

The striking finding that English *why* questions are acquired earlier by Cantonese-dominant bilingual children than monolingual children is consistent with acceleration under Cantonese influence, since the Cantonese equivalents *dim2gaai2* 'why' and *zou6 mat1je5* 'what for' are acquired by the bilingual children at around 27.8 months and 31.4 months respectively (table 4.6). If the bilingual children proceed in accordance with the monolingual schedules for Cantonese and English, they are expected to acquire *why* questions earlier in Cantonese (at 31.3 months, vs. 35 months for English). Not only do Cantonese-dominant bilingual children acquire Cantonese *why* questions earlier, our only English-dominant child Charlotte also shows this pattern. The fact that Cantonese *why* questions emerge earlier than English ones in both Cantonese-dominant and English-dominant children provides a nice illustration for developmental asynchrony independent of overall language dominance. The early acquisition of *why* questions in Cantonese sets the stage for transfer to English in bilingual development, resulting in the earlier emergence of *why* questions in English as predicted by the developmental asynchrony hypothesis (section 2.5.3). The earlier emergence of Cantonese *why* questions may be due to language-specific reasons. Cantonese *dim2gaai2 why* questions *zou6 mat1je5* 'why/what for' questions are relatively transparent morphologically since the form *dim2gaai2* is made up of morphemes meaning *dim2* 'how' and *gaai2* 'explain' and *zou6 mat1je5*, an expression that literally means 'do what', may also lend itself to transfer (see section 4.3.4), thus accounting for the early acquisition of Cantonese *why* questions. Cantonese *dim2gaai2* and *zou6 mat1je5 why* questions are recorded in Alicia's diary data as early as 22 and 24 months respectively:

(65)   a. Dim2gaai2 sik6 ni1   go3 gaa3?
           why   eat this CL   SFP
           'Why eat this one?'   (Alicia 1;10;23)

        b. Ni1 go3 tek6 go3 bo1 zou6 mat1je5?
           this CL kick CL ball do   what
           'What is that person kicking the ball for?'
                                              [watching World Cup soccer]
                                                          (Alicia 2;00;25)

In the following sections we pursue qualitative analysis of peculiar features of *wh*-questions produced by individual bilingual children.

4.3.1   Split *what questions*

The prevalence of *wh*-in-situ in *what* questions has been discussed in section 4.2.5 above. A particular problem is posed by questions with *what* modifying a noun in the form [*What X*] where the whole noun phrase has to be fronted. Kathryn's fronted *what* questions include [*what* + N] phrases:

(66)   What tights is your colour?   (Kathryn 3;02;19)

(67)   What song is it?   (Kathryn 4;02;17)

(68)   What number is this?   (Kathryn 4;02;17)

(69)   What word is your English first word?   (Kathryn 4;04;29)

(70)   What colour are you two wearing, ah?   (Kathryn 4;05;10)

In the earliest example (66), Kathryn selects the wrong constituent for movement, fronting *what tights* in place of *what colour*. The remaining examples are well-formed. By contrast, Timmy and Sophie passed through a stage in which they split such *wh*-phrases, applying *wh*-movement to *what* while leaving the remainder of the modified noun phrase in situ:

(71)   *What* does he find a *new name*?
        [i.e. 'What new name does the monkey get?']   (Timmy 3;11;06)

(72)   *What* does the rabbit make *noise*?
       [i.e. 'What noise does the rabbit make?']   (Timmy 3;11;08)

(73)   Daddy, *what* do you like *insect*, ladybird or mosquito?
       [i.e. 'What insect do you like?']   (Sophie 5;04;29)

(74)   Father: They're looking for orchids. Flowers.
       Sophie: *What* are they looking for *flowers*? [watching TV]
       [i.e. 'What flowers are they looking for?']   (Sophie 4;11;11)

(75)   Daddy, *what* we read *story*? [i.e. 'What story shall we read?]
       What we read *story* about? How about the cat and his hat?
       [i.e. 'What story shall we read about or 'What shall we read a story about?']
                                                              (Sophie 5;05;05)

One possible example of this kind is produced by Charlotte:

(76)   *What* you want me to draw # *body*?   (Charlotte 2;09;04)

These split questions represent an intermediate stage in the transition from *wh*-in-situ to *wh*-movement, one which is not described in monolingual corpus studies such as Stromswold (1995). In experimental studies, however, Crain and Thornton (1998: 40) report similar split questions with *whose*, where the possessive and head noun inside the [*whose*-N] phrase are split in forming long-distance [*whose*-N] questions as in:

(77)   Who do you think's porridge Pocahontas tried?
       [i.e. 'Whose porridge do you think Pocahontas tried?']

Gavruseva and Thornton (2001) found the same phenomenon in an elicited production task, where preschool children aged 4;5 to 6 made use of split *wh*-questions as in (77) in addition to full pied-piping of the entire *whose* phrase. However, the preschool children who split *whose* questions did not split *what*-questions as in our bilingual data.[25] Thus the split *what* questions in our diary data represent original empirical data that have not to our knowledge been documented in acquisition studies.

The development of possessive *whose* questions is discussed in section 4.3.3. Such split-question formation with *who* extracted out of a possessive NP is a grammatical option in some languages such as Hungarian (Crain & Thornton 1998: 40). A similar case, where a transitional stage in the bilingual data corresponds to an option attested in adult languages, is that of partial *wh*-movement as discussed in section 4.3.6.

4.3.2   Where *questions*

When Timmy first asks *where* questions he uses the phrase *to the what* in place of *where*. This creative usage is attested in diary data from age 2;05 to 2;07:[26]

(78)   The cars going to what? [watching traffic outside]
        [i.e. 'Where are the cars going?']   (Timmy 2;05;14)

(79)   You go to the what, you went to the what? [to Daddy coming home]
        [i.e. 'Where did you go?']   (Timmy 2;05;15)

(80)   He climb up to the what? [watching animal on TV]
        [i.e. 'Where did he climb up?']   (Timmy 2;06;02)

(81)   Press to the what?
        [i.e. 'Where do you press (the torch)?']   (Timmy 2;07;12)

The emergence of *where* questions in Sophie is represented by the following exchange:

(82)   CHI: What they sleep, where?
        INV: Where?
        INV: Yeah, where do they sleep.
        CHI: What they sleep where?   (Sophie 2;06;12)

Here Sophie apparently wants to ask a *where* question but is not able to do so, as evidenced by her use of *what* instead of *where* to begin the question. Even after the investigator reformulates her question by fronting *where* and filling in the *do* support, Sophie still begins with *what* as a question marker, then uses *where* in situ. The initial *what* may be functioning as a scope marker, as discussed in section 4.3.6 below.[27]

Like other locative expressions in Cantonese (see chapter 7), *bin1dou6* 'where' can occur either before or after the verb, depending on the verb and the semantic role of the locative phrase. This is reflected in Sophie's use of *where* which appears either after the verb as in (83) or between subject and verb (85), both being in situ:

(83)   I put in the where? [trying to fit spare photo into album]
        Put in the where? [10 minutes later, with another photo]   (Sophie 2;05;25)

(84)   Po4po2 where? [i.e. 'Where is Grandma?']   (Sophie 2;06;09)

(85)   [Father has told Sophie he bought her a purple 'dress']
        You . . . where buy . . . this dress?   (Sophie 3;02;24)

The Cantonese equivalents are illustrated by:

(86)   Heoi3 bin1dou6 le1?
        go   where   SFP
        'Where shall we go?'   (Sophie 2;03;25)

(87)   Bin1dou6 kam2   pei5   aa3?
        where   cover   blanket SFP
        'Where shall we put the blanket?'   (Sophie 2;06;12)

Another problem involves the syntax of *where*. Sophie uses the prepositional phrase *in where* where English would use *where*:

(88)   [with lotion on palm] Put in where?   (Sophie 2;06;20)

(89)   Drink something in where we?[28] We drink something in where?
        [returning from playground]   (Sophie 3;11;09)

Here Sophie's use of *in where* is the result of cross-linguistic influence. In English *where* is a pro-PP, i.e. it substitutes for a prepositional phrase such as *in the house*. In Cantonese *bin1dou6* 'where' is a NP and cannot substitute directly for a PP: a preposition *hai2* is required to form a PP [*hai2 bin1dou6*], parallel to *in where* in Sophie's English.

Alicia often wavers between moving *where* and leaving it in situ:

(90)   Where Timmy? Where Timmy? Timmy where?   (Alicia 2;03;08)

(91)   Where Timmy ball? The Timmy ball where?   (Alicia 2;07;24)

Together with the variation in usage, these cases suggest that for a period Alicia treats *wh*-movement as optional in English. The optionality of *wh*-movement in English poses a problem of learnability, as the target grammar requires obligatory movement in *wh*-questions.

4.3.3   *Possessive* whose *questions*

The possessive form *whose* poses particular problems. Although conventionally written *whose*, to children it is a case of the genitive clitic *'s* (and as such could be represented as *who's*). Sophie and Alicia both use *who* in a possessive function:

(92)   This is who that? [points to unfamiliar object]
        [i.e. Whose is this?]   (Sophie 3;01;15)

(93)   This one is who? [finds clothes intended to be presents]
        [i.e. Whose is this one?]   (Alicia 3;11;16)

(94)   This is who present? The big present is who, Daddy?
        [i.e. Whose present is this? Whose is the big present?]   (Alicia 4;10;25)

The absence of the possessive clitic is not unexpected, since at this age the children regularly produce possessive noun phrases without the possessive clitic:

(95)   Father: Is that Mummy's hair?
        CHI: Mummy hair. Mummy hair is like this. [draws on board]
        [drawing Daddy] You the hair is so messy, see?   (Sophie 3;07;04)

When *whose* is acquired it regularly appears in situ, like the Cantonese counterpart *bin1go3 ge3* ('who' + possessive marker):

(96)   This is whose violin?
        [i.e. 'Whose violin is this?']   (Timmy 3;03;08)

(97)   This one is whose? [points to bag of nuts]
        [i.e. 'Whose is this one?']   (Sophie 3;05;11)

The acquisition of *whose* questions is closely tied to that of the possessive clitic *'s*. At this age Sophie also over-extends the clitic to the possessive pronoun *you*, producing a possessive form *yous*:

(98)   Daddy, this one is whose? [holds up pair of shoes]
        [i.e. 'Whose is this one?']
        Is that yous, this one?
        [i.e. 'Is that yours, this one?']   (Sophie 3;07;11)

4.3.4   Why *questions*

Like many children, Sophie began to use *why* questions in English just before she turned 3. However, initially she constructed *why* questions using *what are doing*:

(99)   Daddy, what are doing?[29] What are doing hurt?
        [i.e. 'What's the matter? Why are you hurt?']
        [seeing plaster on father's finger]   (Sophie 2;10;18)

(100)   Father: Let's go up.
        CHI: *What are doing* go up? [i.e. 'why go up?']   (Sophie 2;10;18)

(101)   I want to eat. [holding packet of nuts]
        What are doing no eat? Daddy, *what are doing* no eat?
        [i.e. 'Daddy, why aren't you eating?']   (Sophie 2;10;18)

(102)   *What are doing* you carry me?
        [i.e. 'Why are you carrying me across the road?']   (Sophie 2;11;09)

The phrase *what are doing?* is evidently calqued on the Cantonese equivalent with *zou6 mat1je5* (literally 'do what') which appears in the same period:

(103)   INV: Daa2-gaau1 aa3!
              fight   SFP
              'Fighting!'

        CHI: Hai6 aa3, *zou6 mat1* daa2-gaau1 aa3?
              yes SFP do   what hit-fight   SFP
              'Yes, why are you fighting?'   (Sophie 2;10;10)

(104)   *Zou6 mat1* mit1 hoi1 keoi5 aa3?
        do   what tear open it   SFP
        'Why are you tearing it open?'   (Sophie 2;11;18)

This is a common alternative to *dim2gaai2* (literally 'how to explain?', 'how come') in forming *why* questions in Cantonese (Matthews & Yip 1994: 329). Sophie demonstrates the equivalence in her English by reformulating such a question with *why*:

(105)   *What are doing* is wet, Daddy? Is wet, *why*? [feeling wet tissue]
                                                             (Sophie 2;11;10)

Soon after age three, *why* replaced *what are doing* in Sophie's English, and the *why* period familiar to all parents began in earnest:

(106)   Why you don't go? [seeing parents not going out after all]

(Sophie 3;03;21)

(107)   Why you must like this? [seeing father swirl wine in glass]

(Sophie 3;06;14)

Developmentally, the brief period of *what are doing* in the sense of *why* suggests Bilingual Bootstrapping (Gawlitzek-Maiwald & Tracy 1996): before the target construction has been acquired, a construction modelled on the child's stronger language is used as a stopgap measure. The case of prenominal relative clauses in English discussed in chapter 6 provides another example of bootstrapping that shows a similar but longer lived pattern.

Sophie's questions with *what are doing* in her bilingual development have parallels in contact languages: as Salikoko Mufwene (p.c.) has pointed out, this pattern resembles that in English creoles with *wa-mek* (deriving from *what makes*) and French creoles with *kife* (from French *qui fait*), literally 'what makes?' These are instances of the common pattern whereby contact languages (re-)create *wh*-words made up transparently of two morphemes (Muysken & Veenstra 1995). The pattern is common in Caribbean creoles (e.g. *wa-mek* in Guyanese and Jamaican creole). Consistent with this distribution, Holm (2000: 120) hypothesizes substrate influence from West African languages such as Ibo and Yoruba in which *why* questions are expressed as 'what it makes?' The substrate account is consistent with the developmental phenomenon whereby Sophie's earliest *why* questions are calqued on the Cantonese *wh*-phrase.

4.3.5   Multiple wh-*questions*

Multiple *wh*-questions, in which more than one *wh*-phrase is questioned, occur relatively rarely in natural discourse because they require very specific contexts. Such multiple questions with a moved *wh*-phrase and the other *wh*-phrase in situ are typically answered with pairings of different members. Thus an appropriate answer to *who brought what?* would be *Mary brought the dessert, and Bill the salad.* Nevertheless some examples do appear in the diary data:

(108)   What day you going to where? [to father as he holds calendar]

(Timmy 2;05;13)

(109)   What we wrap for who? [wrapping presents]   (Sophie 4;11;20)

Timmy is recorded using multiple *wh*-questions in both languages on the same day:

(110)   Mother: Sai3lou2 waa6 sik1   zing2 ge3 wo3.
                brother   say   know   make   SFP SFP
                'Younger brother says he knows how to do it.'

CHI: Bin1go3 waa6 sik1   zing2 mat1je5?
      who   say   know   make   what
      'Who says he knows how to do what?'   (Timmy 3;04;29)

(111)   Where do you buy which one?   (Timmy 3;04;29)

Although in cases such as (108) and (109) the auxiliary verb is missing (see section 4.3.8 on the acquisition of inversion), these multiple questions are remarkably well-formed as far as the interrogative elements are concerned. It is possible that the presence of *wh*-in-situ in Cantonese, and the *wh*-in-situ stage in the children's English, facilitates acquisition of multiple *wh*-questions, where the second *wh*-phrase must be left in situ. This question deserves further study, testing the full range of multiple *wh*-configurations and relevant constraints.[30]

4.3.6   *Partial* wh-*movement*

In English, long-distance *wh*-movement is called for when the constituent being questioned originates in an embedded clause. In generative grammar, such long-distance movement is treated as involving successive applications of *wh*-movement, such that *who* moves initially to the front of the embedded clause:[31]

(112)   Who do you think [$_{CP}$ __ [$_{IP}$ I met __]]?

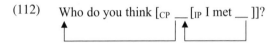

The acquisition of long-distance movement offers an interesting window into the child's developing grammatical competence. *Wh*-questions in general and long-distance *wh*-questions in particular have drawn the attention of both syntacticians and language acquisition researchers because these constructions 'exemplify some of the most significant principles of grammar' (de Villiers 1995: 1). Long-distance *wh*-questions such as (112) are of particular interest because in addition to full *wh*-movement vs. *wh*-in-situ, the possibility of partial movement arises: that is, moving a *wh*-phrase to some intermediate position, such as the beginning of the embedded clause. Partial *wh*-movement is attested in several languages, and as a developmental phenomenon in the acquisition of English by monolingual children. In some dialects of German, for example, the *wh*-word *was* 'what' in (113) begins the sentence (serving as *scope-marker*, in the analysis of McDaniel 1989) but the true question word *wie* 'how' moves only as far as the beginning of the embedded clause:

(113)   *Was* glaubst,   *wie* alt   sie   ist?
         what   think-2sg   how   old   she   is
         'How old do you think she is?'   (Austrian German)

The variant *wh*-copying construction places the same *wh*-phrase at the front of both the main clause and the embedded clause, as in Romani:

(114)   *Kas*   mislin-e   *kas*   o   Demir-i   dikh-ol
        who-Acc think-2sg who-Acc the-Nom Demir-Nom see-3sg
        'Who do you think that Demir sees?'

Although no such question forms occur in adult English, Thornton (1990) found children producing these spontaneously while McDaniel, Chiu and Maxfield (1995) showed that for a period between age 2;11 and 5;07, many children acquiring English will accept one or both these options as grammatical under experimental conditions. Using elicitation experiments, Thornton and Crain (1994) and Crain and Thornton (1998) found that subjects aged between three and four produced questions with a medial *wh*-phrase such as (115) with subject extraction, and (116) with object extraction (Thornton & Crain 1994: 220):[32, 33]

(115)   Who do you think *who* _ is in the box?
(116)   What do you think *what* babies drink _?

According to Stromswold (1995: 42), monolingual children have not been shown to produce partial *wh*-movement spontaneously. Timmy, however, occasionally produces questions of the *wh*-copying type:

(117)   It's broken. *Who* did you t'ink *who* broken it?
        [to father, referring to broken car]   (Timmy 3;10;30)

Another option, not discussed in the above monolingual studies but used productively by all three bilingual siblings, is to move the *wh*-phrase only as far as the beginning of the embedded clause, leaving the main clause without any indication that a question is being asked:

(118)   You t'ink *where* do you put it? [asking Daddy to find candies]
                                                                 (Timmy 3;11;20)

(119)   You think *what nut* I am getting now? [picking nut out of mixed tin]
                                                                 (Timmy 4;01;29)

(120)   You think . . . you think *what* is Kasen school?
        [i.e. 'which do you think is Kasen's school?']   (Alicia 3;09;24)

(121)   You think *where* is Sophie? [hiding under table]   (Sophie 5;03;02)

(122)   Father: What are you making, Sophie?
        CHI: You want *what* do I make?   (Sophie 5;04;19)

In one case, Sophie begins by producing an embedded question with *wh*-in-situ, then revises her question by applying partial *wh*-movement to *what*; as indicated by the acute accent in (123), Sophie stresses *what*, perhaps to draw attention to the change, or to focus on the *wh*-phrase despite its medial position:

(123)   You like I write *what*? [drawing on board]
         [later in the same activity] You like *whát* I write?
         [i.e. what would you like me to write?]   (Sophie 5;03;27)

These data suggest that developmentally, partial movement is an intermediate step between *wh*-in-situ and full application of *wh*-movement. This is consistent with the view of partial *wh*-movement as a 'transitional behavior' (McDaniel, Chiu & Maxfield 1995: 725), except that our children's behavior involves producing questions with partial movement spontaneously in natural discourse, rather than merely accepting them under experimental conditions. With regard to the goal of providing 'an account of cross-linguistic variation with respect to *wh*-movement types that would include adult languages as well as . . . child English data' (McDaniel, Chiu & Maxfield 1995: 710), the bilingual data suggest that a further type of partial *wh*-movement not attested in monolingual development needs to be recognized, namely the type seen in (118)–(122) without an initial *wh*-word serving as scope marker. Similar partial *wh*-movement and *wh*-scope marking constructions are reported by Schulz (2005) in adult German and Japanese L2 learners of English where she argues that *wh*-scope marking can either be grounded in IL competence or a reflection of processing capacities, depending on the learner's L1.

4.3.7   Indirect Questions

Indirect questions require movement of the *wh*-phrase to the front of the embedded clause. In Sophie's earliest attempts at indirect questions, the *wh*-phrase in the embedded clause is left in situ, just as in direct questions:

(124)   Mother: Timmy le1?
         Timmy SFP
         'Where's Timmy?'
         CHI: No. I don't know Timmy is where, no.   (Sophie 2;08;25)

(125)   . . . I know, I know, I know it's where.   (Sophie 3;03;18)

(126)   I don't know you lost what. [Her brother has lost something]
                                                                    (Sophie 3;09;25)

(127)   Let me to see this is who. [looking inside passport]   (Sophie 4;02;15)

At age 4;03, Sophie begins to produce indirect questions with fronted *wh*-phrases:

(128)   I want to see Alicia, what he doing.
         [since gender is not distinguished, *he* here refers to *Alicia*]
                                                                    (Sophie 4;03;28)

(129)   Mother: Why did she open that one? [referring to Christmas present]
         CHI: So that I can know what is it?   (Sophie 4;09;10)

(130)   I can't peek. Because if it's Christmas I know what is it.   (Sophie 4;09;18)

(131)   Daddy, I got a problem. [sings] I don't know where is the batteries.
                                                               (Sophie 4;11;20)

(132)   [picking up phone] Daddy, I don't know who is this.   (Sophie 5;02;06)

(133)   I know where is it. [goes to fetch diary]   (Sophie 5;05;00)

Kathryn produced quite a number of embedded questions:

(134)   . . . you don't know *what*'s in here.   (Kathryn 3;02;19)

(135)   What do you know *how* to play?   (Kathryn 3;11;27)

(136)   She told me my name. She told me *what* name is she.
                                                               (Kathryn 4;02;17)

All six fronted *where* questions produced by Kathryn involve embedded
questions such as the following:

(137)   No one, I know where does it go.   (Kathryn 4;01;05)

(138)   No, I know where is the park.   (Kathryn 4;04;29)

(139)   I'll show you where you press it.   (Kathryn 4;06;07)

Three embedded questions were attested in Llywelyn's corpus as he turned
three:

(140)   . . . I don't know what is this.   (Llywelyn 3;00;27)

(141)   INV: What did he say?
         CHI: He said what do you want.   (Llywelyn 3;00;27)

(142)   . . . I show you which way the way is the way.   (Llywelyn 3;01;04)

Two embedded questions appear in Charlotte's corpus:

(143)   I don't know where is Ma.   (Charlotte 2;09;04)

(144)   I don't know what [/] I don't know where's the money.   (Charlotte 2;10;29)

To summarize, the first emergence of embedded questions in the six bilingual
children ranges from around age 2;08 to 3;02, with a majority of *what* and
where questions as the complement of the matrix verb *know* and all are tensed
clauses except one infinitival one in Kathryn's (135). An overwhelming majority of the bilingual children's embedded questions show subject – auxiliary
inversion just as in main clause questions. These patterns resemble the earliest

embedded questions in Singapore Colloquial English (SCE), many of which are complements of the verb *know* (Gupta 1994: 135; see section 4.5 below).

4.3.8   Subject – auxiliary inversion and wh-questions

When there is an auxiliary verb in the *wh*-question, subject – auxiliary inversion (SAI) is required (145), just as it is in *yes-no* questions (146):

(145)   What can I eat?

(146)   Can I eat?

Early *wh*-questions in both monolingual and bilingual children generally do not include auxiliary verbs, thus precluding the possibility of subject – auxiliary inversion.

O'Grady (1997: 161) discusses 'the most celebrated generalization about the development of inversion in *wh* questions', namely that inversion in *wh*-questions emerges only after it has appeared in *yes-no* questions (Klima & Bellugi 1966). This generalization is a developmental corollary of Greenberg's typological Universal 11:

Inversion of statement order so that verb precedes subject occurs only in languages where the question word or phrase is normally initial. This same inversion occurs in yes-no questions only if it also occurs in interrogative word questions.

(Greenberg 1963: 111)

Bellugi (1971) reported that in Adam's development at 3;05, an overwhelming number of auxiliaries underwent inversion in his *yes-no* questions (198 inverted vs. 7 uninverted) while relatively few did so in *wh*-questions (9 inverted vs. 22 uninverted). As Adam's language developed, auxiliaries were mostly inverted in *wh*-questions too (33 inverted vs. 5 uninverted at age 3;08 and 27 inverted vs. 4 uninverted at age 4;03). This pattern led to the hypothesis that inversion develops later in *wh*-questions since two movement rules are involved: both the auxiliary verb and the *wh*-word have to move. However, current views suggest that there is no universal preference among monolingual English-speaking children for inversion to occur in either *yes-no* questions or *wh*-questions, and individual variation points to a lack of uniform developmental order with respect to inversion (O'Grady 1997: 163; Stromswold 1995). One interesting hypothesis considered by Bellugi (1971: 101) is that a simplifying option for children could be to move the auxiliary verb without moving the *wh*-word, producing structures such as (147) in violation of Greenberg's universal:

(147)   * Should I eat what?

Studies of monolingual development have found that children rarely, if ever, apply inversion without *wh*-movement (O'Grady 1997: 162). However, the possibility of inversion without movement arises for our bilingual children: as *wh*-movement is not consistently applied in their *what* and *where* questions, it is possible for inversion to apply with *wh*-in-situ questions. One such example does appear in Alicia's diary data:

(148) Daddy, are you having what? (Alicia 3;09;11)

Such examples raise the theoretical possibility of inversion without movement as an interim strategy in bilingual development. Without further tokens of this type, it is unclear whether inversion without *wh*-movement is in fact adopted by the bilingual children as a productive grammatical option, or merely as an occasional strategy. Future studies could further investigate this issue under experimental conditions.

A further issue involves the limitation of inversion to main clauses. As shown in many of the above examples, the bilingual children frequently apply inversion in embedded clauses, resulting in what looks like a main clause question:

(149) And the ambulance tell you *what* do you go. Go to mall. (Timmy 2;10;25)

(150) Watch me *what* can you do. (Kathryn 4;04;29)

In (150) the child apparently means 'watch me to see what you can do', using *watch* with a complement clause, like the Cantonese translation equivalent *tai2* 'watch/see'.

4.4 Discussion: language dominance, input ambiguity and asymmetry

On the basis of the findings discussed thus far, we propose a three-stage model for our Cantonese-dominant bilingual children's development of *wh*-questions:
  (i) a no-movement stage where *wh*-words are uniformly left in situ. *Wh*-questions with preposed *wh*-words are limited to formulaic expressions such as those with an optional copula *What('s) X?* and *Where('s) X?*
 (ii) an optional *wh*-movement stage where *wh*-movement is applied optionally in some cases but not yet across the board. In multi-clausal *wh*-questions, partial movement is a developmental option with the *wh*-word moving to the intermediate Spec of CP, while full movement to the landing site in the matrix clause is only acquired much later.
(iii) an obligatory *wh*-movement stage where *wh*-movement is applied across the board, with the exception of echo questions.
This constitutes a quite different path of development from that seen in monolingual children. The transfer of *wh*-in-situ from Cantonese to English provides one of the clearest cases of (a) divergence from monolingual development, and (b) cross-linguistic influence in this study. The interpretation of these data and the explanation for why transfer occurs in this domain are not straightforward, however. In the following sections we discuss three factors which may play a role.

4.4.1   Language dominance

In Yip and Matthews (2000a) the transfer of Cantonese-based *wh*-in-situ questions in Timmy's English was essentially attributed to language dominance. Dominance remains a possible factor in the case of the three Cantonese-dominant siblings in whom we have demonstrated systematic transfer of *wh*-in-situ in section 4.2.5. *Wh*-in-situ questions are also found productively in the data from Llywelyn (see table 4.2), who was assessed as Cantonese-dominant from 2;04–2;09 in chapter 3. The prevalence of *wh*-in-situ appears to be related to dominance: qualitatively, Sophie and Alicia consistently leave *where* in situ in the corpus data, while the two children not considered Cantonese-dominant (Kathryn and Charlotte) consistently apply *wh*-movement. Quantitatively, the contrasts in table 4.2 are consistent with the dominance patterns of the children as established in chapter 3. However, even Kathryn and Charlotte show occasional use of *wh*-in-situ. Therefore, several other factors could be playing a role, including ambiguous input and developmental asynchrony.

4.4.2   Input ambiguity

As noted above (section 4.1.2), occasional occurrences of *wh*-in-situ in the English input pose a logical problem: how do children avoid being misled into thinking that *wh*-in-situ is generally allowed in English? This logical problem does not seem to constitute an actual problem for monolingual children, who (as we saw in the case of Eve) use *wh*-in-situ rarely, and generally in appropriate ways. The bilingual counterpart of the problem could be more serious, however. The children are certainly exposed to *wh*-in-situ in English, as in the following exchange:

(151)   CHI: You help me to. I cannot. [holding up pot of paint to be opened]
            Father: Help you to what?
            CHI: Please!   (Sophie 3;03;15)

Here the father elaborates on the child's incomplete sentence by asking a question with *what* in situ. Such *wh*-in-situ questions are well motivated pragmatically and are only grammatical under certain specific conditions in English, whereas in Cantonese *wh*-in-situ is the only grammatical option. Given that Cantonese consistently exhibits *wh*-in-situ and English occasionally shows it, there is a small area of overlap between the two grammars, and a potential ambiguity in the English input which could open the door to transfer by the mechanism discussed in section 2.6.2. The theoretical ambiguity of the input can be illustrated with an actual example. Sophie's first recorded attempt to use *what* in the corpus is in response to the adult investigator presenting her with the same question formulated first with *wh*-movement, and then with *wh*-in-situ:

(152)   INV: What do you want?
         CHI: What I want it
         INV: You want what?
         CHI: I want what
         INV: You want the . . .   (Sophie 2;01;06)

The investigator's use of wh-in-situ *you want what?* here is an echo question, apparently in response to Sophie's strikingly ungrammatical *What I want it.*[34] Perhaps encouraged by the adult's usage, Sophie reverts to the wh-in-situ formulation (*I want what*).

For the monolingual English-speaking child, the two types of wh-questions (with wh-movement, and with wh-in-situ as in echo questions) logically constitute an input ambiguity, but no overlap with another language arises, since there is no other language in contact with English, and no developmental problem ensues. In contrast, the English wh-in-situ echo questions overlap with the Cantonese wh-in-situ questions in the dual input of the bilingual child. This underlines the importance of distinguishing input ambiguity (as a property of a language) from structural overlap (as a property of a language pair) as argued in chapter 2.

4.4.3   Asymmetry in direction of transfer

A further question arising is whether the transfer of wh-in-situ and transfer of wh-movement are symmetrical phenomena. Empirically, transfer of wh-in-situ to English is pervasive in Cantonese-dominant children; the converse, transfer of wh-movement to Cantonese is also attested, though much less systematically (see below). This could be due to the relative paucity of data from English-dominant children in this study, or it could point to an asymmetry in the direction of transfer. Theoretically, transfer of wh-in-situ is favoured by the existence of wh-in-situ in echo questions, constituting a possible ambiguity in the input as discussed above. No such ambiguity arises in Cantonese with regard to the placement of wh-phrases *per se*, although fronting of other constituents (as in topicalization) could provide a precedent for fronting of wh-phrases.[35]

Another possible asymmetry is that between presence and absence of wh-movement. Other things being equal, it may be simpler to treat all objects alike and leave them in situ than to select certain '+wh' items for fronting in interrogatives. O'Grady (1997: 156) observes that children's preference for sentences without gaps may explain why their early wh-questions involve formulaic copula constructions. This preference can be extended to the wh-in-situ structures in our bilingual children: there is no gap in these in-situ structures where the wh-phrase remains unmoved. The change from the declarative sentence to the interrogative counterpart is minimal, with no change in word order required: all that is needed is to substitute the question word for the questioned constituent. Typological evidence on this point is inconclusive, since the presence or absence of *wh*-movement is closely tied to word order typology: many Verb-Object (VO) languages have *wh*-movement, while Object-Verb (OV) languages generally lack it (Hawkins 1999: 274), so that no overall preference emerges for either *wh*-in-situ or *wh*-movement.

Any combination of these factors could conspire to induce transfer of *wh*-in-situ. To tease them apart would require systematic studies of different types of children: do balanced or English-dominant bilinguals also transfer *wh*-in-situ? Is there an asymmetry between transfer of *wh*-in-situ by Cantonese-dominant bilinguals and transfer of *wh*-movement by English-dominant bilinguals? Some evidence comes from our sole English-dominant subject, Charlotte, who produces only two clear cases of *what* in situ:

(153)   CHI: this one.
         CHI: this is what
         INV: huh?   (Charlotte 2;01;22)

(154)   CHI: Claire has what?
         CHI: Daddy has swimming suit.   (Charlotte 2;09;06)

There is also one instance of code-mixing where *what* appears in situ in an otherwise Cantonese utterance:

(155)   Li1dou6, li1   go3   what?
         here   this CL   what
         'What is this here?' (Charlotte 1;08;28)

No other *wh*-phrases are found in situ in the corpus for Charlotte. Conversely, Charlotte apparently applies *wh*-movement to both *where* and its Cantonese counterpart *bin1dou6* 'where' in mixed utterances (Lai 2005):

(156)   Where's dang6?
         Where's chair
         'Where's the chair?'   (Charlotte 1;10;09)

(157)   Bin1dou6 chair?
         Where   chair
         'Where's the chair?'   (Charlotte 1;11;05)

While these two examples do not make for a clear generalization, it appears that Charlotte may be applying *wh*-movement to both languages (perhaps optionally, given examples of *wh*-in-situ as in (153)–(154)), consistent with the dominance of English. By contrast, in all our voluminous corpus data for the three Cantonese-dominant siblings, there is no trace of *wh*-movement being applied to Cantonese. Just two examples appear in Sophie's diary data, after the end of the regular recording period. The first involves an embedded question, where *bin1dou6* 'where' is fronted as far as the beginning of the embedded clause, in accordance with English syntax:

(158)   Zi1-m4-zi1dou6 *bin1dou6* ngo5 zeoi3 zung1ji3 aa3?
        know-not-know *where*   I   most like   SFP
        'Do you know where I like most?'   (Sophie 5;02;03)

The second example is a clearer case of *wh*-movement, with *mat1je5* 'what' at the beginning of the clause:

(159)   Maa1mi4, *mat1je5* lei5 zung1ji aa3, gam1jat6
        Mummy   *what*   you like   SFP today
        'Mummy, what would you like today?'   (Sophie 5;05;05)

Coming at the end of the study period, these examples are consistent with the shift of dominance towards English which occurs in all three siblings from around age five, when they begin all-day English-medium schooling (see chapter 3). These examples are closely comparable to Kwan-Terry's (1986) data from Singapore (see section 4.5 below).

4.5   *Wh*-in-situ in contact languages

Considering the bilingual child as a microcosm of language contact, we now examine parallel cases of *wh*-in-situ in contact languages. Pidgins and creoles based on European languages typically show *wh*-movement, or fronting of *wh*-phrases in interrogatives (Veenstra & den Besten 1994). However, contact languages with Chinese substrate influence show *wh*-in-situ phenomena comparable to those observed in the bilingual children. We shall look at how *wh*-in-situ constructions found in the bilingual data are paralleled in two contact languages, Singapore Colloquial English and Chinese Pidgin English.

4.5.1   Singapore Colloquial English

Relevant case studies of the acquisition of interrogatives in Singaporean children have been carried out by Kwan-Terry (1986), Harrison and Lim (1988) and Gupta (1994). Kwan-Terry (1986: 23) reports examples of *wh*-in-situ in a Cantonese-English bilingual child in Singapore, which are very similar to those produced by the Hong Kong bilingual children:

(160)   You are doing what?   (Elvoo 3;06)

(161)   This is for making what?   (Elvoo 3;09)

(162)   We are going to eat where?   (Elvoo 3;09)

When the same child began to prepose *wh*-words in English, his Cantonese was affected and he produced non-target interrogatives like the following:

(163)   Mat1je5 lei5 zung1ji3?
        what   you like

'What do you like?'   (Elvoo 4;09)

We also have suggestive evidence of this kind from Sophie (159) and from our English-dominant subject, Charlotte (157).

The crucial difference between the Singapore and Hong Kong studies lies in the nature of the input. Harrison and Lim (1988: 149) show that *wh*-in-situ is used by adults to the children involved in their study, as in the following questions:

(164)   Doll lie down where?
(165)   This one what hah?[36]

Therefore, in addition to *wh*-in-situ being produced under direct influence from Chinese, 'Singaporean children's English interrogative structures are open to influence from the form of English motherese they hear' (Harrison & Lim 1988: 149). The children alternate between *wh*-movement and *wh*-in-situ, as in the following pair produced by the same child in Harrison & Lim's study (from the age group 2;11–3;01):

(166)   What the girl doing?
(167)   This is what?

That is, much as we argued in the case of Timmy and Alicia, *wh*-movement is essentially optional. The alternation may be partly a matter of register, with *wh*-movement more likely to apply in acrolectal SCE.

Gupta (1994) also provides extensive evidence for *wh*-in-situ in Singaporean children. In the case of Singapore, this could be attributed either to direct transfer from Chinese dialects, and/or to acquisition of SCE, in which *wh*-in-situ is present (as a substrate feature derived from Chinese dialects). *Wh*-in-situ is a prominent feature of adult Singaporean usage: 'in SCE x-interrogatives with *what*, *where* and *who* may have the *wh*-word either in the declarative position or fronted' (Gupta 1994: 94). *Wh*-in-situ is also documented in an adult SCE corpus by Fong (2004: 91):

(168)   So you get what?
         'So what do you get?'

(169)   Talking about who?
         'Who are you talking about?'

Gupta (1991: 131) records a mother asking her child *you study where?* with *where* left in situ. *Where* is commonly left in situ by the Singaporean children (Gupta 1994: 98):

(170)   Aunty want to go where?   (EG 2;11)
(171)   Press where?   (YG 3;06)

(172)   Powder put where?   (EB 7;08)

(173)   So I put where this?   (EG 5;11)

The generalization based on Singaporean children's development shows that 'where the *wh*-word is the object of the verb, or the complement of a preposition, it is likely to maintain its declarative position', i.e. the *wh*-word remains in situ (Gupta 1994: 98).

A detailed account of Singaporean children's development of embedded interrogatives is provided in Gupta (1994: 130–142). The *wh*-word in the embedded interrogatives produced by Gupta's subjects is fronted in every case but one, and 'the earliest embedded interrogatives follow experiential verbs, especially *know*, and are *how* interrogative clauses' (1994: 134–135):

(174)   Don't know how to read.   (YB 4;00)

(175)   I don't know what is this.   (EB 4;07)

The acquisition sequence for *wh*-words based on Gupta's study of four Singapore children's longitudinal development bears strong resemblance to that of our Hong Kong bilingual children: *what* and *where* are acquired before *why* and *who* while *when* and *which* are acquired late (Gupta 1994: 88). The *wh*-phrases *what for* and (with *wh*-in-situ) *for what* are used in SCE in the sense of 'why' (Gupta 1994: 100):

(176)   What for you use the straight type?   (EB 6;02)

This usage may be attributed to transfer and/or substrate influence since in the local dialects (Hokkien and Teochew as well as Cantonese) *why* questions are typically expressed by a compound expression meaning 'do what' as in Cantonese (see section 4.3.4).

4.5.2   Chinese Pidgin English

Chinese Pidgin English (CPE) was spoken in Cantonese-speaking communities including Canton, Hong Kong and other trading ports in the eighteenth and nineteenth centuries. It was used for limited, largely mercantile interaction between European traders and Chinese merchants. CPE is no longer spoken in Hong Kong and is thought to have become extinct soon after the Second World War. It is known mainly from English language sources such as travellers' memoirs. Recently, however, Chinese language sources have come to light which add greatly to the available database. In particular, data from a phrase book, *The Chinese-English Instructor*, published in Chinese in Guangzhou around 1862 have been transcribed in Li, Matthews and Smith (2005).

English-language sources for CPE typically show fronting of *wh*-phrases, as in (177):

(177)   *How muchee* you gib? [how much are you offering]   (Dier 1860)

The Chinese data present a different and more varied picture. These data show *wh*-questions with *wh*-in-situ as in (178), optional *wh*-movement (179) and partial *wh*-movement (180) in which the *wh*-phrase is moved only as far as the beginning of the embedded clause:

(178)   You give *what price* [what price do you give]

(179)   a. *How muchee* more you wantchee? [what more do you want]
         b. You wantchee *how muchee*? [how much do you want]

(180)   You thinkee *what time* ship can come
         [when do you expect the ship's arrival]

All three options are found in Cantonese-dominant bilingual children as described above. *Wh*-in-situ therefore reflects the influence of Cantonese as substrate language in CPE, and as dominant language in bilingual development.

4.6   Conclusions

Interrogative sentences with *wh*-in-situ provide a clear case of syntactic transfer from Cantonese. In many respects the bilingual data contrast with monolingual data, where non-echo questions with *wh*-in-situ are vanishingly rare: even when such questions are found in monolingual children, they are generally not spontaneous but modelled on the adult's input, unlike the copious examples in our bilingual corpus and diary data that are entirely spontaneous. We have shown that four Cantonese-dominant children go through a *wh*-in-situ stage where *wh*-words are not moved; and that subsequently when *wh*-movement is acquired, it remains optional for a period before it becomes obligatory in their grammar. Partial *wh*-movement, attested in monolingual English-speaking children's spontaneous production and experimental studies, is also produced as an intermediate stage in the acquisition of *wh*-movement by bilingual children. Our diary data on spontaneously produced split *what* questions represent an original finding which has thus far not been reported in monolingual development.

The novel use of *what are doing* questions in the sense of *why* by some bilingual children exemplifies Bilingual Bootstrapping (Gawlitzek-Maiwald & Tracy 1996): before the target construction has been acquired, a Cantonese construction modelled on *zou6 mat1je5* 'why', literally 'do what', is used as a stopgap measure. In this connection, it is noteworthy that on the average, English *why* questions emerge at 30.3 months in bilinguals, 5 months earlier than monolingual children at 35 months. The acceleration in bilingual children's acquiring *why* questions can be attributed to the early acquisition of Cantonese *why* questions with *dim2gaai2* and *zou6 mat1je5* 'what for'.

Language dominance plays a clear role here: the Cantonese-dominant children contrast qualitatively and quantitatively with our English-dominant child Charlotte and the balanced child Kathryn, who produce lower rates of *wh*-in-situ in English. A second factor may be input ambiguity: the existence of echo questions in the input to children provides evidence for *wh*-in situ as an option in English, encouraging the children to apply it to English as well as Cantonese.

This case study also has implications for language contact. When two typologically different languages are in contact, *wh*-in-situ questions in Cantonese-type languages prove to be transferable to English-type languages which require *wh*-movement in forming interrogatives. Due to the influence of Cantonese as substrate language, in both SCE and CPE *wh*-in-situ is attested with similar properties to those observed in our bilingual acquisition data. The optional *wh*-movement stage in bilingual development is paralleled by the optionality of *wh*-movement in SCE. Transfer of *wh*-questions is not unidirectional from a *wh*-in-situ language to a language with *wh*-movement; the converse is also attested: *wh*-movement in English-type languages is amenable to transfer to Cantonese-type languages, as evidenced in our children's occasional questions with fronted *wh*-word in Cantonese and a Singapore child's *wh*-questions in Kwan-Terry's (1986) study.

NOTES

1. *Wh*-questions and relative clauses share many structural properties and involve similar processes: both constructions typically involve a gap and similar *wh*-words e.g. *who, where, whose* in English. Even in languages without overt *wh*-movement, these two constructions are shown to have many similarities. Demuth (1995) investigates the acquisition of *wh*-questions and relative clauses in Sesotho, a Bantu language with no *wh*-movement in either questions or relatives. She argues that children initially treat relative clauses as IPs, rather than CPs, just as *wh*-questions are IPs. Similarly, the bilingual children's *wh*-in-situ questions discussed in this chapter and prenominal relative clauses in chapter 6 may be analysed as IPs just like declarative sentences.

2. Our discussion will not touch on *how* and *when* questions in the bilingual corpus since they are not sufficiently frequent in the period during which the recording was conducted. Questions asking time relations are known to be late acquired cross-linguistically. For example, out of six children, only one clear token of a *when* question is attested in the oldest child Kathryn's corpus:

(i)   When can we go to your house?   (Kathryn 3;03;16)

Kathryn also produced one token of the Cantonese counterpart asking *gei2 dim2zung1* 'what time':

(ii)	. . . Ngo5	man6	sin1saang1	gei2	e6	gei2	dim2zung1	sin1
	I	ask	teacher	what	INT	what	hour	then
	faan1	sin1	faan1	lei4	sin1			
	return	then	return	come	first			

'I ask the teacher what time (we) return.'   (Kathryn 4;02;17)

A couple of 'time' questions are recorded in Timmy's diary data:

(iii)   You what time will go to work? Which day you will go to work?

                                                              (Timmy 3;02;14)

The *wh*-phrase *what time* appears after the subject *you*, reflecting the Cantonese word order while *which day* is appropriately fronted in the immediately following question. One instance of Cantonese *gei2 dim2* literally 'what hour' is found in Timmy's corpus:

(iv)	Gei2	dim2	lei4	sin1?
	what	hour	come	first

'What time does (he) come?'   (Timmy 3;05;28)

3. It is widely assumed that even the subject *wh*-phrases undergo *wh*-movement: for example, *who* in (3) occupies the same position as the displaced object in (1). In generative grammar this position is taken to be the Specifier of CP (see e.g. Haegeman & Guéron 1999: 172). However, not all theoretical approaches assume a movement analysis of subject *wh*-questions (Stromswold 1995: 13).

4. The two separate questions in (9) can also be turned into a multiple question:

(i)	Lei5	tung4	bin1go3	gei2	dim2	hai2	bin1dou6	dang2	ngo5	waa2?
	you	with	who	what	hour	at	where	wait	me	SFP

'You'll be waiting with who, when and where?'

5. While there are debates about whether monolingual children exhibit a *wh*-in-situ stage (Radford 1990; Stromswold 1995), we are not aware of any studies on the acquisition of target-like *wh*-in-situ questions as in (10)–(13).

6. An utterance containing the two words *what else* is also excluded from analysis since no syntactic structure is implicated.

7. Eve was a precocious child whose 'speech developed so much more rapidly than that of Adam and Sarah that 10 months of her transcriptions equalled about 20 months for Adam and Sarah' (Brown 1973: 53). When the MLU values of Brown's three subjects are plotted against chronological age, Eve's development is most consistent, prompting Roger Brown to remark that 'It was almost impossible to fail to find an increment every time two weeks had elapsed' (Brown 1973: 55).

8. Radford (1990: 136) argues that apparent cases of *wh*-movement at this stage are 'semiformulaic utterances', and gives three additional arguments for the lack of CP at this stage:

   (i) Early child clauses lack complementizers;
   (ii) Early child clauses do not contain preposed auxiliaries;
   (iii) Children at this stage are unable to correctly parse clauses containing preposed *wh*-constituents.

9. The base position for *dim2gaai2* 'why' is between subject and verb, as it is for expressions of reason and purpose (Matthews & Yip 1994: 299).

10. Timmy's use of the article as in *a what* and *to the what* may be attributable to Cantonese influence. *What* substitutes for the whole NP in English, but the Cantonese

equivalent *mat1je5* 'what' can be modified by a classifier as in *Lei5 maai5 di1 mat1je5* 'What did you buy?' See note 26.

11. Moreover, there is evidence that children have difficulty understanding and providing an appropriate answer to questions with a non-copula verb that elicits a direct object *wh*-word (Klima & Bellugi 1966: 201; Radford 1990: 129–130).

(i)   a. What have you got? –Eh?   (Dewi 20 months)

       b. What did mummy say? –Mummy.   (Jenny 21 months)

       c. What's he [=caterpillar] doing? –Caterpillar.   (Bethan 20 months)

In (ia)–(ic), the child either responds with a filler *eh*, or repeats a word *mummy* in the adult's question or simply identifies some referent *caterpillar*, referred to by the pronoun in the question. Such abortive answers have led to the hypothesis that children interpret these questions according to the form *What's X?*, 'misanalysing the initial *wh*-pronoun as a base-generated subject rather than a preposed complement' (Radford 1990: 130).

12. The files selected from Timmy's corpus are te950623, te950817, te951019, te951221, te960321, and te960503 for comparison with Eve's corpus including eve05, eve07, eve09, eve11, eve13 and eve 14.

13. The colon notation in *I:t's wha:t?* indicates the lengthening of the vowel in both words.

14. The percentage of *what*-in-situ is calculated in terms of the proportion of in-situ *what* questions out of the total number of *what* questions, including formulaic expressions and other object-fronted questions. Subject questions such as *What happened?* are excluded because there is no way to tell whether *wh*-movement has applied or not.

15. A number of data points (2;06, 2;11, 3;00, 3;02 and 3;03) are not represented in figure 4.1 because no *wh*-questions are found during the months of 2;06, 3;00, 3;02 and 3;03, while only one *wh*-in-situ question is instantiated at 2;11.

16. Although Timmy's *lady what what?* is not quite a target-like echo question, note that it is possible to question part of a compound word:

(i)   A: It's a lady-bug.
       B: A lady-what?

Timmy's question appears to be a variant of an echo question of this type. Artstein (2002) discusses the focus strategy that allows echo questions to focus on parts of words as in (i).

17. Irregular past tense verbs such as *said* in (41) often appear in what is known as 'double tensing' sentences where tense is marked twice, once in the auxiliary *did* and again in the main verb *said* (see O'Grady 1997: 164).

18. The figure for 'fronted' *what* questions produced by Sophie also includes 2 instances where *what* is fronted and *where* remains in situ, as discussed separately under *where* questions and four tokens of *what are doing* meaning 'why?' as discussed under *why* questions.

19. In (47) the dative verb *give* is immediately followed by the PP [to Lulu] and then the in-situ *what*. This is known as a prepositional dative where the PP containing the recipient should be placed after the theme object. The development of word order

phenomena involving dative *bei2* 'give' in Cantonese is extensively discussed in section 7.2.

20. The age of acquisition of a particular *wh*-word in Cantonese is derived by identifying the earliest emergence of a *wh*-word in each child and computing the average age of acquisition. For example, *bin1go3* 'who' is attested in seven out of eight monolingual Cantonese-speaking children; the average age of acquisition is derived by adding the ages at which *bin1go3* 'who' first emerged in the children concerned, and then dividing the total ages by seven.

21. Different functions encoded by Cantonese *wh*-words are distinguished in Cheung (1995): for example *mat1je5* 'what' is used for identification with the copula *hai6* before it is used as object of a transitive verb, while *zou6 mat1je5*, literally 'do what', can mean *what for* or *why* (see also section 4.3.4). Cheung (1995) also investigates Cantonese-speaking children's non-interrogative use of *wh*-words as indefinites, intensifiers and rhetorical questions.

22. A number of interesting findings on monolingual Cantonese development include the following: overall, argument questions are acquired earlier than adjunct questions: an asymmetry in subject-object argument questions is found in Cantonese whereby object questions asking *mat1je5* 'what' and *bin1dou6* 'where' emerged the earliest while subject *bin1go3* 'who' questions emerged earlier than object *bin1go3* 'who' questions (Cheung 1995: 115–116).

23. The dates for Kathryn's first attested *wh*-questions are not included because it is likely that she already used *wh*-questions before the recording period began: the age (3;02;19) is thus not representative of their first emergence.

24. For Llywelyn, the late date of 2;07;04 for both *mat1je5* and *what* may not be representative since his corpus data are less extensive.

25. We thank Rosalind Thornton for drawing our attention to differences between monolingual and bilingual children's split *wh*-questions.

26. Timmy's use of the article as in *a what* and *to the what* may be attributable to Cantonese influence. *What* substitutes for the whole NP in English, but the Cantonese equivalent *mat1je5* 'what' can be modified by a classifier as in *Lei5 maai5 di1 mat1je5* 'What did you buy?' Moreover, there is a partial equivalence between the Cantonese classifier and the English article (Matthews & Pacioni 1997) which could lead the bilingual children to use articles with *what*. It should also be noted, however, that a *wh*-phrase can take a determiner in English *wh*-in-situ questions, as in *it's a WHAT?* Timmy's phrase *to the what* could occur in an echo question, as in *You went to the WHAT?* It is therefore possible that Timmy acquired this pattern from adult input. This would be a case of a child being misled by the occurrence of *wh*-in-situ in English in pragmatically appropriate contexts, as hypothesized in section 4.4.2.

27. In English and many (but not all) languages with *wh*-movement, only one *wh*-phrase can be fronted at a time, so that in multiple questions the remaining *wh*-phrases are left in situ. It might be argued that such a constraint prevents Sophie from fronting *where* in such cases that involve another moved *wh*-word. Sophie's question appears to be a developmental innovation, rather than a multiple question based on adult input (see section 4.3.5 for discussion of multiple *wh*-questions).

28. The postposed *we* in (89) is based on the Cantonese right-dislocation construction, where the subject of the sentence is dislocated and appears at the end of the question (see Matthews & Yip 1994: 71–72, 229, 239).

29. In the context where Sophie produced the question *what are doing?* without any following verb, it is parallel to the Cantonese equivalent *Zou6 mat1je5 aa3?* 'What's the matter?'

30. The question (111) produced by Timmy appears to violate the constraint on multiple questions known as superiority. Superiority dictates that when two *wh*-phrases in the same clause are being questioned, the one in the higher position undergoes *wh*-movement (Huang 1995: 153). Thus English prefers to move the object in (i) rather than (ii) as produced by Timmy:

(i)   [$_{CP}$ Which one$_i$ did [$_{IP}$ you buy t$_i$ where]]?

(ii)   ?*[$_{CP}$ Where$_j$ did [$_{IP}$ you buy which one t$_j$]]?

The explanation may be that in Cantonese, *where* precedes *which one*:

(iii)   Lei5 hai2 bin1dou6 maai5 bin1   go3 aa3?
          you   at   where   buy   which CL SFP
          'Which one did you buy where?'

MacDaniel, Chiu and Maxfield (1995) have investigated the acquisition of multiple questions by English-speaking children in experimental studies.

31. Long-distance *wh*-movement is analysed as a series of successive local movement operations whereby the *wh*-phrase moves across each intermediate landing site (Spec of CP in each clause). The constraint on how far each movement can go is known as subjacency (see Haegeman & Guéron 1999).

32. Thornton and Crain (1994: 220) observed that in their longitudinal studies of several children, subject questions with medial *wh*-phrase persisted even when object questions with medial *wh*-phrase were unlearned. Another nice illustration of *wh*-copying produced by monolingual children is used in the video 'Acquiring the Human Language: Playing the Language Game' Program Two of the Human Language Series by Searchinger (1995):

(i) What do you think what's in here?

A video demo showing how such questions are elicited by experimental techniques in monolingual English-speaking children is available at the Child Language Videos Archive contributed by Stephen Crain and his team:

(ii) What do you think what's in the box?

The point illustrated here is that the non-target structure is not a random error, but an option provided by Universal Grammar (UG) and instantiated in a number of languages such as dialects of German. It is hypothesized that children will only entertain options provided by UG.

33. The finding that 'every child who produced partial movement structures also produced *wh*-copying structures' led Thornton and Crain (1994: 216) to argue that successive cyclic movement was available in the grammar of these children.

34. The pronoun *it* occurs in the object position where the *wh*-phrase originates, and is generally referred to as a resumptive pronoun. While rarely found in *wh*-questions in our data, resumptive pronouns are more extensively attested in the acquisition of relative clauses (see chapter 6).

35. A possible precedent involves *bin1go3* 'which' which can occur as a modifier in a topicalized noun phrase:

(i)   [Bin1go3   ming4-sing1]   lei5   zeoi3   zung1ji3   aa2?
       which   name-star   you   most   like   SFP
       'Which star do you like most?'

This is a case of topicalization, motivated by the noun *ming4sing1* 'star' which happens to be modified by *bin1go3* 'which'. It could, however, be taken as evidence for *wh*-movement in Cantonese, just as echo questions provide a precedent for *wh*-in-situ in English.

36. *Hah* is one of several sentence-final particles in Cantonese which are extensively used in Singapore Colloquial English (Lim 2004).

5 Null objects: Dual Input and Learnability

Alicia: [carrying jar of face cream] I want to put.   (Alicia 2;08;12)
Sophie You want to put on your face?
Alicia: Yeah.   (Sophie 6;11;12)

The above dialogue illustrates the curious case of the missing objects: the object of the verb *put* is never actually stated, but is effectively provided by the children's current topic of conversation, namely a jar of face cream. Following Alicia's use of *put* without its object (*I want to put*), Sophie's response (*You want to put on your face?*) follows suit, adopting the same grammatical device even as late as age 6;11. The null object is thus a feature of the English used by and between the bilingual children, just as it is a feature of Singapore Colloquial English.

In Yip and Matthews (2000a) we showed how in the development of one child, Cantonese influences the developing grammar of English with respect to missing objects of transitive verbs, as in (1):

(1)   You get, I eat . . . [father takes chocolates off shelf]   (Timmy 2;02;03)

In this example, the missing object of the transitive verbs *get* and *eat* refers to certain chocolates which are present in the speech context. In the following example (2), the missing object appears as *it* in the preceding adult utterance:

(2)   INV: Where shall we stick it?
          CHI: Put here.   (Timmy 2;05;05)

This property is transferred from the child's Cantonese, as seen in the child's well-formed reply in (3):

(3)   Mother: Lo2 violin ceot1 lai4   zou6 mat1je5 aa3?
                  take violin out   come do   what   SFP
                'What are you getting the violin out for?'
         CHI: Lo2 ceot1 lai4   taan4 lo1!
               take out   come play SFP
               'I'm taking [it] out to play [it], of course!'   (Timmy 2;04;08)

The object of the verbs *lo2* 'take' and *taan4* 'play' is the violin mentioned in the mother's utterance but omitted in the child's utterance, which involves a serial

133

verb construction consisting of a series of verbs *lo2* 'take', *ceot1 lai4* 'come out' and *taan4* 'play' appearing in succession (see section 5.1 on how such null objects are interpreted).

We shall refer to such missing objects as *null objects*: objects of transitive verbs which are understood, but not pronounced. These null objects are argued to be part of the structure of the sentence, in accordance with the grammar of Cantonese. Yip and Matthews (2000a, 2005) show that the bilingual children's use of null objects in English is quantitatively and qualitatively different from that of monolingual English-speaking children in ways which reflect cross-linguistic influence from Cantonese in this domain. This chapter discusses the analysis of the structures involved in (1)–(3) and the learnability issues given rise by transfer here: why are null objects produced more frequently in bilingual than in monolingual development, and over a longer period? Input ambiguity as defined by Müller (1998) and structural overlap proposed by Hulk and Müller (2000) suggest a mechanism to explain how such interaction takes place between separate systems in bilingual development (see section 5.3.1). However, we will suggest that language dominance also plays a role in accounting for cross-linguistic influence in this domain, which is reflected in quantitative differences between individual children (section 5.3.2).

5.1   Null objects in adult Cantonese

In Cantonese (as in Chinese in general) a transitive verb often appears without an object, as in (4):

(4)   Ngo5 sik6
        I   eat
        'I eat (it).'

In adult Cantonese, a sentence such as *ngo5 sik6* as in (4) can only mean 'I eat it/that' where the object of *eat* is definite; it cannot mean 'I eat (something edible, such as food, dinner etc.)' as in English, where the object of *eat* is indefinite or generic.[1] This implies a phrase structure representation of the following kind, in which the object is represented syntactically as part of the structure of the sentence:

(5)

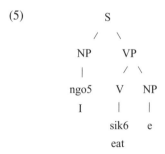

We represent the understood object as an empty category e.[2] An overt pronoun is not used in such cases, since the third person pronoun *keoi5* 'he/she' is generally used only to refer to humans in Chinese.

The null object is understood in one of two ways (see Matthews & Yip 1994: 83):

(a) Referring to an entity which has been explicitly mentioned in the preceding discourse, such as *ni1 gin6 saam1* 'this dress' in (6):

(6)   A: Lei5 zung1-m4-zung1ji3 ni1   gin6 saam1 aa3?
            you   like-not-like   this CL   dress SFP
            'Do you like this dress?'

        B: zung1ji3 aa3!
            like   SFP
            'Yes, [I] like [it]!'

(b) Referring to an entity which is present in the speech context and/or the focus of attention, though it may not be named explicitly, such as 'a gift' in (7):

(7)   A: Sung3 bei2 lei5 gaa3. Lei5 zung1-m4-zung1ji3 aa3?
            give   to   you   SFP   you   like-not-like   SFP
            'This is for you. Do you like [it]?'   [A gives B a gift]

        B: zung1ji3 aa3!
            like   SFP
            'Yes, [I] like [it]!'

This property of Cantonese presents a major contrast with English. Many analyses have connected it to the 'topic-prominent' characteristics of Chinese as a whole (see Cole, Hermon & Sung 1990; Yip 1995:74–78). The idea is that just as a missing object can refer back to an overt sentence topic such as the topicalized object *ni1 gin6 saam1* 'this dress' in (8), so it can refer to a topic which is implied but not stated, as in (9):

(8)   [TOPIC ni1 gin6 saam1]$_i$ ngo5 hou2 zung1ji3 e_i.
               this CL   dress   I   very like   this
        'This dress, I like [it] a lot.'

(9)   [TOPIC Ø]$_i$ ngo5 hou2 zung1ji3 e_i.
                      I   very like
        'I like [it] a lot.'

The importance of this somewhat abstract analysis lies in the nature of transfer: we shall argue that what is transferred in early bilingual acquisition is not merely a general propensity to omit objects, but the whole grammatical organization which we have just outlined for Cantonese, and by which the null object is licensed. A parallel argument is made by Bao (2001) for Singapore Colloquial English (see section 5.4).

5.2   Null objects in English: cross-linguistic influence and learnability

We shall now focus on the development of null objects in the bilingual children's English and Cantonese, before discussing the learnability problem raised by this phenomenon.[3] We begin with a discussion of the complexities regarding the question of object omissibility in the adult input. By *object omissibility* we mean the phenomenon whereby a verb can occur with or without an object as in (10a–e) below; such a missing object is not necessarily a null object as defined above in relation to Cantonese, which is part of the structure of the sentence; if an object is missing, it can simply be that there is no structural position for the object in the argument structure.

5.2.1   Object omissibility in adult English

The traditional classification of verbs into transitive and intransitive subcategories largely masks the problem of object omissibility. The question of what verbs are obligatorily transitive in adult English is far from straightforward: verbs like *eat, read, teach* can be both transitive and intransitive, and the constraints governing each argument structure are determined by a range of semantic and discourse factors (Aarts 1995; Goldberg 2001). Some causative verbs like *kill* and *break* are in most cases transitive but allow optional objects in certain circumstances such as the following (examples from Goldberg 2001: 506):

(10)   a. The chef-in-training chopped and diced all afternoon.
b. Tigers only kill at night.
c. The singer always aimed to dazzle/please/disappoint/impress/ charm.
d. Pat gave and gave, but Chris just took and took.
e. The sewing instructor always cut in straight lines.

Importantly, these cases differ from null objects in Cantonese, and in the bilingual children's English, in that there is no null object as part of the structure of the sentence. This is reflected in a consistent difference in the way the sentences are understood. The unexpressed patient arguments in (10a–e) are interpreted as unspecified entities that are largely predictable based on the context: thus in (10a) the objects of chopping and dicing are assumed to be various cooking ingredients, while in (10c) the object of dazzling and pleasing is the audience. In addition to non-specificity and predictability, Goldberg (2001) observes that the actions designated by the verbs are aspectually iterative (10a, d) or generic (10b, c, e) and construed as atelic or temporally unbounded events. If the sentence refers to a specific rather than a generic event, an object must be present (Fillmore 1986):

(11)   What happened to that carrot?
        I chopped *(it).

(12)   What happened to that gazelle?
        The tiger killed *(it).

These cases (where both the event and the object are specific) in which the object cannot be omitted in English are precisely those where the null object occurs in Cantonese (see above), and in the bilingual children's English, as we shall show.

In English, the missing patient of the verb *eat* as in (13) is understood as something generic like 'food' or 'a meal' but not something specific as 'sandwich', or *peas* in (14) where B's response is not well-formed:

(13)   I ate already.

(14)   A: Did you eat your peas?
        B: *Yes I ate.

Fillmore (1986) points out that the omitted patient is interpreted as 'obligatorily disjoint in reference with anything saliently present in the pragmatic context'. The intransitive use of *eat* in (14) is therefore odd here, since the conversation calls for the maintenance of a definite referent referring to *peas* or else the dialogue becomes incoherent. B's reply is infelicitous since A's question has not been answered: while *I ate* is interpretable as meaning that the speaker ate something, it cannot mean 'Yes, I ate the peas' (whereas it can do so in our bilingual children's English).

Formalizing these observations, Haegeman (1987) proposes a lexical representation (15) for the intransitive sense of verbs like *eat, read* and *teach*:

(15)   eat β
        [+generic]

To acquire target English, the child would have to acquire a representation for intransitive *eat* as in (15), where β represents an implied patient argument (but is not represented in syntax). The semantic feature [+*generic*] would need to be set to constrain the relevant interpretation. The associated discourse properties as discussed by Fillmore (1986) would also need to be acquired.

5.2.2   Object omissibility in monolingual English development

The question of object omissibility in monolingual English-speaking children has been studied by a number of researchers, notably Rispoli (1992) and Ingham (1993). A verb like *eat* poses a problem since it commonly allows both transitive in (16a) and intransitive uses (16b):

(16)   a. Shall we eat these?
         b. It's time to eat.

The intransitive usage is possible only in a context where the omitted object is generic and predictable as in (16b). Monolingual children go through a stage where they inappropriately use the verb *eat* without an object, as in (17) from Rispoli (1992: 589–590):

(17)   [Parent has just opened a bag of popcorn]
         Parent: Popcorn
         Child: I eat
         Parent: You gonna save some for your dad?   (Child 2;06)

In this example, the child's utterance *I eat* without an object sounds odd: from the context, it is natural to assume that *popcorn* is part of the discourse topic which is subsequently referred to again in the parent's reply, in which *some* refers back to the previously mentioned *popcorn*. Rispoli found that children often omitted the object of the verb *eat* when the object has definite reference in the discourse context – exactly when it cannot be omitted in adult English. In the longitudinal transcripts of forty monolingual English-speaking children between 1;0–3;0, Rispoli (1992) found evidence for sensitivity to the relationship between object omission and discourse context at an average age of 2;03 and MLU of 2.4: in discourse contexts which favour an overt object such as (17) the rate of omission is 26%, while in contexts which favour the intransitive usage the object omission rate rises to 45%.[4] Rispoli (1992) suggested that the focal status of the undergoer (patient) in the discourse context may be crucial to the acquisition of the target properties: when the patient is in focus as in (17), the conversation demands continued mention of this explicit patient.

A related set of problems is addressed by Ingham (1993), who discusses the optionality of objects in adult English and in Naomi, a monolingual English-speaking child. He points out that omission of a referential object is grammatical with certain verbs: (Ingham 1993: 96):

(18)   John aimed at the target and missed (it).

(19)   They ran away but we followed (them).

Unlike the generic cases in (10) discussed above, these cases involve missing objects which are specific in reference. Note also that the sentences involve

Table 5.1. *Frequency of null objects in the English of a monolingual child, Adam (based on Huang 1999: 83)*

File name	Age	MLU	No. of null objects	No. of verb-complement structures	% of null objects
06	2;05;12	2.236	3	105	2.86
08	2;06;17	2.904	4	134	2.99
10	2;07;14	2.547	6	145	4.14
12	2;08;16	2.385	4	124	3.23
14	2;09;18	2.383	4	89	4.49
			total = 21	total = 597	
				average over the period = 3.5%	

Table 5.2. *Frequency of null objects with seven transitive verbs in the English of a monolingual child, Adam (based on Huang 1999: 83) (only verbs which appear in 10 or more tokens in the corpus are shown)*

Verb	No. of null objects	Total no. of occurrences of each verb	% of null objects
bite	1	15	6.7
find	1	11	9.1
need	1	15	6.7
push	2	21	9.5
put	7	97	7.2
stir	1	11	9.1
want	2	52	3.8
Total	15	222	6.8

coordinate structures, with *and* (18) or *but* (19), forming a different category of omissible object contexts which we leave aside for this chapter. The verbs Ingham (1993) identifies as allowing an optional object in the monolingual data include *kick, read, touch, bang, draw, push, see, wash* and *eat*. Ingham (1993: 109) showed that Naomi's error rate in omitting obligatory objects was low in the period under study (1;08–1;11): 4.8% (12/251 tokens).[5] Huang (1999: 83) investigated the null objects in a monolingual child, Adam (Brown 1973) and showed that between 2;05–2;09, the average null object rate over the period is 3.5% (table 5.1).[6] Among the verbs which Adam uses with null objects (table 5.2), the frequency varies from 3.8% for *want* to 9.5% for *push*.

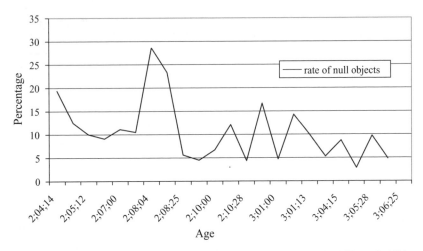

Figure 5.1   Percentage of null objects in the English of a bilingual child, Timmy (based on Huang 1999: 80)

5.2.3   Comparing null objects in bilingual and monolingual English

As we have seen, missing objects appear as a developmental feature in English monolingual children (as in Adam's null objects in tables 5.1 and 5.2). Nevertheless, there are clear quantitative and qualitative differences between the monolingual and bilingual data, as we showed in a case study of Timmy (Yip & Matthews 2000a). To demonstrate these differences we focus on obligatory contexts where the transitive verb must take an object, as in (20) and (21)[7]:

(20)   Father: Timmy, do you want the rest of this?
         CHI: I don't want.   (Timmy 2;07;07)

(21)   Be careful, don't break!
         [cautioning the adult not to break a toy cup]   (Sophie 3;06;06)

These examples show that a specific object is either present in the preceding speech context (*the rest of this* in (20)), or implied in the context (the toy cup which the child is holding in (21)).

Before extending the investigation to the other five bilingual children, let us first consider the longitudinal development of null object rates in Timmy's English as shown in figure 5.1.

The percentage of null objects in the eight recording sessions between 2;04–2;08 ranges from 9.1%–28.6%, a higher range than has been reported in any monolingual studies. In the subsequent period from 2;09–3;06, the rate drops but remains consistently above 5%. The period in which highest null object rates are observed, from 2;04–2;08, is also a period in which his Cantonese is ahead of his English as measured by MLU (see figure 3.3): between 2;04–2;08, the MLU differential between Cantonese and English is as high as 0.87, as against 0.39, the mean differential value for the entire period of study from 2;01–3;06 (see table 3.3).

We now turn to the null object rates across six bilingual children and draw comparisons among them. Table 5.3 shows the rate of null objects for five of the most frequent transitive verbs in the corpora for all six bilingual children.

The overall frequency of null objects for the five verbs studied is highest in Alicia, Sophie and Llywelyn's English (34%, 31.8% and 30.3% respectively) and lowest in Kathryn's (1.4%), with Timmy and Charlotte somewhere between the two ends of the continuum (18.8% and 19.9%). Of these, only the relatively balanced Kathryn lies in the range reported for monolingual English children; the others show null object rates at least twice as high as in monolinguals.

Among the most frequent verbs that take an obligatory object in English, the verb *put* stands out as taking a null object especially frequently (36.6% for Timmy, 71.4% for Sophie, 58.7% for Alicia, 31.4% for Llywelyn, 21.4% for Charlotte but 0% for Kathryn). Typical examples illustrating the null object phenomenon with *put* are (22)–(23):

(22)   <Don't> [>] put here!   (Llywelyn 2;08;08)

(23)   <You can't put> [>] there.   (Charlotte 2;10;15)

This non-target-like structure whereby *put* is directly followed by a locative *here* resembles the Cantonese structure as seen in (24), where both the adult and the child use the verb *baai2* 'place' with a null object.

(24)   Adult: Sik1-m4-sik1   baai2 aa3
                 know-not-know   place   SFP
                 'Do you know how to put it in place?'

         Child: Baai2 aa1
                 place   SFP
                 'Put (it) (in place).'   (Sophie 1;06;00)

That *put* should be the verb showing the highest frequency of null objects may relate to its unique argument structure: as the sole English verb used by the children to require a prepositional phrase as well as a direct object, it calls for a relatively complex and heavy Verb Phrase of the form [V NP PP] if all the arguments are to be overtly realized. Omitting the object therefore simplifies the Verb Phrase to a [V PP] configuration.

For comparison, we analyse the frequency of null objects with the corresponding verbs in Timmy and Sophie's Cantonese. Corresponding to the five English verbs in table 5.3, table 5.4 shows the null object rates with four Cantonese verbs (*lo2* 'get,' *zung1ji3* 'like,' *baai2* 'put' and *jiu3* 'want' since *lo2* corresponds to both 'get' and 'take'). The percentage of null objects for the

Table 5.3. *Frequency of null objects with five transitive verbs in the English of six bilingual children*

Verb	Percentage of null objects					
	Timmy 2;01;02–3;06;25	Sophie 1;06;00–3;00;09	Alicia 1;03;10–3;00;24	Llywelyn 2;00;12–3;04;17	Charlotte 1;08;28–3;00;03	Kathryn 3;01;05–4;06;07
get	21.9	33.3	0	18.9	13.3	1.03
like	7.1	16.7	12.9	25.9	12.5	3.85
put	36.6	71.4	58.7	31.4	21.4	0
take	20.0	56.0	25.0	42.9	14.3	0
want	1.4	26.8	33.8	45.0	22.1	0
Total	18.8	31.8	34.0	30.3	19.9	1.4

Table 5.4. *Frequency of null objects in the Cantonese of two bilingual children, Timmy and Sophie (Timmy: 22 files from 2;01;22 to 3;00;09; Sophie: 28 files from 2;00;07 to 3;00;09)*

Verb	No. of null objects		Total no. of occurrences of each verb		% of null objects	
	Timmy	Sophie	Timmy	Sophie	Timmy	Sophie
lo2 'get'	50	53	93	72	53.8	73.6
zung1ji3 'like'	21	59	32	91	65.6	64.8
baai2 'put'	39	20	43	21	90.7	95.2
jiu3 'want'	62	97	90	136	68.9	71.3
Total	172	229	258	320	66.7	71.6

corresponding verbs in Timmy and Sophie's Cantonese corpus data ranges from 53.8% to 95.2%, and the average rate is 66.7% for Timmy (2;01;22–3;00;09) and 71.6% for Sophie (2;00;07 to 3;00;09),[8] consistently higher than the corresponding frequency of null objects in their English. The frequency of null objects with the verb *baai2* 'put' again tops the other verbs, reaching 90.7% in Timmy and 95.2% in Sophie. Comparing their null object rates with English *put* (36.6% in Timmy and 71.4% in Sophie), it is evident that the rates are much higher in their Cantonese than in English. This implies that although the children are producing null objects under the influence of their Cantonese grammar, they are not merely treating English as Cantonese, as a 'single-system' view would predict. If there were a single system, one would also expect the null object rate to be invariant regardless of language context, i.e. the rate should be the same whether the child is speaking English or Cantonese. In fact there is evidence that the rate varies systematically even within English. Lai (2006) found that Charlotte's rate of object drop in English sentences produced in Cantonese contexts is higher than that in the English contexts (35.1% vs. 19.9%). In the Cantonese contexts (that is, when addressed in Cantonese), Charlotte shows a strong tendency to produce English instead; however, her English in such contexts bears stronger influence from Cantonese, namely, the rate of object drop goes up dramatically compared to the modest rate in the English context. This result is consistent with the hypothesis that the child is more susceptible to transfer when operating in bilingual mode, with both languages activated (Grosjean 1998, 2001a).

A further set of data derives from the investigation of verb-particle constructions as discussed in section 7.3. Verb-particle combinations are identified by searching for potential particles such as *around, away, down, in* and

Table 5.5. *Distribution of null objects in English verb-particle constructions in six bilingual children*

Subject	Timmy	Sophie	Alicia	Llywelyn	Charlotte	Kathryn	Total
No. of null objects	40	27	14	21	26	9	137
No. of transitive [V-PRT] Constructions	79	49	22	38	69	47	304
% null objects	50.6	55.0	63.6	55.3	37.7	19.1	45.0

off. After manually identifying those occurrences which involve verb-particle combinations (such as *turn off*) as opposed to prepositions (as in *off the wall*), these combinations are categorized according to whether the object is between the verb and particle (split order), following the particle (non-split order), or null. Typical examples of null objects in the verb-particle construction include the following, where the context shows that the children are using *take off* in its transitive sense (removing clothes).

(25)   CHI: Take off
        INV: What?   (Charlotte 1;10;09)

(26)   I want take off   (Alicia 2;05;04)

The null object rates in transitive verb-particle combinations are shown in table 5.5, which shows even higher rates of null objects than those already seen in table 5.3.

As a whole, the six bilingual children's average rate of null objects is 45% in verb-particle constructions, a higher rate than for any of the children with simple transitive constructions in table 5.3. Timmy has 50.6% null objects, as against 18.8% for the simple transitive verbs. Charlotte has a lower percentage (37.7%), consistent with lesser influence of Cantonese, but still twice the 19.9% rate for simple transitive constructions in table 5.3. Again, monolingual children show a much lower rate of null objects: as shown in table 5.6, the monolingual children Peter and Allison show lower null object rates of 20% and 4.4% respectively. It is nevertheless interesting that Peter's rate of 20% is well above those reported for null objects of simple transitive constructions in monolingual development. A similar figure is given in Diessel and Tomasello (2005a) who found 21.1% of objects of transitive verb-particle constructions to be null (combining data from Peter and Eve). The fact that null object rates are higher in verb-particle constructions than in simple transitive constructions may have to do with processing span. We have already suggested that the verb *put* shows a higher rate of null objects because it requires a locative PP as well as a direct object. Similarly, the verb-particle combination already constitutes

Table 5.6. *Distribution of null objects in English verb-particle constructions in two monolingual children, Peter and Allison (based on Ho 2003, data from Bloom 1973).*

Subject	Peter 1;09;07–3;01;21	Allison 1;04;21–2;10;00	Total
No. of null objects	203	2	205
No. of transitive [V-PRT] constructions	1012	45	1057
% null objects	20.0	4.4	19.4

two elements of VP, so that to provide the object calls for a VP with three elements, exceeding the span of the two-word stage. Even the most balanced bilingual child in our study, Kathryn, whose null object rate is as low as 1.4%, is found to omit the object of *put in*:

(27)   You can put in 'cause . . . because it's already out.   (Kathryn 3;04;14)

This quantitative picture is complemented by qualitative evidence for transfer. For example, the children coin phrasal verbs using *back* such as *wear back* in (28) and (29), based on combinations with the particle *faan1* 'back' in Cantonese such as *cai3 faan1* 'put back together' in (30) (see Matthews & Yip 1994: 213–214 for more examples in adult Cantonese):

(28)   I want wear back. [holding trousers]   (Timmy 4;00;16)

(29)   Wear back my things.
         [i.e. 'Put my clothes back on.']   (Sophie 5;02;03)

(30)   Lei5 cai3   laa1, cai3   faan1 aa1
         you build SFP   build back   SFP
         'Put it together, put it back together again.'   (Timmy 2;04;12)

There are also cases where the verb is used in a Cantonese sense, like *have* in (31):

(31)   INV: Where's your schoolbag? Any books in it?
         CHI: Still have.   (Timmy 2;07;28)

Apart from the null subject and object in *still have*, suggesting transfer from the Cantonese existential verb *jau5* as in the adult Cantonese sentence (32), we notice the existential use of *have* as seen in (33):

(32)   zung6   jau5
         still   have
         'There are still some (there).'

(33)   There have shark.   (Timmy 2;10;28)

There is also diary data in which an English utterance with null object follows a synonymous Cantonese one as in (34), and where null objects occur in code-switched utterances such as (35):

(34)   [seeing father replacing batteries]
         jiu3   maai5 aa3. Have to buy. Have to buy battery at Mannings.
         need buy   SFP
         'We have to buy some.'   (Timmy 2;10;22)

(35)   Ngo5 jiu3   close . . . I cannot close. [trying to close door]
         I   want close
         'I want to close (it) . . . I cannot close (it).'   (Timmy 2;02.22)

These cases support the assumption that the Cantonese and English structures are parallel for the child.

A further qualitative argument involves the syntactic analysis of null objects and their relationship to null topics. The analysis outlined in section 5.1 above assumes a relationship between topicalization of objects and the occurrence of null objects. We can see in concrete terms how a topicalized object paves the way for a null object in cases like (36):

(36)   Schoolbag put here, put at the door.   (Timmy 2;07;12)

On the first occurrence of *put*, its object [*schoolbag*] has been topicalized; the missing object of the second occurrence of *put* refers back to the same topic, as represented in (37):

(37)   [TOPIC Schoolbag]$_i$ *pro* put e$_i$ here, put e$_i$ at the door.

This is the essence of the analysis of null objects developed by Huang (1984) and widely assumed in studies of language acquisition (Yip 1995: 81; Yuan 1997: 473) as well as language contact (Bao 2001). The notation *pro* represents the subject pronoun which is null (see also section 2.1.2). The same analysis can be extended to cases where the topicalization is implicit rather than overt:

(38)   You bought this for me. Last time you bought. I know you bought.
                                                                   (Timmy 2;07;11)

Here the object *this* is introduced as the object of *bought*, then becomes the (unstated) topic of the following discourse, thereby licensing the null objects in the following two clauses, as shown in (39):

(39)   You bought [this]$_i$ for me. [TOPIC]$_i$ last time you bought e$_i$.
         [TOPIC]$_i$ I know you bought e$_i$.

In representations like (39), the child's use of null objects can be captured precisely by the analysis proposed for Chinese, further supporting the argument for transfer of syntactic structure. Finally, note that the child uses the same structure in his Cantonese from an early age. In (40) the child introduces the object *ni1 di1* 'this', then allows it to function as the null object of *zing2* 'make' in the following clause:

(40)   Ngo5 jiu3 sik6 ni1 di1 aa3. Lei5 zing2 bei2 ngo5 sik6 laa1
         I   want eat this CL SFP you make give me   eat   SFP
         'I want to eat this. Can you make (it) for me to eat?'   (Timmy 2;04;17)

Compared to the monolingual English-speaking children, then, the bilingual children's English shows more frequent and more protracted occurrences of non-target null objects. We have shown *what* is transferred, in terms of syntactic structure and representation. We turn next to *why* transfer occurs in this particular area of grammar.

5.3   Input ambiguity and language dominance

Yip and Matthews (2000a) noted that both input ambiguity and language dominance may be involved in the transfer of null objects. We shall argue that the prevalence of null objects in children with different patterns of dominance suggests a role for input ambiguity. At the same time, variation in the frequency of null objects suggests that language dominance also plays a role.

5.3.1   *Input ambiguity in the transfer of null objects*

As outlined in chapter 2, studies in bilingual development have attributed certain instances of language transfer to ambiguity in the input available to the child. A language A becomes a target of transfer when, in a certain area of its grammar, the input offers ambiguous evidence with respect to the target grammar of A. The possibility for transfer arises when a surface string in the input for language A is compatible with the grammar of B as well as that of A. By hypothesizing that the relevant rules and representations provided by the grammar of B apply to both languages, the child can handle the ambiguous data, but will also produce non-target forms in language A based on the grammar of B.

    The domain of null objects has been argued to present such an ambiguity in the acquisition of French/Italian and Dutch/German (Hulk & Müller 2000). Adult Dutch and German allow empty object topics in clause-initial position, under certain contextual conditions, as in German:

(41)   (Das) weiss ich nicht
        (that) know I   not
        'I don't know.'

The Dutch/German input therefore presents the child with evidence for the validity of a discourse licensing strategy for empty objects. A child acquiring French or Italian, however, receives input which may be confusing as to the validity of this strategy, such as the following:

(42)   ça   j'ai   vu   EC
     that I have seen
     'I've seen that.'

(43)   Je sais   EC
     I   know
     'I know (that).'

(44)   Marie le sait   EC
     Marie it knows
     'Marie knows.'

In (42) the object *ça* 'that' appears as the sentence topic, leaving an empty category (EC, equivalent to *e* in our examples above) in object position following the verb. In (43), the object is null, identified by the discourse topic. This input is consistent with the hypothesis that French, like German or Dutch, allows both overt and null topics which license null objects. This is not the correct hypothesis, however, since a null object generally requires a pronominal clitic as in (44). Bilingual children then produce ungrammatical null object structures such as (45):

(45)   Il   met dans le   bain
     he puts in the bath
     'He puts [her] in the bath.'

A similar ambiguity arises with regard to null objects in the case of Cantonese and English. As discussed in section 5.2.1, the English input includes optionally transitive verbs such as *eat* appearing without an object, as in (46):

(46)   Let's eat.

Such sentences in the input are compatible with at least two analyses:
(a) the target English analysis, in which the missing object is not syntactically present, but interpreted semantically as generic (see section 5.2.1):

    (47)   eat β
            [+generic]

(b) an analysis based on Chinese grammar, in which the missing object is syntactically present, coreferential with a null topic and therefore interpreted as definite (see section 5.1):

    (48)   [TOPIC]$_i$ eat [e]$_i$
               [+definite]

We have ample evidence that our children are applying the Chinese-based analysis (b). For example, in (49) below the 'ambiguous' verb *eat* is accompanied by the unambiguously transitive verb *get*, to which the English analysis (a) would not be applicable. Moreover, the context supplies a specific topic to which the missing objects refer:

(49)   You get, I eat [father takes chocolates off shelf]   (Timmy 2;02;03)

The Chinese-based analysis for this sentence is thus as in (50):

(50)   [$_{TOPIC}$ Ø]$_i$ You get e$_i$, I eat e$_i$
         (chocolates)

This is a case of the topic chain construction (Shi 1989, 2000) in which a single topic licenses multiple null objects coreferential with it. In the following case from Sophie, the topic (a poisoned apple) is actually named in the preceding and following discourse:

(51)   INV: We don't want to eat apple, right?
         INV: Right?
         CHI: Me want to eat.
         INV: What do you want to eat?
         CHI: Apple.   (Sophie 3;00;02)

In the dual input to which the bilingual child is exposed, input ambiguity with respect to object omissibility arises only in English, where verbs like *eat* sometimes appear as transitive and sometimes as intransitive (where the object is unspecified); whereas in the Cantonese input there is across the board optionality, in that all transitive verbs can appear with or without an object (a definite one in this case), as long as it is licensed by a topic (which may be overt or null). If the bilingual child assumes that English transitive verbs behave as in Cantonese and posits a Cantonese-based representation for the objectless sentences as in (50), the learnability problem naturally arises.

5.3.2   Null objects and language dominance

We have shown that null objects in our bilingual children's English are qualitatively and quantitatively different from those occurring in monolingual acquisition of English (section 5.2.3). We have argued that input ambiguity is conducive to transfer of this property from Cantonese (section 5.3.1). This does not mean that language dominance is no longer a relevant factor in transfer, however. A fuller account needs to consider how the two factors interact.

The input ambiguity account outlined above necessarily assumes that the relevant aspect of grammar B has already been acquired, so that it can present a possible analysis for the ambiguous input in language A. Whether this is the case in practice may depend on at least two additional factors:
(a) the child's overall pattern of language dominance;

(b) developmental asynchrony (if any) between the two languages in the relevant grammatical domain (see section 2.5.3).
There is thus scope for interaction between these two factors favouring transfer
and ambiguous input. A child for whom language B is dominant is likely to
have the relevant analysis available to transfer to language A. Conversely, a
child without this pattern of dominance may not have fully acquired the analysis
applicable to language B at the time he or she is confronted with the ambiguous
evidence from language A.

In chapter 3 we reported Mean Length of Utterance (MLU) differentials for
the bilingual children and argued that these figures reflect the dominance of
Cantonese over English in the three siblings and Llywelyn, both in an abso-
lute sense (Cantonese is dominant for these children for part or whole of the
period of study) and in a relative sense (a larger differential MLU indicates a
greater degree of dominance). The MLU figures reported in table 3.3 suggest
that Sophie and Alicia (with MLU differentials of 0.85 and 0.79 respectively)
are more strongly Cantonese-dominant than Timmy and Llywelyn, with MLU
differentials of 0.39 and 0.17.[9] This contrast is borne out when we examine
the relationship between dominance and transfer of null objects. Overall, for
the five verbs studied, Sophie and Alicia have a null object rate of 31.8% and
34.0% respectively, compared to 18.8% for Timmy (see table 5.3 above). The
differences between Timmy and Sophie and between Timmy and Alicia are significant (p < 0.05). The average null object rate is almost twice as high in Alicia's
English (34.0%) as in Timmy's (18.8%). Similar individual differences are seen
in table 5.5 in the case of verb-particle constructions, where Alicia shows the
highest rate of null objects (63.6%) compared to 50.6% for Timmy and 37.7%
for Charlotte. The rate of null objects for Alicia is significantly higher than for
Charlotte (p < 0.05). Kathryn's low frequency of null objects as seen in table
5.3 (1.4%) places her in the range of monolingual English children who cease
to drop objects by the time they are three, about Kathryn's age during the study
(3;01–4;06).

Finally, regarding the possibility of developmental asynchrony, null objects
are a basic feature of Cantonese, highly frequent in the input and acquired early.
Even for an English-dominant child such as Charlotte, the null object property
is acquired early on and can undergo transfer from Cantonese to English, as
reflected in Charlotte's rate of 19.9% null objects in English between 1;08–
3;00: this is markedly lower than the four Cantonese-dominant children, but
still much higher than the English monolingual counterparts.

5.3.3   Resolution of non-target structures

The input ambiguity account explains why transfer occurs in this grammatical
domain. It also suggests why the Cantonese-based analysis is difficult to unlearn:

every time the child hears the intransitive *eat*, he or she may assume a null topic analysis. What evidence could lead the child to reject this analysis? In principle, a context in which no plausible discourse topic is present would cause the child's analysis to 'crash', that is, to fail to assign appropriate reference to the null object. Without a null topic provided by the discourse context, the null object will not be licensed and the sentence will not be fully interpretable. Consider a hypothetical scenario:[10]

(52)   Child: [I'm] hungry!
         Father: Okay, let's eat.

If there is no food around, the father's use of *eat* without an object will be incompatible with the null topic analysis assumed by the child. It remains an empirical question whether such experiences are in fact sufficient to prompt reorganization of the grammar.

Clearly, unlearning the Chinese-based analysis is not straightforward. Whereas other transfer-based structures such as *wh*-in-situ interrogatives and prenominal relatives gradually resolve themselves between ages three to four (see chapters 4 and 6), null objects remain recalcitrant, persisting for a protracted period. The null objects are still observed in our children at age six, albeit with decreasing frequency. The difficulty of unlearning them can be attributed to the challenge posed by the interplay of the ambiguity in the dual input in their environment and the continued dominance of Cantonese over English.

The logical problem here is recognized by accounts which assume conservative learning in monolingual children. To constrain the learnability of object omission, Roeper (1981: 140) hypothesized the following principle:

(53)   All subcategorizations are obligatory until positive evidence shows that they
         are optional.

Although monolingual English-speaking children are not quite as conservative as envisaged by the strong form of Roeper's hypothesis, their object omission rate is far lower than for the bilingual children. Monolingual children tend to avoid dropping objects of verbs which are used only transitively by their caregivers (Roeper 1981; Ingham 1993). To the extent that the null objects in monolingual English children as a class are not grammatically omissible, their occurrence could be attributed to performance limitations (Hyams 1986), thus preserving the null hypothesis that objects are obligatory. In contrast, the null objects in the bilingual data are much more frequent and produced over a protracted period of time relative to the monolingual data. It is clear that the bilingual children go beyond the attested English input and posit null objects where the adult grammar does not sanction them.

5.4   Null objects in Singapore Colloquial English

As might be expected, null objects are observed in Singapore Colloquial English (SCE: Platt & Weber 1980; Ho & Platt 1993). In the following examples from a spoken corpus (Wee & Ansaldo 2004: 71), the null objects are shown as *e*:

(54)   In fact, if you shake the coke okay, I can still open *e*.

(55)   This is not the Chinese sea cucumber, you know. What you call worms. People eat *e* raw, you know.

The syntax of null objects implicates Chinese influence for similar reasons to those which we have discussed in the context of bilingual acquisition. Bao (2001) considers the grammar of null subjects and objects as a case of systemic substrate influence. As in our account, he attributes null objects to the existence of both overt and null topics. Thus, in (56) an overt topic licenses an empty category [e] in object position (Bao 2001: 307–8):

(56)   One time, the flats$_i$, nobody want e$_i$.

In (57), the topic is null, but understood to be an order:

(57)   [(about an order)]$_i$ I don't think I can send e$_i$ to you today.

These examples, and the structure attributed to them, are exactly as we described in the bilingual children's data (see section 5.2.3).

Clearly, null objects, once transferred, can be retained in the development of a contact language as a substrate feature. As argued in chapter 2, bilingual acquisition as well as second language acquisition may be the locus of transfer. The ecology in which SCE evolved includes English-language schools with students from a variety of ethnic backgrounds, with Chinese in the majority (Bao 2001: 285). Such schools provide a socio-historical setting in which transfer could have taken hold.

5.5   Conclusions

We have examined the occurrence of null objects in the bilingual children's English and the learnability issues given rise by transfer from Cantonese. We have shown that null objects are produced more frequently and over a longer period than in the monolingual counterparts. Both quantitative and qualitative evidence points to transfer of the null topic mechanism which licenses null objects in Cantonese. We have suggested that transfer in this domain is facilitated by the ambiguity of the English input which lends itself to a Chinese-style analysis. However, language dominance is also a causal factor: the frequency of null objects is highest in the Cantonese-dominant children, and appears to correlate with degree of dominance.

The bilingual children's English clearly differs from that of monolinguals in that null objects are licensed in their grammar, due to cross-linguistic influence from Cantonese. Compared to other non-target structures such as *wh*-in-situ interrogatives, the use of null objects takes a long time to unlearn as the diary record suggests that they persisted well into age six, though with decreasing frequency. Another reason that makes unlearning difficult is the ambiguity of evidence that English verbs pose – which ones are obligatorily transitive and which ones are not. In the case of adult Chinese learners of English, it has also been noted that null objects are more difficult to detect and unlearn than null subjects (cf. Yip 1995; Yuan 1997). However, young bilingual children stand a better chance of acquiring the target properties than adult second language learners whose grammars may remain fossilized with the recalcitrant null objects. Exactly when, how and to what extent the bilingual children overcome this challenge remains a question for further investigation.

Like *wh*-in-situ (see chapter 4) and other features as discussed in the following chapters, null objects appear as a substrate feature in Singapore Colloquial English. The same mechanism, involving overt and null topics licensing null objects, is applicable to the bilingual and SCE data. Bilingual acquisition is therefore a possible route by which substrate influence may become established in a contact language.

NOTES

1. The object could only be understood as generic where a verb-object compound such as *sik6-faan6* 'eat (rice)' is involved:

   (i)   A: Lei5   sik6-m4-sik6-faan6   aa3?
               you   eat-not-eat-rice   SFP
               'Are you going to eat?'

           B: Ngo5   sik6   aa3
               I   eat   SFP
               'Yes, I am.'

   In B's reply, the object of *sik6* 'eat' is again missing, but is not necessarily to be analysed as a null object (see Huang 1984). On verb-object compounds in Cantonese see Matthews and Yip (1994: 51).

2. In particular models of grammar technical distinctions are made between various null elements: thus the null object might be treated as a variable (x) or a null pronoun (*pro*). Such distinctions are highly theory-dependent, whereas the observations we wish to make about Cantonese grammar transcend such distinctions: in particular, the null object, however represented, is essential to the interpretation of the sentence.

3. We are not directly concerned here with development of null *subjects* in the bilingual children, which raise a rather different set of questions. Huang (1999) found neither qualitative nor quantitative differences between the bilingual child Timmy and his monolingual counterparts as far as null subjects are concerned, although it appears that the unlearning of null subjects may take a longer time for bilingual than for monolingual children.

4. The two year olds were still on their way to full adult competence: not only do they have to acquire the obligatoriness of the object in the case of transitive *eat* but also when to use the intransitive *eat* when the thing eaten is taken to be generic or indefinite. In Rispoli's study, even the older children (three year olds) produced few intransitive forms of *eat* in contexts where the implied undergoer was interpreted as indefinite, referring to anything edible.

5. Unlike subjects, objects in Naomi's developing grammar do not seem to be optional or omissible. Ingham (1993: 111) shows an asymmetry between Naomi's null subject rates vs. null object rates: 52% null subjects at 1;10 and 42% at 1;11, in stark contrast with the low null object rates (4.8%).

6. In monolingual English corpora, different percentages of null objects are found depending on the criteria used. An asymmetry has been widely noted between the prevalence of null subjects on the one hand and the relative rarity of null objects on the other in early child English (see Wang et al. 1992; Hyams & Wexler 1993). According to Hyams and Wexler (1993: 426), the average null object rate for Adam (2;05–3;00) and Eve (1;06–2;01) from Brown's monolingual corpus was about 8%–9%. These figures include a number of optionally transitive verbs (such as *read*, *wash* and *eat*), and thus over-estimate the rate of null objects.

7. A potential complication is that *break* can also be intransitive, though of the unaccusative type. Such an interpretation is ruled out in (21) by the imperative sentence which entails an agent, and thus the transitive rather than the unaccusative sense of *break*.

8. Timmy and Sophie's null object rates closely match the percentages in monolingual Cantonese development reported in Man (1993): 60.0% null objects for CKT (1;10;27–2;02;05) and 44.0% for MHZ (1;09;25–2;02;12) though Sophie's rate 80.6% is higher than the monolingual counterparts.

9. The mean MLUs for both languages are higher in the case of Timmy because the corpus covers a later period of development, extending from 2;01;22–3;06;25.

10. Rispoli (1992: 584) gives a similar example, glossing *eat* as 'satisfy hunger'.

6   Relative clauses: transfer and universals

Child: Where's the Santa Claus give me the gun?
          [i.e. 'Where's the gun Santa Claus gave me?']   (Timmy 2;07;05)

6.1   Introduction

Timmy's 'Santa Clause', reproduced above, is ambiguous if not incomprehensible to an English speaker, misleadingly suggesting the interpretation 'Where's the Santa Claus who gave me the gun?' We shall see that *the Santa Claus give me the gun* is a noun phrase modified by a relative clause, meaning 'the gun that Santa Claus gave me'. This chapter investigates the bilingual children's development of relative clauses, a complex syntactic structure in which the Cantonese word order is found to transfer to the English counterpart in the initial stage of development.[1] The data for this particular structure come primarily from the diary entries made by the authors rather than the longitudinal corpus based on the recordings (why this is so is discussed in section 6.2). The protagonists are our three siblings who show evidence of dominance of Cantonese over English in their preschool years. As seen in previous chapters, aspects of their English show features and structures that are quite unlike their monolingual counterparts, many of which are attributable to transfer from the dominant language, in this case Cantonese. One of the most striking Cantonese-based features observed in these bilingual children is the occurrence of prenominal relative clauses in English where the relative clause precedes the head noun rather than following it as in target English. In the initial stage of development, object relative clauses as in (1a) are produced with the head in final position, i.e. the relative clause (RC) precedes the head noun which it modifies, with the internal structure as shown in (1b):

(1)   a. You buy that tape is English?
          [i.e. 'Is the video tape that you bought in English?']
       b. [_RC_ you buy __] that tape   (Timmy 2;10;22)

Relative clauses, specifically restrictive relatives, serve to restrict the reference of an entity among members of a set (Hamburger & Crain 1982; Crain &

Thornton 1998). The function of the relative clause in (1) restricts the reference of the video tape to the one *that you bought*. To characterize the structure of a relative clause, we focus on the syntactic role of the element that is gapped or relativized inside the relative clause. Thus in (1), the head noun *tape* is understood as the object of the verb *buy* and the gap indicated inside the relative clause represents the object of the transitive verb *buy*, making this an object relative clause.

The case study of transfer of prenominal relative clauses from Cantonese to English is of particular interest for several reasons:

(i) Such prenominal relatives are not known to occur in monolingual English development, nor have they been documented in detail in the acquisition of English by bilingual children. Several types of prenominal relative as produced by our children are, however, paralleled in Singapore Colloquial English, where essentially the same Chinese and English structures are in contact. The case of prenominal relatives thus serves as a case study of how transfer in early bilingual development at the individual level is mirrored in contact languages at the community level.

(ii) In typological terms, prenominal relatives are a universally dispreferred option, and especially rare in SVO languages, with Mandarin Chinese the only case instantiating this combination in many language samples (Hawkins 1990). Cantonese also instantiates the co-occurrence of SVO basic word order and prenominal relatives, as do other Sinitic languages.[2] The rarity of this combination of word order properties is attributable to processing considerations which disfavour it (Hawkins 1994). Nevertheless, Cantonese prenominal relatives prove to be subject to transfer in early bilingual development, as our children each developed prenominal relatives in their Cantonese and English in parallel.

(iii) The prenominal relatives observed in the bilingual children's English are primarily cases of object relativization, counter to the Noun Phrase Accessibility Hierarchy (NPAH, Keenan & Comrie 1977) which would predict that a language or interlanguage allowing object relatives will also allow subject relatives.[3] We shall attribute this unusual phenomenon to the isomorphism between object relatives and main clause word order in Cantonese, which facilitates processing and production of this kind of relative clause. It also raises the intriguing possibility that children are assuming head-internal relative clauses which have internally the syntax of a clause, but externally that of a Noun Phrase (see also Yip & Matthews 2007).

At a later stage of development, postnominal relatives are produced in English which have the target word order but are characterized initially by the occurrence of *resumptive pronouns* indexing the head noun as in (2):

(2)   Maybe *the red thing* that this morning I ate *it*.   (Sophie 5;01;07)

Such resumptive pronouns are also observed in the acquisition of English as a first language by monolingual children (Pérez-Leroux 1995) and as a second language by adult learners from different L1 backgrounds (Gass & Ard 1984), and we shall suggest that they reflect a universal strategy for relative clauses, rather than transfer. The two stages of development illustrate the crucial role played by both transfer and universal factors in early bilingual development.

We shall begin by reviewing background issues including the typological distribution of prenominal relatives in section 6.1.1, and the structure of relative clauses in adult English and Cantonese in section 6.1.2. Section 6.2 describes the emergence of prenominal relative clauses in the children's English and Cantonese. Section 6.3 examines the shift from prenominal to postnominal relatives in English and the role of resumptive pronouns. Section 6.4 discusses internal and external factors which may lead to transfer of prenominal relatives from Cantonese into English. In section 6.5 we compare the transfer of prenominal relatives in bilingual development with Singapore Colloquial English, where similar structures arise as a case of substrate influence. This is followed by conclusions in section 6.6 highlighting the findings of the case study.

6.1.1   *Typological distribution of prenominal relative clauses*

Studies in constituent order typology have demonstrated an overall preference for postnominal relatives over prenominal relatives among the languages of the world. Based on head direction alone, one would expect head-final languages to have prenominal relative clauses. In fact, however, even OV languages show a slight preference for postnominal relatives [N Rel] over prenominal relatives [Rel N], while in VO languages, [N Rel] is ubiquitous and [Rel N] is 'virtually unattested' (Hawkins, 1990). Dryer (1992) found that 98% of VO languages and 58% of OV languages in his sample had postnominal relatives, i.e. there is an overall preference for postnominal relatives, while Chinese languages provide the only clear examples of the rare combination of VO order and prenominal relatives. Hawkins (1994) attributes this asymmetry to parsing considerations. The combination of VO order with prenominal relatives creates configurations as in (3), illustrated by a hypothetical English-based example in (4):

(3) $[_{VP}$ V $[_{NP}$ $[_S$ Relative Clause] N]

(4)   I $[_{VP}$ ate $[_{NP}$ $[_S$ you bought yesterday] the cakes.]

With the relative clause [*you bought yesterday*] intervening between the verb *ate* and its object *the cakes*, this configuration incurs an indefinitely long delay in the parsing of the object NP, and hence also of VP, while the parser awaits the head noun. This delay can be measured using Hawkins' notion of Constituent Recognition Domain:

Constituent Recognition Domain (CRD): The CRD for a phrasal mother node M consists of the set of terminal and non-terminal nodes that must be parsed in order to recognize M and all ICs [Immediate Constituents] of M. (Hawkins 1994: 58)

In the case of (3), VP is a mother node dominating the immediate constituents V and NP. We assume that for NP to be recognized, its head N must be parsed. The CRD for VP then extends from V, through the relative clause to the head N:

(5)   [$_{VP}$ V [$_{NP}$ [$_S$ Relative Clause] N]

Constituent Recognition Domain for VP

The longer and the more complex the relative clause, the longer the CRD and the lower the parsing efficiency achieved by the configuration (some experimental evidence in support of this hypothesis is provided by Matthews & Yeung 2001). The combination of word orders exemplified by (4) is predicted to be strongly dispreferred, as is borne out by Dryer's (1992) statistics cited above. Transfer of prenominal relative clauses in the acquisition of a VO language such as English would create an interlanguage with the anomalous combination of SVO basic word order and [RC N] order, as instantiated in Chinese. We shall see that this can indeed occur, at least in early bilingual acquisition and in Singapore Colloquial English. In section 6.4 we shall suggest a number of factors which might explain this finding.

6.1.2   Relative clauses in adult English and Cantonese

To establish the basis for transfer of prenominal relatives in the bilingual children's English, we need to outline some relevant properties of relative clauses in the two target languages. Relative clauses in English are postnominal, i.e. the clause follows the head noun which it serves to modify, e.g. *clothes* as in (6a) and (6b):

(6)   a. [$_{NP}$ The clothes [$_{RC}$ which I like __]] are expensive
        b. [$_{NP}$ The clothes [$_{RC}$ that I like __]] are expensive

Either the relative pronoun *which* in (6a) or the complementizer *that* as in (6b) is used to introduce the subordinate clause, with the choice depending largely on register. In the colloquial speech addressed to children, the construction with *that* as in (6b) predominates (see section 6.3). The complementizer *that* can be omitted where the head noun is not the subject of the relative clause. English is said to use a 'gap' strategy, that is, the relative clause contains a gap, as indicated in (6) where the object of *like* is missing in the relative clause but corresponds to the noun being modified, *clothes*.

Cantonese uses prenominal relative clauses, in which the modifying clause precedes the head noun *saam1* 'clothes'. Again there are two types differing in structure and in the register to which they belong (Matthews & Yip 1994, 2001). The more formal type uses the particle *ge3* to link the modifying clause to the head noun:

(7)   [NP [S Ngo5 zung1ji3 ___] *ge3*   saam1] hou2 gwai3
        I   like   PRT   clothes   very expensive
        'The clothes I like are expensive.'

This type is often taken routinely as representative of the relative clause in Cantonese, in part because the relative marker *ge3* in (7) corresponds straightforwardly to *de* in Mandarin (8) and in written Chinese:

(8)   Wo xihuan *de*   yifu   hen gui
        I   like   PRT   clothing very expensive
        'The clothes I like are expensive.'

This type is less appropriate as a focus for studies of early language development, however, being characteristic of formal register. While a number of potential tokens of *ge3* relative clauses appear in the children's corpus data (five in Timmy's corpus, one in Sophie's corpus and none in Alicia's), all of these are ambiguous as between relative clauses and attributive clauses (see section 6.4.2).[4]

The type with which we are primarily concerned is the 'classifier relative' (Matthews & Yip 1994, 2001), characterized by the demonstrative *go2* 'that' and an appropriate classifier before the head noun, as in (9):

(9)   [NP [S Ngo5 zung1ji3] go2   di1 saam1] hou2 gwai3
        I   like   DEM   CL   clothes very expensive
        'The clothes I like are expensive.'

This type is characteristic of spoken Cantonese (as opposed to Mandarin and written Chinese), and hence represents the predominant type of relative clause in the language input to young children. A variant of (9) is the 'headless' type as in (10), where the demonstrative and classifier are retained but the noun is omitted, its referent being inferred from the context:

(10)   [NP [S Ngo5 zung1ji3] go2   di1] hou2 gwai3
        I   like   DEM   CL   very expensive
        'The ones I like are expensive.'

An important property of object relatives of this type is that they resemble a main clause. Thus the relative clause in (9) has, at least superficially, the same form as the main clause in (11):

(11)   [s Ngo5 zung1ji3 go2   di1 saam1]
         I   like   DEM CL   clothes
         'I like those clothes.'

This resemblance has a number of implications. Methodologically, it means that object relatives in Cantonese such as (9) and (10) and their transfer-based counterparts in English are not easy to identify in the child data, since they will resemble main clauses in linear order. The earliest possible examples of relative clauses recorded in Alicia's diary data, for example, are less than clear:

(12)   I can see . . . I can see [the Timmy go in the bus].   (Alicia 2;03;22)

(13)   [Child puts on one shoe, looks around for the other; father offers her a
         different pair of shoes]
         The same one. Lulu give me that one.   (Alicia 2;11;16)

There is reason to believe that *the Timmy go in the bus* in (12) means 'the bus that Timmy goes in', hence the use of the article *the*, but other interpretations are possible, including a 'small clause' reading 'I saw Timmy go in the bus'. In (13) the context strongly suggests a relative clause interpretation '[I want] the same one as I'm already wearing, the one that Lulu gave me' but *Lulu give me that one* could also be a straightforward main clause 'Lulu gave me that one'.

In theoretical terms, the identity of main clauses and object relative clauses raises the possibility that children could use such relative clauses without having to acquire any movement rules. While English relatives have been assumed to be formed by *wh*-movement (in the case of *wh*-relatives) or by null operator movement (for *that*-relatives), Cantonese relatives involve no overt movement. Structures resulting from transfer will thus be qualitatively different from a target relative clause derived by *wh*-movement. Indeed, in the case of Cantonese adult second language learners of English, Hawkins and Chan (1997) argue that their Cantonese-based interlanguage representation of English relatives involves pronominal binding by a base-generated null topic, rather than operator movement as in native English.

From a typological perspective, the parallelism between object relatives and main clauses raises the possibility that 'classifier relatives' such as (9) may be internally headed relative clauses:[5] that is, constituents having internally the syntax of a clause, but externally that of a Noun Phrase (cf. Keenan 1985: 161). The dual status of the object relative under such an analysis is shown by the notation NP/S in (14), where S stands for a clause:

(14)   [NP/S Ngo5 zung1ji3 go2   di1   saam1] hou2 gwai3
         I   like   DEM CL   clothes very   expensive
         'The clothes I like are expensive.'

When such an analysis is applied to adult Cantonese, a number of problems arise: while the simplest type of object relative as in (9) and (10) resembles a main clause, evidence from a number of more complex transitive constructions shows that the main clause and relative clause structures are not entirely parallel (Matthews & Yip 2001, 2002). Thus the analysis of classifier relatives as internally headed relative clauses as shown in (14) may not be applicable for adult Cantonese as a whole. Such an analysis remains possible, however, for the case of simple object relatives such as (9) and (10), which are precisely the structures which predominate in the child data. As early as age 2;01, Alicia produces what could either be main clauses or internally-headed relative clauses (see Yip & Matthews 2007 for a more detailed analysis):

(15)   Alicia waak6 go2   di1 je5   [pointing to her own drawings]
        Alicia draw   DEM CL things
        'Alicia drew those things' or '[These are] the things that Alicia drew'
                                                                    (Alicia 2;01;21)

The interpretation of (15) as a relative clause is supported by (16) produced a few days earlier, which unambiguously involves a relative clause since the noun phrase being modified serves as the object of the main verb *zung1ji3* 'like':

(16)   Ngo5 zung1ji3 [Siti zing2 go2   di1 McDonald] aa3
        I   like   Siti make DEM CL McDonald   SFP
        'I like the McDonald's [French fries] that Siti makes.'   (Alicia 2;01;09)

A final piece of suggestive evidence involves child utterances which are not well-formed in terms of adult usage, but consistent with the internally headed analysis, as in (17):

(17)   Ngo5 sik6 joek6   aa3. [Ngo5 sik6 joek6]   hai6 ni1 zek3
        I   eat   medicine SFP I   eat   medicine is   this CL
        'I'm taking medicine. The medicine I take is this one.'   (Alicia 2;08;10)

The second clause here is ill-formed because either the attributive particle *ge3* (as in (7)) or the demonstrative and classifier [*go2* CL] (as in (9)) before the head noun *joek6* 'medicine' would be required for a relative clause interpretation. It is, however, consistent with the analysis whereby the child is using a clause [s *Ngo5 sik6 joek6*] 'I take medicine' as an internally headed relative clause [NP *Ngo5 sik6 joek6*] 'the medicine I take'. Whether this is the case or not, the isomorphism between object relatives and main clauses no doubt facilitates the parsing and production of object relatives, as discussed in section 6.4.3 below.

Table 6.1. *Age of first emergence of subject and object relative clauses in Cantonese and English diary and corpus data in three bilingual children.*

	Prenominal		Postnominal	
	subject relative	object relative	subject relative	object relative
Cantonese*				
Timmy	2;04;28	2;04;28	–	–
Sophie	not attested	2;09;05	–	–
Alicia	4;08;13	2;01;01	–	–
English				
Timmy	not attested	2;07;03	3;10;23	3;04;07
Sophie	3;10;09	3;03;12	5;04;19	4;10;28
Alicia	3;08;01	3;05;06	4;05;03	5;02;17

* Table 6.1 combines clauses with relative marker *ge3* and those formed with a demonstrative and classifier immediately preceding the noun.

6.2   Development of prenominal relative clauses in the bilingual children

The data show two distinct stages in the three siblings' development of English relatives. In the first stage, prenominal object relatives emerge based on a Cantonese pattern. In the second, postnominal relatives appear, initially with resumptive pronouns, as discussed in section 6.3. Relative clauses in the bilingual children's Cantonese data are essentially target-like throughout, showing no apparent influence from English: in particular, there is no sign of postnominal relatives developing in Cantonese under English influence.

Table 6.1 shows the age of first emergence of relative clauses based on the combined corpus and diary data. Since these are naturalistic data and the structures are relatively infrequent in our data, the first attestations are likely to lag behind the actual age of acquisition in each case. Moreover, in some cases subject relatives are not attested at all. In Cantonese, object relatives emerged at about the same time as subject relatives in Timmy, at 2;04;28, and emerged earlier than subject relatives in Sophie (at 2;09;05) and Alicia (at 2;01;01). Cantonese subject relatives are not attested in Sophie's corpus or diary data; in Alicia's diary data the first example was recorded as late as 4;08;13, though it must be assumed that this structure emerged earlier, if only because Alicia transferred it to English from 3;08 onwards. In English, prenominal object relatives emerged earlier than subject relatives in Sophie (3;03;12 vs 3;10;09) and Alicia (3;05;06 vs 3;08;01) while in the case of Timmy, prenominal object relatives emerged as early as 2;07;03 and prenominal subject relatives are not attested. With regard to English postnominal relatives, object relatives preceded subject ones in Timmy (3;04;07 vs 3;10;23) and Sophie (4;10;28 vs 5;04;19) while subject relatives preceded object ones in Alicia (4;05;03 vs 5;02;17).

The ages of first emergence of relative clauses in table 6.1 pose some challenges for the NPAH:

- In the bilingual children's Cantonese, object relatives emerge earlier than or simultaneously with subject relatives,
- In the bilingual children's English, Cantonese-based prenominal relatives first emerged, with object relatives followed by subject relatives,
- When target-like postnominal relatives emerged in the bilingual children's English, object relatives preceded subject ones in two of the three children.

All these findings run counter to the predictions of the NPAH, as discussed in Yip & Matthews (2007).

6.2.1   Functions of relative clauses in the diary data

This chapter relies largely on diary data because clear examples of relative clauses in the longitudinal recordings are infrequent, especially in the English transcripts.[6] By contrast, there are some twenty-five clear cases in the English diary data for Timmy from age 2;07 to 4;05, most of which are cited in this chapter. For Sophie, there are some sixty examples in the diary data between age 3;03 and 5;05, and a similar number for Alicia. The diary data therefore provide the primary basis on which this chapter is built; indeed, this case study makes a striking demonstration that the diary method remains a valuable complement to other methods of data collection.

The paucity of relatives in the longitudinal recordings, compared to their regular attestation in the diary data, calls for explanation. It is partly that relative clauses are a low frequency structure and the regular recording time is not sufficient for such structures to occur naturally. The corpora for Timmy, Sophie and Alicia each contain some 80 files, each representing approximately half an hour's interaction in each language, making for a total of around 40 hours of transcribed speech. In a dense corpus such as ones pioneered by Tomasello and his team (Tomasello & Stahl 2004; Maslen et al. 2004), the likelihood of capturing the child producing relative clauses in the recordings will be greatly increased: in one German monolingual child's dense corpus including 5 one-hour recordings per week from age two to three, 902 relative clauses were identified (Brandt, Diessel & Tomasello forthcoming).

Another factor influencing the frequency of relative clauses involves their functions in discourse: 'Contexts that are uniquely felicitous for a relative clause are ones in which there is a set of objects to restrict from; hence the term restrictive relative clause' (Crain & Lillo-Martin 1999: 397). In speaking to their parents, the children use relatives to identify objects on the basis of shared knowledge, typically involving family members and activities. A typical example is (18) where Timmy is looking for a water pistol given to him by 'Santa Claus' at a Christmas family lunch:

(18)   Where's the Santa Claus give me the gun?
        [i.e. 'Where's the gun Santa Claus gave me?']   (Timmy 2;07;05)

In this utterance, the toy gun is identifiable to the parents, who were present at the Christmas lunch, but not to the research assistants conducting the longitudinal recording, who visited the children at most once per week. The research assistants have a relatively small repertoire of knowledge and experiences shared with the child, hence the opportunities for the child to use relative clauses for purposes of identification as in (18) are limited. The children's spontaneous production of relative clauses is thus heavily dependent on shared knowledge.

6.2.2   Prenominal relatives in Timmy's English

As recorded in the diary data, prenominal relative clauses emerge in Timmy's English at age 2;07:

(19)   Where's the motor-bike? [You buy the motor-bike]? [That you buy the
        motor-bike]. Where's [you buy that one], where's [you buy that one the
        motor-bike]?   (Timmy 2;07;03)

In this example, the utterance *You buy the motor-bike* is not to be interpreted as a full main clause 'Did you buy the motor-bike?', as this interpretation would be incompatible with the child's reformulation of the question *Where's you buy that one?* i.e. 'Where's the one that you bought?' as well as the extra-linguistic context, in which the child is looking for a certain toy. Rather, the utterance is intended as a relative clause 'the motor-bike that you bought' being used to specify reference to a particular toy. The structure for (19) therefore follows the Cantonese prenominal pattern described in (9) and (10) above, as shown in (20):[7]

(20)   Where's [$_{NP}$ [$_S$ you buy] that one],
        where's [$_{NP}$ [$_S$ you buy] that one the motor-bike]?

Similarly in (21), comprehension of the relative clause depends on the addressee's knowledge that uncle Patrick (alias Pet-Pet) bought a certain video-tape for the child:

(21)   I want to watch videotape. Butterfly. [Patrick buy that one].
        I want [Pet-Pet buy that one videotape].   (Timmy 2;11;25)

Here the utterance *Patrick buy that one* is not to be interpreted as a main clause 'Patrick bought that one', but a relative clause 'the one that Patrick bought' being used to specify a particular videotape, implying a modification structure as in (22):

(22)   [NP [S Patrick buy] that one]

Similarly, *I want Pet-Pet buy that one videotape* cannot mean 'I want Pet-Pet to buy that videotape', because the tape concerned has already been bought.

In many of the bilingual children's English relative clauses, *one* serves a generic classifier as in examples (19) and (21) above. This pattern is more extensively attested in Sophie's English (see section 6.2.4). In examples such as (19) and (21) we can see how the child expands a relative with *one* by adding a head noun. In (23), the child replaces *that* with the lexical head noun *tape*:

(23)   This is who buy? Have butterfly? [You bought that] have butterfly?
         [referring to a new video tape with a butterfly on the cover]
         [later] [You buy that tape] is English?   (Timmy 2;10;22)

Here the child's last question, concerning the same videotape, uses a full relative clause with *tape* as the head noun. Note that the demonstrative *that* appears regularly: as in Cantonese relatives such as (9) and (10) illustrated above, this has the force of a definite rather than a deictic determiner (i.e. the distal/proximate distinction is neutralized in this context: similar observations hold for Singapore Colloquial English as discussed in section 6.5).

6.2.3   Prenominal relatives in Timmy's Cantonese

Cantonese relative clauses are recorded in Timmy's diary data during the same week in which prenominal relatives appear in English, the first example being (24):

(24)   [Jan maai5 go2   tiu4]
         Jan buy   DEM CL
         'The one that Jan bought.'   (Timmy 2;07;04)

This is a classifier relative of the type described in section 6.1.2, with the classifier *tiu4* denoting an elongated object (in this case a pair of pants) but the head noun is omitted, as in *Patrick buy that one* (21). Subsequent examples add a head noun, such as *tong4-tong2* 'candy' in (25):

(25)   [Po4po2 maai5 di1   tong4-tong2] ne1?[8]
         grandma buy   CL candy-candy SFP
         'What about the candies Grandma bought?'   (Timmy 2;07;12)

One Cantonese example (26) not only exhibits similar structure to those already described in Timmy's English, but refers to the very same toy gun as the English example (18) above:

(26)   [Santa Claus bei2 lei5 go3 coeng1] le1?
        Santa Claus give you CL gun   SFP
        'Where's the gun Santa Claus gave me?'   (Timmy 2;08;25)

Note that in both (25) and (26) the demonstrative *go2* 'that' is missing where it would be present in adult Cantonese:[9] although inconsistent with adult grammar, this is consistent with the head-internal analysis for child language as outlined in section 6.1.2. Such structures may serve as a precursor to the full-fledged classifier relatives including the demonstrative, classifier and head noun as in (27):

(27)   Go2 di1 Lego le1, [Mannings maai5 go2   di1 Lego] le1?
        DEM CL Lego SFP, Mannings buy   DEM CL Lego SFP
        'What about the Lego, the Lego we bought at Mannings?'
                                                                  (Timmy 2;10;14)

In structure, function and even topic (cf. the 'Santa clause' in (26)) the Cantonese relatives parallel the English examples such as (18) and (19) discussed in section 6.2.2. Given the simultaneous emergence and productive use of prenominal relatives in both languages, the role of transfer in the English examples is firmly established.

6.2.4   Prenominal relatives in Sophie and Alicia

Prenominal relative clauses appear rather later in Sophie's English, at around age 3;03. This relative delay is expected since Sophie's Cantonese was well ahead of her English at this period (she began to produce sentences in Cantonese at eleven months and in English only at around age two). One implication of this timing is that Sophie's production of prenominal relatives cannot easily be attributed to input from the elder sibling. At the time when Timmy was producing them (up to age four: see section 6.3.1) Sophie was between one month and 1;03, well before she had begun to produce English sentences. The development of prenominal relatives in her English can therefore plausibly be considered independent, and the parallel paths taken by both children can be seen as the product of interaction of their developing English and Cantonese grammars under similar input conditions. The same holds for Alicia, whose development recapitulates the same pathway some four years later.

Between ages 3;03 and 4;03, Sophie produces only relatives headed by *one*, without a lexical head noun:[10]

(28)   CHI: [Timmy take that one], I want.
       Father: Which one do you want?
       CHI: [She take that one]. [Timmy take that one].   (Sophie 3;03;12)

(29)   CHI: I also want.
       Father: What do you want?
       CHI: [Timmy said that one].
       [The child has been asking for a piggy-bank]   (Sophie 3;08;21)

(30)   I want [have ear-ear that one].
       [wanting to wear a coat that has ears]   (Sophie 3;10;09)

(31)   Daddy, I want ice-cream. [Carmen eat that one].
       [having seen Carmen eat an ice cream]   (Sophie 4;01;11)

(32)   [I buy in the store that one] is yummy.
       [Talking to her brother about lemon sweets]   (Sophie 4;03;17)

With *one* serving as the head, these are based on the 'headless' Cantonese construction with demonstrative and classifier but no head noun, as discussed in section 6.1.2 and illustrated by Timmy's (24). Whereas Timmy expands the structure with *one* into a full-fledged relative clause by adding a head noun, as in (19) and (21), Sophie replaces *one* with a head noun, as seen in (33):

(33)   Father: Which dress?
       CHI: The . . . [you take for me that one] . . . Where is it, [you said *it* that
       dress]?   (Sophie 4;04;20)

Here the two relative clauses used to specify the same dress are revealing: the first has the pronominal *one* as the head, while the second has *that dress* as the head noun, as well as a resumptive pronoun *it* (see section 6.3.1). The context confirms that *you said it that dress* means 'the dress you mentioned', as the father had recommended a certain dress to go with her gloves and shoes.

    Like Sophie, Alicia begins by producing relative clauses with *one*, first object relatives (34) and later subject relatives (35):[11]

(34)   Daddy, where is that blue bag? My . . . me make that one?
       [i.e. the one I made]   (Alicia 3;05;06)

(35)   Father: What shall we put on you?
       CHI: Have gung1zai2 that one.
       [i.e. 'The dress that has a cartoon character on it.']   (Alicia 3;08;01)

Well before this time, Alicia has already acquired the equivalent object relative construction in Cantonese around 2;01, where a classifier serves as the head in the absence of a head noun:

(36)   Ngo5 waak6 go2   go3 le1?
       I   draw DEM   CL SFP
       'Where's the one I drew?'   (Alicia 2;01;01)

Example (37) contains two object relatives of this type:[12]

(37)   Jan4dei6 sung3   bei2 ngo5 go2   go3 aa3,
        people   present give me   DEM   CL   SFP
        'The one someone gave me as a present,'

        jan4dei6 bei2 ngo5 go2   go3 aa3
        people   give me   DEM   CL   SFP
        'The one [candy] someone gave me.'   (Alicia 3;04;21)

Alicia's development thus replicates that of her siblings, with object relatives emerging first in Cantonese as in (36) and (37) then being transferred to English as in (34) and (35). Being four years and three months younger than Sophie, the possibility of acquiring the English structure directly from her siblings is even less likely than in the case of Sophie's development. We thus have every reason to assume that Alicia's prenominal relatives in English have developed independently, without modelling on her older siblings' speech.

6.2.5   Bilingual and monolingual development of relative clauses compared

In the previous sections we have discussed the initial development of relative clauses in our bilingual children. We now turn to the developmental patterns of monolingual English-speaking children and then compare the two sets of findings.

A study by Diessel and Tomasello (2000) of four monolingual English-speaking children (Peter, Nina, Sarah and Adam) between 1;09 and 5;02 using longitudinal spontaneous speech data examined a total of 329 sentences with a relative clause. An important finding is that 'the earliest relative clauses that English-speaking children learn occur in presentational constructions that are propositionally simple. They consist of a copular clause and a relative that usually includes an intransitive verb' (Diessel & Tomasello 2000: 12). Some examples of the first ten relative clauses produced by the four monolingual English-speaking children are given below (Diessel & Tomasello 2000: 9):

(38)   This is my doggy *cries*.   (Nina 2;00)

(39)   That's a turtle *swim*.   (Nina 2;02)

(40)   What's this *go in there*?   (Peter 2;00)

(41)   This is the fire engine *go 'whoo whoo'*.   (Peter 2;06)

(42)   What is dis *came out*?   (Adam 3;01)

(43)   And that's the birdie *scream*.   (Sarah 4;03)

The examples in (38) to (43) involve a presentational copular clause and a modifying phrase/clause without any relative pronoun or complementizer. While not considered grammatical in standard English, such sentences are found in many dialects of English (Lambrecht 1988). These sentences are the mirror image of our bilingual children's earliest relative clauses: Peter's example (40) *What's this go in there?* resembles our example (20) *Where's you buy that one?* except for the placement of the relative clause: while the monolingual English-speaking children produce postnominal relatives, the bilingual children produce prenominal relatives. Similarly, Peter's (41) would come out in our bilingual children as:

(44)   This is the [go 'whoo whoo'] fire engine.

In fact, 90% of the earliest relative clauses in English are of one of the following types, where the examples are from Diessel and Tomasello (2005a), with bracketing added:
 (i) attached to the predicate nominal of a clause containing a copula:

(45)   This is the sugar [*that* goes in there].   (Nina 3;00)

(46)   What's dat . . . [you have]?   (Adam 2;11)

(ii) attached to an isolated head noun:

(47)   The girl [*that* came with us].   (Nina 3;00)

These points also apply to our bilingual data: for example, Timmy's (18)–(20) involve copula clauses of the form [*where's* NP?], while Alicia's utterances (34)–(37) are isolated noun phrases consisting of a relative clause modifying a noun. Cross-linguistically, these characteristic features have emerged in the early monolingual development of a number of different languages such as French (Hudelot 1980; Jisa & Kern 1998), German (Brandt, Diessel & Tomasello, forthcoming), Hebrew (Dasinger & Toupin 1994), and Indonesian (Cole, Hermon & Tjung 2003, in press; Hermon 2005). To our knowledge, there has not been any systematic investigation of bilingual development of relative clauses, so that cross-linguistic comparison of the development of such structures in other language pairs is not yet feasible.

The theoretical import of these findings is that early relative clauses may be simpler than we thought. The classical examples in discussions of adult grammar, such as our hypothetical example (4), involve a relative clause within a main clause. Examples of this kind are also widely used in experiments on children. In early child language, however, such a complex configuration rarely arises. This is especially true in the case of early object relatives in our data like Alicia's (34)–(37), NPs which have the SVO structure of a main clause (section 6.1.2).

6.3   The emergence of postnominal relatives in English

Having begun with prenominal relatives based on Cantonese in their English, the children face the challenge of switching to the target postnominal relatives. We now focus on how this transition occurs.

6.3.1   Resumptive pronouns

Between the period of prenominal relatives and the eventual emergence of well-formed postnominal relatives, we see an intermediate stage in which relatives are produced in postnominal position, with the target word order but with resumptive pronouns. At the beginning of this stage there is overlapping of the prenominal and postnominal types. The last prenominal relatives produced by Timmy are recorded around age four:

(48)   Daddy, I want the water gun, [the Santa Claus give me that water gun].
                                                                                     (Timmy 3;11;12)

(49)   Actually [I like the best game] is Tetris.   (Timmy 4;00;15)

(50)   Daddy, which [that you record tape]?
            [asking which tape is the one Daddy recorded]   (Timmy 4;02;25)

When postnominal relative clauses begin to appear in Timmy's English, no relative pronoun or complementizer is used, but resumptive pronouns are employed. The first example of this type in Timmy's data is recorded at 3;04:

(51)   It's like the one you bought *it*. [seeing picture of toy car]
            It's not like the one you bought *it*. [seeing difference]   (Timmy 3;04;07)

The possibility of transfer arises again here, since Cantonese allows resumptive pronouns in positions other than that of subject (Matthews & Yip 1994: 110–111). In the case of object relatives the pronoun is not used in simple clauses such as (52), but it is optional in more complex environments such as (53) where there is an embedded clause within the relative clause (cf. Yip & Matthews 2001: 123):

(52)   Ngo5   ceng2   (*keoi5dei6)   go2   di1   pang4jau5
            I   invite   (*them)   DEM   CL   friend
            'Friends that I invite'

(53)   Ngo5   ceng2   (keoi5dei6)   sik6-faan6   go2   di1   pang4jau5
            I   invite   (them)   eat-rice   DEM   CL   friend
            'Friends that I invite to have dinner'

Despite their existence in Cantonese, there are several reasons to believe that the appearance of resumptive pronouns in the children's English is *not* due to transfer. Firstly, while in adult Cantonese the resumptive pronouns are restricted to animate nouns as in (53), the children use them to refer to inanimate nouns as in (54):

(54)   I want the sweet, the sweet that you put *it* there yesterday.

(Timmy 4;00;03)

Secondly, unlike in Cantonese, resumptive pronouns are occasionally used even in the subject position of relative clauses:

(55)   Daddy, where's the thing? Where is the thing *it* hangs? The one *it* says one for me, one for Sophie?
        [looking for coat-hangers with the children's names painted on them]

(Timmy 3;10;23)

Thirdly, the children's Cantonese does not show resumptive pronouns in either subject or object position of relative clauses (see examples in 6.2.3). Finally, the children's English does not show resumptive pronouns when the relative clauses occur in prenominal position (with the single exception of (33)), as would be expected if this property were subject to transfer from Cantonese. All these considerations lead to the conclusion that the resumptive pronouns observed in our children instantiate a universal developmental strategy rather than transfer. Such resumptive pronouns are known to be widely used in second language acquisition by learners regardless of L1 language backgrounds (Hyltenstam 1984; Gass & Ard 1984).

In Sophie's English, resumptive pronouns are again observed in object position when postnominal relatives first appear:

(56)   I got that red flower dress that Jan give *it* to me.   (Sophie 4;10;28)

(57)   This is the homework that I do *it*. But, I done already at school.

(Sophie 4;11;04)

No cases are recorded of resumptive pronouns with subject relatives in Sophie. The scarcity of resumptive pronouns in subject relatives is consistent with the NP Accessibility Hierarchy (Keenan & Comrie 1977), according to which subjects are most accessible to relativization. Resumptive pronouns are used to accomplish relativization based on the less accessible grammatical relations, such as objects of prepositions and direct objects. Resumptive pronouns are thought to facilitate the production and processing of these more complex types of relative clause (Hawkins 1999). There is evidence for such a pattern from language acquisition as well as from language typology. For example, in a picture description task eliciting relative clauses from eleven monolingual English-speaking children from 3;05 to 5;05, Pérez-Leroux (1995) did not find any resumptive pronouns in more than one hundred subject relative clauses, while resumptive pronouns did appear in relative clauses with relativized object and object of preposition.

6.3.2   The transition from prenominal to postnominal relatives

During the shift from the prenominal to postnominal stage, all three children produce transitional structures in their English. In Timmy, such a transitional case is (58):

(58)   But some children buy the boat *it* stands.   (Timmy 4;01;02)

At least two possible analyses present themselves for this utterance. It could be parsed as a prenominal relative with *the boat* as its head, followed by a coreferential subject pronoun as in left-dislocation (59a), or as a postnominal relative with resumptive pronoun in subject position (59b):

(59)   a. But [NP some children buy [NP the boat]] [S *it* stands]
             'But the boats that some children buy, they stand up.'

         b. But some children buy [NP the boat [S *it* stands]]
             'But some children buy boats which stand up.'

At this age, when Timmy uses both prenominal relatives as in (48) and (50) and postnominal ones as in (54), example (58) is genuinely ambiguous. A similar case is recorded in Alicia:

(60)   You know, just now I smell something is not very nice.   (Alicia 3;09;17)

This example could be a prenominal relative modifying *something* as shown in (61a), or an early attempt at a postnominal relative with a missing complementizer (61b):

(61)   a. [NP [S just now I smell] something] is not very nice
         b. just now I smell [NP something [(which) is not very nice]]

One example from Sophie seems to show the same transition taking place in on-line production:

(62)   Where's just now that one I give you?
         [looking for a puzzle done by her father]   (Sophie 5;04;22)

Here the adverbial *just now* belongs semantically in the relative clause, but comes before the head, as if the child starts to construct a typical prenominal relative *Where's [just now I give you that one]?* but then thinks better of it, and postposes the remainder of the relative clause.

A second transition can be observed from the resumptive pronoun strategy to the target gap strategy. Relative clauses using a gap strategy appear shortly before Timmy's fourth birthday; these are ill-formed in the case of subject relatives (63) but target-like in the case of object (64) and prepositional relatives as in (65) and (66):

(63)   Daddy, do you know where is [the thing goes here]?   (Timmy 3;10;25)

(64)   I want to build [the one we saw in Mannings].   (Timmy 3;10;30)

(65)   Daddy, where's [the gun you put water in]?   (Timmy 3;11;01)

(66)   Daddy, we go to [the shop we haven't been to], the mall inside the shop
         [i.e. the shop inside the mall]   (Timmy 4;00;04)

Following the well-formed gap relative [$_{NP}$ *the shop we haven't been to*] in (66), we note the resurgence of prenominal modification in *the mall inside the shop* meaning 'the shop inside the mall' (see section 6.4.2).

When the complementizer *that* appears at age four, object resumptive pronouns are used sporadically, for example in sentences with the verb *put*:

(67)   I want the sweet, [the sweet that you put *it* there yesterday].
                                                                    (Timmy 4;00;03)

(68)   Where is [the thing that I just put here]?   (Timmy 4;01;29)

(69)   Where is [the thing that put inside]?
         Where is [the thing that go inside]?   (Timmy 4;01;30)

A similar shift away from resumptive pronouns is seen in Sophie, though at a slightly later stage. As we have seen, Sophie began to produce postnominal relatives shortly before age five, initially with pronouns in object position as seen in (56) and (57). One month later, similar object relatives appear without the pronouns:

(70)   Thank you for the dress that you give to me, for the dolly. (Sophie 5;00;04)

(71)   Hey, this is the clips that Belma buy.   (Sophie 5;00;05)

Resumptive pronouns reappear in more complex structures, such as an object of an embedded clause within a relative clause:

(72)   Daddy, where's the fox hole, that you said you find *it* yesterday?
                                                                    (Sophie 5;04;15)

Here, the use of the resumptive pronoun in an embedded clause recalls our Cantonese example (53). Such examples can also be explained on universal grounds, however. Compare a similarly complex example from Timmy, in which the pronoun occurs first in object and then subject positions in a coordinate construction:

(73)   I need the train that you push *it* and *it* goes.
         [i.e. 'I want the train that goes when you push it.']   (Timmy 4;03;09)

In such cases the pronouns might be used even in adult English: as Hawkins (1999: 265) observes, 'English gaps in complex NP environments can sometimes be rescued by pronoun retention.'

Sophie eventually achieved mastery of *that*-relatives, appropriately enough, during a visit to Oxford (74), followed by a number of well-formed examples such as (75):

(74)   Then we buy [that lipstick that you want].
         [shopping in Oxford, England]   (Sophie 5;04;19)

(75)   Father: You want to choose something?
         Child: Choose [something that I want to eat].   (Sophie 5;04;20)

Sophie has thus acquired the target English relative clause at age five, as Timmy did at age four. After producing prenominal relatives for a period of up to two years, Alicia began to produce target-like postnominal relatives at 4;05:

(76)   You know Lulu got one too. [waving her fairy wand]
         But here got [a paper that said 'Princess'].   (Alicia 4;05;03)

All three children have, however, reached this point by a very different route from a monolingual child. In McKee, McDaniel and Snedeker's (1998) experimental study of twenty-eight monolingual English-speaking children between 2;02 and 3;10, 80% of relative clauses produced were target-like, while occasional errors involved resumptive pronouns and non-target relative pronouns. In (77), to specify a subset of strawberries, the child uses the non-target relative pronoun *what* and adds the resumptive pronoun *them* in object position (McKee, McDaniel & Snedeker 1998: 586–587, emphasis added):

(77)   Pick those two up *what* the dinosaur is eating *them*.   (child CT 2;10)

McKee, McDaniel and Snedeker (1998: 589) suggest a performance account of the resumptive pronouns on the grounds of their sporadic appearance, and invoke processing demands, just as Hawkins (1999) argues in the case of adult English. By contrast, the productive use of resumptive pronouns in our bilingual children's production data argues for a grammar that systematically generates resumptive pronouns in relative clauses at this transitional stage.[13]

6.4   Accounting for transfer

We now discuss factors involved in the transfer of prenominal relatives from Cantonese to English. One set of factors is external – the dominance of Cantonese over English in our children, which in turn derives from the less-than-balanced input conditions described in chapter 3. Another set of factors involves typological characteristics of Cantonese – the relationship of relative clauses to other prenominal modification structures, and the resemblance between object relatives and main clauses which we noted in section 6.1.2.

6.4.1   Language dominance and developmental asynchrony

The period of transfer of prenominal modification structures in Timmy begins at age 2;07, during a period (2;00–2;10) in which the MLUw for Cantonese utterances is markedly ahead of that for English. Moreover, there is relatively little evidence of transfer from English to Cantonese in these children (see chapter 7), and none at all in the domain of relative clauses. Together, these findings imply dominance of Cantonese as a causal factor. In the case of Sophie and Alicia, dominance of Cantonese is clearer still, based on indicators such as MLUw differential and first use of Cantonese and English (see chapter 3, and section 6.2.4). Language dominance must therefore be considered a major factor favouring transfer from Cantonese to English.

In chapter 2, however, we entertained another possibility raised by Paradis and Genesee (1996), which we formulated as the developmental asynchrony hypothesis. In the case of transfer at issue here, it may be that Cantonese monolingual children's prenominal relatives typically develop earlier than English monolingual children's postnominal ones. If so, it would also be expected that Cantonese relative clauses would develop before English ones in bilingual children, thus fulfilling Paradis and Genesee's condition for transfer. This would constitute a 'developmental asynchrony' in the bilingual child, who would then have reason to transfer the Cantonese structure to English (perhaps as a stopgap measure or 'relief strategy') without dominance necessarily playing a role. Unfortunately we are not able to distinguish between dominance and developmental asynchrony in this case, for two reasons:

(a) the monolingual Cantonese data needed to establish such a baseline for the acquisition of relative clauses are lacking. While corpora for monolingual Cantonese children exist, the rarity of relative clauses in spontaneous production (as noted in section 6.2.1) means that diary and/or experimentally elicited data would be required,

(b) our bilingual children show clear signs of dominance, so that the effects of dominance and language-specific acquisition schedules could not be distinguished. That is, even if it were established that Cantonese object relatives typically develop earlier than their English counterparts, we would be unable to tell whether such a developmental asynchrony is responsible for transfer, as opposed to the general dominance of Cantonese, since the predictions of the two factors coincide in our case study. Studies of relatively balanced and English-dominant children, in whom overall dominance of Cantonese could be excluded, would be needed to test the hypothesis. If transfer of prenominal relatives were indeed observed in such children, the developmental asynchrony hypothesis would be supported.

Finally, we should note that the dominance and asynchrony accounts of transfer are not fundamentally at variance with each other. Dominance essentially means that at a given stage of development language A is ahead of language B in overall complexity, while developmental asynchrony refers to the phenomenon whereby particular aspects of language A are ahead of language B, for language-specific reasons. The actual mechanisms of transfer could well be the same in each case, i.e. the child has competence in language A which he or she lacks in language B, and some property of language A is transferred to language B as an interim strategy.

6.4.2   Relative clauses and other prenominal modifiers

As we noted in section 6.1.1, Sinitic languages are virtually unique in the co-occurrence of SVO basic order with prenominal relatives. Part of the explanation for the exceptional status of Sinitic in this regard lies in the fact that relative clauses follow a consistent pattern of prenominal modification. Indeed, it can be argued that there is a continuum from adjectival modification to relative clauses, with some structures being of indeterminate or intermediate status as between adjectival modifiers and relative clauses. Thus example (78) may be translated with an adjective or a relative clause:

(78)   Hou2 ceot1meng2 go2   gaan1 caan1teng1 zap1-zo2-lap1   laa3
         very famous   DEM CL   restaurant close-PFV-down SFP
         'That famous restaurant has closed down.'
         or 'That restaurant which is famous has closed down.'

This unity of noun-modifying structures is a typological feature widespread in Asian languages (Comrie 1996, 1998, 2002). Such an areal perspective proves to be a fruitful way of looking at our children's relative clauses. Alicia had already acquired this Cantonese structure as early as 1;10, well before she produced the corresponding structure in English, as seen in (79) and (80):

(79)   Ngo5 zung1ji3 sai3   go2   go3 carrot
         I   like   small DEM CL   carrot
         'I like the small carrot.'   (Alicia 1;10;26)

(80)   Father: Do you want the small violin?
         Child: I want small that one.   (Alicia 3;03;09)

Alicia's syntax here is that of the Cantonese structure as illustrated in (79), with the adjective *small* occupying the same position as a relative clause. In the following examples in Cantonese and English respectively, the modification structure with adjective (*wu1zou1* 'dirty' in (81), *blue* in (82)) is recast as one with an object relative, underlining the parallelism between the two:

(81)

Wu1zou1	go2	di1	si2	aa3,	o1	ceot1	lai4	go2	di1	si2	le1
dirty	DEM	CL	faeces	SFP,	excrete	out	come	DEM	CL	faeces	SFP

'[It looks like] those dirty faeces, you know, the faeces one excretes.'

(Alicia 3;08;18)

(82)   Daddy, where is that blue bag? My . . . me make that one?
         In Baptist that blue bag.   (Alicia 3;05;06)

In Timmy's data, we find examples which might be seen as intermediate between adjectival modifiers and full relative clauses:

(83)   I like to eat no seeds inside the grapes. [i.e. seedless grapes]

(Timmy 3;09;24)

(84)   This is a nobody can find me place.   (Timmy 4;00;19)

The modifying 'clause' *no seeds inside* in (83) lacks a verb, while (84) lacks a preposition or other indicator of the spatial relationship between the head noun and the modifying clause *nobody can find me*.

The developmental parallel between relative clauses and other modifiers also finds support in English monolingual development, albeit this time in postnominal position. Tager-Flusberg (1989) describes an experiment in which younger children tended to produce prepositional phrases as modifiers, as in (85), rather than relative clauses (86):

(85)   The boy gave the dog to [$_{NP}$ the bear [$_{PP}$ with the wagon]]

(86)   The boy gave the dog to [$_{NP}$ the bear [$_{CP}$ who is holding the wagon]]

Tager-Flusberg concludes:

Children may be using their knowledge of simpler constructions to guide the acquisition of more complex constructions. In this [elicitation] task both forms, prepositional phrases and relative clauses, fulfill the function adequately, but younger children used primarily simpler prepositional phrases, while older children used primarily relative clauses. Perhaps the developmental roots of relative clauses lie in simpler constructions. (1989: 157)

A particular case of the continuum scenario outlined by Comrie (1996, 1998) with regard to Japanese involves prenominal modifying phrases which are clearly clausal (rather than adjectival) and yet not prototypical relative clauses, in the sense that there is no grammatical relation between the head noun and the clause; rather, there is a looser relation of association between them, analogous to that which obtains in topic-comment constructions. Such structures, which Comrie terms attributive clauses, are equally possible in adult Cantonese.[14] In (87), for example, the instrumental relationship between the head noun *bat1* 'pen' and the predicate *waak6-waa2* 'draw pictures' is unexpressed, while in

(88) there is no grammatical relation at all between *soeng2* 'pictures' and *waat6-syut3* 'ski':

(87)   Ngo5 waak6-waa2 go2 zi1 bat1
         I   draw-picture that CL pen
         'The pen that I draw pictures [with]'

(88)   Lei5 waat6-syut3 go2   di1 soeng2
         you   slide-snow   those CL   pictures
         'The pictures of you skiing; your skiing pictures'

There is good evidence that the children's developing grammar allows modifying clauses of this type, which involve no grammatical relationship between the head and the relative clause. A rare example of a clausal modifier in the longitudinal corpus data for Timmy is (89):

(89)   Co5 fei1gei1 go2 di1 ze4ze1   bei2 ngo5 gaa3
         sit plane   DEM CL   big-sister give me   SFP
         '(The toy was) given to me by those ladies on the plane.'   (Timmy 3;02;26)

Referring to a toy given to the child by the flight attendants (*ze4ze1* 'big sisters'), the clause in (89) could in principle be analysed as a subject relative 'the big sisters who take the plane', with a gap in subject position. More plausibly, however, the child means 'the big sisters associated with taking the plane', in which case the head noun *ze4ze1* 'big sisters' would bear no grammatical relation to the predicate *co5 fei1gei1* 'sit plane' (meaning to take a plane). Rather, it would be a relationship by way of association, of the kind often found in Chinese topic-comment structures: there would be no gap, and the structure would be an attributive clause, intermediate between a relative clause and other premodifying phrases:

(90)   [NP [S co5 fei1gei1] go2   di1 ze4ze1]   bei2 ngo5 gaa3
                sit plane   DEM   CL   big-sister give me   SFP
         'The ladies on the plane gave (the toy) to me.'

A similar example is recorded in Sophie's English:

(91)   The go to Australia things!
         [pointing to things packed for trip to Australia]   (Sophie 4;03;24)

This example could be a subject relative ('the things which are going to Australia') but again it is more plausibly taken as an associative clause ('the things involved in (our) going to Australia'). On this analysis, the children would be extending Comrie's 'Asian' type of noun-modifying clause to their English. Further examples from Sophie clearly call for such an 'associative' analysis:

(92)   Where's my medicine? That here painful that one.
        [pointing to gums]   (Sophie 4;09;11)

(93)   I want that blue thing, I go to Chinese school that.   (Sophie 4;11;17)

The relative clause in (92) is intended to mean 'the medicine that I use when it hurts here', in which there is no grammatical relation between the modifying phrase *here painful* and *that one* (the medicine). Similarly:

(94)   How 'bout . . . I wear the go PE shoes, that one.   (Sophie 4;10;18)

Here *the go PE shoes* are clearly not shoes which go to PE (Physical Education) lessons themselves, but those which the child wears when going to such lessons. This is not a subject relative, but an associative one of the kind we identified in Timmy's Cantonese (90) and Sophie's English (91). Alicia also produced such examples in both Cantonese and English:

(95)   Oh, so many eat something. [sees pictures of foodstuffs in book]
        [i.e. so many things to eat!]   (Alicia 2;10;04)

(96)   Mother: Lei5 soeng2 heoi3 Ou3mun2 waan2 mat1je5?
                you   want   go   Macau   play   what
                'What do you want to play with when you go to Macau?'

        Child: Waan2 jau4-seoi2   go2 go3 je5
                play   swim-water DEM CL thing
                'The thing for swimming [i.e. my inflatable toy].'   (Alicia 2;11;07)

(97)   Where is Sophie Baptist school that one?
        [i.e. Where is the videotape of Sophie at the Baptist school?]
                                                              (Alicia 3;06;29)

What is being transferred, then, is not merely the Cantonese relative clause, but the overall strategy of pronominal modification.

The unity of relative clauses and other modifiers has implications for the theory of transfer. Up to this point we have not invoked input ambiguity as a factor favouring transfer of prenominal relatives, because English relative clauses are unambiguously postnominal. Adjectives and other modifiers such as participles, however, precede the noun, as in *the crumbling edifice*. There is therefore a potential ambiguity of evidence in that modifiers of the noun are split between those which precede and those which follow the noun. This potential ambiguity is made more real in the case of bilinguals by the fact that in Cantonese there is no clear division between adjectives and relative clauses (especially if adjectives are in fact a sub-class of verbs, as is often argued, cf. Francis & Matthews 2005). We therefore have a rather complex case of input ambiguity: a latent property of the non-dominant language (inconsistent ordering of modifiers in English) is exacerbated by a property of the dominant language (unity of relative clauses, adjectives and other attributive modifiers in Cantonese).[15] As noted for the case of dominance versus developmental asynchrony above, the relative roles of dominance and input ambiguity could be further illuminated by studies of balanced and English-dominant bilinguals acquiring Chinese and English.

6.4.3   Object relatives and parsing

The earliest prenominal relatives recorded, in both English and Cantonese, are object relatives – those in which the head noun functions as the object of the relative clause. As we showed in connection with adult Cantonese (see section 6.1.2), it is precisely in the case of object relatives that the relative clause matches the main clause order. This resemblance has consequences for production and processing:

(i) prenominal object relatives are easily constructed using the canonical SVO word order of a main clause (and possibly the actual structure of a main clause, if the internally headed analysis as sketched in section 6.1.2 is applicable);

(ii) if the child should parse the relative clause as a main clause, the sentence will still be readily intelligible (though the restrictive sense will be lost). Our example (9) above would allow such a conjoined clause interpretation, as shown in (98):

(98)   [$_S$ Ngo5   zung1ji3   go2   di1   saam1] [$_S$ hou2   gwai3]
         I   like   DEM CL clothes   very   expensive
         'I like the clothes (and/but) they are expensive.'

The finding that prenominal object relatives are first to emerge in our bilingual children may be compared with English monolingual development in which postnominal *subject* relatives are acquired earliest, and also most readily processed under experimental conditions (Tavakolian 1981). Given the combination of SVO and postnominal relatives, the situation in English is the reverse of that in Cantonese, and it is in subject relatives that the word order matches that of a main clause. As argued by Tavakolian (1981), a relative clause such as (99) can be given a conjoined clause interpretation as in (100):

(99)   The rabbit [that kissed the duck] is happy.

(100)   The rabbit kissed the duck, (and) is happy.

The isomorphism between object relatives and main clause word order in Cantonese therefore facilitates the production of prenominal object relatives at the expense of subject relatives. Based on this isomorphism, Matthews and Yip (2002) predicted that object relatives in Cantonese should be (a) produced earlier than subject relatives by monolingual children, and (b) processed faster and/or more accurately by both children and adults. For monolingual Cantonese development, an experimental study by Lau (2006) suggests an advantage for subject relatives over object relatives in Cantonese, while longitudinal corpus-based studies await future investigation. Recent results from adult processing of relatives in Mandarin Chinese are mixed. Using a moving-window reading task, Hsiao and Gibson (2003) found that Mandarin object relatives were indeed processed faster than subject relatives in the critical regions of the sentence examined. As the authors note, this finding is contrary to the NPAH but is consistent with Gibson's (1998) processing account, as well as with the canonical word order account suggested above. A study by Lin, Fong and Bever (2005), by contrast, found an advantage for Mandarin subject relatives over object relatives, consistent with the NPAH.

6.5   Relative clauses in Singapore Colloquial English

The influence of Chinese on English relative clauses may be observed in at least one other context, namely that of Singaporean Colloquial English (SCE), where it is attested in both child language and adult usage. In this, speech community transfer, parallel to that observed in our bilingual children, eventually gives rise to substrate influence.

6.5.1   Relatives with one

Relative clauses similar to those in our bilingual children's English are attested in Singaporean children's English (Gupta 1994). These children are exposed to several varieties of Chinese including Mandarin, Cantonese, Hokkien and Teochew (Chiu Chow), and in some cases also Malay, alongside English. The English of Singaporean children is strikingly similar to that observed in our Hong Kong bilingual children: although the sociolinguistic situations differ considerably, the influence of southern Chinese dialects through transfer and as substrate languages results in similar effects on the structure of Singaporean Colloquial English. In particular, we find relative clauses with *one* as a pronominal head in Singaporean children's developmental data (Gupta 1994: 90):

(101)   My this can change one ah.
         [i.e. 'Mine is the sort that can change']   (Child EB 5;11)

Such examples are, to say the least, not immediately recognizable as relative clauses. The morpheme *one* has a complex array of functions in SCE, which Gupta (1992: 328) attributes to the interaction of the English pronominal *one* and the Chinese nominalizer (Mandarin *de*, Hokkien *e*, Cantonese *ge*). One of these functions is to form relative clauses, as described by Alsagoff and Ho (1998: 134–135) in adult SCE:

(102)   They grow one very sweet.
'The fruit that they grow is very sweet.'

(103)   Don't have car one, I don't want.
'I don't want [a man] who does not own a car.'

Like Gupta, Alsagoff and Ho (1998: 127) argue that these relative clauses 'show an amalgamation of both substrate (i.e. Chinese) and superstrate (i.e. English) grammatical features'. The substratal influence manifests itself in the use of *one* as a relative marker, which is argued to arise through calquing of the Chinese nominalizer (Mandarin *de*, Hokkien *e*, Teochew *kai*, etc.) into English. Such structures make a particularly strong case for substrate influence in SCE, since the range of configurations with *one* closely matches the Chinese, and is not otherwise predicted by universal considerations (Gupta 1992: 328, 335). This analysis is partially applicable to our children, but in addition to the nominalizer *ge3*, their grammar is influenced specifically by the Cantonese classifier relative as discussed in section 6.1.2. Code-mixed examples from our children suggest that *that one* as in (104) corresponds to the Cantonese demonstrative + classifier complex *go2 go3* as in (105):

(104)   Where's Jane-Jane sung3 bei2 ngo5 that one?
[i.e. where's the one that Jane gave me?']   (Alicia 4;01;19)

(105)   Lo2 go2   go3, go2   go3 pay money go2   go3 [picks up wallet]
take DEM CL, DEM CL pay money DEM CL
'I'm taking the thing for paying money.'   (Alicia 3;10;13)

The use of *one* in this and other grammatical functions is discussed further in section 8.3.

6.5.2   Head-initial vs. head-final relatives

In the SCE examples discussed so far, *one* appears at the end of the relative clause. When extended to include a lexical head noun, however, the relative clause typically follow the noun, as in the following adult examples from Alsagoff and Ho (1998: 134):

(106)   [NP The fruit they grow one] very sweet.

(107)   [NP That boy pinch my mother one] very naughty.

In addition to postnominal relatives of this type, Gil (2003: 496) cites examples in which a nominal head follows the relative clause:

(108)   Ah Chew buy yesterday Lisa choose that house.

Here *that* is used in a restrictive function ('the house that Lisa chose'), which Gil (2003: 493) identifies as distinct from the demonstrative *that*. Indeed, as many as three tokens of *that* can occur in the same sentence (Gil 2003: 495):

(109)   Ah Chew buy *that* yesterday Lisa choose *that* Jamil like *that* one.

Matthews and Yip (2002) came to similar conclusions independently, discussing similar examples in Sophie's English:

(110)   Where is that 'mou tiu', that Mummy wrote that paper?   (Sophie 4;09;08)

(111)   Daddy, I haven't got that Mickey Mouse, that Chloe gave me that one.
                                                                    (Sophie 5;04;24)

In these examples we seem to have three distinct occurrences of *that*:[16]
(a) demonstrative *that* (*that mou tiu, that Mickey Mouse*);
(b) complementizer *that* (*that Mummy wrote, that Chloe gave me*), representing emergence of the target English relative;
(c) a restrictive use of *that* (*that paper, that one*) corresponding to the demonstrative *go2* in Cantonese classifier relatives such as (105) above.

The very specific and detailed parallels between our bilingual data and SCE support the case for substrate influence of Chinese on SCE, which (in this and other cases) remains a matter of controversy. For example, Gil observes that 'premodifier constructions with *that* do not seem to possess close analogues in any of the Singapore substratum languages' (Gil 2003: 494). We have shown that the necessary analogues do exist: taking account of colloquial Cantonese classifier relatives as discussed in section 6.1.2, even the restrictive use of *that* can be traced back to Cantonese (and the corresponding constructions in Min dialects such as Chiu Chow).

Overall, the relative clause presents a particularly strong case for substrate influence in SCE. Prenominal relatives are typologically exceptional in a VO language, as reviewed in section 6.1.1. Unlike many cases of putative substrate influence, there would seem to be no competing universalist explanation for these phenomena.

6.5.3   That-*relatives vs.* wh-*relatives*

A further parallel between our bilingual acquisition data and contact varieties such as SCE involves the absence of *wh*-relatives. While monolingual children acquiring English use *wh*-relatives extensively (and indeed misuse them, as in (77)), the postnominal relative clauses produced by our children are overwhelmingly *that*-relatives or zero-relatives, with *wh*-relative pronouns essentially absent from both the longitudinal recordings and diary data.

An exception to prove the rule is illustrated by a rare example of an apparent *wh*-relative in Timmy's data:

(112)   The one who breaks is the not-winner. ·
          [playing with toy trains]   (Timmy 4;10;16)

Although (112) looks superficially like a *wh*-relative, it is in all probability influenced by the Cantonese construction as in (113) which does use a *wh*-word, *bin1go3* 'who':

(113)   Bin1go3   zing2 laan6   zau6 syu1
          who   make broken then lose
          'Whoever breaks (it), loses.'

The structure in (113) is treated as a free relative in Matthews and Yip (1994: 113). To the extent that the only apparent examples of *wh*-words in relatives are such free relatives, the child's example (112) may owe as much to this Cantonese construction as it does to English *wh*-relatives. A series of utterances produced by Sophie clearly demonstrates transfer of such free relatives with *wh*-words:

(114)   [entering apartment] I bath! I always come back I bath.
          Who bath tomorrow can go in . . .
          [makes bed] Who want to sleep over here, then you can sleep.
          If who want to sit on this, you can.
          Daddy, you can sit on this thing, if you like.   (Sophie 5;01;03)

As Sophie's paraphrases with *if* show, the construction has an implicitly conditional function, which is characteristic of the Cantonese construction as in (113).

The predominance of *that*-relatives again matches findings for Singaporean children who are observed to produce only *that*-relatives (Gupta 1994: 90). Register may be an important factor here: the colloquial spoken English addressed to our children contains largely *that*-relatives. More generally, it is found that *that*-relatives predominate over *wh*-relatives in English interlanguages and emerging Asian varieties of English (Newbrook 1999; Gisborne 2000). This is attributable in part to the lack of *wh*-relatives in the Asian languages which act as substrates in these new Englishes. In addition, the invariant form of *that* makes it a straightforward relative marker for a learner to use, whereas in *wh*-relatives the form of the relative pronoun varies according to animacy and even case.

6.6   Conclusions

Two main findings have emerged from this study of the development of relative clauses in three Cantonese-dominant bilingual children. Firstly, prenominal relative clauses in Cantonese prove to be readily transferable to English. These prenominal relatives are predominantly object relatives, in which the word order resembles that in main clauses, facilitating processing and production of this structure. Secondly, the development of postnominal relatives shows the use of resumptive pronouns in object and occasionally also in subject position. While the prenominal relatives represent a clear case of transfer, the resumptive pronoun strategy cannot plausibly be attributed to transfer as resumptive pronouns are not attested in the children's Cantonese. To the extent that different groups of learners including simultaneous bilingual children, monolingual English-speaking children and adult second learners of English all make use of resumptive pronouns in their production of relative clauses at a certain developmental stage, the resumptive pronoun strategy appears to represent an option universally available to the language learner.

A number of developmental and typological factors conspire together to favour transfer of prenominal relatives in the bilingual children's English. The dominance of Cantonese over English, as indicated by the MLUw differential, largely determines the directionality of transfer in the acquisition of relative clauses (see section 3.3.2). At the same time, an element of input ambiguity exists in that prenominal modification is found in English with modifiers other than relative clauses. The prenominal relatives in Cantonese share important properties with other types of prenominal modification, which surface as interlanguage structures with phrases and clauses of all kinds modifying the head noun. Comrie's (1996) suggestion of a continuum of prenominal modification structures finds developmental confirmation in the parallel development of relative clauses and other prenominal modifiers. In particular, a type of modifying clause instantiated both in the children's Cantonese and their English involves a kind of association rather than strict grammatical relationship between the head and the predicate in the prenominal modifying clause.

In addition, the prenominal object relatives share the canonical word order of the main clause, which may offset the parsing difficulty of prenominal relatives predicted by Hawkins (1990, 1994). This also explains why it is object relatives which predominate in the bilingual children's English: prenominal relatives with other relativized positions such as subject relatives would not preserve the canonical word order of a main clause. Canonical word order offers a powerful strategy that overrides the theoretical difficulties presented by prenominal relatives in an SVO language.

Lastly, we have shown that the transfer of relative clause structures from Cantonese to English is parallel in many respects to the Chinese-influenced relative clauses in Singapore Colloquial English. The similar outputs at the individual and community levels provide strong support for substrate accounts of these phenomena.

NOTES

1. This chapter is based on Matthews and Yip (2002) with substantial elaboration, including data from a third child (Alicia) and more extended discussion of the implications for language contact as seen in Singapore Colloquial English (section 6.5).

2. We use the term 'Sinitic languages' for what have traditionally been called 'Chinese dialects' in order to reflect the magnitude of structural differences between varieties of Chinese (cf. Chappell 2001).

3. Yip and Matthews (2007) discuss a theoretical issue in applying typological universals such as the Noun Phrase Accessibility Hierarchy to acquisition studies regarding whether and how the learner has access to generalizations of a typological nature. We thank Salikoko Mufwene for drawing our attention to this important issue. Yip and Matthews (1995) argue that to impute a typological generalization to learners is to assume that they have access to whatever knowledge underlies the typological characteristics in question. In order to be explanatory, typological universals must be expressed in terms which can be attributed to the learner's competence. For example, the linguistic knowledge concerned may be encoded in Universal Grammar, or in the learner's L1. Another alternative is to derive the relevant grammatical properties from processing principles which are independent of UG (Hawkins 1994, 2004) and specifically, 'the increasing complexity of the processing domains for different relativizable positions' which motivates the Noun Phrase Accessibility Hierarchy (Hawkins 2004: 177). These processing factors are assumed to be applicable equally to children, monolingual or bilingual, and to adults.

4. The five potential cases of *ge3* relatives found in the Timmy corpus include the following:

(i) <hai6 hai6 hai6> [/] hai6 jiu3 lei4 daa2-gaau1 ge3 je5 lei4
     is   is   is   is   need come fight   PRT thing SFP
     '(It) is a thing for fighting.'   (Timmy 2;07;28)

(ii) mou5   go3 kam2 lok6 heoi3 ge3 je5
     not-have CL   cover down go   PRT thing
     '(I) don't have the thing to use as a cover.'   (Timmy 2;08;18)

(iii) hai2 li 1dou6 ge3 trap
      at   here   PRT trap
      'The trap (that's) here.'   (Timmy 3;02;03)

Two examples in one of Timmy's transcripts are ambiguous as to whether the modifying elements before the head noun constitute adjectival or clausal modification:

(iv) go2 di1 jai5   ge3 siu2 pang4jau5 . . . [repeated a few lines later]
     that CL   naughty   PRT little children
     'those naughty little children' or 'the children who are naughty' (Timmy 3;05;14)

The only *ge3* relative found in Sophie's corpus is (v):

(v) jau5 duk6   ge3 ping4g(w)o2 li1 go3 aa3
     have poison PRT apple   this CL   SFP
     'the apple that is poisonous, this one'   (Sophie 2;02;03)

Example (v) is actually ambiguous since *jau5 duk6* 'have poison' can be treated as a compound adjective, thus resulting in adjectival modification before the head, i.e.

'a poisonous apple, this one'. All the examples in (i)–(v) represent indeterminate cases falling on the continuum between attributive and relative clause constructions as discussed in section 6.4.2.

5. We thank Lisa Cheng, Peter Cole and Gabriella Hermon for discussion of the analysis of Cantonese relatives as internally headed relative clauses.

6. The number of potential relative clauses attested in the three siblings' Cantonese corpora is 8 in Timmy, 4 in Sophie and 9 in Alicia. It is remarkable that all 8 relative clauses in Alicia's corpus data come from one early file at age 1;10;16 (see section 6.4.2 for discussion):

(i)   Zaa1 ce1 go2 go3
       drive car that CL
       'The one who drives'   (Alicia 1;10;16)

The following example is ambiguous:

(ii)   Jam2 go2 go3 # li1dou6
       Drink that CL   here
       'The one I'm drinking is here.' = object relative or
       'The thing that is used for drinking.' = attributive clause or
       '(I) drink that one, here.' = main clause. (less preferred reading)   (Alicia 1;10;16)

Some of the utterances produced by Timmy are ambiguous between main clause and relative clause interpretation given that the context does not provide sufficient cue to disambiguate them:

(iii) Ngo5 bei2 lei5 tai2 go2 go3
       I   give you see that CL
       'I let you see that one.' = main clause reading or
       'The one I let you see.' = relative clause   (Timmy 2;09;08)

The main clause reading of (iii) naturally arises since early child Cantonese in monolingual, and especially in bilingual children favours the non-target order in double object *bei2* 'give/let' constructions with the recipient preceding the theme (see detailed discussion in chapter 7).

(iv)   Ngo5 zung1ji3 lei5 maai5 go2 di1 zyu1gaak1lik6 (i.e. zyu1gu1lik1)
       I   like   you buy   that CL chocolate
       'I like you to buy those chocolates.' = main clause reading or
       'I like the chocolates that you bought.' = relative clause reading   (Timmy 2;07;00)

7. The structure is shown conventionally as a head-final relative with a clause (S) modifying a head noun. As discussed in section 6.1.2, an alternative analysis would posit a head-internal structure [$_{NP/S}$ *you buy that one*] with the SVO clause functioning simultaneously as S and NP.

8. Questions of the form [NP *ne1/le1?*] in Cantonese (corresponding to [NP *ne?*] in Mandarin) conventionally mean either 'what about x? or 'where's x?' (Matthews & Yip 1994: 348).

9. Here the child appears to use the default classifier *go3* for *coeng1* 'gun', where adult Cantonese would use a more specific classifier such as *zi1* or *baa2*. The pronoun *lei5* 'you' is a case of pronoun reversal: the child clearly intends reference to himself, so that the target is *ngo5* 'I'.

10. There is also one example of what appears to be a headless free relative:

(i) You already eat is what? [i.e. What is it that you already ate?]

(Sophie 3;11;12)

Note that the *wh*-word *what* is left in situ, as discussed in chapter 4.

11. Possible examples produced by Alicia appear as early as 2;03, as discussed in section 6.1.2. Such early emergence is consistent with the fact that the Cantonese counterparts have been acquired by 2;01, as seen in (36).

12. The second clause [*jan4dei6 bei2 ngo2 go2 go3*] is in fact potentially ambiguous: given that the children tend to use the non-target order [*bei2* 'give' – recipient – theme] (see 7.2 on the development of dative constructions), it can be interpreted as a main clause 'Someone gave me that (present)', as in (i):

(i) Jan4dei6 [$_{VP}$ bei2 [ngo5] [go2 go3]] aa3
     people   give   me   that CL   SFP
     'Someone gave me that one.'   (main clause analysis)

(ii) [$_S$ Jan4dei6 bei2 ngo5] [$_{NP}$ go2 go3] aa3
       people   give   me   that CL   SFP
      'The one that someone gave me.'   (relative clause analysis)

In (i) *go2 go3* 'that one' is the recipient of the main verb *bei2* 'give' whereas in (ii) *go2 go3* is the head of the relative clause. The context shows that a relative clause reading (ii) is intended, since the child is identifying a certain present given to her by another person. Once again, the ambiguity is consistent with the head-internal relative clause analysis as sketched in section 6.1.2.

13. This is not to say that performance factors are irrelevant. On the contrary, we believe that the principal motivation for pronoun retention is to facilitate parsing and production, as argued by Hawkins (1999). The point is that pronoun retention in our bilingual children is a developmental stage, rather than a sporadic phenomenon induced by on-line constraints or experimental pressures.

14. We are grateful to the late Professor Rudolf de Rijk of Leiden University for drawing our attention to relative clauses which lack strict grammatical relations and their significance for Cantonese grammar.

15. We thank Nik Gisborne, Usha Lakshmanan and Yasuhiro Shirai for discussion of this point.

16. While in adult speech the complementizer usage would be distinguished by reduction of the vowel to schwa, in Sophie's speech these uses of *that* are all pronounced alike, with the full vowel [æ].

7   Vulnerable domains in Cantonese and the directionality of transfer

Child: Je4sou1 bei2 (ng)o5 cin2 aa3[1] 'Jesus gave me money.'
Adult: Je4sou1 bei2 cin2 lei5 aa4? 'Jesus gave you money?'
Child: Hai6 aa3 'Yes he did.'
Adult: Bin1go3 bei2 cin2 lei5 aa3? 'Who gave you money?'
Child: Hai6 Je4sou1 bei2 (ng)o5 cin2 'It was Jesus who gave me money.'

(Sophie 2;05;02)

The above Cantonese dialogue between Sophie at two years five months and the adult researcher illustrates how the child's grammar is different from the adult's. Sophie's sentence shows a non-target word order: *Je4sou1 bei2 ngo5 cin2* 'Jesus gave me money,' where the recipient *ngo5* 'me' immediately follows the verb *bei2* 'give' and the object *cin2* 'money' in turn follows the recipient. She repeats this despite the adult's word order in *Je4sou1 bei2 cin2 lei5 aa4?* 'Jesus gave you money?' and *Bin1go3 bei2 cin2 lei5 aa3?* 'Who gave you money?' where the object *cin2* 'money' immediately follows the verb *bei2* 'give' and the recipient *lei5* 'you' appears as the second object. In section 7.2.1 we shall see that our bilingual children have a strong tendency to produce the Cantonese double object construction with *bei2* 'give' in the non-target word order, which in turn resembles the English counterparts. This is one of the few grammatical domains that show cross-linguistic influence from English, the weaker language to Cantonese, the dominant language: the reverse of the typical pattern of transfer as discussed in the preceding chapters.

The clear cases of transfer discussed in the preceding chapters involve Cantonese structures being transferred to English. This pattern is consistent with the language dominance hypothesis (see section 2.4), although other factors may also play a role, including input ambiguity (in the case of null objects discussed in chapter 5) and developmental asynchrony (as discussed in the case of *why* questions in chapter 4 and relative clauses in chapter 6). It also resembles the typical pattern in second language acquisition, where transfer is generally unidirectional since the first language is already well in place (see section 2.1.2). In the case of bilingual acquisition, bidirectional transfer is a distinct possibility since both languages are still developing. In this chapter we focus on cases where the direction of influence is reversed: the grammar of English, the weaker language, appears to be influencing that of Cantonese, the dominant language. Since such influence is not predicted by language dominance, other factors must be involved, including in particular properties of the input such as input ambiguity as discussed in chapter 2.

On initial observation, while our Cantonese-dominant children's English shows clear signs of Cantonese influence, their Cantonese appears similar to that of monolingual Cantonese-speaking children. Apart from cases of code-mixing where English words are inserted into Cantonese sentences, there is little sign of influence from English. In fact, to see English influence will require careful qualitative and quantitative comparison with monolingual Cantonese development. We shall pursue three case studies of increasing complexity, including prepositional phrases with *hai2* 'at' (section 7.1), *bei2* 'give' dative constructions (section 7.2) and verb-particle constructions (section 7.3). These will be argued to constitute 'vulnerable domains' as defined in chapter 2: specific areas of grammar prone to cross-linguistic influence regardless of patterns of dominance.

The question of directionality of cross-linguistic influence also has implications for language contact. Just as there is often a dominant language in the bilingual child, so there is typically a socially dominant language in most language contact situations (Aikhenvald & Dixon, 2006). To the extent that mutual influence is observed in bilingual children, this provides a mechanism by which grammatical convergence can occur between languages in contact (Backus 2004) and hence in the emergence of linguistic areas (Thomason 2001; Dahl 2001).

7.1   Placement of prepositional phrases in bilingual children's Cantonese

Yip and Matthews (2000a: 206) observed that Timmy commonly placed locative prepositional phrases with *hai2* 'at' after the verb, as in (1) with non-target [V PP] order:

(1)   Ngo5 saang1-zo2 hai2 ji1jyun2 go2dou6
       I   born-PFV   at   hospital there
       'I was born in the hospital.'   (Timmy 2;08;07)

The target order in Cantonese in this case is [PP V], as in:

(2)   Ngo5 [hai2 ji1jyun2 go2dou6] saang1 ge3
       I   at   hospital there   born   SFP
       'I was born in the hospital.'

The non-target word order [V PP] in (1) is one area where influence of English on Cantonese may be implicated, since the child's placement of the PP after the verb corresponds to English word order. However, at least two alternative explanations are available for the non-target order in (1):

(i) Cantonese also allows postverbal *hai2*-prepositional phrases, albeit as a minority pattern. The non-target order could result from over-generalization of grammatical [V PP] structures such as:

(3)   Ngo5 tip3 [hai2 bun2 syu1 go2dou6]
        I   stick at   CL   book there
        'I'm sticking [it] in the book.'

(ii) In terms of language universals, Chinese is apparently unique among SVO languages in having prepositional phrases before the verb as in (2). The non-target order [V PP] could result from universal factors favouring the postverbal PP order, whether these factors involve innate Universal Grammar or functional principles such as iconicity and processing efficiency. Both of these alternative accounts predict that monolingual children should make similar [V PP] errors to the bilingual children. They also raise the possibility that some interaction of (i) and/or (ii) with cross-linguistic influence from English leads to the developmental errors such as (1) in bilingual children. In the following sections we test these predictions, comparing data on bilingual and monolingual development.

7.1.1   Placement of prepositional phrases in English and Cantonese

Locative prepositional phrases (PPs) constitute an area where English and Cantonese exhibit clear contrasts, but also partial overlap. In terms of categorical status, English has a distinct category of prepositions, while Cantonese has a class of 'coverbs' which function like prepositions but retain many properties of verbs. The word *hai2* 'at' with which we will be concerned here is one such coverb, so-called because it typically occurs with another verb such as *zou6* 'do' in (4):

(4)   Keoi5 hai2 daai6hok6 zou6-je5
        She   at   university do-things
        'She works at the university.'

A coverb like *hai2* 'at' in (4) may be analysed either as a preposition or the first of two verbs in a serial verb construction (Francis & Matthews 2006; Matthews 2006a: 71). Regardless of this issue, the coverb phrase is functionally parallel to a locative prepositional phrase in English, and bilingual children apparently make an interlingual identification between the two. We will therefore refer to phrases consisting of [*hai2* + NP] as PPs in the following discussion.

In English, locative PPs occur in postverbal position within the VP, yielding [V NP PP] order as in (5), but never immediately before the verb [PP V] as in (6):

(5)   The mailman put the newspaper [at the doorstep].

(6)   *The mailman [at the doorstep] put the newspaper.

By contrast, Cantonese locative PPs may appear in preverbal or postverbal positions depending on the verb concerned, as well as on various semantic and pragmatic factors. In Cantonese [PP V] order is used where the PP encodes location of action, while the order [V PP] occurs when the locative PP represents a goal towards which the action is directed (Cheung 1990, 1991). For example, in (7a) the picture ends up on the wall, which therefore has the role of goal, while in (7b) the wall represents the location in which the action of hanging the picture takes place:[2]

(7)   a. Keoi5 gwaa3-zo2 fuk1 waa2   hai2 bung6 coeng4 dou6
            she   hang-PFV CL picture at   CL   wall   there
            'She hung the picture on the wall.'

       b. Keoi5 hai2 bung6 coeng4 dou6 gwaa3-zo2 fuk1 waa2
            she   at   CL   wall   there hang-PFV CL picture
            'She hung the picture on the wall.'

The functional principle of iconicity may play a role in the placement of PPs. Iconicity refers to a non-arbitrary match between form and meaning. When the PP is placed at the end of the sentence, it mirrors the end result of the event. This contrast can be understood under the view that these constructions are (or at least derive historically from) serial verb constructions (SVCs), since in certain types of SVCs the ordering of verbs tends to reflect the progress of the events described in time (Aikhenvald 2006: 35). The postverbal placement of goal PPs is thus in accordance with iconicity: the expression representing the goal or result of the action is placed at the end of the clause describing that action, as described by Tai (1975) for Mandarin and Kwan (2005a, 2005b) for Cantonese. With verbs of placement such as *baai2* 'put' and *fong3* 'put' which select a goal PP, the preferred order is accordingly [V (NP) PP] as in (7a). With posture verbs such as *co5* 'sit' and *kei5* 'stand', either order is possible:[3]

(8)   a. Keoi5 hai2 go2dou6 co5
            she   at   there   sit
            'She's sitting over there.'

       b. Keoi5 co5 hai2 go2dou6
            she   sit at   there
            'She sat down there.'

In the context of acquisition, such verbs may play a role in leading the child to assume that either preverbal or postverbal placement of *hai2* 'at' phrases is possible. In this respect, the Cantonese input is ambiguous, opening the door to cross-linguistic influence (see section 7.1.3).

7.1.2   Placement of Cantonese locative prepositional phrases with hai2 'at' in bilingual and monolingual children

We now compare the placement of Cantonese PPs with *hai2* 'at' in monolingual and bilingual development. For monolingual Cantonese-speaking children, the challenge is to identify the constraints which limit the occurrence of [V PP] order. While we might expect monolingual children to have difficulty here, we have not found any such non-target orders in Cancorp (Lee et al. 1996) which would suggest over-generalization of [V PP] order. Monolingual Cantonese-speaking children appear to be conservative learners in this respect, taking [PP V] to be the basic order in accordance with its predominance in the input, and using [V PP] order only in cases where they have heard it instantiated. Bilingual children, however, have the additional motivation to use [V PP] order as in English. Diary data from Alicia provide extensive evidence of [V PP] order under English influence. On one occasion a family friend came to dinner for a second time, provoking Alicia to remark:

(9)   Jau6   sik6 hai2 li1dou6 aa4, lei5
         again eat   at   here   SFP   you
         'Eating here again, are you?'   (Alicia 4;00;21)

This remark is grammatically ill-formed as well as pragmatically inappropriate: [V PP] order is not licensed because the PP [*hai2 li1dou6*] 'here' has the role of location rather than goal. Similarly, using *sik* 'eat' with an object, Alicia produces the order [V NP PP]:

(10)   Keoi5 sik6 min6-min6   hai2 po4po2   go2dou6 aa3
         she   eat   noodle-noodle at grandma   there   SFP
         'She's eating noodles at Grandma's.'   (Alicia 3;11;17)

In some cases Alicia uses parallel [V PP] structures in both languages, first addressing her mother in Cantonese and then switching to English to address her father:

(11)   Ngo5 waan2 bubble hai2 soeng6min6 go2dou6 aa3 [to Mother]
         I   play   bubble at   up-side   there   SFP
         'I was playing with bubbles upstairs.'
         I'm play bubble in there. [to Father]   (Alicia 2;10;01)

The verbs involved here, *sik6* 'eat' in (9)–(10) and *waan2* 'play' in (11), do not involve a goal argument and never allow [V PP] order in Cantonese. These cases are therefore not likely to be the result of over-generalization of a Cantonese pattern. As we have seen, however, posture verbs allow both orders. The verb

Table 7.1. *Placement of Cantonese locative PPs with* hai2 *'at' in six bilingual children*

	Timmy	Sophie	Alicia	Llywelyn	Kathryn	Charlotte
PP V	58	5	14	6	18	0
V PP	79	15	52	27	29	2
% V PP	58	75	79	82	62	N/A

V = verb, PP = prepositional phrase

fan3-gaau3 'sleep' is actually a verb-object compound based on *fan3* 'lie', but this is not obvious (since the word *gaau3* is seldom used independently) and the child apparently treats it as a posture verb, as in the ill-formed (12):

(12)   Ngo5 gin3 dou2 lei5 kam4maan5 fan3-gaau3 hai2 Sophie go2dou6
        I   see PRT you last night lie-sleep   at   Sophie there
        'I saw you sleeping in Sophie's (bed) last night.'   (Alicia 4;02;26)

Compare the use of *fan3* 'lie' as a simplex verb, which (being a posture verb) does allow [V PP] order in Cantonese, as in the adult sentence (13):

(13)   Ngo5 kam4maan5 gin3 dou2 lei5 fan3 hai2 Sophie go2dou6
        I   last night see PRT you lie at   Sophie there
        'I saw you sleeping in Sophie's bed last night.'

We might expect to find patterns in monolingual child Cantonese with quasi-posture verbs such as *fan3-gaau3* 'sleep' as in (12), since the pattern exists in adult Cantonese, whereas we would not expect such orders with verbs such as *waan2* 'play' and *sik6* 'eat'. The Cancorp data in fact show no evidence of monolingual children over-extending [V PP] order with the preposition *hai2* 'at'. A study by Leung (2005) compared data from the bilingual children Timmy and Sophie with those from the eight monolingual children from Cancorp. In quantifying the data, unclear cases were excluded, such as incomplete utterances and instances which could represent the grammaticalized usage of preverbal *hai2dou6* 'here' to express progressive aspect (Matthews & Yip 1994: 202).

Table 7.1 shows the distribution of [V PP] and [PP V] orders in the bilingual children's corpus. All six bilingual children produce primarily [V PP] orders, with an overwhelmingly high proportion in Llywelyn (82%), followed by Alicia (79%), Sophie (75%), Kathryn (62%) and Timmy (58%). Since Charlotte produced only two tokens of [V PP] and none of [PP V], no meaningful percentage can be computed.

Table 7.2 shows the distribution of [V PP] and [PP V] orders in the eight monolingual children from Cancorp. Among the children whose number of tokens allows generalization, CCC and LLY use both [PP V] and [V PP] orders

Table 7.2. *Placement of Cantonese locative PPs with* hai2 *'at' in eight monolingual children in Cancorp (Lee et al. 1996)*

Child	CCC	CKT	CGK	HHC	LTF	LLY	MHZ	WBH
PP V	8	0	3	1	0	13	0	0
V PP	6	0	2	2	38	14	2	2
% V PP	43	N/A	40	66	100	52	N/A	N/A

V = verb, PP = prepositional phrase

Table 7.3. *Placement of Cantonese locative PPs with* hai2 *'at' in six bilingual and six monolingual children*

	Bilingual (n = 6)	Monolingual (n = 6)
PP V	101	25
V PP	204	28
% V PP	67	53

with approximately equal frequency: 43% [V PP] order for CCC and 52% for LLY. One child, LTF, seems to behave very differently from the rest: LTF produced exclusively [V PP] structures, a total of thirty-eight tokens, topping the monolingual corpus finding. LTF's categorical use of [V PP] order stands out from among the children. The likely explanation is that LTF is not truly monolingual: as recorded in the CHILDES database manual, she used 'something English-like' with her Filipina domestic helper and was thus exposed to influence from English. The quantitative figures reported below for monolingual Cantonese children therefore exclude LTF, as well as CKT who produced no relevant tokens, thus leaving a total of six monolingual children for comparison with the six bilingual children.

Table 7.3 shows the group comparison between the bilingual and monolingual children's patterns of PP placement using *hai2* 'at'. While monolinguals use both orders with approximately equal frequency (53%), bilinguals show a clear preference (67%) for [V PP] order. The difference is significant on a χ^2 test of the hypothesis that the bilinguals should produce a larger proportion of [V PP] order than monolinguals ($\chi^2 = 3.91$, $p < 0.05$, one-tailed).

Qualitative comparison complements this picture, showing that the monolingual children use [V PP] only where it is well-formed. Table 7.4 shows that apart from Charlotte (who produced only two tokens of [V PP] order) the other five bilingual children all produced non-target [V PP] Cantonese sentences, with the percentage ranging from 3.4% for Kathryn, 8.9% for Timmy, 13.3% for

Table 7.4. *Non-target placement of Cantonese locative PPs with* hai2 *'at' in six bilingual children*

Child	Timmy	Sophie	Alicia	Llywelyn	Kathryn	Charlotte	Total
Non-target [V PP]	7	2	8	6	1	0	24
Target [V PP]	79	15	52	27	29	2	204
% non-target	8.9	13.3	15.4	22.2	3.4	N/A	11.8

Sophie, 15.4% for Alicia to 22.2% for Llywelyn. Overall, 11.8% of the [V PP] utterances produced by bilingual children are judged to be non-target. This is in striking contrast to the pattern in monolingual Cantonese development where no clear examples of non-target [V PP] order are attested in the corpus data. Examples illustrating the [V PP] non-target order in the bilingual Cantonese data include the following:[4]

(14)   e6,   lei5dei6 waan2 jat1 zan6 hai2 ji1dou6 hou2 mou2   aa3
        INT   you   play   a   while at   here   good-not-good SFP
        'Would you play here for a while?'   (Timmy 3;01;01)

(15)   Ngo5   lok6   heoi3   <hai2> [/] hai2 ji1dou6 aa3
        I   go   down   at   at   here   SFP
        'I go down there.'   (Sophie 3;00;09)

(16)   Gan1zyu6 saan1   maai4 go3   baak6sik1 goi3   hai2 dou6
        then   close   PRT   CL   white   cover at   here
        'Then close the white cover here.'   (Alicia 2;07;10)

(17)   Sik6   faan6 hai2   ni1dou6 aa1, hou2-m4-hou2   aa3
        eat   rice   at   here   SFP   good-not-good SFP
        'Shall we eat (dinner) here?'   (Kathryn 3;04;14)

(18)   (Ng)o5   daa2   din6waa2 hai2 li1dou6
        I   call   telephone at   here
        'I'm making a call here.'   (Llywelyn 2;08;08)

(19)   Waan2   hai2 #   li1dou6
        play   at   here
        'Play here.'   (Llywelyn 2;08;08)

The monolingual data from Cancorp include just one possible instance of non-target [V PP] order, where LTF uses *waan2* 'play' (Leung 2005):

(20)   Ngo5   jiu3 #   jau5 di1   waan2 je5   hai2 nei1dou6 aa3
        I   need #   have some play   thing at   here   SFP
        'I need to . . . have some . . . play something here.'   (LTF 2;08;24)

With *waan2* 'play' followed by a PP, this utterance may be comparable to example (14) from Timmy and (19) from Llywelyn. However, in (20) it is not clear whether the PP [*hai2 nei1dou6*] modifies the verb *waan2 je5* 'play (with) things' in a [V NP PP] configuration, as implied by the translation; the sentence could also be interpreted as 'I need to have some play-things here.' If (20) is indeed an instance of ill-formed [V PP] order, this is consistent with the assumption that LTF is a 'bilingual in disguise', as already suggested based on the quantitative data in table 7.2.

7.1.3   Discussion: structural overlap and input ambiguity

As noted above, the placement of PPs with *hai2* 'at' in adult Cantonese presents some ambiguity of evidence, in that (a) both [PP V] and [V PP] orders are productive, and (b) certain verbs allow both orders. Table 7.5 shows the distribution of PPs with *hai2* 'at' in the adult speech in two adult Cantonese corpora (Kwan 2005a) and both the adult and child Cantonese in the Hong Kong Bilingual Child Language Corpus.

Table 7.5 shows that that adult Cantonese strongly favours [PP V] over [V PP] order: in the Cantonese Radio Corpus (Francis et al. 2002), the predominance of [PP V] order is as high as 53.1% [PP V] vs. 8.3% [V PP], with the remaining 38.5% of PPs being in topic position as in (21):

(21)
[TOPIC hai2 gwo3heoi3 ge3 jat6zi2], ngo5 zeon6-zo2 ngo5 ge3 nang4lik6
       at   past   PRT days   I   try-PFV   my   PRT ability
'In the past days, I have done my best.'

In the Hong Kong Cantonese Adult Language Corpus (Leung & Law 2002), the distribution of PP orders is 39.9% [PP V] vs. 15.8% [V PP], with 43.2% topic PP and 1.1% right-dislocated PP. In the input to children, however, the balance is different: as measured by the child-directed speech in our bilingual corpus,[5] there is 35.4% [PP V] vs 62.0% [V PP], with 0.6% topic PP and 2.0% right-dislocated PPs. The proportion of [V PP] is much higher than in the adult Cantonese corpora. The distribution of PPs with *hai2* 'at' in the bilingual children's Cantonese shows a close match to the patterns of the child-directed adult speech: 67% of the PPs show [V PP] order, against 33% for [PP V].

Although the adult speech represented in the corpus provides only a small proportion of the overall input available to the children, it is clear that child-directed speech differs from adult-to-adult Cantonese. First, topic PPs such as (21) are rarely used in interacting with children.[6] Second, [V PP] is much more prevalent in child-directed speech, largely because it makes extensive use of the placement verbs such as *baai2* 'put' which require this order, and posture verbs such as *co5* 'sit' which allow it (see section 7.1.1). The bilingual children

Table 7.5. *Distribution of locative PPs with hai2 'at' in two adult Cantonese corpora (based on Kwan 2005a) and the Hong Kong Bilingual Child Language Corpus*

	Cantonese Radio Corpus	Hong Kong Corpus of Adult Cantonese	Hong Kong Bilingual Child Language Corpus	
	adult-to-adult Cantonese	adult-to-adult Cantonese	adult-to-child Cantonese	bilingual children's Cantonese
% PP V	53.1	39.9	35.4	33
% V PP	8.3	15.8	62	67
% topic PP	38.5	43.2	0.6	0
% others	0.1	1.1	2	0

reflect this bias, producing a majority of [V PP] utterances (67% overall, as shown in table 7.3 above).

While these figures might suggest that the prevalence of [V PP] in the bilingual children is merely a response to the input, two differences between the bilingual and monolingual children remain to be explained:

(i) quantitatively, the bilinguals show a higher proportion of [V PP] order (table 7.3);

(ii) qualitatively, the bilingual children show developmental errors, specifically non-target instances of [V PP] which the monolingual children do not (table 7.4).

These differences suggest that for a monolingual child, the Cantonese input is sufficient to induce the correct generalization, limiting [V PP] order to certain classes of verb and preventing overextension. To a bilingual child, however, the Cantonese input provides two options, one of which [V PP] coincides with the invariant order of English. The ambiguity of evidence (as defined in section 2.6.3) in Cantonese here opens the door to English influence, even in Cantonese-dominant children such as our three siblings and Llywelyn, and possibly also in the not-quite-monolingual child LTF. Some fluctuation in usage suggests that this ambiguity does lead to uncertainty in the bilingual children. Alicia shows ambivalence, for example, using a PP both before and after the verb in the same sentence with the verbs *co5* 'sit' (22) and *zyu6* 'live' (23), verbs which allow both orders in Cantonese (see section 7.1.1):

(22)   Lei5 *hai2dou6* co5 *hai2dou6*
        you   here   sit here
        'Sit here.'   (Alicia 2;03;02)

(23)   Dog-dog *hai2 li1dou6* zyu6 *hai2 gaan1 uk1 go2dou6*
        dog-dog at   here   live at   CL   house there
        'The dog lives here, in the house.'   (Alicia 2;06;09)

In one example Timmy reformulates a sentence, first producing a target-like [PP V] and, after some hesitation, replacing it with a non-target [V PP] structure:

(24) Lei5 li1 go3 hai2 go2dou6 go2 # waan2 # *hai2* ... *li1dou6* waan2
      you this CL   at   there   that   play   at   here   play

      hai2 go2dou6 gaa3
      at   there   SFP
      'Your one is there . . . here . . . play here.'   (Timmy 2;03;17)

7.1.4   Word order universals

A final factor to be considered in the placement of locative PPs with *hai2* 'at' involves the role of language universals. In a sample of some 600 languages, Dryer (2003) finds only three SVO languages with [PP V] order, all being dialects of Chinese. The rarity of the combination [SVO] and [PP V] is readily explained in the processing perspective of Hawkins (1990, 1994): the combination of VO (verb-object) and [V PP] order results in consistently head-initial phrases and more efficient parsing, while the combination of VO (head-initial) and [PP V] (head-final) phrases is less efficient in terms of early recognition of the constituents of a sentence (Hawkins 1994). Given that the placement of locative PPs is one of very few areas in which English influences Cantonese even in Cantonese-dominant children, there is an intriguing parallel between the typological rarity of [PP V] order and its vulnerability in bilingual acquisition. Clearly, the children have no way of knowing that Cantonese is so unusual in preferring [PP V] order, just as they have no way of knowing that prenominal relative clauses are unexpected in a VO language (see chapter 6). A more plausible hypothesis would be that the same factors which underlie the rarity of [PP V] in VO languages also render it vulnerable in bilingual acquisition. One possibility which might be explored is that [PP V] order is especially difficult for children to parse and/or produce due to their limited processing capacity. If so, the same processing factors which underlie the rarity of [PP V] in VO languages would underlie the vulnerability of [PP V] in bilingual acquisition. Similarly, to the extent that [PP V] order is inefficient in a VO language, it may be vulnerable to contact-induced change (though apparently not to internal change, to the extent that no such tendency can be observed in monolinguals).

7.1.5   Summary

The placement of Cantonese prepositional phrases with *hai2* 'at' shows both qualitative and quantitative influence from English. Qualitatively, bilingual children produce ill-formed [V PP] structures which monolingual Cantonese-speaking children do not. Quantitatively, English influence shifts the balance in favour of [V PP] order in the bilingual children's Cantonese. Bilingual acquisition therefore provides a mechanism by which shifts in basic word order can occur. It is well known that changes in word order do occur in language contact situations. Thomason (2001: 88) discussed a number of cases: Akkadian, a Semitic language with inherited VSO word order and Ethiopic Semitic languages with inherited SVO word order acquired SOV word order from Sumerian and Cushitic languages respectively; similarly Finnish, a Uralic language, is thought to have shifted from SOV to SVO order under Indo-European influence.

7.2   Dative constructions with *bei2* 'give' in bilingual children's Cantonese

We now return to the case of dative constructions with the verb *bei2* 'give' with which this chapter began. The phenomenon involves the non-target word order in double object constructions with *bei2* 'give':

(25)   Bei2 keoi5 zyu1gu1lik1 laa1
       Give him   chocolate   SFP
       'Give him chocolate.'   (Timmy 2;07;04)

(26)   Je4sou1 bei2 (ng)o5 cin2   aa3
       Jesus   give me   money SFP
       'Jesus gave me money.'   (Sophie 2;05;02)

The recipients (R) *keoi5* 'him' in (25) and *ngo5* 'me' in (26) precede the theme (T) objects *zyu1gu1lik1* 'chocolate' and *cin2* 'money' respectively, resulting in the non-target [V-R-T] order which contrasts with the target [V-T-R] order (see further discussion in section 7.2.1 below):

(27)   Bei2 di1 zyu1gu1lik1 keoi5 laa1
       give CL chocolate   him   SFP
       'Give him some chocolate.'

Given that the non-target order coincides with that in English, one may suspect that it might be due to cross-linguistic influence from English. As in the case of postverbal placement of PPs (section 7.1), however, the possibility of English influence on bilingual children's Cantonese involves several complications:
  (i) The order [V-R-T] which the bilingual children are using does exist in adult Cantonese as a variant order;
  (ii) monolingual children also use the non-target [V-R-T] word order;
  (iii) universal factors appear to favour the order [V-R-T] over the target Cantonese structure [V-T-R].
In many respects the case of the *bei2* 'give' dative is parallel to the case of locative prepositional phrases already discussed in section 7.1: the picture is complicated by the existence of [V-R-T] order in the input where the order of

R and T is subject to processing constraints (see section 7.2.2). The fact that parallel non-target structures are indeed attested in monolingual acquisition of Cantonese also renders the question of cross-linguistic influence in this domain correspondingly more complex (see section 7.2.3). Moreover, cross-linguistic investigation of similar constructions suggests that [V-R-T] is the order more frequently attested in languages of the world (see section 7.2.4).

7.2.1 The dative construction in English and Cantonese

Cantonese differs from both English and Mandarin Chinese in the order of objects with the verb 'give'. Characterizing the objects in semantic terms, we will refer to the direct object as theme (T) and the dative or indirect object as recipient (R):

(28) Wo gei ni   qian
      I   give you money
      'I give you money.'
      gei 'give': [_ NP NP][7]
                    recipient theme   (Mandarin)

(29) Ngo5 bei2 cin2   lei5
      I   give money you
      'I give you money.'
      bei2: [_ NP NP]
              theme recipient   (Cantonese)

The dative construction [V-T-R] has often been singled out as an 'aberrant' property of Cantonese, topping the list of grammatical points of divergence from Mandarin (e.g. Chao 1968: 13; Browning 1974). The term 'Inverted Double Object Construction' for Cantonese (Tang 1998) reflects the perception that the order [V-R-T], as in English and Mandarin, is normal for dative object constructions, while the order [V-T-R] as in Cantonese is 'inverted'.

In Cantonese, *bei2* 'give' is essentially the only verb participating in the double object dative construction with [V-T-R] order.[8] The issue of which verbs participate in the dative alternation thus does not arise as it does in English (Pinker 1989).[9] Other dative predicates, such as *gei3* 'send' and *maai5* 'buy' (see section 7.2.6), are used in a serial verb construction together with *bei2* 'give' as the second verb:[10]

(30) Ngo5 gei3 seon3 bei2 keoi5
      I   mail letter give him
      'I send him a letter.'

The uniqueness of *bei2* 'give' is in turn connected with this serial verb construction. If *bei2* 'give' were to be used as the first verb in this construction, the resulting sentence would use *bei2* 'give' twice:

(31)   ?*Bei2* lai5mat6 *bei2* keoi5dei6
         give present give them
         'Give a present to them.'

Such repetition is resisted, unless a substantial distance intervenes between the two instances of *bei2* as in (32):

(32)   Ngo5 *bei2*-zo2 bun2 jung6 Zung1man2 se2   ge3 jyu5faat3
         I   give-PFV CL   use   Chinese   write PRT grammar
         syu1 *bei2* keoi5
         book give   her
         'I gave a grammar book written in Chinese to her.'

As pointed out by Tang (1998: 44), the grammaticality of this type of sentence improves as the distance between the two instances of *bei2* 'give' increases. This is consistent with a formal analysis in which the second *bei2* is deleted (Xu & Peyraube 1997; Tang 1998) as in (33):

(33)   bei2 NP bei2 NP   → bei2 NP [e] NP

Deletion of the second *bei2* 'give' (leaving a null dative case marker in Tang's analysis) thus gives rise to the surface word order of the 'canonical' Cantonese dative construction [V-T-R] with one *bei2* 'give' only. Although positing a somewhat abstract source for such a basic construction of the language, such an analysis is plausible for a number of reasons:
(a) the dropping of the second *bei2* 'give' can be attributed to haplology (for which there are other precedents in Chinese: Tang 2000), whereby two phonologically identical morphemes are reduced to one;
(b) the 'underlying' structure [*bei2* NP *bei2* NP] can occur when the first object is very long, as in (32);
(c) it explains why *bei2* 'give' is the only verb to consistently allow [V-T-R] order, since it is only with *bei2* 'give' that the repetition arises as in (31).

Developmental evidence that the Cantonese [V-T-R] order is based on a serial verb construction, and on *bei2* ... *bei2*, as in (32), in particular, comes from children's use of *bei2* 'give'. Chan (2003) found that both monolingual and bilingual children produce the [*bei2*-T-*bei2*-R] constructions. Some early examples from Cancorp are given in Chan (2003: 102):

(34)   Bei2 cin2   bei2 lei5 aa1
         give money give you SFP
         '(I) give money to you.'   (CGK 2;03;04)

(35)   Baa1baa1 bei2 hung1sung1beng2 bei2 Hou6zeon1
         daddy   give muffin   give Hou6zeon1
         'Daddy gives a muffin to Houzeon (child's name).'   (MHZ 2;03;09)

This 'double-*bei2*' construction is of particular interest since it appears to 'spell out' the underlying structure posited in (33), before haplology applies to delete the second *bei2* 'give.' For two out of eight monolingual children represented in Cancorp, the earliest use of *bei2* with both T and R overtly present took the form [*bei2* NP *bei2* NP], as illustrated in (34) and (35) (Chan 2003: 77). In the later stages of acquisition this double-*bei2* construction continues to appear sporadically, alongside the other options (more commonly, the children produce the non-target order [V-R-T] as in (25) and (26) above). Data from our bilingual children show similar use of the [*bei2* NP *bei2* NP] serial verb construction:

(36)   Ji1   go3 *bei2* ji1   go3   *bei2* lei5
        this CL   give   this   CL   give   you
        'This one, I give you this one.'   (Timmy 2;07;28)

(37)   *Bei2* jat1 go3 *bei2* lei5 aa1
        CL   one   CL   give   you   SFP
        'I give you one.'   (Sophie 2;11;18)

In the case of Alicia, as with the monolingual children CGK and MHZ, the first full datives attested take this form:

(38)   *Bei2* jat1 go3 *bei2* ngo5, jat1 go3 . . .
        give   one   CL   give   me,   one   CL
        'Give one to me, one . . .'   (Alicia 1;11;05)

7.2.2   *Variants of the canonical dative construction*

Though [V-T-R] is the default order in adult Cantonese, the alternative word order [V-R-T] is also used in some environments. In Hong Kong Cantonese, at least, the more basic form must be assumed to be [V-T-R] as in (39), since in the simplest case [V-R-T] order is ill-formed (40):

(39)   Bei2 min2 ngo5
        give face me
        'Give me face.'   [V-T-R]

(40)   ?*Bei2 ngo5 min2
        give   me   face
        'Give me face.'   *[V-R-T]

When the direct object is longer than the indirect object, both orders are possible, especially if the direct object is the focus of contrast (41c):

(41)   a. Keoi5dei6 bei2 hou2 do1   cin2   ngo5
           they   give very much money   me
           'They give me a lot of money.'

b. ?Keoi5dei6 bei2 ngo5 hou2 do1   cin2
   they   give me   very much   money
   'They give me a lot of money.'

c. Keoi5dei6 bei2 ngo5 hou2 do1   cin2,   m4hai6 hou2 siu2 cin2
   they   give me   very much   money   not-be very little money
   They give me a lot of money, not very little money.'

In cases like (41b & 41c) the Theme NP is displaced to the right, comparable to Heavy NP Shift in English.

Another point to be considered is that although the [V-T-R] order can be considered the canonical dative construction with *bei2* 'give', the full dative configuration with both objects in place is not overwhelmingly frequent in discourse. In fact, based on the Cancorp data, it constitutes only 29.5% of *bei2* datives in child-directed speech (Chan 2003: 53). There are a number of reasons for this:

(i) Cantonese allows null objects (see chapter 5), which means that the theme argument is often not realized in the *bei2* 'give' dative construction:[11]

(42)   Lei5 bei2 [e] ngo5 laa1
        you   give   me   SFP
        'Give (it) to me.'

Such utterances with a null theme surfacing as [*bei2*-R] sequences constitute some 48.5% of usages in child-directed speech (Chan 2003: 53). In Cancorp, when *bei2* 'give' is followed by another argument, it is often the recipient (75 tokens = 82.4%)) but less frequently the theme (16 tokens = 17.6%) as shown by Chan (2003: 75). The theme in the [*bei2*-T] sequences is typically *cin2* 'money' used as fixed expressions by the monolingual children while the recipient in the [*bei2*-R] expressions is realized as different pronouns and lexical NPs. The bilingual children show an even greater preference for [*bei2*-R]: there is a total of 100 tokens (80%) of [*bei2*-R], and 25 tokens (20%) of [*bei2*-T] in the bilingual Cantonese data. The English-dominant child Charlotte produced as many as 15 tokens of [*bei2*-R], but no [*bei2*-T] or full *bei2* datives. The fact that Charlotte only produced [*bei2*-R] during 1;08–3;00 and the other five bilingual children overwhelmingly use [*bei2*-R] suggests that it is the precursor to the acquisition of the full *bei2* datives.

(ii) Cantonese is a topic-prominent language where topicalization is highly productive, which together with focusing and other movement operations results in frequent displacement of the theme argument. In (43) the theme object *bun2 syu1* 'the book' appears displaced in topic position, the result of topicalization of the object as shown in (44):

(43)   Bun2 syu1 ngo5 bei2 lei5 ge3
         CL   book I   give you SFP
         'I give the book to you.'

(44)   [Bun2 syu1] ngo5 bei2 [e] lei5 ge3

As a consequence of the frequently missing and displaced theme objects, the 'basic' order [V-T-R] is not readily visible to the child. This has implications for the explanation of the non-target forms based on properties of the input (see section 7.2.4).

7.2.3   Bilingual and monolingual children's full bei2 'give' datives compared

Here we compare the frequencies of 'full datives', i.e. those where both objects are present after the verb *bei2* 'give' in the bilingual and monolingual corpus (recall that objects are often null or displaced in Cantonese, as discussed in section 7.2.2 above: it is only when both objects are overtly realized in postverbal position that their order can be determined). Table 7.6 shows the distribution of Cantonese full *bei2* datives (with both T and R present in postverbal position) produced by the six bilingual children.

In general, the number of full *bei2* datives is low since the theme is often null or displaced in Cantonese. Apart from the English-dominant child, Charlotte, whose corpus does not contain any relevant tokens, the five remaining bilingual children produced a total of 51 full *bei2* datives (13 in Timmy, 19 in Sophie, 5 in Alicia, 7 in Llywelyn and 7 in Kathryn). The proportion of non-target [*bei2*-R-T] orders is 84.6% in Timmy, 94.7% in Sophie, 100% in Alicia and 85.7% in Llywelyn. Kathryn's non-target rate of 71.4% is lower than the other bilingual children. Overall the distribution of non-target [*bei2*-R-T] vs. target [*bei2*-T-R] orders is 45 (88.2%) vs. 6 (11.8%): the non-target forms far outnumber the target ones in our Cantonese-English bilingual child language corpus.

We now turn to the distribution of full *bei2* datives in eight monolingual Cantonese-speaking children from Cancorp, as shown in table 7.7. Three out of eight monolingual Cantonese-speaking children (CCC, CKT, MHZ) did not produce any *bei2* 'give' datives with both T and R present. Two children (HHC and WBH) produced only one token of non-target [*bei2*-R-T] and no target [*bei2*-T-R] forms, while three children (CGK, LTF and LLY) produced eight or more tokens. Among these three children's total of 31 full datives, 19 (61.3%) take the non-target [*bei2*-R-T] form while 12 (38.7%) take the target [*bei2*-T-R]

Table 7.6. *Frequency of Cantonese full bei2 'give' datives in six bilingual children*

Child	Timmy	Sophie	Alicia	Llywelyn	Kathryn	Charlotte	Total
Age	2;01.22–3;06;25	1;06;00–3;00;09	1;03;10–3;00;24	2;00;12–3;04;17	3;06;18–4;06;07	1;08.28–3;00.03	
Non-target [*bei2*-R-T]	11 (84.6%)	18 (94.7%)	5 (100%)	6 (85.7%)	5 (71.4%)	0	45 (88.2%)
Target [*bei2*-T-R]	2 (15.4%)	1 (5.3%)	0	1 (14.3%)	2 (28.6%)	0	6 (11.8%)
Total no. of full datives	13	19	5	7	7	0	51

Table 7.7. *Frequency of Cantonese full bei2 'give' datives in eight monolingual children in Cancorp (Lee et al. 1996, based on Chan 2003:79)*

Child	CCC	CKT	CGK	HHC	LTF	LLY	MHZ	WBH	Total
Age	1;10;08–2;10;27	1;05;22–2;07;22	1;11;01–2;09;09	2;04;08–3;04;14	2;02;10–3;02;18	2;08;10–3;08;09	1;07–2;08;06	2;03;23–3;04;08	
Non-target [*bei2*-R-T]	0	0	9 (69%)	1(N/A)	4 (50%)	6 (60%)	0	1 (N/A)	21 (63.6%)
Target [*bei2*-T-R]	0	0	4 (31%)	0	4 (50%)	4 (40%)	0	0	12 (36.4%)
Total no. of full datives	0	0	13	1	8	10	0	1	33

form. Overall, the distribution of non-target [*bei2*-R-T] vs. target [*bei2*-T-R] orders in five children who produced at least one full dative is 21 (63.6%) vs. 12 (36.4%): the proportion of non-target forms is nearly twice that of the target forms.

While the non-target order appears as the majority even in monolingual children, the proportion of full datives showing non-target order is still higher in the bilingual children. Comparing the frequency of the non-target [*bei2*-R-T] order in the bilingual and monolingual corpus data, it can be seen that the bilingual percentages are greater than their monolingual counterparts (88.2% vs. 63.6%). This difference is significant on a χ^2 test ($\chi^2 = 7.2$, $p < 0.05$, 2-tailed).[12]

Next, we compare the age of first emergence of the forms under investigation in the two groups of children. The results are given in table 7.8 and table 7.9. Table 7.8 shows that the non-target [*bei2*-R-T] form emerges before the [*bei2*-T-R] form in three children (Sophie at 2;03, Alicia at 2;03 and Llywelyn at 2;09); target forms are not attested in Alicia's corpus, while both forms are attested from Kathryn in the same file at 3;03. The target [*bei2*-T-R] form emerges earlier than the non-target [*bei2*-R-T] form in Timmy by two and a half months. As no relevant tokens are attested in the Charlotte corpus, the age of emergence cannot be determined. Full *bei2* datives were first attested in the corpus data at around 2;03 in two of the monolingual children (CGK and LTF, whose recording started at 1;11;01 and 2;02;10 respectively). Generalizing across the results of the monolingual children in table 7.9, it seems that non-target [*bei2*-R-T] order is attested either earlier than or at the same time as the target order [*bei2*-T-R] in all five children who produced at least one token of these forms. None of the eight monolingual children use the target [V-T-R] order when they first express both the theme and the recipient. These children instead use the non-canonical forms: the [T-*bei2*-R] form with preposed theme in CCC, HHC and WBH; the [*bei2*-R-T] order in LTF and LLY; and the serial verb form [*bei2*-T-*bei2*-R] in CGK and MHZ.

The bilingual and monolingual corpus findings suggest that the non-target [*bei2*-R-T] form emerges before the target [*bei2*-T-R] form almost by default. Furthermore, none of the eight monolingual Cantonese children produced the target word order [V-T-R] on their first use of a full *bei2* dative, despite its relatively high frequency among the adult full datives.

7.2.4   Discussion: properties of the input

The case of PP placement discussed above (section 7.1) presents a clear instance of ambiguity of evidence as defined in section 2.6.3: both orders, [PP V] and [V PP] are commonly instantiated in the Cantonese input, creating overlap between the English and Cantonese grammars and a potential ambiguity with regard to

Table 7.8. *Age of first emergence of Cantonese full* bei2 *'give' datives in six bilingual children*

Child	Timmy	Sophie	Alicia	Llywelyn	Kathryn	Charlotte
bei2-R-T	2;07;14	2;03;24	2;03;16	2;09;07	3;03;16	not attested
bei2-T-R	2;04;28	2;08;00	not attested	2;10;14	3;03;16	not attested

Table 7.9. *Age of first emergence of Cantonese full* bei2 *'give' datives in eight monolingual children in Cancorp (Lee et al. 1996)*

Child	CCC	CKT	CGK	HHC	LTF	LLY	MHZ	WBH
bei2-R-T	not attested	not attested	2;03;11	2;10;13	2;03;30	2;11;01	not attested	2;09;19
bei2-T-R	not attested	not attested	2;03;11	not attested	2;07;20	3;02;06	not attested	not attested

the target Cantonese grammar. For the case of the *bei2* dative, ambiguity of this kind is less clear-cut: while the input may be said to be ambiguous in the sense that both [V-T-R] and [V-R-T] orders are attested in the input, the latter option is relatively rare. The adult input findings reported in Chan (2003: 55) show that the [*bei2*-R-T] orders are infrequent (9.33%) in adult-to-adult speech in Leung and Law's (2002) Hong Kong Cantonese Adult Language Corpus, and are used even less frequently in Cancorp in Cantonese child-directed speech: the [*bei2*-R-T] amounts to only 0.27%, while the canonical [*bei2*-T-R] form represents 29.52% of the total *bei2* dative constructions. Consequently, to invoke ambiguity of evidence in Cantonese on the basis of such variation is questionable. However, a further case of input ambiguity involves sentences with a relative clause (RC) containing *bei2* 'give'. Consider the following hypothetical example:

(45)   A: Lei5 jiu3   bin1   fan6 lai5mat6 aa3?
            you   want which CL   present   SFP
            'Which present do you want?'

          B: [RC Ngo5 kam4jat6 bei2 keoi5] go2   fan6 lai5mat6
              I   yesterday give   her   DEM   CL   present
              'The present that I gave her yesterday.'

In (45), the relative clause in B's reply has exactly the same surface order as a main clause where the verb *bei2* is followed by R and T as in child Cantonese.

In terms of adult grammar, the [V-R] sequence *bei2 keoi5* 'give her' modifies the Theme object, hence the apparent [V-R-T] word order. As discussed in chapter 6, however, children may not know this, especially if they are applying the internally headed relative clause analysis in which relative clauses share the structure of main clauses. To such children, relative clauses such as that in (45) would exemplify [V-R-T] order. Although not the canonical order of *bei2* datives, there is a precedent for this order in adult Cantonese: the order [V-R-T] does occur as an alternative order, especially when the indirect object is a heavy NP (Matthews & Yip 1994: 137). There is thus some ambiguity in the input data. The fact that monolingual as well as bilingual children produce non-target [V-R-T] constructions suggests that there is an inherent difficulty in Cantonese which gives rise to non-target datives as a developmental phenomenon. This difficulty is compounded in the case of bilingual children by the presence of English dative constructions which uniformly instantiate the very order [V-R-T] which occurs naturally as a developmental phenomenon in Cantonese. The *bei2* dative is thus a 'vulnerable domain' of the kind discussed in section 2.7.

A further type of ambiguity in the Cantonese input was pointed out in Chan (2003). As we have seen, full datives (with both objects in situ following the verb 'give') are a minority pattern in the input. More commonly, the direct object is null as in (46), (see chapter 5) or displaced as in (47), where *li1 go3* 'this' is topicalized in the adult utterance):

(46)   INV: Bei2 ngo5
              give   me
              'Give (it) to me.'

        CHI: Bei2 jat1 go3 bei2 ngo5, jat1 go3
              give   one CL   give   me   one CL
              'Give one to me, one . . .'   (Alicia 1;11;05)

(47)   INV: Li1 go3 bei2 bin1go3 aa3?
              this CL give   who   SFP
              'Who is this for?'

        CHI: bei2 lei5 lo1
              give   you SFP
              'for you'   (Alicia 2;04;20)

In either case, the adult sentence fails to show where exactly the theme object belongs: before, or after the Recipient? That is, faced with [V-R] as in the above examples, it is not clear whether the underlying structure would be [V-(T)-R] or [V-R-(T)]. Worse still, such sentences present the Recipient immediately following the verb, creating an apparent [V-R] complex. This constitutes a type of input ambiguity which helps to explain the occurrence of errors in monolingual as well as bilingual acquisition. In the case of the bilingual children, the ambiguity in the Cantonese input opens the door for English influence: the invariant English [V-R-T] order boosts Cantonese [V-R-T] order as one of the possible orders sanctioned by Cantonese grammar.

7.2.5   Code-mixing in dative constructions

One further difference between bilingual and monolingual children is that a substantial proportion of the non-target [V-R-T] datives produced by bilinguals are cases of code-mixing, in which the theme object is an English noun phrase:[13]

(48)   Ngo5 m4 bei2 lei5 *tickser book*
        I   not give you sticker book
        'I'm not giving you the sticker book.'   (Alicia 2;10;29)

(49)   Jyu4gwo2 lei5 m4 gwaai1, ngo5 m4 bei2 lei5 *sticker*
        if   you not good   I   not give you sticker
        'If you don't behave, I won't give you stickers.'   (Alicia 3;08;11)

(50)   Timmy, tau4sin1 Lulu m4 bei2 ngo5 *slime* aa3!
        Timmy just now Lulu not give me   slime SFP
        'Timmy, just now Lulu didn't give me slime!'   (Alicia 3;10;13)

In (48)–(50), the verb *bei2* 'give' is immediately followed by the recipient *lei5* 'you' and then by the theme object in English (*tickser book, sticker, slime* – all objects of interest for children of this age). Sophie continues to produce such examples (albeit with different objects of interest) as late as at age 7, as recorded in diary data:

(51)   Belma bei2 ngo5dei6 *lipstick*
        Belma give us   lipstick
        'Belma gave us lipstick.'   (Sophie 7;00;16)

It thus appears that the [*bei2*-R-T] is particularly prevalent where the object (T) is code-mixed. This can be interpreted in at least two ways: perhaps use of an English noun phrase in sentence planning activates English syntax, and/or use of [V-R-T] order favours code-mixing, by virtue of congruence with English syntax. In adult usage, too, code-mixing of the theme NP is one factor favouring [V-R-T] order, as in the following example:[14]

(52)   Zik1 hai6 hou2 general gam2 joeng2 bei2 lei5 jat1 go3
        that is   very general such way   give you a   CL
        ge3 guideline gam2 joeng2
        PRT guideline such way
        'That is, to give you a guideline in a general way.'

Note that code-mixing of pronouns is not found, and not expected, since pronouns are closed-class items which generally do not participate in code-mixing. We therefore do not see examples where the pronoun after *bei2* 'give' is in English such as:

(53)   *Bei2   *me* jat   go
         give   me one CL
         'Give me one.'

7.2.6   Other dative verbs: novel use of buy and maai5 'buy' in the bilingual data

While the verb *bei2* 'give' is unique in Cantonese, other dative verbs present problems for the bilingual children. In Sophie's Cantonese, non-target order is found in the use of *maai5* 'buy' followed by *bei2*, Recipient and Theme. The *bei2* here has the same form of the verb *bei2* 'give' in the *bei2* dative:

(54)   CHI: You want hamburger, I want two ice cream.
         INV: Okay, you want ice cream.

         CHI: Maai5 bei2 ngo5dei6 go2 . . .
              buy   for   us   DEM . . .
              'buy us that . . .'

     Grandma: Gong2 je5   zau6 ting1jat6 maai5
               talk   thing then tomorrow   buy
               'If you talk (a lot), then I'll buy (you) (this) tomorrow.'

         CHI: *Lei5 maai5 bei2 ngo5 go3 syut3gou1*
              you   buy   for   me   CL   ice cream
              'You buy ice cream for me.'   (Sophie 2;08;22)

In cases such as (54), the target structure requires that the theme object immediately follow the verb *maai5* 'buy' as in:[15]

(55)   Lei5 maai5 go3 syut3gou1 bei2 ngo5
         you   buy   CL   ice cream for   me
         'You buy ice cream for me.'

Another complex structure involving *maai5* 'buy' which invites the non-target order is the serial verb construction where a series of verbs are involved:

(56)   Ngo5 m4   maai5 bei2 lei5 sik6 ice cream gaa3
         I   not buy   for   you   eat   ice cream SFP
         'I'm not buying ice cream for you to eat.'   (Sophie 2;05;16)

The target order for (56) again requires that the theme object *ice cream* be adjacent to the verb *maai5* 'buy' as in (57):

(57)   Ngo5 m4 maai5 ice cream bei2 lei5 sik6 gaa3
        I   not buy   ice cream for you eat SFP
        'I'm not buying ice cream for you to eat.'

In (57), a total of three verbs occur in close succession: *maai5* 'buy' is followed by *bei2* 'give' and then *sik6* 'eat'. Here *bei2* is glossed as 'for' but is in fact ambiguous between a verb and a preposition. If *bei2* is perceived as the equivalent of English *for* in these constructions, it suggests an account for the English sentences below, where *buy* is followed by [pp *for* NP]. Interestingly, shortly before producing example (56), the child produced (58) with the target word order (but with a missing classifier after the demonstrative *li1* 'this'):

(58)   Ngo5 m4 maai5 li1 bei2 lei5 sik6 gaa3 wo3
        I   not buy   this for you eat SFP SFP
        'I'm not buying this for you to eat.'   (Sophie 2;05;16)

It seems that Sophie's grammar allows both word orders. Since the simpler structure with [*maai5-bei2*-R-T] is rather entrenched, it is likely that the complex structure with yet another verb [*maai5-bei2*-R-V-T] will only be reinforced given the robustness of the simpler structure.

    Parallel structures to those in (54) and (56) also appear in the bilingual children's English. Out of six bilingual children, non-target word order involving the dative verb *buy* is found in two children, who place the PP [*for* NP] immediately after the verb while the theme NP follows the PP, resulting in [V PP NP] order as in (59)–(60):

(59)   I buy for you the bear okay?   (Sophie 2;05;30)

(60)   Will buy for Kenny that.   (Llywelyn 3;04)

These sentences are in striking contrast to the target forms where the theme object appears immediately after the verb in the order [V NP PP] as in (61):

(61)   Mummy next time buy sunglasses for me?   (Sophie 2;03;18)

One implication of these data is that there is bidirectional influence in this domain. On the one hand, the Cantonese dative construction with *bei2* 'give' is influenced by the English. On the other hand, the non-target Cantonese dative with *maai5* 'buy' as in (54) is transferred to English dative with *buy*.

7.2.7   Resolution

We have already suggested that quantitative differences between bilingual and monolingual children imply cross-linguistic influence from English. Further evidence comes from the eventual resolution of the errors. In monolingual children, the non-target structure is superceded by the target dative structure by age three or four (Chan 2003). In the bilingual children's Cantonese, however, the non-target structure persists until age seven and beyond, apparently due to the influence of English which instantiates the [V-R-T] order. Although regular recording of Timmy ended after age four, he makes occasional appearances in Sophie's corpus data, and happens to use a non-target dative construction at 5;08:

(62)   Ngo5 m4   bei2 lei5 tong2tong2
         I   not give you   candy
         'I won't give you any candy.'   (Timmy 5;08;00)

Similarly, diary data show Sophie using [V-R-T] as late as age seven:

(63)   Ngo5 bei2 lei5 bin1go3 hou2 aa3?
         I   give you   which   good SFP
         'Which one should I give you?'   (Sophie 7;01;30)

(64)   Hai6 laa3, Jan bei2 ngo5 laam4sik1, Jan bei2 lei5 caang2sik1 ge3
         is   SFP   Jan give me   blue   Jan give you   orange   SFP
         'Yes, Jan gave me the blue one, Jan gave you the orange one.'
                                                                    (Sophie 7;11;03)

In addition, there are a few surprising examples where *maai5* 'buy' is used like English *buy* in a double object construction (see section 7.2.6):

(65)   Maai5 ngo5 jat1 go3 aa1
         buy   me   one   CL   SFP
         'Buy me one.'   (Sophie 9;03;00)

A further factor here is a gradual shift in language dominance: from age five onwards, Timmy and Sophie attended an English primary school all day, and English influence increased. It seems likely that their Cantonese will remain marked by more extensive use of non-target features such as [*bei2*-R-T] order than in monolinguals.

7.2.8   Datives in typology and in contact languages

The [V-T-R] double object construction appears to be dispreferred in the world's languages. The [V-T-R] double object form is attested in certain areas: in Southeast Asia, it is found in Cantonese and some other Chinese dialects (Tang 1998; Liu 2001), and in Thai as well as other Tai languages (Matthews 2006a); in West Africa, most languages have [V-R-T] while Ewe is unusual in also allowing [V-T-R] (Essegbey 2002). As these are all serializing languages, the distribution is consistent with analyses which relate the [V-T-R] double object construction to serial verb constructions (see section 7.2.1).

The [V-R-T] word order has also been identified as the unmarked word order from a functional-typological perspective in Kozinsky and Polinsky (1993), who proposed a tentative universal on coding of the thematic recipient and theme in ditransitive constructions: in *Agent-before-Patient* languages, the recipient precedes the theme; and in *Patient-before-Agent* languages, the theme precedes the recipient. In this regard, Cantonese is an exception with respect to the verb-recipient-theme/agent-before-patient correlation, since Cantonese is an *Agent-before-Patient* language with [V-T-R] order.

As to why the recipient should precede the theme in the dative construction, a functional account is offered by Givón (1984: 139), who proposed the topic hierarchy where dative/benefactive roles rank high (second to agents) since like agents, they are likely to be human/animate argument (Givón 1984: 371), which in turn suggests that their animacy makes them more accessible as topics.[16]

Bruyn, Muysken and Verrips (1999) argue that the [V-R-T] construction is universally unmarked in Universal Grammar (UG), based on its cross-linguistic frequency in creole languages and its early emergence in acquisition data:

The ease of acquisition of DOCs [i.e. double object constructions] in Dutch and English, as well as their widespread distribution in creole languages suggest that UG provides children with DOCs as an unmarked value. (363)

Dutch children produce the first DOCs at around 2;05–2;06. Bruyn, Muysken and Verrips (1999) noted that DOCs are generally rare in the Dutch CHILDES corpora they looked at and that 'the scarcity of double-object data is not only due to lack of data in general but also to the fact that these constructions apparently emerge very slowly' (Bruyn, Muysken & Verrips 1999: 360).

In a study of both Creole and non-Creole child grammar, Adone (2002) shows that there is a preference for the [V-R-T] order over the [V-T-R] order in DOCs. Evidence from cross-linguistic comparison of acquisition data of English, Dutch, Chinese, Morisyen and Seselwa is adduced to support her claim that DOC with [V-R-T] order is a default pattern in child language acquisition. Michaelis and Haspelmath (2003) suggest an alternative explanation, pointing out that creoles show double object constructions where the relevant substrate languages also have them.

7.2.9   Contact-induced word order change

As we suggested for the case of [PP V] order, the ambiguity with the dative makes the [V-T-R] construction vulnerable to contact-induced change. Killingley (1993) argues that in Malayan Cantonese, the basic order is in fact [*bei2*-R-T] rather than [*bei2*-T-R]. This may be explained by contact with Min dialects such as Hokkien and Teochew in which [*give*-R-T] prevails. Hulk and Van der Linden make a similar point about the effect of language contact on the frequency of object fronting in French-Dutch bilinguals (see section 1.6).

7.2.10   Summary

While both monolingual and bilingual children produce non-target [*bei2*-R-T] structures, the bilinguals produce it more frequently and over a longer period of development. Properties of the input make this a vulnerable domain: the Cantonese input is often ambiguous with respect to placement of the theme, which is frequently null or displaced. The non-target [*bei2*-R-T] order which is adopted as the default appears to be universally preferred in terms of cross-linguistic distribution as well as acquisition. In the case of bilingual children, influence of English is an additional factor that favours the non-target [*bei2*-R-T] order, irrespective of language dominance. The English target [*bei2*-R-T] order coincides with and reinforces the universally preferred order, making it difficult to unlearn in the bilingual children's Cantonese grammar. The vulnerability of dative constructions thus poses especially challenging learnability problems for bilingual children who have to learn to override the combined force of English order and universally preferred order in order to acquire the [*bei2*-T-R] order.

7.3   Bidirectional transfer in verb-particle constructions in bilingual development

Yip and Matthews (2000a: 206–207) noted two areas in Timmy's bilingual development in which influence of English on Cantonese might be implicated. One is the postverbal placement of prepositional phrases as discussed in section 7.1. The other involves non-target word order in Cantonese verb-particle constructions, as in (66) where the pronoun *keoi5* 'her' separates the verb *baai2* 'put' from the particle *dai1* 'down':

(66)   M4hou2 *baai2* keoi5 *dai1*   laa1
         don't   put   her   down   SFP
         'Don't put her down!' (referring to a child being carried)   (Timmy 3;09;09)

The target Cantonese structure does not allow the pronoun *keoi5* 'her/him' in between *baai2* 'put' and *dai1* 'down' but requires it to be placed after the particle as in *baai2 dai1 keoi5* (literally 'put down her'). The non-target word order in these Cantonese verb-particle constructions is attributed to English influence on Cantonese. At the same time, in the same domain, there is also evidence of transfer from Cantonese to English as in (67):

(67)   Why no light? You turn on it. [i.e. Mid-Autumn Festival lantern]
                                                              (Timmy 3;04;05)

The placement of the pronoun *it* after the particle *on* is ungrammatical in English, but consistent with Cantonese syntax as in (70) below. Since there is overlap between English and Cantonese verb-particle constructions and ambiguity in the input in both languages, this case is more complex than those discussed so far in that the input is variable in both languages. We therefore see cross-linguistic influence in both directions.

7.3.1   Verb-particle constructions in English and Cantonese

Here we compare the verb-particle constructions in English and Cantonese in order to shed light on the analysis of the bilingual data. There are two types of verb-particle constructions (VPCs) in English which we shall term split VPC (68) vs. non-split VPC (69):

(68)   a. Pick the book up.
        b. Pick it up

(69)   a. Pick up the book.
        b. *Pick up it.

The split VPC refers to the cases where the verb and the particle are separated by a lexical noun phrase (68a) or a pronoun (68b) while the non-split VPC refers to those cases where the verb and the particle are adjacent to each other without anything intervening (69a). One well-known fact about this construction is that an unstressed pronoun following the non-split verb-particle resulting in [V-PRT-pronoun] is ungrammatical as in (69b).[17] What happens in the bilingual children's verb-particle constructions is that the ungrammatical order in (69b) is attested in their English as shown in (67). There has been much theoretical discussion about whether the underlying form of this construction should be the split or non-split type. Recent proposals tend to treat the split type as the underlying form and the non-split type as the derived form.[18] In Cantonese, by contrast, the basic order is for the verb and particle to be adjacent as in (70), rather than split as in (71):[19]

(70)   *Baai2 dai1*   go3 bi4bi1/keoi5 laa1
        put   down CL   baby/her   SFP
        'Put down the baby/her!'   (adult Cantonese)

(71)   *Baai2* go3 bi4bi1/keoi5 *dai1*   laa1
        put   CL   baby/her   down SFP
        'Put the baby/her down!'   (adult Cantonese)

There are, however, certain Cantonese constructions in which the verb and particle are separated, notably by the modal *dak1* 'can' as in (72a) and the negator *m* 'not' as in (73a). This construction then allows a further degree of separation, whereby the object (typically a pronoun) also intervenes between the verb and the particle, as in (72b) and (73b).

(72)   a. Ngo5 *pou5* dak1 *hei2* keoi5
           I   carry can   up   her
           'I can carry her (manage to do so)'

        b. Ngo5 *pou5* dak1 keoi5 *hei2*
           I   carry can   her   up
           'I can carry her (manage to do so)'

(73)   a. Ngo5 *pou5* m4 *hei2* keoi5
           I   carry not up   her
           'I can't carry her' (she's too heavy')

        b. Ngo5 *pou5* keoi5 m4 *hei2*
           I   carry her   not up
           'I can't carry her.' (she's too heavy)

Given the lexical-semantic resemblances between verb-particle combinations in the two languages and the syntactic similarities with respect to separability as in (72)–(73), there is considerable overlap between the English and Cantonese constructions, and a precedent in Cantonese for separating the verb and particle. Such overlap constitutes one of the conditions for transfer identified by Hulk and Müller (2000); and as they point out, this factor is in principle independent of language dominance. That bilingual children perceive this overlap is suggested by cases of code-mixing such as the following, where they insert English verb-particle combinations into Cantonese frames:

(74)   Ji1 zek6 slide m4 dou2 down aa3
        this CL   slide not able down SFP
        'With these (shoes) one can't slide down.'   (Timmy 2;11;18)

(75)   Dim2gaai2 lei5 throw ni1 go3 away ge2?
        why   you throw this CL away SFP
        'Why do you throw this one away?'   (Kathryn 3;07;13)

In (74) Timmy uses the English verb-particle combination *slide down* separated by the Cantonese negative *m4* 'not' and the potential particle *dou2*. In (75), Kathryn inserts the combination *throw away* into a Cantonese utterance, separating it in accordance with the preferred order in English [V-NP-PRT] but stretching the grammar of Cantonese in the process since Cantonese does not allow the object NP to appear in this configuration.

7.3.2   Bilingual development of verb-particle constructions

In Timmy's example (66), the separation of verb and particle in Cantonese is consistent with influence from English, where the verb and particle can be freely separated. A similar case is recorded in the diary in which Alicia separates the verb *lau4* 'leave' and the particle *dai1* 'down':

(76)   *Lau4* lei5 *dai1*   hai2 ji1dou6   hou2-m4-hou2   aa3?
       leave you down at   here   good-not-good   SFP
       'Is it okay if we leave you behind here?'   (Alicia 3;02;25)

Although this phenomenon is apparently quite rare in our data, it points to some factors which may underlie transfer in such cases. In particular, to the extent that both languages can be said to have verb-particle constructions (as argued in section 7.3.1 above), there is overlap between the two grammars. In examples such as (66) and (76), the Cantonese verb-particle combination is separated by a pronoun following the English pattern. In the same grammatical domain (verb-particle constructions) there is also influence, both qualitative and quantitative, from Cantonese to English. Like Timmy as seen in (67), Sophie and Alicia use verb-particle constructions such as the following:

(77)   She wake up *me*.   (Sophie 2;05;16)

(78)   Let me to take out *it*, to see. [opens present]   (Sophie 4;02;23)

(79)   CHI: Put in.
       CHI: This put in.
       CHI: Put in *this*.   (Alicia 2;00;26)

The [V-PRT-pronoun] constructions in (77)–(79) are ungrammatical in adult English because the pronouns *me, it* and *this* (unless stressed) must occur between the verb and particle. The bilingual children's grammar reflects the order in Cantonese, as illustrated in (80) and (81):[20]

(80)   Keoi5 giu3   seng2   ngo5
       she   call   awake   me
       'She woke me up'

(81)   Lo2   zau2   li1   go3
       take   away   this   CL
       'Take this away.'

Where there is a choice, the predominant order in monolingual children's English is [V-NP-PRT] as in (82a), while the order in (82b) is the result of 'particle shift' and is more likely to occur when the object is a heavy Noun Phrase (Lohse et al. 2004).[21]

(82)   a. Pick the baby up
       b. Pick up the darling little baby

The basic status of (82a) is reflected in monolingual English-speaking children, who overwhelmingly favour the [V-NP-PRT] order. Sawyer (2001) investigates the distribution of split vs. non-split verb-particle constructions in monolingual English-speaking children.[22] The overall results show an overwhelming preference for the split [V-NP-PRT] order: between 90% and 95% in Adam, Eve and Sarah from ages 1;06–5;01 from Brown (1973) and between 70% and 87% in Adam's late stage files and Ross (2;06–7;09) from MacWhinney (2000a); for details, see Sawyer (2001: 183). In a corpus study of monolingual children's verb-particle constructions, Diessel and Tomasello (2005: 101) analyse the distribution of both pronominal and lexical NPs in Peter (Bloom 1973) and Eve (Brown 1973). Overall, the split [V-NP-PRT] order is overwhelmingly preferred for the two children, in accordance with the adult input. The distribution of lexical NPs in [V-NP-PRT] and [V-PRT-NP] is 86.6% vs. 13.4%. If lexical NPs, personal pronouns and other pronouns are included, the total number of [V-NP-PRT] tokens is 421 (93.6%) and [V-PRT-NP] tokens is 29 (6.4%). Crucially, all 200 (100%) personal pronouns appear in the target split [V-pronoun-PRT] order, i.e. none appears in the non-split order [V-PRT-pronoun], which is ungrammatical in adult English but used by some of our bilingual children as in (77)–(79).

Diessel and Tomasello (2005b) conducted a multifactorial analysis of six linguistic variables correlated with particle placement in adult English based on Gries (1999, 2003). Two variables turned out to be significant, namely the NP type of the direct object and the meaning of the particle. The majority of objects are short and simple, consisting of one or two words as a pronoun, a bare noun, or a noun and a determiner (96%) (Diessel & Tomasello 2005:100). Some verb-particle constructions are used by the two children with both split and non-split orders:

(83)   Pick them up.   (Peter 2;00)

(84)   Pick up my cup.   (Peter 2;01)

(85)   Turn that on.   (Eve 2;03)

(86)   You turn on the fan.   (Eve 2;01)

Other combinations involve fixed particle position in the split order, as in *put NP down/back/in/away* and *have NP on*. Diessel and Tomasello (2005b) attribute the overwhelming predominance of the split orders to the high frequency of spatial particles, which tend to follow the direct object.

In bilingual children, by contrast, the ratio of split [V-NP-PRT] to non-split [V-PRT-NP] orders is much closer. A quantitative study by Ho (2003) compared Timmy and Sophie with the monolingual children, Peter and Allison (Bloom 1973). The comparison shows that bilingual children are far more likely than monolingual children to use the structure [V-PRT-NP] which matches Cantonese. We now look at the distribution of lexical NPs in the bilingual children's verb-particle constructions. The six bilingual children are separated

Table 7.10. *Distribution of lexical NPs and pronouns in four Cantonese-dominant bilingual children's English verb-particle constructions*

Child	Timmy	Sophie	Alicia	Llywelyn	Total
V-NP-PRT (split order)	5	0	1	0	13
V-PRT-NP (non-split order)	12	5	6	4	33
% non-split	70.6	100	85.7	100	71.7
V-pronoun-PRT (split order)	22	7	0	11	60
V-PRT-pronoun (non-split order)	0	10	1	2	24
% non-split	0	58.9	100	15.4	28.6

Table 7.11. *Distribution of lexical NPs and pronouns in two non-Cantonese-dominant bilingual children's English verb-particle constructions*

Child	Charlotte	Kathryn
V-NP-PRT (split order)	7	16
V-PRT-NP (non-split order)	5	0
% non-split	41.7	0
V-pronoun-PRT (split order)	20	21
V-PRT-pronoun (non-split order)	11	1
% non-split	35.5	4.5

into Cantonese-dominant (the three siblings plus Llywelyn) vs. non-Cantonese-dominant groups (Kathryn and Charlotte) as the influence of Cantonese is clearly reflected in the former group.

Table 7.10 shows the distribution of the different word orders in VPCs in four Cantonese-dominant bilingual children. The table separates lexical NP objects (where English offers the choice of orders) from pronouns (where only the split order is permitted in English). The results show that, in contrast to the monolingual findings, the Cantonese-dominant children prefer the non-split order, which makes up 71.7% of the total with lexical NPs. With pronouns as objects, 28.6% appear in the non-split VPCs, but note that this entails ill-formed structures of the kind *she wake up me* which were not found at all in Diessel and Tomasello's (2005b) monolingual study. Of the Cantonese-dominant children only Timmy exhibits categorical use of the target-like split order with pronouns in the corpus data; note, however, that non-target non-split order is attested in diary data for Timmy, as illustrated in (67).

Contrasting findings for the two non-Cantonese-dominant children are shown in table 7.11. Charlotte shows no clear preference (41.7% non-split) for

Table 7.12. *Distribution of lexical NPs and pronouns in the English verb-particle constructions of two monolingual children, Peter and Allison (Bloom 1973, based on Ho 2003: 33)*

Child	Peter	Allison	Total
V-NP-PRT (split order)	288	17	305
V-PRT-NP (non-split order)	29	4	33
% non-split	9.2	19	9.8
V-pronoun-PRT (split order)	487	22	509
V-PRT-pronoun (non-split order)	5	0	5
% non-split	1	0	1

constructions with a lexical NP, and produces ill-formed non-split constructions with pronouns at a similar rate (35.5%) to the Cantonese-dominant children. Kathryn shows a clearly distinct pattern, namely producing exclusively split [V-NP-PRT] order with lexical NP objects (100%) and only a single case of non-split order with pronoun as object. The pattern seen in Kathryn is identical to the monolingual data from Peter and Allison, shown in table 7.12.[23] The two monolingual children produce only 9.8% non-split constructions with lexical NPs, and very rarely with pronouns as objects (1%).

In the transcripts Sophie uses the supposedly 'basic' structure [V-NP-PRT] only when the intervening object is a pronoun (as in *put this away*), and never with a full NP object (as in *put these things away, pick the baby up*). Instead she uses the order [V-PRT-NP] as in Cantonese (*put away these things, pick up the baby*). Being bilingual therefore changes the 'dynamics' of particle shift by affecting the balance between two variant word order patterns. In an extreme case such as that of Sophie, it may even change the basic order to that which matches Cantonese, thus licensing [V-NP-PRT] even with pronominal objects as in (77)–(78), which are ungrammatical in adult English. Such a change in basic order has clear implications for language contact at a societal level: the mechanism which we have seen at work in bilingual children could change the dominant order, as in contact-induced word order shifts which are known to be common. A specific prediction resulting from this case study would be that in Singapore Colloquial English, the balance should move in the direction of the non-split order, relative to standard English as represented by the monolingual studies discussed above.

7.3.3   Summary

To conclude, verb-particle constructions constitute an area of overlap between the two target grammars which leads to syntactic transfer in both directions.

If language dominance were the only factor determining transfer in bilingual development, then we would not expect to see syntactic transfer in the reverse direction. The predominant direction of transfer, however, is still from Cantonese to English, consistent with the language dominance hypothesis (section 2.5.2).

7.4 Conclusions

We have identified three domains of grammar in Cantonese that are vulnerable in bilingual development, regardless of language dominance. Even Cantonese-dominant children are influenced by English, the weaker language, with regard to the placement of Cantonese locative PPs with *hai2* 'at'. This influence is visible both quantitatively, in the preponderance of [V PP] over [PP V] orders, and qualitatively, in the existence of ill-formed [V PP] orders which are not found in the available monolingual child Cantonese data.

The case of non-target word order in Cantonese dative construction with *bei2* 'give' is more complex in that the developmental problem appears in monolingual as well as bilingual development where the non-target forms are more frequent and persist over a much longer period. The vulnerability of this grammatical domain is attributed to properties of the Cantonese input, namely ambiguity of input with respect to placement of the theme object: in particular, the prevalence of null and displaced theme objects makes the target order difficult to establish. The non-target [V-R-T] order coincides with the universally preferred word order and is in turn reinforced by the English order which is invariant. The vulnerability of Cantonese *bei2* 'give' datives poses learnability problems for the bilingual children, causing quantitative differences and protracted use of the non-target forms relative to the monolingual counterparts.

The third case, that of verb-particle constructions, shows bidirectional influence, consistent with the overlap between the two languages and ambiguity of evidence in both languages with respect to separability of the verb and particle. The influence of English is seen in freer separation of the verb and particle in bilingual children's Cantonese. At the same time, influence of Cantonese, the dominant language, on bilingual children's English, the weaker language, is pervasive. Quantitatively, the influence of Cantonese shifts the preferred order from the split [V-NP-PRT] order as in English towards the non-split [V-PRT-NP] order; qualitatively, it leads to ill-formed developmental structures such as [V-PRT-Pronoun] which are very rarely found in monolingual child English data.

Taken together with the cases covered in the preceding chapters, these phenomena show that cross-linguistic influence can be found in both directions in the same children, although it may be asymmetrical as in our Cantonese-dominant bilingual children. At the level of language contact at large, such interactive development represents a possible mechanism of convergence between languages in contact.

NOTES

1. The first person pronoun *ngo5* in Cantonese is often pronounced as *o5* by children and many adult speakers. The initial *ng* sound is variably dropped in other words with this initial as part of a general phenomenon of sound change in Cantonese (Matthews & Yip 1994: 29–30).

2. Phrases consisting of *hai* + NP are often completed by a 'localizer' such as *dou6* 'there' in (7). Localizers are formally nouns but function like postpositions (Matthews & Yip 1994: 117).

3. The difference (if any) is subtle, but often involves iconicity: being located in a position favours [PP V], while sitting down such that one ends up in that position favours [V PP].

4. Leung (2005) investigated the verbs used in non-target examples of [V PP] order with *hai2* 'at' by three bilingual children and LTF, the alleged bilingual child from Cancorp. Timmy produced seven non-target tokens with the following verbs: *daa2-zam1* 'have an injection', *dan(g)2* 'wait', *waan2* 'play', *zaa1-ce1* 'drive', *sik6* 'eat', and *gaan2* 'choose'; Sophie produced 2 such tokens with *tai2* 'see', and *lok6 heoi3* 'go down'. Kathryn and LTF each produced one such token with *sik6* 'eat' and *waan2* 'play' respectively. In addition, we found eight tokens produced by Alicia with *beng6* 'get sick', *fei1* 'fly', *man(g)1* 'tug', *so1* 'comb', *mit1* 'pinch', *zuk1* 'catch', *saan1* 'close', and *co5-fei1gei1* 'take the plane'. Llywelyn produced six tokens with *caai2* 'tread/cycle', *caat3ngaa4* 'brush teeth', *waan2* 'play', *tai2* 'look', and *daa2-din6waa2* 'telephone'.

5. The results are based on the child-directed speech in the corpus data for four bilingual children (Timmy, Sophie, Alicia and Kathryn).

6. Kwan (2005a: 60) found that topic PPs are used more frequently where the PP is relatively complex. They also tend to be used for abstract senses of *hai2* such as the temporal sense as seen in (21). These findings suggest that the rarity of topic PPs in child-directed speech reflects the relatively low complexity of PPs in this register and the more concrete senses in which they are used.

7. The category label NP adopted here may be taken as equivalent to DP (Determiner Phrase) in works in the generative paradigm; assuming a functional projection DP does not affect the argument.

8. A few other verbs do participate in double object constructions but these are infrequent, especially in the input to children. For example, the colloquial verb *sing2* as in *sing2 lei5 jat1 zoeng1 fei1* 'reward you with a ticket' (Tang 1998). Note that in this case the order is [V-R-T].

9. In the literature on the acquisition of datives, one controversial issue involves the relationship between double object datives (i) and prepositional datives (ii):
   (i) I give you money.
   (ii) I give money to you.
   Many dative verbs participate in the alternation between the two types of dative constructions but others do not. Researchers are interested in learnability issues such as whether and to what extent there is overgeneralization of the alternation in developmental data (see Gropen et al. 1989).

10. The morpheme *bei2* in this position can also be analysed as a preposition (Matthews 2006a: 77). This does not necessarily affect the argument. However, as Salikoko Mufwene points out, *bei2* as a verb allows a null object, whereas *bei2* as a preposition should not.

11. The missing theme NP after the verb is shown conventionally as [e] indicating some empty category, without implying any particular analysis at this point. The case of null anaphora can be assimilated to that of topicalization by assuming that the null anaphor is bound by a null topic (see chapter 5).

12. Overall the number of full datives with *bei2* 'give' is rather low considering that the total number of Cantonese child utterances produced by eight monolingual children amount to 85,375, but the number of full datives is only 33. There is a total of 43,588 lines in six bilingual children's Cantonese files, and the number of full datives is 51.

13. In this example the child aims to pronounce *sticker book*. The target word *sticker* contains the consonant cluster [st] which Alicia avoids by using metathesis as in *tickser*.

14. We thank Richard Wong for pointing out this code-mixed example from the Hong Kong Cantonese Adult Language Corpus, available at http://shs.hku.hk/corpus/corpus.asp

15. The classifier *bui1* 'cup' is used instead of *go3* in the noun phrase [*go3 syut3gou1*] 'ice cream' in adult Cantonese as in (i). The alternative is to have a bare NP as in (ii):

(i)   Lei5   maai5   bui1   syut3gou1   bei2   ngo5
         you   buy   CL   ice cream   for   me
         'You buy ice cream for me.'

(ii)   Lei5   maai5   syut3gou1   bei2   ngo5
         you   buy   ice cream   for   me
         'You buy ice cream for me.'

Sophie and the other bilingual children often overgeneralize the use of *go3* as a general classifier in many contexts, as is well known in monolingual Cantonese development.

16. We thank William O'Grady for drawing our attention to the animacy of the recipient in the topic hierarchy.

17. When the pronoun following the [V-PRT] is stressed, the interpretation is grammatical (*I said pick up HIM*).

18. In principle, the non-split type can be derived by two alternative means: (a) movement of the NP to the right of the particle (cf. Heavy NP Shift)

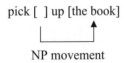

pick [ ] up [the book]

NP movement

(b) movement of the particle to the left of the NP

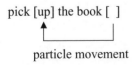

pick [up] the book [ ]

particle movement

19. The equivalent constructions in Mandarin Chinese are conventionally described as 'resultative verbal complements' (Li & Thompson 1981). However, Matthews and Yip (1994: 64–5, 213) point out several parallels between English verb-particle (or 'phrasal verb') constructions and these Cantonese constructions.

20. The Cantonese *giu3 seng2* 'wake up' and *lo2 zau2* 'take away' are arguably resultative verbal compounds, somewhat different from typical verb-particle constructions, but have similar behaviour: for example, *giu3 seng2* 'wake up' is separable as in *ngo5 giu3 keoi5 m4 seng2* 'I cannot wake him up'.

21. The preference for [V-NP-PRT] is connected with the fact that (72)–(74) are ungrammatical with an unstressed pronoun: given the preference for short constituents before longer ones, where the object is a pronoun there is no motivation for shifting the word order from [V-NP-PRT] to [V-PRT-NP] (Hawkins 1994).

22. Sawyer (2001) argues that the traditionally unified verb-particle constructions bifurcate into two classes: (1) verb-adverb construction (VAC) with a verb, a complement and an adverb and (2) verb-particle construction (VPC) with a verb, a complement and a particle. She shows evidence from monolingual English data that children treat the two constructions differently from early on. We collapse the VAC and VPC subtypes as one category since both show a strong preference for the split [V-NP-PRT] order; whether our bilingual children treat the two subtypes differently awaits further investigation. Sawyer's analysis predicts that the split form of the VAC would be learned before the non-split form and that 'VACs are learned early and produced in large numbers' due to the productivity of many adverbs freely combining with many verbs (Sawyer 2001: 152). These predictions are largely borne out in her corpus study of monolingual English-speaking children. An interesting finding is that the overwhelming error in VAC is object drop, which conforms in rate and timing to subject drop during the null subject stage.

23. The age span for Ho's (2003) study of Peter's development of verb-particle construction is from 1;09;07–3;01;21 and that for Allison is from 1;04;21–2;10;00.

8   Bilingual development and contact-induced grammaticalization

Alicia: [squashes ant] The ant, is die already.   (Alicia 4;05;24)
Sophie: What did Alicia say?
Father: 'The ant is die already.'
Sophie: Got the wrong tense.   (Sophie 8;08;21)

As the eight-year-old Sophie has noticed, her sister Alicia at age four has her own way of dealing with tense. Sophie is puzzled by Alicia's use of *is die* with the adverb *already*. The form *is die already* is not among those used at school, where the concept of tense has recently been imparted to Sophie; nor is it obviously 'Chinese English' (to use Sophie's term) as some phenomena discussed in this book are. Where, then, does Alicia's own 'grammar' come from? This and similar questions are the subject of our penultimate chapter.

In chapter 1 we discussed how developments in bilingual individuals parallel, and ultimately underlie, those taking place in the course of contact-induced change. In bilingual individuals we can observe processes such as code-switching, transfer and other forms of grammatical interaction; in languages in contact we observe processes such as lexical borrowing, calquing and contact-induced grammaticalization, while the outcomes include language shift, pidginization and creolization. The relationship between the individual and language-level processes is not well understood, as we shall see in the domain of grammaticalization. It is, however, widely recognized that 'the bilingual individual is the ultimate locus of language contact' (Romaine 1996: 573).

In this chapter we focus on the process of grammaticalization in circumstances of language contact, and the corresponding processes in bilingual development at the individual level. In section 8.1, we first outline a framework for analysis in which these notions are defined. Section 8.2 discusses grammatical phenomena that are among the most salient of many potential cases in the bilingual data: the emergence of *already* as a marker of aspect presents a case of 'ordinary' contact-induced grammaticalization. Section 8.3 discusses the development of grammatical functions of *give* which represents a case of replica grammaticalization and the case of *one* illustrates the further grammaticalization of an already grammatical item in section 8.4.

227

8.1   Contact-induced grammaticalization

Grammaticalization has typically been viewed as a process internal to a language, as opposed to external or contact-induced changes such as structural borrowing, calquing and substrate influence. Indeed, linguists have often debated whether a particular development was to be attributed to contact or to internal development through grammaticalization. This dichotomy is still evident in current textbooks: for example, the treatment of contact-induced change in Thomason (2001) does not mention grammaticalization, while the treatment of grammaticalization in Trask (1996) does not mention language contact, and Winford (2003: 350) retains the traditional assumption that 'grammaticalization involves grammatical change that is internally motivated'. In recent work this dichotomy has broken down, due to findings in two areas in particular:

(a) areal typology, where it became clear that similar instances of grammaticalization show strong geographical clustering, implicating mutual influence as a factor in the process (Ansaldo 1999; Dahl 2001; Enfield 2003; Heine & Kuteva 2005);

(b) creoles and other contact languages, where it became clear that apparent cases of grammaticalization could result from substrate influence: 'what at first sight looks like internal grammaticalization may well be due to influence from other languages as well' (Arends, Muysken & Smith 1994: 120).

Both these points can be illustrated by the grammaticalization of the verb 'say'. In areas such as West Africa and Southeast Asia, a verb originally meaning 'say' serves as a complementizer meaning 'that'. Typically this change occurs through reanalysis of a serial verb construction, as in Cantonese where the verb *waa6* 'say' follows another verb such as *gong2* 'talk' in (1):

(1)   Keoi5 tung4 ngo5 gong2 waa6 lei5 mou5   cin2
        he   with   me   talk say you not.have money
        'He told me you had no money.'

The second verb *waa6* has a lexical meaning 'say' but in this position serves a structural function: to introduce a complement clause. This becomes clear when it follows a verb such as *soeng2* 'want' whose meaning does not involve speech at all:

(2)   Keoi5 soeng2 waa6   ting1jat6 heoi3 taam3 lei5
        she   want   say/that tomorrow go   visit you
        'She wants to visit you tomorrow.'

Here *waa6* no longer means 'say' but serves as a complementizer, comparable to *that*. This grammatical use of 'say' recurs in many Chinese dialects with different 'say' verbs, which are grammaticalized as complementizers to different degrees: for example, in the case of *kóng* 'say' in Taiwanese southern Min, the grammaticalization process is more advanced than in that of Cantonese *waa6* (Chappell 2006). Moreover, the same process applies to the verb *shuo* 'say' in the variety of Mandarin spoken in Taiwan which is under substrate influence from Taiwanese southern Min (Cheng 1997a). Clearly the pattern has spread from one dialect to another – a prima facie instance of contact-induced grammaticalization.

In the extreme case of language contact represented by creoles such as Sranan, a similar use of the verb 'say' with a grammatical function is observed. In Sranan the word *taki*, derived from English *talk*, is used as a complementizer meaning 'that' in a similar pattern to *waa6* 'say' in Cantonese (1)–(2). The substrate model for Sranan is provided by West African languages such as Gbe and Twi in which the complementizer 'that' derives from the verb 'say' (Plag 1995). Whether these developments constitute grammaticalization has been a matter of some debate. Bruyn (1996) suggested that such cases involve 'apparent grammaticalization', where the appearance of grammaticalization results from a three-stage process:

(i) Grammaticalization of item X has already occurred in language A
(ii) Item Y in language B is identified with item X
(iii) A range of functions is transferred from item X to item Y

According to this model, no process of grammaticalization actually takes place in the contact language. Rather, a term such as 'say' in the lexifier language is identified with an equivalent in the substrate language, based on the lexical meanings rather than grammatical functions of these words. Stage (ii) of Bruyn's model formalizes the traditional notion of interlingual identification, as used by Weinreich (1953) and widely adopted in the field of second language acquisition. The whole range of functions of the substrate item X, including grammatical as well as lexical usages, is transferred to the developing contact language.[1]

The model advanced by Bruyn and Plag is questioned by Mufwene (2006) on several grounds. Much of the development of contact languages such as creoles is gradual, with the current state of classical creoles such as Mauritian and Haitian being the result of development over several centuries. Grammaticalization can be internally or externally motivated; indeed, many 'classical' cases of grammaticalization may have been contact-induced. For example, the compound perfect tenses formed with 'have' and 'be' in several European languages offer textbook cases of grammaticalization, but these cases occurred in circumstances of contact-induced restructuring and are unlikely to have been entirely independent of each other.

Especially relevant to the present study is the notion of 'idiogrammaticization' (Mufwene 2006) i.e. the innovation whereby an individual speaker uses an item in a new, incipiently grammatical function:

There are no group selections without individual selections and therefore no grammaticization process at the communal language level without requisite idiogrammaticizations. (27)

From this perspective, bilingual children can be seen as producing idiogrammaticizations of a kind which logically precedes contact-induced grammaticalization.

8.1.1   'Ordinary' contact-induced grammaticalization

Heine and Kuteva (2003, 2005) have taken on the challenge of rethinking grammaticalization to take account of the role of language contact. They propose a relatively explicit model which makes a useful point of departure, although several aspects of this model invite debate. Their 'ordinary contact-induced grammaticalization' defines a process similar to Bruyn's (1996) 'apparent grammaticalization', but Heine and Kuteva consider it to be a case of grammaticalization, meaning that the usual principles of grammaticalization apply. The process assumes a model language M and a replica language R in which a grammatical phenomenon is reproduced.

'Ordinary' contact-induced grammaticalization
a. Speakers of language R notice that in language M there is a grammatical category Mx.
b. They develop an equivalent category Rx in language R on the basis of patterns available in R.
c. To this end, they draw on universal strategies of grammaticalization, using construction Ry in order to develop Rx.
d. They grammaticalize category Ry to Rx.   (Heine & Kuteva 2005: 81)

The fact that this definition explicitly refers to what individual speakers do, as opposed to what happens in languages (the focus of much research on language contact), makes the model potentially applicable to bilingual acquisition. As it stands, however, the definition incurs a certain monolingual bias: 'Speakers of language R' in step (a) seems to imply that R is the first or privileged language for the speakers concerned.[2] To apply the model to bilingual acquisition we will need to replace 'Speakers of language R' with 'Speakers with knowledge of at least two languages, M and R'. There is also an important question of metalinguistic awareness raised by 'notice' in step (a), which we shall discuss further in connection with replica grammaticalization (see section 8.1.2).

An example given by Heine and Kuteva (2005) involves aspect marking in Bislama, the English-based pidgin of Vanuatu. The Austronesian languages serving as models for Bislama have a durative aspect marker, a prefix *u-* in the case of Vetmbao (Keesing 1991: 328):

(3)   Naji ng-u-xoel   dram
       he   he-DUR-dig   yam
       'He's in the process of digging yams'

In Bislama, an aspectual category equivalent to that in the substrate languages is formed by using the verb *stap* 'stay' (derived from English *stop*) before the main verb:

(4)   Em   i   stap   pik-im   yam
       he   PRED   DUR   dig-TRS   yam
       'He's in the process of digging yams'

While the aspectual prefix in languages such as Vetmbao is opaque, having only a grammatical function, Bislama co-opts the lexical verb *stap* 'stop, stay' but uses it in a grammatical function. The case of *already* as an aspect marker to be discussed in section 8.2 represents 'ordinary contact-induced grammaticalization' of this kind. It may be noted that such cases appear incompatible with the 'apparent grammaticalization' model according to which the range of functions from lexical to grammatical is transferred to the contact language based on interlingual identification: there is no lexical item in the substrate language with which the verb *stap* can be identified.

8.1.2   Replica grammaticalization

Replica grammaticalization is proposed as a special case of contact-induced grammaticalization in which not only is an equivalent grammatical category created in the replica language R, but it is derived through the same pathway of grammaticalization from lexical to grammatical (or from grammatical to more grammatical) as in the model language M:

'Replica grammaticalization'
a. Speakers of language R notice that in language M there is a grammatical category Mx.
b. They develop an equivalent category Rx, using material available in their own language (R).
c. To this end, they replicate a grammaticalization process they assume to have taken place in language M, using an analogical formula of the kind [My > Mx]: [Ry > Rx].
d. They grammaticalize category Ry to Rx.   (Heine & Kuteva 2003: 539)

We have already noted the monolingual bias of 'Speakers of language R' in step (a), for which we may substitute 'Speakers with knowledge of at least two languages, M and R'. Similarly, for 'available in their own language (R)' in step (c) we would substitute the simpler 'available in language R'. Deeper problems with this model involve the assumptions that speakers 'notice' a grammatical category (step a) and 'replicate a grammaticalization process they assume to have taken place in language M' (step c). These formulations imply a metalinguistic awareness (in steps a and c) and a historical perspective (in step c) which are available to the linguist, but not (at least not directly) available to a bilingual speaker, let alone a bilingual child. In order for the model to be viable, these notions will have to reformulated or glossed in such a way that it is plausible to attribute steps (a)–(d) to individual speakers. For step (a), it will suffice to say there is a pattern in language M which speakers try to adapt in order to express similar content in language R. A more profound problem is posed by step (c): the processual nature of the formula [My > Mx], meaning that a change has taken place in the model language (possibly centuries ago) which cannot possibly be accessible to speakers without explicit study. To identify such a process (such as a shift from 'say' to 'that') requires evidence of a kind that for most languages is not available even to linguists, who in the absence of historical records can only hypothesize such changes. It is therefore not feasible to assume that speakers 'replicate a grammaticalization process *they assume to have taken place* in language M' (Heine & Kuteva 2003: 539, step (c) in the above model; our emphasis), as if the speakers responsible for the changes were budding historical linguists.[3] The changes that can be identified historically take place as a result of cumulative innovations made by individual speakers (Mufwene 2001).

What is available to the speaker is the implicit knowledge that a single phonological form is associated with more than one function: for example, the form *waa6* in Cantonese serves both as a verb meaning 'say' and as a complementizer 'that'. We would therefore replace the analogical formula [My > Mx]:[Ry > Rx] in step (c) by a formula such as [My ~ Mx]:[Ry ~ Rx], where ~ represents a continuum from a lexical sense y to a grammatical function x, both associated with the same phonological form (or at least with phonologically relatable forms). Such a continuum arises with the development from lexical 'give' to passive, where the pathway of grammaticalization is set out by Lord, Yap and Iwasaki (2002):

(5)   Lexical verb: Permissive: Passive:
       'give'   > 'allow'   > 'by'

As the arrows (>) indicate, this schema represents a historical course of development, reconstructed on the basis of comparative evidence. It is, however, possible to state this situation in synchronic terms, thus avoiding the 'budding historical linguist' paradox.[4] A synchronic manifestation of the pathway can be found in languages in which all three functions are performed by the same word, as in the Min dialect of Chaozhou (Matthews, Xu & Yip 2005: 270):

(6)   Ua tsau-ze? k'e? i   puŋ tsɯ
        I   yesterday give 3sg CL book
        'I gave him a book yesterday.' (lexical 'give')

(7)   I   bo k'e? ua t'õi tsi puŋ tsɯ
        3sg not give 1sg read this CL book
        'He didn't let me read this book.' (permissive 'let')

(8)   Puŋ tsɯ k'e? naŋ   boi k'ɯ lau
        CL book give person buy RVC SFP
        'The book has been bought already.' (passive)

We have already suggested that this should be seen as a continuum rather
than, say, three distinct functions. Evidence for such a continuum comes from
intermediate cases compatible with more than one interpretation of the 'give'
verb:

(9)   k'e?   i   t'õi tse? e
        give/let 3sg see one while
        'Give (it) to him to read for a while.' (lexical 'give')
        OR 'Let him read (it) for a while.' (permissive)

(10)   Mai   k'e?   naŋ   lia? tio? lɯ
        not-want let/PASS people catch RVC 2sg
        'Don't let anyone catch you.' (permissive)
        OR 'Don't get (yourself) caught.' (passive)

Such cases are termed *bridging contexts* by Evans and Wilkins (2000: 156)
and incorporated as a crucial step in the grammaticalization process by Heine
(2002).

8.1.3   *Contact as catalyst and principles of grammaticalization*

As argued above, the model outlined by Heine and Kuteva (2003; 2005) appears
viable to the extent that it can be reformulated without the assumption that
diachronic processes are accessible to speakers. By reformulating their analogical formula in terms of polyfunctionality, we come closer to the alternative
models of Bruyn (1996) and Lefebvre (1998) and to the polysemy copying
model considered by Heine and Kuteva (2005: 100). We differ from Bruyn's
notion of 'apparent grammaticalization' and Lefebvre's Relexification model
in assuming that general principles of grammaticalization are applicable, not
only to the substrate language(s) in which grammaticalization originally took
place, but also to the contact language affected by it. These principles include
the following (Hopper 1991):

Directionality: change is overwhelmingly from lexical to grammatical, or from grammatical to more grammatical, while changes in the converse direction are relatively rare;

Persistence: a grammaticalized form may retain characteristics of the lexical source from which it derives;

Divergence: grammaticalized forms gradually diverge from their lexical sources in form (for example, by undergoing phonological reduction) and other properties;

Layering: grammaticalization introduces a new layer which may coexist with older layers within the same functional domain, often resulting in specialization.

Because these principles are relevant to the language contact phenomena at issue, we retain the notion of *contact-induced grammaticalization*. Recall that different Chinese dialects have grammaticalized the 'say' complementizer to different extents (see section 8.1). It is therefore not the case that the set of structures and functions associated with a grammaticalized item has been transferred wholesale from one language to the next, as Bruyn's and Lefebvre's models imply (see section 8.1). Rather, the partial equivalences established on the basis of interlingual identification have led to parallel developments along a single pathway, or (more precisely) a number of related pathways of grammaticalization, as we shall argue in section 8.3.4. We thus see contact as a catalyst driving change along pathways of grammaticalization.

While the same general principles remain applicable, it is also possible that contact-induced grammaticalization in circumstances of intensive contact differs from typical 'language-internal' grammaticalization with respect to certain of these principles. For example, in connection with layering, Hopper and Traugott observe:

Typically, grammaticalization does not result in the filling of any obvious functional gap. On the contrary, the forms that have been grammaticalized compete with existing constructions so familiar in function that any explanation involving 'filling a gap' seems out of the question. (Hopper & Traugott 1993: 125)

By contrast, in contact-induced grammaticalization 'gap-filling' is recognized as a factor:

With the replication of a category on the model of another language, the replica language may acquire a category for which previously there was no or no appropriate equivalent. (Heine & Kuteva 2005: 124)

Contact-induced changes of this kind are system-altering changes as described in the Amazon region by Aikhenvald (2002). Heine and Kuteva (2005) give many examples from contact languages including pidgins and creoles; this is to be expected in an expanding pidgin such as Tok Pisin, where various grammatical categories may previously have been missing. In bilingual acquisition, especially where there is a dominant language, contact-induced grammaticalization may serve to fill temporary gaps where the target language structure has yet to be acquired: we shall see evidence for this in the case of verbal aspect (section 8.2.2) and the passive (section 8.3.3).

8.2   *Already* as marker of perfective aspect

Tense and aspect constitute an area in which substrate effects are commonly identified in contact languages, as in the case of Bislama discussed in 8.1.1 above. An extreme case is offered by Singapore Colloquial English (SCE), where Bao (2005) argues for systemic transfer of the whole aspectual system from the Chinese substrate. The development of *already* as a marker of perfective aspect in SCE is paralleled in the bilingual data. In terms of Heine and Kuteva's model, this constitutes a case of 'ordinary' contact-induced grammaticalization, whereby a category in the model language is replicated using equivalent material in the replica language, but without recapitulating the same pathway of grammaticalization.

8.2.1   Already *in Singapore Colloquial English (SCE)*

Several studies have described the use of *already* to indicate aspect in SCE. Ho and Platt (1993) and Bao (1995, 2005) relate this usage to perfective aspect marking in Hokkien and other Chinese dialects. Examples of SCE from Bao (2005) include:

(11)   I wash my hand *already*
         'I (have) washed my hands.'

(12)   The tongue red *already*
         'The tongue has turned red.'

Bao stresses that *already* with an adjective as in (12) denotes a change of state: 'The tongue has turned red.' He also notes that whereas in standard English *already* can precede or follow the verb, SCE *already* consistently follows the verb, just like the perfective marker *le* in Mandarin Chinese. Mandarin *le* in fact appears in two positions with somewhat different but related meanings: when immediately following the verb [V-*le*] it expresses perfective aspect as in (13), while following a stative verb it expresses change of state (14):

(13)   Wo xi-le   shou
         I   wash-PFV   hand
         'I (have) washed my hands.'

(14)   Yanjing hong le
         eye   red   PFV
         'The eyes have turned red.'

Bao concludes that 'the substrate source of *already* is unmistakable' (Bao 2005: 243). Bao's account of the SCE aspectual system relies heavily on comparisons with Mandarin, which played only a limited role in the formation of SCE; in this case, however, the general argument remains valid since similar models exist in the relevant substrate dialects: in particular, the dominant Hokkien dialect has the aspect marker *liau* (cognate with Mandarin *le*) in both postverbal and sentence-final positions, comparable to (13)–(14).

In terms of Heine and Kuteva's (2005) model, this would be a case of 'ordinary' contact-induced grammaticalization (see section 8.1.1). The Mandarin aspect marker *le* (and its equivalents in other dialects such as *liau* in Hokkien and *zo2* in Cantonese) lack a lexical sense which can be extended through replica grammaticalization as in the case of *give* discussed below (see section 8.3).[5] Instead, the nearest equivalent in English to the Hokkien perfective *liau* is sought in the adverb *already*.

8.2.2   Already *in bilingual development*

In her Singapore case study, Kwan-Terry (1989) related the use of the adverb *already* to the acquisition of the Cantonese perfective marker *zo2* in her bilingual child Elvoo's development (Kwan-Terry 1989: 38):

(15)   You eat your cream already?   (Elvoo 3;06)

(16)   Alice fell down in the hole already.   (Elvoo 3;06)

(17)   Now my school is close already.   (Elvoo 3;10)

(18)   The car is stop already.   (Elvoo 4;00)

In the following example Elvoo produced Cantonese *zo2* in a code-mixed sentence which is syntactically parallel to an English sentence with *already* (Kwan-Terry 1989: 39):

(19)   Ngo5 sik6 go3 cake zo2
         I   eat   CL   cake PFV
         'I've eaten the cake already.'   (Elvoo 3;09)

(20)   I eat the cake already.   (Elvoo 3;09)

It is ungrammatical to put the suffix *zo2* in sentence-final position as in (19), but to Elvoo, *zo2* and *already* are treated as equivalent as a result of interlingual identification. Elvoo was observed to use *zo2* and *already* alongside each other, providing further evidence for interlingual processes. In a dialogue with his mother, for example, Elvoo used the verb *die* together with *already* (Kwan-Terry 1989: 40):

(21)   Mother: O! Ngo5 sei2-zo2 laa3
                        Oh I   die-PFV   SFP
                        'Oh! I have died!' (i.e. Oh! I am dead!)'

         CHI: Die, die already.   (Elvoo 3;08)

Elvoo's English utterance is a translation of the mother's prior Cantonese utterance, with both *zo2* and *already* in the postverbal position, suggesting that the two forms are equivalent for him. Elvoo also used *already* with stative verbs to denote a new situation or state reached (Kwan-Terry 1989: 40):

(22)   The tongue red already, you see?
         [The tongue has turned red, you see?]   (Elvoo 3;06)

(23)   Ze Ze is not here already.
         [Ze Ze isn't here anymore.]   (Elvoo 3;08)

In our bilingual data, all three Cantonese-dominant siblings use *already* with uninflected verbs. They differ somewhat in the position of *already*, and in their use of combinations of *already* with adverbs such as *now* and *all*. Timmy uses *already* both before and after the verb, in accordance with its syntax in English. The following are typical examples from diary data:

(24)   I already eat. [pointing to plate of fruit]   (Timmy 2;04;09)

(25)   I find already the glasses.   (Timmy 2;07;10)

Much as in SCE, the use of *already* expresses the perfective aspect: 'I've found the glasses.' Both the contexts of use and the time course of acquisition suggest that he is following the Cantonese model. The perfective marker *zo2* is consistently the first aspect marker to be acquired in Cantonese, and Timmy uses it productively by age 2:[6]

(26)   Faan1 lai4 zo2, hei2-san1 zo2
         come   back PFV   raise-body PFV
         'I'm back, I've got up.'   (Timmy 2;01;16)

Evidence that Timmy's use of *already* as an aspect marker is modelled on Cantonese *zo2* comes from an idiomatic usage of *already* following a modal verb:

(27)   I give you to eat apple. Have to cut already first. (Timmy 2;11;16)

Here *already* is unexpected to the extent that the apple has yet to be cut, but in fact corresponds exactly to the adult usage of the perfective marker *zo2* with a modal verb as in:

(28)   Jiu3   cit3-zo2   sin1
          need   cut-PFV   first
          'You have to cut it first.'

Timmy also commonly uses the combination *already now*:

(29)   I drink this already now. I drink already this. I drink this already now.
          [holding beer can]   (Timmy 2;06;17)

(30)   I open already now. [holding up opened present]   (Timmy 2;07;04)

(31)   I want balloon, the green one broke already now.   (Timmy 2;07;30)

A possible model for the combination *already now* is the combination [V-*zo2 laa3*], where *zo2* is the perfective aspect and *laa3* a sentence particle expressing current relevance (like Mandarin *le* as discussed in section 8.2.1): apparently *now* represents the closest approximation to this meaning available in English. A pair of parallel utterances by Timmy (32), recorded on the same day as (29), suggests that Timmy makes the interlingual identification that is a crucial step in all models of the process:

(32)   [To father] Lei5   sik6-zo2   laa3
                        you   eat-PFV   SFP
                        'You've eaten (already).'

          [To helper] He has eat already now.   (Timmy 2;06;17)

Here, although the verb *eat* itself remains uninflected, the appearance of *has* in the position of perfect auxiliary shows Timmy on the way to developing a target-like tense/aspect system. Between ages two and three, Sophie frequently uses an uninflected verb followed by *already*:

(33)   She wake already.   (Sophie 2;06;09)

(34)   INV: Where are they?
          CHI: Eat already.
          INV: Ah, eat already. [laughs]   (Sophie 2;07;22)

(35)   Daddy, I ask already.   (Sophie 3;00;21)

At this stage Sophie has yet to acquire the English present perfect form as in *He's gone* and the use of *already* fills the gap, as shown by the following exchange where the adult researcher models the target form *has gone* but Sophie proceeds to ignore it:[7]

(36)   INV: Where is monster now?
          CHI: He go already. He go already.
          INV: The monster has gone already.
          Brother: < He's dead again > [>] dead again.
          INV: What did Timmy say?
          CHI: < He > [/] he go already the monster.   (Sophie 2;10;21)

In addition to *laa3* which is comparable to sentence-final *le* in Mandarin and *liau* in Hokkien, Cantonese has the quantificational particle *saai3* indicating completion or exhaustive effect.[8] The combination [V *saai3 laa3*] as seen in (37) appears to underlie the frequent co-occurrence of *all* and *already* in Alicia's and Sophie's English:

(37)   Jam2 saai3 laa3!
        drink all   SFP
        'I've drunk it all!' [holding up glass]   (Alicia 2;05;18)

(38)   Daddy drink all already?   (Alicia 2;08;29)

(39)   CHI: He eat the . . . he eat all already.
        INV: He has < eaten > [/] eaten up all of the food. Okay . . .
                                                                (Sophie 2;09;24)

A precocious example of 'impromptu translation' by Alicia shows how she treats the construction [V *saai3 laa3*] as equivalent to *already*, thus making the interlingual identification necessary for contact-induced grammaticalization (step (b) in section 8.1.1):

(40)   Father: It's dark already.
        CHI: hak1 saai3 laa3!
                dark all   SFP
                'It's all dark already.'   (Alicia 1;10;16)

Other examples confirm Bao's point that *already* following an adjective denotes a change of state:

(41)   [coming in wearing pink dress] I today wear pink. I today wear pink.
        [later, reappearing in red dress] I all red already.   (Alicia 2;09;05)

Here Alicia is pointing out a change of state: instead of pink she is now wearing red.

To summarize, the bilingual children's development recapitulates the development of *already* as a marker of perfective aspect in SCE. *Already* is used in postverbal or clause-final position to express change of state and other perfective notions. Both in SCE and in the bilingual data, the status of the model is less straightforward than in cases of replica grammaticalization such as that of *give* (see section 8.3). In SCE, verbal and/or sentence final *le* (in Mandarin) and/or *liau* (in Hokkien) serve as the models; in Cantonese, the models include [V *zo2 laa3*] and [V *saai3 laa3*], all of which are grammatically optional: that is, there are variants such as [V *saai3*] and [V *laa3*].

8.3   *Give*-passives and replica grammaticalization

Replica grammaticalization is a special case of contact-induced grammaticalization where the development of grammatical functions in a lexical item follows the same pathway of grammaticalization as in the model language (see section 8.1.2). This is well illustrated by the development of grammatical functions of 'give' verbs in various Chinese dialects. Cantonese instantiates the three stages illustrated for Chaozhou in section 8.1.2 above:

Cantonese *bei2* 'give' > permissive > passive

In Taiwanese southern Min (Tsao 1988), in addition to passive, the permissive gives rise to a causative usage as in (42):

Taiwanese *ho* 'give' > permissive > causative
                        permissive > passive

(42)   I   hō   goá   chin   siong-sim
        he   give   me   truly   sad
        'He made me sad.'   (Cheng 1997b: 203)

In the Chaozhou dialect, the grammaticalized *give* extends from passive constructions to unaccusative verbs as in (43) (Matthews, Xu & Yip 2005: 268):

Chaozhou *k'eʔ* 'give' > permissive
                          permissive > passive
                                        passive > unaccusative

(43)   tsaŋ   hue   k'eʔ   i   si   k'ɯ
        CL   flower   give   3sg   die   RVC
        'The flower has died.'

Replica grammaticalization (as defined by Heine and Kuteva but with the modifications outlined in section 8.1.2 above) can apply to any segment of these various pathways. For example, the progression [give > permissive > causative] can spread in the form of a polysemy [give ∼ permissive ∼ causative] or (more perspicuously, using lexical concepts) [give ∼ allow ∼ make]. A bidialectal speaker can, for example, apply the set of meanings and functions associated with the verb *ho* 'give' in Taiwanese to the equivalent verb *k'eʔ* 'give' in Chaozhou. The result will be a case of 'idiogrammaticization' (Mufwene 2006): in this speaker's usage, Chaozhou *k'eʔ* is grammaticalized, having causative functions alongside its lexical sense of 'give' and other grammaticalized functions.

   A striking feature of these cases of grammaticalization is the continued existence of the 'give' verb itself alongside its grammaticalized counterparts. It is characteristic of grammaticalization in Southeast Asian languages that the lexical item remains in use alongside its grammaticalized counterpart. This relates to the typology of these languages in which (a) affixes are rare and dispreferred, preventing the grammaticalized item from becoming an affix, and (b) lexical tone must be preserved on all syllables, preventing phonological reduction of the grammaticalizing forms (Ansaldo 1999). The continued existence of the lexical verb thus inhibits divergence, but may facilitate interlingual identification: this in turn would help to explain why the Southeast Asian linguistic area is characterized to such an extent by recurrent patterns of grammaticalization (Heine & Kuteva 2005: 203; Matthews 2006b).

Finally, the continued existence of the lexical verb makes it difficult to maintain that grammaticalization merely involves reanalysis, as suggested by Lefebvre (1998: 42). Grammaticalized verbs have acquired new functions, but have not necessarily been reanalysed: for example, Cantonese *bei2* and Chaozhou *k'e?* have been argued to remain verbs in their permissive and even passive functions (Tang 2001; Matthews, Xu & Yip 2005: 270).

8.3.1   Give-*passives in Malay contact varieties*

Give-passives recur in several varieties of Malay, again with a number of different '*give*' verbs. In at least some of these varieties it is clear that Chinese, specifically Southern Min and/or Cantonese influence is involved. Baba Malay, for example, has a clear Hokkien substrate and uses *kasi* 'give' in passives (Ansaldo & Matthews 1999):

(44)   Lu   punya favourite girl nanti kasi lain   orang book out
         you POSS favourite girl later give other man   book out
         'Your favourite girl will be booked out by another man.'

In Kedah Malay the verb *bagi* is used similarly (Yap & Iwasaki 1998, 2003):

(45)   Rumah kita habis bagi api jilat!
         house   we   finish give fire lick
         'Our house was completely "licked" by the fire!'

A particularly Sinitic property of these *give*-passives is that the agent phrase (*api* 'fire' in (45)) is obligatory. This can be attributed to retention of the subcategorization of the lexical source verb 'give' as a three-place predicate (Matthews, Xu & Yip 2005: 272–273). It is therefore a case of persistence, a puzzling but pervasive feature of grammaticalization (see section 8.1.3).

Another notable point is that in Malay, just as in Chinese, different 'give' verbs are used in each dialect; actual borrowing of forms is the exception to the rule that what is spreading is the pattern of grammaticalization. A question arising here is whether the Chinese model has spread directly to the various Malay dialects, or whether it has spread from Chinese to one Malay dialect and thence into others. Heine and Kuteva (2005) observe that it is often impossible to distinguish between these two patterns, (i) where a model M is replicated independently in two languages R_1 and R_2 and (ii) where the model is replicated in language R_1 which in turn serves as the model for a replica language R_2:

(i) M > R_1
    > R_2
(ii) M > R_1 > R_2

To the extent that direct influence of Chinese varies from one dialect area to another within Malaysia, it is likely that the indirect pattern (ii), M > R_1 > R_2 has applied in at least some of the varieties concerned.

8.3.2   Give-*passives in Singapore Colloquial English*

Bao and Wee (1999: 5) describe two passive constructions in SCE, *give*-passive as in (46) and the *kena* passive (where *kena* is borrowed from Malay) as in (47):

(46)   John give his boss scold.
        'John was scolded by his boss.'

(47)   The durian kena eat by him already.
        'The durian has been eaten by him.'

As in the southern Chinese dialects discussed above, the agent (*his boss* in (46)) is required in the *give*-passive, whereas in the *kena* passive it is optional. There is thus layering and specialization in the domain of the passive (see section 8.1.3). The agent requirement may be attributed to the *give*-passives in the Chinese substrate dialects as in Hokkien *hor* and Cantonese *bei* (Bao & Wee 1999: 7):[9]

(48)   Ah Hock tapai   hor   lang   me
        Ah Hock always   give people scold
        'Ah Hock always gets scolded by people.'

(49)   Keoi5 seng4jat6 bei2 jan4   laau6
        he   always   give people scold
        'He is always being scolded.'

While it is clear that the substrate Chinese dialects somehow underlie the *give*-passive, it is not obvious whether this is a case of simple calquing or of contact-induced grammaticalization. Some observations on the SCE *give*-passive made by Bao and Wee suggest that, as noted in section 8.1.3 above, the functions of the substrate items are not simply transferred *en masse*:

> We suggest that *hor/bei* and *give* may have undergone different degrees of grammatical-ization. The lexical meaning of *give* or *hor/bei* requires an animate subject. In Hokkien or Cantonese, *hor/bei* is fully grammaticalized, losing the meaning of animacy. In SgE [SCE], *give* is only partially grammaticalized. As such, it is less productive, and retains the animacy requirement. (Bao & Wee 1999: 8)

The requirement for an animate subject is one that naturally applies to permissive functions: the sense 'allow oneself to be scolded' implies responsibility for the action. In SCE, however, the requirement for an animate subject extends to the *give*-passive. This is evidence of persistence, the phenomenon whereby the lexical source of a grammaticalized item constrains its grammatical functions (Hopper & Traugott 1993: 3), and is thus consistent with Heine and Kuteva's account in which general principles of grammaticalization (such as persistence) apply to contact-induced grammaticalization as they do to grammaticalization in general (see section 8.1.1). This in turn argues for retaining the term 'grammaticalization' in such cases, and is consistent with the contact-as-catalyst model outlined in section 8.1.3.

8.3.3   Ontogenetic grammaticalization of give in bilingual children

Parts of the pathway of grammaticalization discussed above are paralleled in the language development of individual children. A particularly clear case is that of Sophie, who uses *give* in all three functions associated with *bei2* 'give' in Cantonese:

I. Lexical *give*

(50)   Give you one.   (Sophie 2;01;17)

(51)   I give you. I want to watch this one. [holding video]   (Sophie 2;05)

(52)   You give me that one, one only. [pointing to after-shave]

(Sophie 2;06)

The contextual indications show that the lexical meaning of transfer of possession is intended.

II. Permissive *give*

(53)   You open give me see. [giving Daddy Father's Day present]

(Sophie 3;03;20)

(54)   Daddy I give you see. [appearing in swimsuit]   (Sophie 3;04;06)

(55)   If Timmy don't give me to play this one, then I not be her brother.
        [i.e. If Timmy doesn't let me play with this, I won't be his sister].

(Sophie 3;07;06)

Here the contexts indicate that transfer of possession is not involved, but *give* means 'let'.

III. Passive *give*

(56)   [father holds up broken pen]
        This one . . . give Timmy . . . give Timmy break it.   (Sophie 3;03)

(57)   Here is give Timmy scratch [points to scratched leg]   (Sophie 3;06)

(58)   Daddy, I already give the mosquito to bite [shows bite]   (Sophie 4;09)

(59)   Father: How about your coat?
        CHI: Give Popo taken.   (Sophie 4;11)

These examples (from diary data) are less frequent than instances of the permissive usage of *give*, but suffice to show that Sophie extends her use of *give* to passive functions just as in SCE. She does so to fill a gap, in that at this stage she does not command the English passive. This can be seen from her attempts to express passive meanings at a slightly later age, which lack morphological or other indicators of passive voice:

(60)   Last night I bite here . . . The mosquito bite, last night. [showing a mosquito
        bite]   (Sophie 5;00;26)

(61)   Daddy, I cut! [showing a cut in her finger]   (Sophie 5;00;28)

Just as we argued with regard to Chinese dialects (see section 8.1.2), Sophie's English shows evidence of bridging contexts – usages consistent with more than one interpretation along the pathway of grammaticalization. Thus the following examples can be read as lexical 'give' as in 'give it to me to see', or permissive 'let' as in 'let me see':

(62)   Give me see, give me see.   (Sophie 2;02)

(63)   Daddy, I give you to drink *caa4-caa4* (i.e. tea).
        I give you to drink my *caa4*. Okay Daddy . . .   (Sophie 3;08)

Later examples allow either a permissive or a passive reading:[10]

(64)   Daddy, wake up. Otherwise you got nothing to eat.
        Give all body . . . everybody to eat already.   (Sophie 4;11)

Here Sophie is warning her father that there will be nothing left to eat if he does not get up quickly. A passive reading '[The food] will have been eaten' is possible, but this can be seen as an extension of the permissive reading 'You'll let everyone eat it all (and it will be your fault)', where the subject retains responsibility for the action, as in the case of SCE discussed in section 8.3.2 above.

To summarize, the developmental sequence seen in Sophie's English is consistent with contact-induced grammaticalization in:

(a) Order of acquisition: the lexical stage precedes the permissive and the passive usages of *give*;

(b) Mode of progression: bridging contexts mediate between the various senses in which *give* is used.

Under the view of contact as catalyst (section 8.1.3), it is not predicted that a bilingual child will transfer the whole range of uses of Cantonese *bei2* to English *give*, as Sophie did. Rather, we expect to see segments of the pathway undergoing transfer. Consistent with this prediction, Timmy and Alicia are recorded as using *give* in the permissive, but not in the passive function:

(65)   Ghost have dinner, and give ghost eat dinner and . . .   (Timmy 2;09;02)

(66)   How about a apple? I give you to eat apple.   (Timmy 2;11;16)

(67)   Give me go there [pulls Sophie's hand]   (Alicia 2;09;19)

We can see why Timmy has no need of the *give* passive, since unlike Sophie, he produces target-like passives as early as 3;02:

(68)   My space rocket is crashed up. The house was crashed. This is broken. This was crashed. This was crashed by the car. [referring to Lego models]
         (Timmy 3;02;17)

One question arising here is whether a bilingual child could use passive *give* without also using permissive *give*, thereby missing a step in the process. If no grammaticalization is involved, as with 'apparent grammaticalization', there would seem to be no reason why this should not occur. If contact-induced grammaticalization is taking place in ontogeny, however, then the following strong hypotheses can be derived:
  (i) earlier stages of grammaticalization must exist for the child, subject to an implicational hierarchy: passive → permissive → lexical 'give,'
  (ii) bridging contexts (see section 8.1.2) must exist at the individual level in order for the child to extend lexical 'give' to permissive, or permissive to passive function.

Some relevant questions here concern:
(a) monolingual Cantonese development: to what extent does ontogenetic grammaticalization recapitulate historical developments (see Ziegeler 1997)? Wong (2003, 2004) shows that the sequence in monolingual Cantonese is as follows: transfer (lexical 'give') > permissive > dative > passive. Although this is consistent with ontogenetic grammaticalization, Wong (2004: 337) notes that it also matches the frequency of the respective constructions in the input, so that other explanations for the developmental sequence are possible, including those based on input frequency and syntactic complexity.
(b) individual variation: some bilingual children exhibit more transfer effects than others; are these the innovators responsible for propagation of change (Enfield 2004: 294)? One factor contributing to individual variation is, once again, language dominance. Only the Cantonese-dominant children are recorded as using grammaticalized *give*: Timmy and Alicia used *give* in the permissive function, while Sophie used both permissive and passive *give*. In the corpus, Charlotte is recorded as using only lexical *give*; Kathryn also used primarily lexical *give*, with one possible example of permissive *give*:

(69)   It was just my Mum, my and, and my # and # and # and Alasdair give
me to eat.   (Kathryn 3;04;14)

This is a potential bridging context, consistent with a lexical reading 'Alisdair
gave it to me to eat' as well as a permissive one 'Alisdair let me eat (it).'

Meanwhile, the children's Cantonese exhibits all the relevant functions of
bei2 'give' as well as bridging contexts such as the following, which allows a
permissive or a passive interpretation:

(70)   Lei5 siu2sam1 m4 bei2 jan4   zuk1 lei5 aa3!
you careful   not give people catch you SFP
'Be careful not to let people catch you./Be careful not to get caught.'
(Timmy 2;09;01)

8.3.4   Dative constructions with bei2 *'give'*

Apart from its permissive and passive functions, Cantonese *bei2* 'give' is grammaticalized as a dative marker (arguably becoming a preposition). This occurs
when *bei2* appears as the second verb of a serial verb construction (Matthews
2006a: 77):

(71)   Lei5 waan4 faan1 bei2 ngo5
you return back give me
'Give [it] back to me.'

This represents a separate pathway of grammaticalization from that which leads
to the permissive and passive functions, which involves grammaticalization of
bei2 as the *first* verb in a serial verb construction. Lord, Yap & Iwasaki (2002)
recognize a second pathway of grammaticalization:

Lexical 'give' > dative > benefactive

The Cantonese-dominant children transfer this usage too. Examples where they
repeat the same message in both languages clearly demonstrate the equivalence
between English *give* and Cantonese *bei2* in this function:

(72)   I cut will give you [cutting water melon].

(73)   Lei5 tsiah, ngo5 zoi6 cit3 bei2 lei5 sik6
you eat   I   again cut give you eat
'Eat it, and I'll cut some more for you to eat.'   (Timmy 2;11;21)[11]

(74)   Po4po2 buy   give me.
Po4po2 maai5 bei2 ngo5 ge3
grandma buy   give me   SFP
'Grandma bought these for me.'   (Alicia 3;02;26)

Another example suggests that Alicia treats *give* as equivalent to the preposition *for*:

(75)   Daddy, this one give you. [presents dish of toy food]
        Daddy, this one for you.   (Alicia 3;04;04)

The reformulation here (from *give* to *for*) may suggest that Alicia is aware that this use of *give* is non-native-like. A similar case is recorded in Sophie's diary data, where the mother's comment on her use of *give* prompts Sophie to reformulate her point using *for*:

(76)   CHI: This is give Mummy's.

        Mother: Keoi5 cyun4bou6 waa6 give ge3
                she   everything say   give SFP
                'She says 'give' for everything.'

        CHI: This one for Mummy, Daddy.   (Sophie 3;07;09)

Alicia nevertheless continues to use dative *give*, especially in serial verb constructions parallel to the Cantonese (70):

(77)   You know, I got a Swan Lake book give Lulu.   (Alicia 4;05;15)

Later examples include the copular construction [*It's give* NP] which is no longer a serial verb construction but suggests a later stage of grammaticalization:

(78)   Father: What have you got?
        [Alicia carries bag containing stamps]
        CHI: It's give Lulu. Later. On Saturday.   (Alicia 4;00;30)

Alicia even quotes herself using dative *give*:

(79)   CHI: Where is the Christmas surprise give Lulu?
        Father: In Mummy's room.
        CHI: I want to see. It says 'Lulu' so it's Lulu's surprise.
             When we go to Lulu, surprise, 'It's give you,' like that.
                                                             (Alicia 4;06;11)

The equivalent construction in Cantonese uses *bei2* 'give' without the copular verb:

(80)   Ni1 di1 bei2 lei5, ni1 di1 bei2 lei5 laa1
        this CL give you   this CL give you   SFP
        'This is for you, this is for you.'   (Alicia 3;02;01)

Llywelyn also used dative *give*:

(81)   This one is give Winnie, you take . . . [?]   (Llywelyn 2;03;14)

The case of dative *give* illustrates an important general point: different pathways of grammaticalization may develop based on the same verb, occurring in different syntactic environments. This is a common pattern especially in isolating languages of Southeast Asia, as discussed in the introduction to section 8.3.

8.4   *One* as nominalizer

Definitions of grammaticalization typically specify that it involves development 'from lexical to grammatical and from grammatical to more grammatical forms' (Heine & Kuteva 2005: 14). In practice most discussion focuses on striking cases of lexical-to-grammatical shifts such as *say*-complementizers (see section 8.1) and *give*-passives (see section 8.3). Yet contact-induced grammaticalization can equally apply to the development from grammatical functions to more grammaticalized ones. A case in point involves English *one*, which serves both as a numeral as in *one person*, and as a pronoun with a more grammatical function, substituting for the remainder of a noun phrase following the determiner as in *this one*, *the red one*, etc. Since the use of *one* as a numeral is ancient (going back to Indo-European and cognate with Latin numeral *unus*, etc.) it may be assumed that the pronominal use as in *this one* is the result of grammaticalization of the numeral *one* as in *one person*. In contact languages such as SCE, *one* has developed further grammatical functions including those of nominalizer and relative marker (Wee & Ansaldo 2004). In bilingual development, we have seen that *one* plays a prominent role in relative clauses (section 6.5).

8.4.1   *Grammaticalization of* one *in Singapore Colloquial English (SCE)*

Studies of SCE have established the functions of *one* ranging from nominalizer to pragmatic particle. (Alsagoff & Ho 1998: 134–145) describe the extension of *one* from nominalizer to relative marker:

(82)   Don't have car one, I don't want.
         'I don't want (a man) who does not own a car.'

(83)   They grow one very sweet.
         'The fruit that they grow is very sweet.'

The use of *one* to nominalize the preceding clause as in [*don't have car*] *one* in (82) is an extension of the English pronominal use as in *a red one*. Since there is no categorical distinction in Chinese between adjectival modification and modification by a relative clause (see section 6.4.2), this extension can be achieved by straightforward substitution of the modifier. Thus *one* comes to serve as a marker of a relative clause as in [*They grow*] *one* in (83).

Yap, Matthews and Horie (2003) analyse the development of morphemes from nominalizers to relative clause markers and pragmatic markers of 'stance' in a number of Asian languages (Japanese, Malay, Mandarin and Cantonese).

The following examples from a novel replete with dialogue in SCE illustrate how this development may take place.

(84) The batter they use – very funny one.
    (dialogue from *Mammon Inc* by a Singaporean author, Tan 2001: 155)

(85) Hey, Ah Girl, phone call from England very expensive one. (Tan 2001: 35)

These are potential bridging contexts (see section 8.1.2), syntactically compatible with the relative clause analysis ('the batter they use is one which is very funny') but functioning pragmatically to express the speaker's stance ('the batter they use is really funny, the way I see it'). The following examples represent switch contexts in the sense of Heine (2002): they are no longer compatible with the relative clause reading. For example, *we're sure to fight one* in (86) cannot be parsed as a relative clause ('we are one which is sure to fight'), and *one* must be taken instead as a marker of stance: 'we're sure to fight, I'm telling you'.

(86) You *cannot* spend all the day at home. We spend too much time together, we're sure to fight one. (Tan 2001: 219)

(87) But only you smart enough to get the scholarship. You sure can pass the test one. (Tan 2001: 220)

All these developments replicate the functions of Chinese (and to some extent Malay) grammatical words: *e* in Hokkien, *kai* in Teochew, *ge3* in Cantonese, *de* in Mandarin and *punya* in Malay.

Relative clauses such as (82)–(83) in SCE are said to show 'an amalgamation of both substrate (i.e. Chinese) and superstrate (i.e. English) grammatical features' (Alsagoff & Ho 1998: 127). The substratal influence manifests itself in the use of *one* as a relative marker, which is argued to arise through calquing of the Chinese nominalizer (Mandarin *de*, Hokkien *e*, Teochew *kai*, etc.) into English. To spell out how 'amalgamation' works in such cases, and how contact-induced grammaticalization differs from the traditional notion of calquing, the process can be described as one of replica grammaticalization (see section 8.1.2), similar to the case of *give*-passives except that the relevant items are already grammaticalized in both English and Chinese, so that the replication applies to a set of grammatical functions. The necessary steps would be as follows:

a. Speakers of Chinese dialects use a nominalizing morpheme (Hokkien *e*, Cantonese *ge*, Mandarin *de*) to construct relative clauses, as in the case of Cantonese *ge3*:

(88) [NP Lei5 bei2 ngo5 ge3]
    you give me NOM
    'The one you gave me.' (Cantonese)

b. Bilingual speakers set up an equivalence [M_{NOM}]:[R_{NOM}] between the Chinese nominalizer and the pronoun *one* based on overlapping functions as in (89):

(89)   hung4-sik1 ge3
        red-colour NOM
        'a/the red one'

c. Bilingual speakers follow an analogical formula [$M_{NOM} \sim M_{REL}$]:[$R_{NOM} \sim R_{REL}$] resulting in a continuum including nominalizing and relative clause structures in the replica language:

(90)   [the red one $\sim$ you give me one]

d. Grammaticalization of *one* can proceed by extending the construction with *one* from adjectival nominalization (89) to clausal nominalization as in (91), parallel to (88):

(91)   you give me one

These steps suffice to derive the *one*-relative as discussed in chapter 6 by contact-induced grammaticalization.

8.4.2   One-*relatives in Cantonese-English bilingual children*

As shown in chapter 6, the bilingual children use *one* in relative clauses, parallel in some respects to SCE. Thus Alicia uses *one* to construct first object relatives (92) and later subject relatives (93):

(92)   Daddy, where is that blue bag? My . . . me make that one?
        [i.e. the one I made]   (Alicia 3;05;06)

(93)   Father: What shall we put on you?
        CHI: Have gung1zai2 that one.
        [i.e. 'The dress that has a cartoon character on it.']   (Alicia 3;08;01)

The equivalent relative construction in Cantonese has already been acquired by Alicia, as illustrated by the following examples:

(94)   Ngo5 waak6 go2   go3 le1
        I   draw   DEM   CL   SFP
        'What about the one I drew?'   (Alicia 2;01;01)

(95)   jan4dei6 sung3   bei2 ngo5 go2 go3 aa3,
        people   present give me   DEM CL   SFP
        'the one someone gave me as a present,'

        jan4dei6 bei2 ngo5 go2   go3 aa3
        people   give me   DEM   CL   SFP
        'the one someone gave me'   (Alicia 3;04;21)

The model for replica grammaticalization therefore exists for the child, consistent with the steps outlined in section 8.4.1 above.

8.4.3   SCE and bilingual development compared

As in the case of *already* (see section 8.2), the structures involved in SCE and in our children's bilingual development are similar but the models are somewhat different in each case. For Cantonese-dominant children, two nominalizing strategies which may serve as models are the following (see section 6.1.2 for discussion):

(a) nominalizing morpheme (as in (88)–(89) above)

> (96)   [$_{NP}$ lei5 bei2 ngo5 ge3]
>   you   give me   NOM
>   'the one you gave me'   (Cantonese)

(b) demonstrative + classifier complex as in (97):

> (97)   [$_{NP}$ lei5 bei2 ngo5 go2   go3]
>   you   give me   DEM   CL
>   'the one you gave me'   (Cantonese)

While accounts of SCE generally assume strategy (a), option (b) is also available in the relevant substrate Chinese dialects, including Hokkien, Teochew and Cantonese. Furthermore, strategy (b) is more colloquial in Cantonese and therefore more relevant to child language development, as argued in chapter 6.

8.5   Discussion

We have shown that a range of developmental phenomena in bilingual children are compatible with Heine and Kuteva's model of contact-induced grammaticalization, subject to the modifications introduced in section 8.1.1 and section 8.1.2: in particular, the model cannot plausibly refer to the speaker's knowledge of grammaticalization processes. Instead, what is transferred must involve synchronically identifiable patterns of polyfunctionality.

These parallel developments may also be compatible with other models such as the traditional notion of 'calquing' or with 'polysemy copying' as discussed by Heine and Kuteva (2005: 100). We have pursued the grammaticalization account because of evidence that general principles of grammaticalization apply (such as persistence: see section 8.1.3), and because the model makes the necessary steps more explicit than the traditional notion of 'calquing'. We have shown that bilingual children can and do replicate the process by which certain grammatical patterns spread across languages: the process by which substrate influence of Chinese dialects affects Singapore Colloquial English, and by which patterns of polyfunctionality such as the 'epidemic' of 'acquire' modals spread throughout Southeast Asia (Enfield 2003). More specifically, we have verified several parts of the process as described by Heine and Kuteva (2005), including:

(i) Interlingual identification: the children's parallel usage as in the case of *already* (see section 8.2.2) and dative *give* (see section 8.3.4) supports the perceived equivalence between the model and replica languages;

(ii) Intermediate steps: children's development shows that *give*-passives develop via permissive usages, mediated by bridging contexts (see section 8.3.3, and Heine & Kuteva 2005: 102);

(iii) Gap filling: the children create perfective (see section 8.2.2) and passive forms (see section 8.3.3) to plug gaps where they have yet to acquire the target language strategies. Gap filling is argued to be a motivation for contact-induced grammaticalization, especially in contact languages (Heine & Kuteva 2005: 124).

One implication of these findings is that bilingual first language acquisition is a possible route for substrate influence, both in general and specifically in the development of contact languages such as pidgins and creoles. Parallel phenomena in bilingual development and in Singapore Colloquial English (SCE) illustrate this possibility. We do not mean to suggest that SCE is a creole, or that the bilingual children are developing a 'home creole'. While SCE has in fact been considered 'almost a creole' (Ho & Platt 1993; Gupta 1994), this is no longer a substantive issue to the extent that creoles are no longer seen as a structurally distinct class of languages (Corne 1999; Mufwene 2001). The mechanisms of interaction between English and the substrate grammars remain essentially the same, whether we consider the resulting language to be a variety of English, an English-lexifier creole, or some other form of mixed language.

One remaining difference between the ontogenetic development of bilingual acquisition and the historical development of contact languages involves the differential outcomes. From age five, the bilingual children attended international schools where the teachers and many of the children are more or less monolingual native speakers of English. In this environment, grammatical peculiarities such as Sophie's *give*-passive and Alicia's uninflected verbs with *already* give way to more familiar English voices and tenses. The contact-induced features which occur as developmental stages in these children never develop into a contact language. But what would happen given a whole community of similar children? Just such a community is thought to have given rise to SCE, which has its origins in English-medium schools in ethnically mixed districts including Eurasians, Jews, Armenians and Straits Chinese (Gupta 1994: 33). The teachers included Chinese and Eurasians whose English would have been Chinese-influenced. The Straits Chinese spoke Baba Malay which was itself heavily influenced by Hokkien (Ansaldo & Matthews 1999). In such a social environment, features which develop through interactive development in bilingual and multilingual children can feed into the feature pool of a developing contact language.

NOTES

1. A similar view is suggested by the Relexification model of creole formation, in which words of the lexifier language are assigned lexical entries from the corresponding lexical item in the substrate language, thus taking on the grammatical as well as lexical functions of the substrate item. In such a model, there is no need to assume that grammaticalization takes place (Lefebvre 1998: 40). Instead, 'what is being transferred into the creole is a lexical item with all of its functions, thus a multifunctional lexical entry' (Lefebvre 2004: 180).

2. Heine and Kuteva (2005: 237–239) distinguish L1 > L2 replication, where the speaker's first language forms the model and a second language acts as the replica language, from L2 > L1 replication, where the second language itself serves as the model and the first as the replica. However, this distinction still assumes first and second languages rather than simultaneous bilingualism. The distinction also proves difficult to draw, especially since in some situations the same language serves as both model and replica language (239).

3. The problem here is analogous to that facing the property of persistence, which refers to the way in which grammaticalized items apparently retain characteristics of the lexical item from which they developed (Hopper 1991). The paradox is that speakers cannot know that such a development has occurred. The challenge is to explain these phenomena without attributing such knowledge to speakers of the language. Either the properties of the grammaticalized item are somehow fossilized, or there must be some ontogenetic mechanism which recapitulates or mimics aspects of the historical development (Ziegeler 1997).

4. Those recognizing this problem sometimes appeal to a notion of 'panchrony' intended to subsume diachronic and synchronic perspectives. We avoid this concept since it circumvents the problem rather than tackling it head-on, and introduces intractable new problems (Newmeyer 1998: 284). We believe that the Jakobsonian insight of diachrony-in-synchrony can be more effectively pursued by distinguishing diachronic processes from (a) their synchronic reflexes, and (b) their ontogenetic counterparts.

5. However, the Malay *sudah* 'already' may be regarded as an adverb tending to grammaticalize into a marker of perfective aspect. To the extent that Malay *sudah* serves as an additional model for *already* in SCE, replica grammaticalization could be involved.

6. Timmy places the aspect marker *zo2* after the verbal complex (*faan1 lai4 zo2, hei2-san1 zo2*), whereas in adult usage it would attach to the first verb of each complex (*faan1-zo2 lai4, hei2-zo2 san1*). This developmental error is also found in monolingual children.

7. The use of right-dislocation as in *he go already the monster* (36) is highly productive in both child and adult Cantonese. Right-dislocation is also possible in English, as in *He's already gone, the monster*; the frequency of the phenomenon suggests Cantonese influence, although the congruence between the English and Cantonese structures no doubt favours its use by the bilingual children.

8. The particle *saai3* has been identified as a substrate word from the Miao-Yao language family (Yue-Hashimoto 1991), which helps to explain why it lacks equivalents in other dialects (Matthews 2006b). See also Matthews and Yip (1994: 222–223).

9. The passive marker is typically spelt *hor* in Singapore following English orthography, reflecting the Hokkien pronunciation [hɔ] with an open vowel.

10. Note that the infinitive in *give . . . everybody to eat* is consistent with the passive reading, since some of Sophie's *give*-passives use the infinitive, as in *I already give the mosquito to bite* in (58).

11. Timmy uses the word *tsiah* 'eat' from the Chiu Chow dialect as spoken by his grandmother. This is one of the few Chiu Chow words that he uses, often for jocular effect.

9   Conclusions and implications

Mother: [looking at child's diary] What's this word?
Child: You . . . you always talk about the children's language, and you
         don't know?   (Sophie 7;03;27)

With a quizzical look and a hint of disdain for her parents' academic enterprise,
Sophie puts them on the spot. How much do we [now] know about our bilingual
children's language? How much will we ever know? And how do we know it
anyway?

Having written this book, we believe we at least know more than we did
before regarding the process our six bilingual children, in particular our own
three children, go through in acquiring two languages and the striking features
that show up during this process. In this chapter we review the highlights of our
investigation and explore some implications for research in bilingual acquisition
and language contact. We have examined a range of grammatical features in the
development of bilingual children exposed to Cantonese and English from birth.
Though representing only a modest subset of the children's overall grammatical
development, these provide a window into the processes in bilingual acquisition
and language contact.

In chapter 1 we posed some basic questions:

• How do children acquire two languages simultaneously in the first years of
  life?
• Do the two languages develop independently or do they influence each other
  in systematic ways?
• How does bilingual development differ from acquisition of the same two
  languages by monolingual children?
• What role does bilingual development play in language contact and the development of contact languages?

To address these fundamental issues in the development of childhood bilingualism, we have outlined some central theoretical and methodological issues
and presented the aggregate findings on our bilingual children's acquisition of
a number of grammatical domains. On the basis of a systematically collected
and analysed body of empirical data arising out of successive projects spanning

over ten years, we have shown how childhood bilingualism develops naturally in six bilingual children growing up in Hong Kong; how a dominant language influences the development of a weaker language and vice versa in a number of grammatical domains, resulting in bidirectional cross-linguistic influence; and how bilingual children may take strikingly different paths from monolingual children to reach the target grammar.

9.1   Theoretical issues

Our study of early development in Cantonese-English bilingual children is intended to contribute to the respective fields of bilingual acquisition and language contact by clarifying the common threads that draw the two fields together, discussing how the cross-fertilization of these fields deepens our understanding of each, and comparing language contact in the bilingual child at the individual level and language contact at the societal level as seen in languages such as Singapore Colloquial English. We have raised a number of theoretical issues beginning with the epistemological status of the bilingual child's knowledge of language and the intriguing relationship between bilingual first language acquisition and child second language acquisition. While acknowledging the important differences in the two acquisition contexts, we view them as constituting a continuum rather than a dichotomy. We adopt the position that a theoretical model, whether nativist or nonnativist (emergentist or other variants) is necessary to spell out the content of what is acquired in order to properly frame the questions of bilingual acquisition. Both the child's innate endowment, the bilingual instinct and the properties of the dual input in the environment work together to make the development of two languages in the mind of the child such a natural and inexorable process. To what extent the bilingual instinct is domain-specific or domain-general remain very much open to investigation and we expect this profound, perennial research question to continue to generate even more interdisciplinary research in the years to come.

Our work is grounded on the complementarity of generative and typological approaches, whose combined insights illuminate much of our grammatical analysis of various constructions in bilingual development and language contact. It is our experience that the two seemingly divergent frameworks share ample common ground that provides useful tools for the investigation of the grammatical phenomena of interest.

Another theoretical issue raised in chapter 2 is the logical problem of bilingual acquisition and the poverty of the dual stimulus. Compared with the monolingual child, the acquisition task poses a more severe challenge to the bilingual child in that two different languages are to be acquired in more or less the same span of time. Two sides of the logical problem need to be distinguished: the case of the bilingual child successfully acquiring knowledge of two languages that goes beyond the limited dual input, and the converse case of the bilingual child *not* acquiring the equivalent knowledge to the monolingual child in the same time span. While cases of success in attaining bilingual competence strengthen the argument from the poverty of stimulus, since the deficiency of input is more acute and the success all the more remarkable, cases of uneven development, where the course of development of one or both languages may be less rapid and uniform than the monolingual counterparts, also call for explanation.

9.1.1   Bilingual development of grammatical systems

We have assumed from the outset that the bilingual child's two systems constitute two separate systems. It is worth recapitulating why we adopt the assumption that the bilingual child has two separate and differentiated systems. If the systems were not separate we should see the same grammar applying to both languages. But this is not what we see at all. For example, if there were a single undifferentiated system for both languages, we would expect to see *wh*-questions formed with and without *wh*-movement (see chapter 4) or relative clauses sometimes preceding and sometimes following the noun (see chapter 6), in both languages. What we see is highly frequent *wh*-in-situ questions and prenominal relative clauses in English as a developmental stage in the Cantonese-dominant children under the influence of Cantonese. In the case of Cantonese locative prepositional phrases with *hai2* 'at', regardless of dominance, all the bilingual children tend to place the PP after the verb in Cantonese under English influence, but do not place prepositional phrases before the verb in their English (see section 7.1). The bilingual children produce *bei2* 'give' dative constructions in the [V-R-T] order which coincides with the English target order and universally preferred order but do not produce English dative constructions in Cantonese order with [V-T-R] (see section 7.2). If there were a unitary system for both languages, we would expect both orders to occur in both languages but this is not what we find.

At the same time, we have seen strong evidence for interaction between the two developing grammatical systems. Areas of grammar in which influence of Cantonese on English is evident include the formation of *wh*-questions and relative clauses, the omission of objects, and the word order in verb-particle constructions. The study of these areas argues for an interactive view of early bilingual development. Cross-linguistic influence has been attributed to factors including language dominance and aspects of the language input the children receive, notably ambiguous input in the language subject to influence.

We would stress that the study of interaction between developing grammatical systems is still young. We do not yet know why interaction is observed in some children and not in others. There are two main possibilities:

(i) ecological differences in the children's language environment
(ii) individual variation.

Differences in the environment can in turn be separated into:

(a) family structure: nuclear vs. extended families, single children vs. children with siblings, etc.
(b) input patterns: language separation by caregivers vs. language alternation and code-mixing.

Some European studies such as that of De Houwer (1990) take place in a nuclear family, where a one parent – one language situation may mean just that. In Asian societies an extended family is traditionally the norm, with relatives and caregivers other than the parents contributing significantly to the input. In our case study, these additional sources of input tip the balance in favour of Cantonese.

Similar considerations apply to the reasons why interaction occurs, in those cases when it does. In our data, transfer is strongly asymmetrical. In a number of constructions, we see pervasive influence of the dominant language on the weaker language: in the Cantonese-dominant siblings there is systemic transfer of *wh*-in-situ, null objects and relative clauses. By contrast, the weaker language's influence on the dominant language is limited: influence of English on Cantonese as in the placement of PPs with *hai2* 'at', word order of theme and recipient in the dative construction with *bei2* 'give' and verb particle constructions, discussed in chapter 7, is limited to 'vulnerable domains' where properties of the Cantonese input create problems of learnability for bilingual and, in the case of the dative, also for monolingual children.

Overall our findings support Grosjean's (1989) view that 'bilinguals are not two monolinguals in one'. The bilingual children in our study have a distinct and unique linguistic profile that cannot be characterized as a composite of two monolinguals housed in the same mind. The trajectory of developmental changes and acquisition processes in the bilingual child are more complex and intricate as a result of the contact and interaction of two languages in the same mind/brain.

9.1.2   Language dominance and input ambiguity

Language dominance has not been a fashionable topic of research, and some have even argued that it is superfluous as an explanation. This may be correct to the extent that certain structures are susceptible to transfer independent of dominance. For example, the placement of locative PPs with *hai2* 'at' in Cantonese as described in chapter 7 is susceptible to influence from English, or (presumably) any language with consistently postverbal PPs. These are 'vulnerable domains' for reasons which can be identified, such as potentially ambiguous input data. Such cases do not invalidate language dominance, however. The concept will still be needed, if only because there is no clear and categorical way to draw a line between bilingual first language acquisition and child second language acquisition. That is, at a certain point in the continuum, a dominant language is likely to be described as a first language and the weaker language as a second language. There is no compelling conceptual or empirical reason to believe that at any point a qualitative gap opens up between bilingual children with a dominant language and children with first and second languages. The language dominance hypothesis proposed in section 2.5.2 serves to highlight the significant role of dominance in childhood bilingualism which predicts that cross-linguistic influence will occur (in some but not all domains of grammar) when one of the languages assumes dominance over the other. We have shown that the degree of dominance as measured by the MLU differential can account for some phenomena including the different proportions of *wh*-in-situ and null objects in the English of the bilingual children depending on how far Cantonese is ahead of English.

Another proposal is the developmental asynchrony hypothesis which suggests that independent of the overall dominance of one language over the other, a particular domain of grammar in a language may develop faster in accordance with the monolingual timetable which happens to be earlier due to language-specific reasons. For example, Cantonese *dim2gaai2* 'why' questions *zou6 mat1je5* 'why/what for' questions are relatively transparent morphologically since the form *dim2gaai2* is made up of morphemes meaning *dim2* 'how' and *gaai2* 'explain' and *zou6 mat1je5* literally means 'do what', which may account for an advantage in the acquisition of Cantonese *why* questions by monolingual and bilingual children alike (see section 4.3). When the two monolingual developmental schedules are compared, Cantonese *why* questions emerge 3.7 months earlier than English ones (see tables 4.3 and 4.4). If the bilingual child develops in accordance with the monolingual schedule, it is expected that Cantonese *why* questions will be acquired earlier than English *why* questions by the bilingual child, which then sets up a situation whereby the knowledge of Cantonese *why* questions can transfer to English, as a stopgap measure, resulting in the accelerated emergence of *why* questions at 30.8 months in our bilingual children's English (table 4.5) relative to their emergence at 35.0 months in monolingual English development (table 4.3).

We have proposed to clarify the notion of input ambiguity (Müller 1998; Müller & Hulk 2001) by identifying two types of ambiguity (see section 2.6.3): (i) ambiguity of analysis, whereby a given form is compatible with different structural analyses; (ii) ambiguity of evidence, whereby the input provides variable orders, providing ambiguous evidence concerning the placement of constituents such as PPs with *hai2* 'at' and word order of *bei2* 'give' dative constructions in Cantonese (see chapter 7). When a language presenting such ambiguities is in contact with another language where there is no ambiguity of evidence, i.e. the word order is uniform, then the language with ambiguity is subject to influence from the language without ambiguity.

9.2   Methodological issues

Although a century has passed since serious studies of bilingual child language acquisition began, it is only in recent decades that the research questions have come into focus, and the advent of corpora has made it possible to document and quantify aspects of development in detail and with systematicity. Our study has combined state-of-the-art multimedia corpora with the traditional diary method, which continues to be fruitful.

Corpora of the kind generally used today, including our Cantonese-English bilingual corpus, give only a general, incomplete picture of the complex development of childhood bilingualism. For example, our corpora do not provide sufficient tokens of relative clauses, which are richly represented in our diary data (see chapter 6). Some of the limitations of such corpora can be overcome by using sufficiently dense corpora (Tomasello & Stahl 2004; Noji 1973–1977). This solution is extremely demanding in terms of resources, however, and it is not obvious that it renders the diary method obsolete. For example, diary data could help to establish which acquisition situations would best repay the substantial investment required for a dense corpus or experimental study.

At the same time, large-scale corpora are valuable in enabling systematic quantitative investigation to be conducted. They allow us to show, for example, how the rate of null objects differs between monolingual and bilingual children, as well as between bilingual children showing different degrees of dominance (chapter 5). Subtle cases of cross-linguistic influence, such as those of English on Cantonese as discussed in chapter 7, call for statistical comparisons with monolingual baseline data.

9.3   Implications for first and second language acquisition

As Brian MacWhinney has observed, the study of bilingual acquisition can refine the theory of first language acquisition: 'One promising application is the use of child bilingualism as a way of informing our theories of monolingual acquisition' (MacWhinney 2001: 263). A related point is made by Fred Genesee:

Theories of language acquisition are currently based largely on monolingual children, but must ultimately incorporate the 'facts' of BFLA if they are to be comprehensive. While most theories do not exclude the possibility of learning two languages at the same time, they do not address it explicitly or in detail. Research on BFLA can fill this gap in our knowledge. (Genesee 2006: 45)

While the field of BFLA regularly adopts methods and insights from (monolingual) first language acquisition, the relationship between these two fields is a two-way street. Many cases in this book demonstrate this point. In the domain of *wh*-interrogatives, for example, the bilingual data shed light on:

- the acquisition of English *wh*-in-situ questions as an intermediate stage of bilingual development, as well as a subsequent optional *wh*-movement stage in the acquisition of *wh*-questions (section 4.2.5);
- intermediate grammars such as split *what* questions (section 4.3.1) and partial *wh*-movement, where the bilingual children spontaneously produce non-target structures which monolinguals are not known to produce (see section 4.3.6).

If English is considered one of the first languages of our bilingual children, then these developmental stages will have to be taken into consideration in the overall model of acquisition of English as a first language. Moreover, the ambiguity of evidence posed by echo *wh*-questions in English and their overlap with Cantonese *wh*-in-situ questions raise new questions regarding the relationship between echo and non-echo *wh*-questions in bilingual and monolingual development: how are echo questions acquired, and how do children distinguish them from questions formed by *wh*-movement?

MacWhinney also points out that 'studies of children learning two languages of markedly different structure can shed light on basic issues in language processing' (2001: 264). The case of relative clauses bears out this point: we have suggested that object relatives develop early in the children's English because the structure transferred from Cantonese exploits the canonical SVO structure of a main clause. Consequently, processing difficulties that are an obstacle in monolingual English-speaking children's acquisition of object relative clauses may not arise.

The parallels between bilingual acquisition and second language acquisition are a recurrent theme in the literature. Exactly how similar the bilingual child's weaker language is to the L2 in second language acquisition awaits further research and refinement. It seems unlikely that there will emerge any discrete way to categorize individual child learners as having two first languages or a L1 with a L2. These are among the challenging epistemological issues that the fields of bilingual and second language acquisition have to address in building an overall theory of language acquisition.

9.4 Implications for language contact

Though the data come from two specific languages, Cantonese and English, the theoretical claims made go beyond these languages and potentially apply to any combination of languages in a contact situation. These implications are illustrated by the parallels between our children's English and emerging varieties of English, in particular Singapore Colloquial English (SCE). In both SCE and our bilingual children's English, we see systematic divergences from standard English, many of them attributable to the interaction of English with Chinese including *wh*-in-situ questions (chapter 4), null objects (chapter 5) and prenominal relatives (chapter 6). These parallels would be of interest to the study of emerging varieties of English. SCE is seen as a nativized variety of English born of a multilingual situation with several varieties of Chinese prevalent in the environment, along with Malay and other languages such as Tamil. The linguistic ecology in which the bilingual children's English develops may thus be seen as a microcosm of the more complex ecology which gave rise to SCE and other English-based contact languages (see Chinese Pidgin English in section 4.5.2).

Given these parallels, it can be concluded that cross-linguistic influence in the course of bilingual development represents a possible mechanism for substrate influence as seen in SCE, and other contact languages including creoles such as Hawaiian Creole English. The extent to which bilingual children have been an agent of influence must depend on local socio-historical circumstances. Given the similarities and the continuum between bilingual language acquisition and second language acquisition, we assume that such influence takes place alongside classical transfer in SLA. Nevertheless the bilingual child bridges the dichotomy between child and adult contributions to the formation of creoles and other contact languages.

Another dichotomy which breaks down is that between internal and external change. In the case of contact-induced grammaticalization (chapter 8), parallel developments in bilingual development and in contact languages imply that no such distinction is tenable. Rather, changes along natural pathways of development may be triggered or accelerated by contact with another language in which grammaticalization along a similar pathway has resulted in patterns of polyfunctionality which can undergo transfer. We thus come to see contact as a catalyst for grammaticalization.

9.5   Prospects for future research

Our study offers a window into the rich diversity and heterogeneity of bilingual children, their developmental processes and acquisition outcomes. Far from demonstrating the full range of variability in bilingual development, we have shown that individual bilingual children can develop in very different ways from each other. Compared with monolingual development, bilingual development is necessarily more diverse given the variables related to two different languages and the bilingual environment. Some of these differences can be accounted for in principled ways: for example, the different null object rates in our bilingual children's English may reflect the bilingual child's degree of dominance in

Cantonese over English (see section 5.3). Language-specific properties of the target languages investigated in light of linguistic theory and typology, and properties of child-directed input in the bilingual environment, will be among the topics of future research in order to pin down the source of variability in bilingual development.

Our study lies close to the beginning of the investigation of bilingual acquisition of an important language pair: a Chinese language together with English. Even with the data in our corpus, many more grammatical domains remain to be investigated: argument structure, definiteness, number and gender agreement, tense and aspect, are just a few domains where contact phenomena have been noted in this study but not pursued in depth. More studies investigating childhood bilingualism pairing a Chinese language with a language other than English will be important in extending the empirical database and addressing theoretical issues related to language contact and cross-linguistic interaction. Childhood bilingualism will be better understood when investigated against a rich background of diverse language pairs, including Chinese and other Asian languages. The transfer of Cantonese-based prenominal relative clauses into English discussed in chapter 6 is a case in point: it is only when a Chinese language is paired with English, a language with different typological characteristics, that the phenomenon has been documented.

The study of bilingual acquisition will continue to thrive on being interdisciplinary, drawing on different fields as well as making contributions to them. Bilingual acquisition research will continue to address central issues of interest to the field of language acquisition at large: the contribution of the child's innate capacity for language and general cognitive development, the input properties of each language in the child's environment, and the complex interplay between these factors in the course of bilingual development. Other general questions for future studies include: how do different dominance patterns shape the development of different language pairs? What are the effects of factors such as age of first exposure, imbalance, interruption or temporary deprivation of input? What are the qualitative and quantitative differences between bilingual and monolingual acquisition? In what way is the simultaneous acquisition of two languages similar to and different from the successive acquisition of two languages in childhood? To what extent is the difference between the bilingual child's dominant and non-dominant languages of a similar magnitude to that between a first and second language in early child second language acquisition? These questions should be testable empirically, based on studies of children with different patterns of language dominance.

Apart from longitudinal corpus data based on case studies, experimental data are called for to investigate unexplored territory in bilingual acquisition in terms of language perception, production and comprehension. Studies of language differentiation in phonology, in terms of segmental and suprasegmental features (including tone and prosody), are especially lacking compared to the growing literature on the development of bilingual lexicon and syntax. The acquisition of tone in bilingual children is one area where studies of Chinese can contribute to the overall understanding of bilingual development. Another area of research that is unique to bilingual contexts and which awaits investigation in the Chinese context involves bilingual children's code-mixing patterns (Lanza 2004) and the emergence of structural constraints governing early code-mixing (Paradis, Nicoladis & Genesee 2004).

The case studies presented in the book may be used for comparison with children learning other language pairs, or with atypical children such as those with language delay or disorders, who may also be bilingual (Genesee, Paradis & Crago 2004). Basic research of this kind also serves to inform educational administrators in formulating policies that have an impact on the linguistic future of children, as well as parents and caregivers who would like to bring up their children bilingual. As the eminent psycholinguist and champion of bilingualism Francois Grosjean (2001b) remarked, 'One never regrets knowing several languages but one can certainly regret not knowing enough.' Speaking two languages is widely considered an asset, not just for adults but more importantly for children: in the age of globalization, children with knowledge of more than one language would be better equipped to live in an increasingly multilingual and multicultural world.

References

Aarts, Bas. 1995. Secondary predicates in English. In Bas Aarts and Charles F. Meyer (eds.), *The Verb in Contemporary English: Theory and Description*. Cambridge: Cambridge University Press, pp. 75–100.

Adone, Dany. 1994. *The Acquisition of Mauritian Creole*. Amsterdam: John Benjamins.
2002. Double object constructions in creole acquisition. Paper presented at the Society for Pidgin and Creole Linguistics Meeting. San Francisco: USA.

Adone, Dany and Ingo Plag (eds.). 1994. *Creolization and Language Change*. Tübingen: Max Niemeyer Verlag.

Aikhenvald, Alexandra Y. 2002. *Language Contact in Amazonia*. Oxford: Oxford University Press.
2006. Serial verb constructions in typological perspective. In Alexandra Aikhenvald and R. M. W. Dixon (eds.), *Serial Verbs: A Cross-linguistic Typology*. Oxford: Oxford University Press, pp. 1–68.

Aikhenvald, Alexandra Y. and R. M. W. Dixon (eds.). 2006. *Grammars in Contact*. Oxford: Oxford University Press.

Albom, Mitch. 2003. *The Five People You Meet in Heaven*. UK: Time Warner.

Alsagoff, Lubna and Ho Chee Lick. 1998. Relative clauses in Singapore English. *World Englishes* 17: 127–138.

Andersen, Roger W. 1983a. *Pidginization and Creolization as Language Acquisition*. Rowley, MA: Newbury House.
1983b. Transfer to somewhere. In Susan Gass and Larry Selinker (eds.), *Language Transfer in Language Learning*. Rowley, MA: Newbury House, pp. 177–221.

Ansaldo, Umberto. 1999. A typology of comparatives in Sinitic: areal typology and patterns of grammaticalization. PhD thesis, Stockholm University.

Ansaldo, Umberto and Stephen Matthews. 1999. The Min substrate and creolization in Baba Malay. *Journal of Chinese Linguistics* 27: 38–68.
2001. Typical creoles and simple languages: the case of Sinitic. *Linguistic Typology* 5: 311–325.

Aoun, Joseph and Audrey Y. H. Li. 2003. *Essays on the Representational and Derivational Nature of Grammar: the Diversity of Wh-Constructions*. Cambridge, MA: MIT Press.

Arends, Jacques, Pieter Muysken and Norval Smith (eds.). 1994. *Pidgins and Creoles: An Introduction*. Amsterdam: John Benjamins.

Artstein, Ron. 2002. A focus semantics for echo questions. In Agnes Bende-Farkas and Arndt Riester (eds.), *Workshop on Information Structure in Context*, IMS, University of Stuttgart, pp. 98–107.

Backus, Ad. 2004. Convergence as a mechanism of language change. *Bilingualism: Language and Cognition* 7: 179–181.

Baker, Carl Lee. 1979. Syntactic theory and the projection problem. *Linguistic Inquiry* 10: 533–581.

Baker, Carl Lee and John McCarthy (eds.). 1981. *The Logical Problem of Language Acquisition*. Cambridge, MA: MIT Press.

Baker, Colin. 2001. *Foundations of Bilingual Education and Bilingualism* 3rd edition. Clevedon: Multilingual Matters.

Baker, Colin and Sylvia Prys Jones. 1998. *Encyclopedia of Bilingualism and Bilingual Education*. Clevedon: Multilingual Matters.

Bakker, Peter. 2002. Some future challenges for pidgin and creole studies. In Glenn Gilbert (ed.), *Pidgin and Creole Linguistics in the Twenty-first Century*. Frankfurt: Peter Lang, pp. 69–92.

Bao, Zhiming. 1995. *Already* in Singapore English. *World Englishes* 14: 181–188.

2001. The origins of empty categories in Singapore English. *Journal of Pidgin and Creole Languages* 16: 275–319.

2005. The aspectual system of Singapore English and the systemic substratist explanation. *Journal of Linguistics* 41: 237–267.

Bao, Zhiming and Lionel Wee. 1999. The passive in Singapore English. *World Englishes* 18: 1–11.

Bates, Elizabeth. 1998. Construction grammar and its implications for child language: comment on Tomasello. *Journal of Child Language* 25: 462–466.

Bates, Elizabeth and Brian MacWhinney. 1989. Functionalism and the Competition Model. In Brian MacWhinney and Elizabeth Bates (eds.), *The Cross-linguistic Study of Sentence Processing*. Cambridge: Cambridge University Press, pp. 3–76.

Bauer, Robert and Paul Benedict. 1997. *Modern Cantonese Phonology*. Berlin: Mouton de Gruyter.

Bellugi, Ursula. 1971. Simplification in children's language. In Renira Huxley and Elizabeth Ingram (eds.), *Language Acquisition: Models and Methods*. New York: Academic Press, pp. 95–119.

Bernardini, Petra. 2003. Child and adult acquisition of word order in the Italian DP. In Natascha Müller (ed.), *(In)vulnerable Domains in Multilingualism*. Amsterdam: John Benjamins, pp. 41–81.

Bernardini, Petra and Suzanne Schlyter. 2004. Growing syntactic structure and code-mixing in the weaker language. *Bilingualism: Language and Cognition* 7: 49–69.

Bialystok, Ellen. 2001. *Bilingualism in Development: Language, Literacy and Cognition*. Cambridge: Cambridge University Press.

Bickerton, Derek. 1981. *Roots of Language*. Ann Arbor: Karoma.

2003. Refuting the Bioprogram is easy . . . Paper presented at the Society for Pidgin and Creole Linguistics, University of Hawaii at Manoa.

Bley-Vroman, Robert. 1986. Hypothesis testing in second language acquisition theory. *Language Learning* 36: 353–376.

Bloom, Lois. 1973. *One Word at a Time: The Use of Single-word Utterances before Syntax*. The Hague: Mouton.

Bloom, Lois, Susan Merkin and Janet Wootten. 1982. *Wh*-questions: linguistic factors that contribute to the sequence of acquisition. *Child Development* 53: 1084–1092.

Bloomfield, Leonard. 1933. *Language*. New York: Henry Holt.

Bosch, Laura and Núria Sebastián-Gallés. 1997. Infant bilingual language questionnaire. Unpublished instrument, Universitat de Barcelona, Barcelona, Spain.
    2001. Early language differentiation in bilingual infants. In Jasone Cenoz and Fred Genesee (eds.), *Trends in Bilingual Acquisition*. Amsterdam: John Benjamins, pp. 71–93.
    2003. Simultaneous bilingualism and the perception of a language-specific vowel contrast in the first year of life. *Language and Speech* 46: 217–243.
Bowerman, Melissa. 1988. The 'no negative evidence' problem: how do children avoid constructing an overly general grammar? In John Hawkins (ed.), *Explaining Language Universals*. Oxford: Blackwell, pp. 73–101.
Brandt, Silke, Holger Diessel and Michael Tomasello. Forthcoming. The acquisition of German relative clauses: a case study.
Braunwald, Susan. R. and R. W. Brislin. 1979. The diary method updated. In Elinor Ochs and Bambi Schieffelin (eds.), *Developmental Pragmatics*. New York: Academic Press, pp. 11–42.
Brown, Roger. 1973. *A First Language: The Early Stages*. Harvard University Press.
Browning, Larry. 1974. The Cantonese dialect with special reference to contrasts with Mandarin as an approach to determining dialect relatedness. PhD thesis, Georgetown University.
Bruyn, Adrienne. 1996. On identifying instances of grammaticalization in creole languages. In Philip Baker and Anand Syea (eds.), *Changing Meanings, Changing Functions: Papers Relating to Grammaticalization in Language Contact*. London: Westminster University Press, pp. 29–46.
Bruyn, Adrienne, Pieter Muysken and MaaikeVerrips. 1999. Double-object constructions in the creole languages: development and acquisition. In Michel DeGraff (eds.), *Language Creation and Language Change: Creolization, Diachrony, and Development*. Cambridge, MA: MIT Press, pp. 329–374.
Cenoz, Jason and Fred Genesee (eds.). 2001. *Trends in Bilingual Acquisition*. Amsterdam: John Benjamins.
Chan, Angel Wing-Shan. 2003. The development of *bei2* dative constructions in early child Cantonese. Unpublished MPhil. thesis, Chinese University of Hong Kong.
Chan, Brian Hok-Shing. 1998. How does Cantonese-English code-mixing work? In Martha Pennington (ed.), *Language in Hong Kong at Century's End*. Hong Kong: Hong Kong University Press, pp. 191–216.
    2003. *Aspects of the Syntax, the Pragmatics, and the Production of Code-Switching*. New York: Peter Lang.
Chang-Smith, Meiyun. 2005. First language acquisition of functional categories in Mandarin nominal expressions: a longitudinal study of two Mandarin-speaking children. Unpublished PhD thesis, The Australian National University.
Chao, Yuan-Ren. 1968. *A Grammar of Spoken Chinese*. Berkeley: University of California Press.
    1976. The Cantian idiolect: an analysis of the Chinese spoken by a twenty-eight-months-old child. In *Aspects of Chinese Sociolinguistics: Essays by Yuen Ren Chao*. Stanford, CA: Stanford University Press, pp. 204–228.
Chappell, Hilary (ed.). 2001. *Sinitic Grammar: Synchronic and Diachronic Perspectives*. Oxford: Oxford University Press.

Chappell, Hilary. 2006. Variation in the grammaticalization of *verba dicendi* in Taiwanese Southern Min and other Sinitic languages. Ms. Ecole des Hautes Etudes en Sciences Sociales, Paris.

Chen, Ee-San. 2002. 'You play with me, then I friend you': development of conditional constructions in Chinese-English bilingual preschool children in Singapore. Unpublished PhD thesis, University of Hong Kong.

2003. Language convergence and bilingual acquisition: the case of conditional constructions. *Annual Review of Language Acquisition* 3: 89–137.

Cheng, Lisa. 1997. *On the Typology of Wh-Questions*. Garland Publishing, New York & London.

Cheng, Robert L. 1997a. Taiyu yu Taiwan Guoyu li de ziju jiegou biaozhi 'jiang' yu 'kan' [The complementation markers 'say' and 'see' as complementizers in Taiwanese and Taiwan Mandarin]. In Robert L. Cheng (ed.), *Taiwanese and Mandarin Structures and Their Developmental Trends in Taiwan*. Vol. II, pp. 105–132.

1997b. Causative constructions in Taiwanese. In Robert L. Cheng (ed.), *Taiwanese and Mandarin Structures and Their Developmental Trends in Taiwan*, Vol. II. Taipei: Yuan-Liou Publishing, pp. 201–251.

Cheung, Hung-Nin Samuel. 1972. *Xianggang Yueyu Yufa de Yanjiu (Studies on Cantonese Grammar as Spoken in Hong Kong)*. Hong Kong: Chinese University of Hong Kong Press.

Cheung, Kwan Hin and Robert Bauer. 2002. *The Representation of Cantonese with Chinese Characters. Journal of Chinese Linguistics*, Monograph Series Number 18. Berkeley: University of California.

Cheung, Shuk-Yee Alice. 1995. Acquisition of *wh*-words by Cantonese-speaking children. Unpublished MPhil. thesis, Hong Kong Polytechnic University.

Cheung, Sik-Lee. 1990. The acquisition of locative constructions by Cantonese Children. *Papers & Reports on Child Language Development*. Vol. XXIX. Stanford University, pp. 20–27.

1991. The notion of 'result' in Cantonese children. *Papers & Reports on Child Language Development*. Vol. XXX. Stanford University, pp. 17–24.

Chiat, Shula. 2000. *Understanding Children with Language Problems*. Cambridge: Cambridge University Press.

Chomsky, Noam. 1965. *Aspects of the Theory of Syntax*. Cambridge, MA: MIT Press.

1980. *Rules and Representations*. New York: Columbia University Press.

1986. *Knowledge of Language*. New York: Preger Books.

Clark, Herbert and Eve Clark. 1977. *Psychology and Language: An Introduction to Psycholinguistics*. New York: Harcourt Brace Jovanovich.

Cole, Peter and Gabriella Hermon. 1994. Is there LF movement? *Linguistic Inquiry* 25: 239–262.

Cole, Peter, Gabriella Hermon and Li May Sung. 1990. Principles and parameters of long-distance reflexives. *Linguistic Inquiry* 21: 1–22.

Cole, Peter, Gabriella Hermon and Yassir Nassanius Tjung. 2003. The acquisition of relative clauses in colloquial Jakarta Indonesian. Paper presented at the Workshop on Indonesian Linguistics, Max Planck Institute for Evolutionary Anthropology, Leipzig.

In press. The formation of relative clauses in Jakarta Indonesian. In A. van Engelenhoven and H. Steinhauser (eds.) *Selected Studies on Indonesian/Malay Linguistics*.

Dewan Bahasa dan Pustaka (Kuala Lumpur) and the International Institute for Asian Studies (Leiden/Amsterdam).

Comrie, Bernard. 1996. The unity of noun-modifying clauses in Asian languages. *Proceedings of the 4th International Symposium on Pan-Asiatic Linguistics*, pp. 1077–1088.

1998. Attributive clauses in Asian languages: towards an areal typology. In Winfried Boeder, Christoph Schroeder, Karl Wagner, & Wolfgang Wildgen (eds.), *Sprache in Raum und Zeit, in Memoriam Johannes Bechert, Band 2*. Tübingen: Gunter Narr, pp. 51–60.

2002. Typology and language acquisition: the case of relative clauses. In Anna Giacalone (ed.), *Typology and Second Language Acquisition*. Berlin: Mouton de Gruyter, pp. 19–37.

Corne, Chris. 1999. *From French to Creole: The Development of New Vernaculars in the French Colonial World*. London: University of Westminster Press.

Crain, Stephen and Diane Lillo-Martin. 1999. *Linguistic Theory and Language Acquisition*. Oxford: Blackwell.

Crain, Stephen and Paul Pietroski. 2002. Why language acquisition is a snap. *The Linguistic Review* 19: 163–183.

Crain, Stephen and Rosalind Thornton. 1998. *Investigations in Universal Grammar: A Guide to Experiments on the Acquisition of Syntax and Semantics*. Cambridge, MA: MIT Press.

Dahl, Östen. 2001. Principles of areal typology. In Martin Haspelmath, Ekkehard König, Wulf Österreicher and Wolfgang Raible (eds.), *Language Typology and Language Universals: An International Handbook*. Berlin: Mouton de Gruyter, pp. 1456–1470.

Dasinger, Lisa and Cecile Toupin. 1994. The development of relative clause functions in narratives. In Ruth A. Berman and Dan I. Slobin (eds.), *Relating Events in Narrative: A Cross-linguistic Developmental Study*. Hillsdale, NY: Erlbaum, pp. 457–514.

De Houwer, Annick. 1990. *The Acquisition of Two Languages from Birth: A Case Study*. Cambridge: Cambridge University Press.

1995. Bilingual language acquisition. In Paul Fletcher and Brian MacWhinney (eds.), *The Handbook of Child Language*. Oxford: Blackwell, pp. 219–250.

1998a. By way of introduction: methods in studies of bilingual first language acquisition. *The International Journal of Bilingualism* 2: 249–263.

1998b. Comparing error frequencies in monolingual and bilingual acquisition. *Bilingualism: Language and Cognition* 1: 173–174.

de Villiers, Jill. 1995. Introduction to the special issue on the acquisition of *wh*-questions. *Language Acquisition* 4: 1–4.

de Villiers, Jill and Peter de Villiers. 1985. The acquisition of English. In Dan Slobin (ed.), *The Cross-linguistic Study of Language Acquisition*. Hillsdale, NJ: Lawrence Erlbaum, pp. 27–139.

de Villiers, Jill, Thomas Roeper and Anne Vainikka. 1990. The acquisition of long-distance rules. In Lynn Frazier and Jill de Villiers (eds.), *Language Processing and Language Acquisition*. Dordrecht: Kluwer, pp. 257–297.

DeGraff, Michel. 1999. Creolization, language change, and language acquisition: a Prolegomenon. In Michel DeGraff (ed.), *Language Creation and Language Change: Creolization, Diachrony, and Development*. Cambridge, MA: MIT Press, pp. 1–46.

2003a. Against creole exceptionalism. *Language* 79: 391–410.

2003b. 'Creolization' is acquisition. Paper presented at the Society for Pidgin and Creole Linguistics, University of Hawaii at Manoa.

Demuth, Katherine. 1995. Questions, relatives, and minimal projection. *Language Acquisition* 4: 49–71.

Denham, Kristen. 2000. Optional wh-movement in Babine-Witsuwit'en. *Natural Language and Linguistic Theory* 18: 199–251.

Deuchar, Margaret and Rachel Muntz. 2003. Factors accounting for code-mixing in an early developing bilingual. In Natascha Müller (ed.), *(In)vulnerable Domains in Multilingualism*. Amsterdam: John Benjamins, pp. 161–190.

Deuchar, Margaret and Suzanne Quay. 1998. One vs. two systems in early bilingual syntax: two versions of the question. *Bilingualism: Language and Cognition* 1: 231–243.

2000. *Bilingual Acquisition: Theoretical Implications of a Case Study*. Oxford: Oxford University Press.

Dier, John K. 1860. Pigeon-English. *Knickerbocker* 55: 300–303.

Diessel, Holger and Michael Tomasello. 2000. The development of relative clauses in English. *Cognitive Linguistics* 11: 131–151.

2005a. A new look at the acquisition of relative clauses. *Language* 81: 882–906.

2005b. Particle placement in early child language: a multifactorial analysis. *Corpus Linguistics and Linguistic Theory* 1: 89–112.

Dixon, R. M. W. and Alexandra Y. Aikhenvald (eds.). 2002. *Word: A Cross-linguistic Typology*. Cambridge: Cambridge University Press.

Döpke, Susan. 1992. *One Parent, One Language: An Interactional Approach*. Amsterdam: John Benjamins.

1997. Is the simultaneous acquisition of two languages in early childhood equal to acquiring each of two languages individually? In Eve Clark (ed.), *Proceedings of the 28th Annual Child Language Research Forum*. Stanford Linguistic Forum, pp. 95–113.

1998. Competing language structures: the acquisition of verb placement by bilingual German-English children. *Journal of Child Language* 25: 555–584.

Döpke, Susan (ed.). 2000. *Cross-linguistic Structures in Simultaneous Bilingualism*. Amsterdam: John Benjamins.

Dryer, Matthew. 1992. The Greenbergian word order correlations. *Language* 68: 81–138.

2003. Word order patterns in Sino-Tibetan. In Graham Thurgood and Randy LaPolla (eds.), *The Sino-Tibetan Languages*. London: Routledge, pp. 43–55.

Elman, Jeffrey, Elizabeth Bates, Mark Johnson, Annette Karmiloff-Smith, Domenico Parisi and Kim Plunkett. 1996. *Rethinking Innateness: A Connectionist Perspective on Development*. Cambridge, MA: MIT Press.

Elster, Jon. 1993. *Political Psychology*. Cambridge: Cambridge University Press.

Enfield, N. J. 2003. *Linguistic Epidemiology: Semantics and Grammar of Language Contact in Mainland Southeast Asia*. London: Routledge Curzon.

2004. Areal grammaticalization of postverbal 'acquire' in mainland Southeast Asia. In Somsonge Burusphat (ed.), *Papers from the XIth Annual Meeting of the*

Southeast Asian Linguistics Society. Tempe: Arizona State University, pp. 275–296.

Essegbey, James. 2002. Inherent Complement Verbs Revisited: Towards an Understanding of Argument Structure in Ewe. PhD dissertation, Max Planck Institute for Psycholinguistics.

Evans, Nicholas and David Wilkins. 2000. In the mind's ear: the semantic extensions of perception verbs in Australian languages. *Language* 76: 546–592.

Fernald, Anne. 2006. When infants hear two languages: interpreting research on early speech perception by bilingual children. In Peggy McCardle and Erika Hoff (eds.), *Childhood Bilingualism: Research on Infancy through School Age*. Clevedon: Multilingual Matters, pp. 19–29.

Fillmore, Charles J. 1986. Pragmatically controlled zero anaphora. *Berkeley Linguistics Society* 12: 95–107.

Fodor, Janet Dean. 1998. Unambiguous triggers. *Linguistic Inquiry* 29: 1–36.

Fodor, Janet Dean and Carrie Crowther. 2002. Understanding stimulus poverty arguments. *The Linguistic Review* 19: 105–145.

Fodor, Jerry. 1981. *Representations*. Cambridge, MA: MIT Press.

Fong, Vivienne. 2004. The verbal cluster. In Lisa Lim (ed.), *Singapore English: A Grammatical Description*. Amsterdam: John Benjamins, pp. 75–104.

Foster-Cohen, Susan. 2001. First language acquisition . . . second language acquisition: 'What's Hecuba to him or he to Hecuba?' *Second Language Research* 17: 329–344.

Francis, Elaine and Stephen Matthews. 2005. A multi-dimensional approach to the category 'verb' in Cantonese. *Journal of Linguistics* 41: 267–305.

2006. Serial verbs and object extraction in Cantonese. *Natural Language and Linguistic Theory* 24: 751–801.

Francis, Elaine, Winnie Yiu Sze-Man, Stephen Matthews and Gene Chu. 2002. Cantonese Radio Corpus. University of Hong Kong.

Gass, Susan and Josh Ard. 1984. Second language acquisition and the ontology of language universals. In William Rutherford (ed.), *Language Universals and Second Language Acquisition*. Amsterdam: John Benjamins, pp. 33–68.

Gavruseva, Elena and Rosalind Thornton. 2001. Getting it right: *whose* questions in child English. *Language Acquisition* 9: 229–267.

Gawlitzek-Maiwald, Ira and Rosemary Tracy. 1996. Bilingual bootstrapping. *Linguistics* 34: 901–926.

Genesee, Fred. 1989. Early bilingual development: one language or two? *Journal of Child Language* 6: 161–179.

2006. Bilingual first language acquisition in perspective. In Peggy McCardle and Erika Hoff (eds.), *Childhood Bilingualism: Research on Infancy through School Age*. Clevedon: Multilingual Matters pp. 45–67.

Genesee, Fred, Elena Nicoladis and Johanne Paradis. 1995. Language differentiation in early bilingual development. *Journal of Child Language* 22: 611–631.

Genesee, Fred, Johanne Paradis and Martha Crago. 2004. *Dual Language Development and Disorders: A Handbook on Bilingualism and Second Language Learning*. Baltimore: Paul H. Brookes.

Gibson, Edward. 1998. Linguistic complexity: locality of syntactic dependencies. *Cognition* 69: 1–76.

Gibson, Edward and Kenneth Wexler. 1994. Triggers. *Linguistic Inquiry* 25: 407–454.

Gil, David. 2003. English goes Asian: Number and (in)definiteness in the Singlish noun phrase. In Frans Plank (ed.), *Noun Phrase Structure in the Languages of Europe*. Berlin: Mouton de Gruyter, pp. 467–514.

Gisborne, Nikolas. 2000. Relative clauses in Hong Kong English. *World Englishes* 19: 357–371.

Givón, Talmy. 1984. *Syntax: A Functional-Typological Introduction*. Vol. I Amsterdam: John Benjamins.

Gleitman, Lila R. 1990. The structural sources of verb meanings. *Language Acquisition* 1: 3–55.

Goldberg, Adele. 2001. Patient arguments of causative verbs can be omitted: the role of information structure in argument distribution. *Language Sciences* 23: 503–524.

Gordon, Raymond G. (ed.). 2005. *Ethnologue: Languages of the World*. 15th edition. Dallas, Texas: Summer Institute of Linguistics. Internet version: http://www.ethnologue.com/

Grammont, Maurice. 1902. Observations sur le langage des enfants. In D. Barbelenet & Paul Boyer (eds). *Mélanges Linguistiques Offerts à M. Antoine Meillet*. Paris: Klincksieck, pp. 61–82.

Greenberg, Joseph H. 1963. Some universals of grammar, with particular reference to the order of meaningful elements. In Joseph Greenberg (ed.), *Universals of Language*. Cambridge, MA: MIT Press, pp. 73–113.

Gries, Stefan Th. 1999. Particle movement: a cognitive and functional approach. *Cognitive Linguistics* 10: 105–145.

2003. *Multifactorial Analysis in Corpus Linguistics: A Study of Particle Placement*. London, New York: Continuum Press.

Gropen, Jess, Steven Pinker, Michelle Hollander, Richard Goldberg and Ronald Wilson. 1989. The learnability and acquisition of the dative alternation in English. *Language* 65: 203–255.

Grosjean, François. 1989. Neurolinguists, beware! The bilingual is not two monolinguals in one person. *Brain and Language* 36: 3–15.

1995. A psycholinguistic approach to code-switching: the recognition of guest words by bilinguals. In Lesley Milroy and Peter Muysken (eds.), *One Speaker, Two Languages*. Cambridge: Cambridge University Press, pp. 259–275.

1998. Transfer and language mode. *Bilingualism: Language and Cognition* 1: 175–176.

2001a. Bilinguals' language modes. In Janet Nicol (ed.), *One Mind, Two Languages: Bilingual Language Processing*. Oxford: Blackwell, pp. 1–22.

2001b. The right of the deaf child to grow up bilingual. *Sign Language Studies* 1: 110–114.

Gupta, Anthea Fraser. 1991. Acquisition of diglossia in Singapore English. In Anna Kwan-Terry (ed.), *Child Language Development in Singapore and Malaysia*. Singapore: Singapore University Press, pp. 119–160.

1992. Contact features of Singapore Colloquial English. In Kingsley Bolton and Helen Kwok (eds.), *Sociolinguistics Today: International Perspectives*. London: Routledge, pp. 323–345.

1994. *The Step-tongue: Children's English in Singapore*. Clevedon: Multilingual Matters.

Haegeman, Liliane. 1987. The interpretation of inherent objects in English. *Australian Journal of Linguistics* 7: 223–248.

Haegeman, Liliane and Jacqueline Guéron. 1999. *English Grammar: A Generative Perspective*. Oxford: Blackwell Publishers.

Hamburger, Henry and Stephen Crain. 1982. Relative acquisition. In Stan Kuczaj (ed.), *Language Development* Vol. I. Hillsdale, NJ: Lawrence Erlbaum, pp. 245–274.

Harrison, Godfrey and Soo Lin Lim. 1988. The acquisition of English questions by young Singaporean children. In Joseph Foley (ed.), *New Englishes: The Case of Singapore*. Singapore: Singapore University Press, pp. 149–168.

Hawkins, John A. 1990. A parsing theory of word order universals. *Linguistic Inquiry* 21: 223–262.

1994. *A Performance Theory of Order and Constituency*. Cambridge: Cambridge University Press.

1999. Processing complexity and filler-gap dependencies across grammars. *Language* 75: 244–285.

2004. *Efficiency and Complexity in Grammars*. Oxford: Oxford University Press.

Hawkins, Roger and Cecilia Yuet-Hung Chan. 1997. The partial availability of Universal Grammar in second language acquisition: the 'failed functional features Hypothesis'. *Second Language Research* 13: 187–226.

Heine, Bernd. 2002. On the role of context in grammaticalization. In Ilse Wischer and Gabriele Diewald (eds.), *New Reflections on Grammaticalization*. Amsterdam: John Benjamins, pp. 83–101.

Heine, Bernd and Tania Kuteva. 2003. On contact-induced grammaticalization. *Studies in Language* 27: 529–72.

2005. *Language Contact and Grammatical Change*. Cambridge: Cambridge University Press.

Hermon, Gabriella. 2005. The acquisition of relative clauses in colloquial Jakarta Indonesian. Paper presented at the Workshop on the Typology, Processing and Acquisition of Relative Clauses. Max Planck Institute for Evolutionary Anthropology, Leipzig, Germany.

Ho, Mian-Lian and David Platt. 1993. *Dynamics of a Contact Continuum: Singapore English*. Oxford: Clarendon Press.

Ho, Samantha Shuk Kwan. 2003. Syntactic transfer in Cantonese-English bilingual development: a corpus-based study of phrasal verbs. Unpublished Bachelor of Cognitive Science thesis, University of Hong Kong.

Hoffmann, Charlotte. 1991. *An Introduction to Bilingualism*. London: Longman.

Holm, John. 2000. *An Introduction to Pidgins and Creoles*. Cambridge: Cambridge University Press.

Hopper, Paul. 1991. On some principles of grammaticalization. In Elizabeth Traugott and Bernd Heine (eds.), *Approaches to Grammaticalization*. Vol. I. Amsterdam: John Benjamins, pp. 17–35.

Hopper, Paul and Elizabeth Traugott. 1993. *Grammaticalization*. Cambridge: Cambridge University Press.

Hornstein, Norbert and David Lightfoot. (eds.). 1981. *Explanation in Linguistics: The Logical Problem of Language Acquisition*. London: Longman.

Hsiao, Franny and Edward Gibson. 2003. Processing relative clauses in Chinese. *Cognition* 90: 3–27.

Huang, C. T. James. 1982. Move *wh* in a language without *wh*-movement. *The Linguistic Review* 1: 369–416.

1984. On the distribution and reference of empty pronouns. *Linguistic Inquiry* 15: 531–574.

1995. Logical form. In Gert Webelhuth (ed.), *Government and Binding Theory and the Minimalist Program*. Oxford: Blackwell, pp. 127–175.

Huang, Pai-Yuan Simon. 1999. The development of null arguments in a Cantonese-English bilingual child. Unpublished MPhil thesis, Chinese University of Hong Kong.

Hudelot, Christian. 1980. Qu'est-ce que la complexité syntaxique? L'exemple de la relative. [What is syntactic complexity? The case of the relative clause.] *La Linguistique* 16: 5–41.

Hulk, Aafke and Elizabeth van der Linden. 1996. Language mixing in a French-Dutch bilingual child. In Eric Kellerman, Bert Weltens and Theo Bongaerts (eds.), *EUROSLA 6: A Selection of Papers*. Utrecht: Vereniging voor Toegepaste Taalwetenschap, pp. 89–101.

Hulk, Aafke and Natascha Müller. 2000. Bilingual first language acquisition at the interface between syntax and pragmatics. *Bilingualism: Language and Cognition* 3: 227–244.

Hyams, Nina. 1986. *Language Acquisition and the Theory of Parameters*. Dordrecht: Reidel.

Hyams, Nina and Kenneth Wexler. 1993. On the grammatical basis of null subjects in child language. *Linguistic Inquiry* 24: 421–459.

Hyltenstam, Kenneth. 1984. The use of typological markedness conditions as predictors in second language acquisition: the case of pronominal copies in relative clauses. In Roger Andersen (ed.), *Second Languages: A Cross-linguistic Perspective*. Rowley, MA: Newbury House, pp. 39–58.

Ingham, Richard. 1993. Input and learnability: direct-object omissibility in English. *Language Acquisition* 3: 95–120.

Jisa, Harriet and Sophie Kern. 1998. Relative clauses in French children's narrative texts. *Journal of Child Language* 25: 623–652.

Keenan, Edward. 1985. Relative clauses. In Timothy Shopen (ed.), *Language Typology and Syntactic Description*. Vol. II: *Complex Constructions*. Cambridge: Cambridge University Press, pp. 141–170.

Keenan, Edward and Bernard Comrie. 1977. Noun phrase accessibility and Universal Grammar. *Linguistic Inquiry* 8: 63–99.

Keesing, Roger M. 1991. Substrates, calquing and grammaticalization in Melanesian pidgin. In Elizabeth C. Traugott and Bernd Heine (eds.), *Approaches to Grammaticalization*. Vol. I. Amsterdam: Philadelphia: John Benjamins, pp. 315–342.

Killingley, Siew-Yue. 1993. *Cantonese*. München, Germany: Lincom Europa.

Klee, Thomas, Stephanie F. Stokes, Anita M-Y. Wong, Paul Fletcher and William J. Gavin. 2004. Utterance length and lexical diversity in Cantonese-speaking children with and without SLI. *Journal of Speech, Language and Hearing Research* 47: 1396–1410.

Klima, Edward and Ursula Bellugi. 1966. Syntactic regularities in the speech of children. In John Lyons and Roger J. Wales (eds.), *Psycholinguistic Papers*. Edinburgh: Edinburgh University Press, pp. 183–208.

Kozinsky, Isaac and Maria Polinsky. 1993. Causee and patient in the causative of transitive: coding conflict or doubling of grammatical relations. In Bernard Comrie and Maria Polinsky (eds.), *Causatives and Transitivity*. Amsterdam: John Benjamins, pp. 177–240.

Krashen, Stephen D. and Tracy D. Terrell. 1983. *The Natural Approach: Language Acquisition in the Classroom*. Oxford: Pergamon Press.

Kupisch, Tanja. 2003. The DP, a vulnerable domain? Evidence from the acquisition of French. In Natascha Müller (ed.), *(In)vulnerable Domains in Multilingualism*. Amsterdam: John Benjamins, pp. 1–39.

Kwan, Wing Man Stella. 2005a. On the word order of locative prepositional phrases in Cantonese: processing, iconicity and grammar. Unpublished MPhil. thesis, University of Hong Kong.

2005b. Placement of locative prepositional phrases in Cantonese: a processing perspective. In Chuanren Ke (ed.). *Proceedings of the 16th North American Conference on Chinese Linguistics (NACCL-16)*, GSIL: University of Southern California, pp. 170–186.

Kwan-Terry, Anna. 1986. The acquisition of word order in English and Cantonese interrogative sentences: a Singapore case study. *RELC Journal* 17: 14–39.

1989. The specification of stage by a child learning English and Cantonese simultaneously: a study of acquisition processes. In Hans W. Dechert and Manfred Raupach (eds.), *Interlingual Processes*. Gunter Narr Verlag Tübingen, pp. 33–48.

Labov, William. 1972. *Language in the Inner City*. Philadelphia: University of Pennsylvania Press.

Lai, Regine Yee-King. 2005. Asymmetrical code-mixing in a case study of uneven development: Bootstrapping hypothesis or ivy hypothesis? Paper presented at the 5th International Symposium on Bilingualism, Barcelona.

Lai, Regine Yee-King. 2006. Language mixing in an English-Cantonese bilingual child with uneven development. Unpublished MPhil. thesis, The University of Hong Kong.

Lakshmanan, Usha. 1995. Child second language acquisition of syntax. *Studies in Second Language Acquisition* 17: 301–329.

Lakshmanan, Usha and Larry Selinker. 2001. Analyzing interlanguage: how do we know what learners know? *Second Language Research* 17: 393–420.

Lam, Victoria Yuk Ping. 2006. The lexical development of a Cantonese-English bilingual child. Unpublished MA report, Chinese University of Hong Kong.

Lambrecht, Knud.1988. There was a farmer had a dog: syntactic amalgams revisited. *Berkeley Linguistics Society* 14: 319–339.

Lanvers, Ursula 1999. Lexical growth patterns in a bilingual infant: the occurrence and significance of equivalents in the bilingual lexicon. *International Journal of Bilingual Education and Bilingualism* 2: 30–52.

Lanza, Elizabeth. 2004. *Language Mixing in Infant Bilingualism: A Sociolinguistic Perspective*. Extended paperback edition. Oxford: Oxford University Press.

Lass, Roger. 1997. *Historical Linguistics and Language Change*. Cambridge and New York: Cambridge University Press.

Lau, Elaine. 2006. The acquisition of relative clause by Cantonese children: an experimental approach. Unpublished MPhil. thesis, University of Hong Kong.

Lee, Hun-Tak Thomas and Colleen Wong. 1998. Cancorp: The Hong Kong Cantonese Child Language Corpus. *Cahiers de Linguistique Asie Orientale* 27: 211–228.

Lee, Hun-Tak Thomas, Colleen Wong, Samuel Leung, Patricia Man, Alicia Cheung, Kitty Szeto and Cathy S. P. Wong. 1996. The development of grammatical competence in Cantonese-speaking children. Report of RGC earmarked grant 1991–94.

Lefebvre, Claire. 1998. *Creole Genesis and the Acquisition of Grammar*. Cambridge: Cambridge University Press.

2001. What you see is not always what you get. *Linguistic Typology* 5: 186–213.

2004. *Issues in the Study of Pidgin and Creole Languages*. Amsterdam: John Benjamins.

Leopold, Werner. 1939, 1947, 1949a, 1949b. *Speech Development of a Bilingual Child: a Linguist's Record* (Vols. 1–IV). Evaston: Northwestern University Press.

Leung, Man Tak and Sam Po Law. 2002. HKCAC: The Hong Kong Cantonese Adult Language Corpus. *International Journal of Corpus Linguistics* 6: 305–325.

Leung, Shuk Ching Fiona. 2005. Syntactic transfer in Cantonese-English bilingual development: a corpus-based study on prepositional phrases in Cantonese. Bachelor of Cognitive Science thesis. University of Hong Kong.

Li, Charles and Sandra Thompson. 1981. *Mandarin Chinese: A Functional Reference Grammar*. Berkeley: University of California Press.

Li, David. 1996. *Issues in Bilingualism and Biculturalism: A Hong Kong Case Study*. New York: Peter Lang.

Li, David and Sherman Lee. 2004. Bilingualism in East Asia. In Tej K. Bhatia and William C. Ritchie (eds.), *The Handbook of Bilingualism*. Oxford: Blackwell, pp. 742–779.

Li, Michelle, Stephen Matthews and Geoff Smith. 2005. Pidgin English texts from the Chinese English Instructor. *Hong Kong Journal of Applied Linguistics* 10: 79–167.

Li, Ping. 2006. Modeling language acquisition and representation: connectionist networks. In Li Ping, Tan Li-Hai, Elizabeth Bates and Ovid Tzeng (eds.), *Handbook of East Asian Psycholinguistics*. Vol. 1. Cambridge: Cambridge University Press, pp. 320–329.

Li, Ping and Igor Farkas. 2002. A self-organizing connectionist model of bilingual processing. In Roberto Heredia and Jeanette Altarriba (eds.), *Bilingual Sentence Processing*. Dordrecht: Elsevier, pp. 59–85.

Li, Ping, Tan Li-Hai, Elizabeth Bates and Ovid Tzeng (eds.). 2006. *Handbook of East Asian Psycholinguistics*. Vol. 1. Cambridge: Cambridge University Press.

Li, Wei and Sherman Lee. 2002. L1 Development in an L2 environment: the use of Cantonese classifiers and quantifiers by young British-born Chinese in Tyneside. *International Journal of Bilingual Education and Bilingualism* 4: 359–382.

Light, Timothy. 1977. Clairetalk: a Cantonese-speaking child's confrontation with Bilingualism. *Journal of Chinese Linguistics* 5: 261–275.

Lightfoot, David. 1982. *The Language Lottery: Towards a Biology of Grammars*. Cambridge, MA: MIT Press.

1991. *How to Set Parameters: Arguments from Language Change*. Cambridge, MA: MIT Press.

1999. *The Development of Language: Acquisition, Change and Evolution*. Oxford: Blackwell.

Lim, Lisa (ed.). 2004. *Singapore English: A Grammatical Description*. Amsterdam: John Benjamins.

Lin, Charles, Sandiway Fong and Thomas G. Bever. 2005. Constructing filler-gap dependencies in Chinese possessor relative clauses. *Proceedings of PACLIC 19, the 19th Asia-Pacific Conference on Language, Information and Computation*. Taipei: Academia Sinica, pp. 143–154.

Liu, Danqing. 2001. Hanyu 'gei' zi lei shuang jiwu jiegou de leixingxue kaocha. [A typological study of double object give constructions in Chinese] *Zhongguo Yuwen* 284: 387–397.

Lleó, Conxita and Margaret Kehoe. 2002. On the interaction of phonological systems in child bilingual acquisition. *International Journal of Bilingualism* 6: 233–237.

Lohse, Barbara, John A. Hawkins, and Tom Wasow. 2004. Domain minimization in English verb-particle constructions. *Language* 80: 238–261.

Lord, Carol, Foong-Ha Yap and Shoichi Iwasaki. 2002. Grammaticalization of 'give': African and Asian perspectives. In Ilse Wischer and Gabriele Diewald (eds.), *New Reflections on Grammaticalization*. Amsterdam: John Benjamins, pp. 217–235.

MacWhinney, Brian (ed.). 1999. *The Emergence of Language*. Mahwah, NJ: London: Lawrence Erlbaum Associates.

MacWhinney, Brian. 2000a. *The CHILDES Project: Tools for Analyzing Talk*. (3rd edition). Mahwah, NJ: Lawrence Erlbaum.

2000b. Emergence from what: comments on Sabbagh and Gelman. *Journal of Child Language* 27: 727–733.

2001. Last words. In Jasone Cenoz and Fred Genesee (eds.), *Trends in Bilingual Acquisition*. Amsterdam: John Benjamins, pp. 257–264.

Major, Roy. 1992. Losing English as a first language. *The Modern Language Journal* 76: 190–208.

Man, Yuk Hing Patricia. 1993. Subject – object distinctions and empty categories in child Cantonese. Unpublished MPhil. thesis. Hong Kong Polytechnic.

Maratsos, Michael. 2000. More overregularizations after all: new data and discussion on Marcus, Pinker, Ullman, Hollander, Rosen & Xu. *Journal of Child Language* 27: 183–212.

Marcus, Gary. 1999. Poverty of stimulus arguments. In Robert Wilson and Frank Keil (eds.), *The MIT Encyclopedia of the Cognitive Sciences*. Cambridge, MA: MIT Press, pp. 660–661.

Maslen, Robert, Anna Theakston, Elena Lieven and Michael Tomasello. 2004. A dense corpus study of past tense and plural overregularization in English. *Journal of Speech, Language and Hearing Research* 47: 1319–1333.

Matthews, Stephen. 2003. Verb-fronting in Sinitic and French vernaculars: a comparative study inspired by Chris Corne. *Te Reo* 46: 3–17.

2006a. On serial verbs in Cantonese. In Alexandra Aikhenvald and R. M. W. Dixon (eds.), *Serial Verbs: A Cross-linguistic Typology*. Oxford: Oxford University Press, pp. 69–87.

2006b. Cantonese grammar in areal perspective. In Alexandra Aikhenvald and R. M. W. Dixon (eds.), *Grammars in Contact*. Oxford: Oxford University Press.

Matthews, Stephen and Patricia Pacioni. 1997. Specificity and genericity in Cantonese and Mandarin. In Lie-Jiong Xu (ed.), *The Referential Properties of Chinese Noun Phrases*. Paris: Ecole des Hautes Etudes en Sciences Sociales, Centre de Recherches Linguistiques en Asie Orientale, pp. 45–59.

Matthews, Stephen, Huiling Xu and Virginia Yip. 2005. Passive and unaccusative in the Jieyang dialect of Chaozhou. *Journal of East Asian Linguistics* 14: 267–298.

Matthews, Stephen and Louisa Yeung. 2001. Processing motivations for topicalization in Cantonese. In Kaoru Horie and Shigeru Sato (eds.), *Cognitive-functional Linguistics in an East Asian Context*. Tokyo: Kurosio Publishers, pp. 81–102.

Matthews, Stephen and Virginia Yip. 1994. *Cantonese: A Comprehensive Grammar*. London: Routledge.

2001. The structure and stratification of relative clauses in contemporary Cantonese. In Hilary Chappell (ed.), *Sinitic Grammar: Synchronic and Diachronic Perspectives*. Oxford: Oxford University Press, pp. 266–281.

2002. Relative clauses in early bilingual development: transfer and universals. In Anna Giacalone (ed.), *Typology and Second Language Acquisition*. Berlin: Mouton de Gruyter, pp. 39–81.

McBride-Chang, Catherine. 2004. *Children's Literacy Development* (Texts in Developmental Psychology series). London: Edward Arnold/Oxford: Oxford University Press.

McCardle, Peggy and Erika Hoff (eds.). 2006. *Childhood Bilingualism: Research on Infancy Through School Age*. Clevedon: Multilingual Matters.

McDaniel, Dana. 1989. Partial and multiple *wh*-movement. *Natural Language and Linguistic Theory* 7: 565–604.

McDaniel, Dana, Bonnie Chiu and Thomas L. Maxfield. 1995. Parameters for *wh*-movement types: evidence from child English. *Natural Language and Linguistic Theory* 13: 709–753.

McDaniel, Dana, Cecile McKee and Helen Smith Cairns (eds.). 1996. *Methods for Assessing Children's Syntax*. Cambridge, MA: MIT Press.

McKee, Cecile, Dana McDaniel and Jesse Snedeker. 1998. Relative clauses children say. *Journal of Psycholinguistic Research* 27: 573–596.

McLaughlin, Barry. 1978. *Second Language Acquisition in Childhood*. Hillsdale, NJ: Lawrence Erlbaum.

McWhorter, John H. 2001. The world's simplest grammars are creole grammars. *Linguistic Typology* 5: 125–166.

2005. *Defining Creole*. Oxford: Oxford University Press.

Meisel, Jürgen. 1989. Early differentiation of languages in bilingual children. In Kenneth Hyltenstam and Lorraine Obler (eds.), *Bilingualism Across the Lifespan: Aspects of Acquisition, Maturity, and Loss*. Cambridge: Cambridge University Press, pp. 13–40.

Meisel, Jürgen. 1990. *Two First Languages: Early Grammatical Development in Bilingual Children*. Dordrecht: Foris.

Meisel, Jürgen (ed.). 1994. *Bilingual First Language Acquisition: French and German Grammatical Development*. Amsterdam: John Benjamins.

Meisel, Jürgen. 2001. The simultaneous acquisition of two first languages: early differentiation and subsequent development of grammars. In Jasone Cenoz and Fred Genesee (eds.), *Trends in Bilingual Acquisition*. Amsterdam: John Benjamins, pp. 11–41.

2004. The bilingual child. In Tej K. Bhatia and William C. Ritchie, (eds.), *Handbook of Bilingualism*. Oxford: Blackwell, pp. 90–113.

Menn, Lise and Nan B. Ratner (eds.). 2000. *Methods for Studying Language Production*. New Jersey: Lawrence Erlbaum Associates.

Mervis, Carolyn B., Cynthia A. Mervis, Kathy E. Johnson and Jacquelyn Bertrand. 1992. Studying early lexical development: the value of the systematic diary method.

In Carolyn Rovee-Collier and Lewis Paeff Lipsitt (eds.), *Advances in Infancy Research*. Vol. VII. Norwood, NJ: Ablex, pp. 291–378.

Michaelis, Susanne and Martin Haspelmath. 2003. Ditransitive constructions: creole languages in a cross-linguistic perspective. Creolica 23/4/2003. http://www.creolica.net

Montrul, Silvina. 2004. Subject and object expression in Spanish heritage speakers: a case of morphosyntactic convergence. *Bilingualism: Language and Cognition* 7: 125–142.

Mufwene, Salikoko S. 1999. The language bioprogram hypothesis: hints from Tazie. In Michel DeGraff (ed.), *Creolization, Diachrony, and Language Acquisition*. Cambridge, MA: MIT Press, pp. 95–127.

2001. *The Ecology of Language Evolution*. Cambridge: Cambridge University Press.

2004. Multilingualism in linguistic history: creolization and indigenization. In Tej K. Bhatia and William C. Ritchie (eds.), *Handbook of Bilingualism*. Oxford: Blackwell, pp. 460–488.

2005. *Créoles, écologie sociale, évolution linguistique*. Paris: l'Harmattan.

2006. Grammaticization is part of the development of creoles. Ms. University of Chicago.

Müller, Natascha. 1998. Transfer in bilingual first language acquisition. *Bilingualism: Language and Cognition* 1: 151–71.

Müller, Natascha. (ed.). 2003. *(In)vulnerable Domains in Multilingualism*. Amsterdam: John Benjamins.

Müller, Natascha. 2004. Null-arguments in bilingual children: French topics. In Philippe Prévost and Johanne Paradis (eds.), *The Acquisition of French in Different Contexts: Focus on Functional Categories*. Amsterdam: John Benjamins, pp. 275–304.

Müller, Natascha and Aafke Hulk. 2001. Cross-linguistic influence in bilingual language acquisition: Italian and French as recipient languages. *Bilingualism: Language and Cognition* 4: 1–21.

Muysken, Pieter and Tonjes Veenstra. 1995. Haitian. In Jacques Arends, Pieter Muysken and Norval Smith (eds.) *Pidgins and Creoles: An Introduction*. Amsterdam: John Benjamins, pp. 153–164.

Nettle, Daniel. 1999. *Linguistic Diversity*. Oxford: Oxford University Press.

Nettle, Daniel and Suzanne Romaine 2000. *Vanishing Voices: The Extinction of the World's Languages*. Oxford: Oxford University Press.

Newbrook, Mark. 1999. Which way? *That* way – relative clauses in Asian Englishes. *World Englishes* 17: 43–59.

Newmeyer, Frederick J. 1998. *Language Form and Language Function*. Cambridge, MA: MIT Press.

Nicoladis, Elena. 2003. Cross-linguistic transfer in deverbal compounds of preschool bilingual children. *Bilingualism: Language and Cognition* 6: 17–31.

2006. Cross-linguistic transfer in adjective-noun strings by preschool bilingual children. *Bilingualism: Language and Cognition* 9: 15–32.

Noji, Junya. 1973–1977. *Yooziki no Gengo Seikatu no Zittai, I–IV*. [The Language Development of a Child, I–IV]. Hiroshima: Bunka Hyooron.

O'Grady, William. 1997. *Syntactic Development*. Chicago: University of Chicago Press.

2005a. *How Children Learn Language*. Cambridge: Cambridge University Press.

2005b. *Syntactic Carpentry: An Emergentist Approach to Syntax*. Lawrence Erlbaum.

Ozeki, Hiromi & Yasuhiro Shirai. 2005. Semantic bias in the acquisition of relative clauses in Japanese. In Alejna Brugos, Manuella R. Clark-Cotton, and Seungwan Ha (eds.), *Proceedings of the 29th Annual Boston University Conference on Language Development*, Vol. II. Somerville, MA: Cascadilla Press, pp. 459–470.

Packard, Jerome. 2000. *The Morphology of Chinese: A Linguistic and Cognitive Approach*. Cambridge: Cambridge University Press.

Pallotti, Gabriele. 1996. Towards an ecology of second language acquisition: SLA as a socialization process. In Eric Kellerman, Bert Weltens and Theo Bongaerts (eds.), *EUROSLA 6: A Selection of Papers*. Utrecht: Vereniging voor Toegepaste Taalwetenschap, pp. 121–134.

Paradis, Johanne. 2000. Beyond 'one system or two': degrees of separation between the languages of French-English bilingual children. In Susanne Döpke (ed.), *Crosslinguistic Structures in Simultaneous Bilingualism*. Amsterdam: John Benjamins, pp. 175–200.

    2001. Do bilingual two-year-olds have separate phonological systems? *The International Journal of Bilingualism* 1: 19–38.

Paradis, Johanne and Fred Genesee. 1996. Syntactic acquisition in bilingual children: autonomous or interdependent? *Studies in Second Language Acquisition* 18: 1–25.

Paradis, Johanne, Elena Nicoladis and Fred Genesee. 2000. Early emergence of structural constraints on code-mixing: evidence from French-English bilingual children. *Bilingualism: Language and Cognition* 3: 245–261.

Pavlenko, Aneta 2000. L2 influence on L1 in late bilingualism. *Issues in Applied Linguistics* 11: 175–205.

Pavlenko, Aneta and Scott Jarvis. 2002. Bidirectional transfer. *Applied Linguistics* 23: 190–214.

Pavlovitch, Ivan. 1920. *Le Langage Enfantin: Acquisition du Serbe et du Français Par un Enfant Serbe*. Paris: Champion.

Pearson, Barbara, S. C. Fernandez and D. K. Oller. 1995. Cross-language synonyms in the lexicons of bilingual infants: One language or two? *Journal of Child Language* 22: 345–368.

Peng, Ling Ling Linda. 1998. The development of *wh*-questions in a Cantonese/English bilingual child. MPhil. thesis, Chinese University of Hong Kong.

Pérez-Leroux, Ana. 1995. Resumptives in the acquisition of relative clauses. *Language Acquisition* 4: 105–138.

Peters, Stanley. 1972. The projection problem: how is a grammar to be selected? In Stanley Peters (ed.), *Goals of Linguistic Theory*. Engelwood Cliffs, NJ: Prentice-Hall, pp. 171–188.

Petersen, Jennifer. 1988. Word-internal code-switching constraints in a bilingual child's grammar. *Linguistics* 26: 479–493.

Pinker, Steven. 1989. *Learnability and Cognition: the Acquisition of Argument Structure*. Cambridge, MA: MIT Press.

    1994. *The Language Instinct*. New York: Basic Books.

Plag, Ingo. 1995. The emergence of *taki* as a complementizer in Sranan: on substrate influence, universals and gradual creolization. In Jacques Arends (ed.), *The Early Stages of Creolization*. Amsterdam: John Benjamins, pp. 113–148.

Platt, Jennifer. 1988. What case studies can do? *Studies in Qualitative Methodology* 1: 1–23.

Platt, John and Heidi Weber. 1980. *English in Singapore and Malaysia: Status, Features, Functions*. Kuala Lumpur: Oxford University Press.

Platzack, Christer. 2001. The vulnerable C-domain. *Brain and Language* 77: 364–377.

Plunkett, Kim. 1998. Language acquisition and connectionism. *Language and Cognitive Processes* 13: 97–104.

Pollock, Karen, Johanna Price and K. C. Fulmer. 2003. Speech-language acquisition in children adopted from China: a longitudinal investigation of two children. *Journal of Multilingual Communication Disorders* 1: 184–193.

Poulin-Dubois, Dianne and Naomi Goodz. 2001. Language differentiation in bilingual infants: evidence from babbling. In Jasone Cenoz and Fred Genesee (eds.), *Trends in Bilingual Acquisition*. Amsterdam: John Benjamins, pp. 95–106.

Pullum, Geoffrey K. and Barbara C. Scholz. 2002. Empirical assessment of stimulus poverty arguments. *The Linguistic Review* 19: 9–50.

Quirk, Randolph, Sidney Greenbaum and Jan Svartvik. 1972. *A Grammar of Contemporary English*. London: Longman.

Radford, Andrew. 1990. *Syntactic Theory and the Acquisition of English Syntax*. Oxford: Blackwell.

Reinecke, John E. 1969. *Language and Dialect in Hawaii: A Sociolinguistic History to 1935*. Honolulu: Hawaii University Press.

Rispoli, Matthew. 1992. Discourse and the acquisition of *eat*. *Journal of Child Language* 19: 581–595.

Roberts, Jenny, Karen Pollock, Rena Krakow, Johanna Price and Paul Wang. 2005. Language development in preschool-age children adopted from China. *Journal of Speech, Language and Hearing Research* 48: 93–107.

Roberts, Sarah Julianne. 1998. The role of diffusion in the genesis of Hawaiian Creole. *Language* 74: 1–39.

1999. Serial verb distribution. Creolist posting, 5 August 1999. http://listserv. linguist.org/archives/creolist.html

2000. Nativization and the genesis of Hawaiian Creole. In John McWhorter (ed.), *Language Change and Language Contact in Pidgins and Creoles*. Amsterdam: John Benjamins, pp. 257–300.

Roeper, Thomas. 1981. On the deductive model and the acquisition of productive morphology. In Carl Lee Baker, and John MacCarthy (eds.), *The Logical Problem of Language Acquisition*. Cambridge, MA: MIT Press, pp. 129–150.

1999. Universal bilingualism. *Bilingualism: Language and Cognition* 2: 169–186.

Romaine, Suzanne. 1995. *Bilingualism*. Second Edition. Oxford: Basil Blackwell.

1996. Bilingualism. In William C. Ritchie and Tej K. Bhatia (eds.), *Handbook of Second Language Acquisition*. New York: Academic Press, pp. 571–605.

Ronjat, Jules. 1913. *Le Développement du Langage Observé Chez un Enfant Bilingue*. Paris: Champion.

Rutherford, William. 1989. Preemption and the learning of L2 grammars. *Studies in Second Language Acquisition* 11: 441–457.

Sabbagh, Mark and Susan Gelman. 2000. Emergence is what? *Journal of Child Language* 27: 763–766.

Sampson, Geoffrey. 2002. Exploring the richness of the stimulus. *The Linguistic Review* 19: 73–104.

Satterfield, Teresa. 2005. The bilingual bioprogram: evidence for child bilingualism in the formation of creoles. *Proceedings of the 4th International Symposium on Bilingualism*, pp. 2075–2094.

Sánchez, Liliana. 2004. Functional convergence in the tense, evidentiality and aspectual systems of Quechua Spanish bilinguals. *Bilingualism: Language and Cognition* 7: 147–162.

Saunders, George. 1988. *Bilingual Children: From Birth to Teens*. Clevedon: Multilingual Matters.

Sawyer, Joan. 2001. Bifurcating the verb particle construction: evidence from child language. *Annual Review of Language Acquisition* 1: 119–156.

Schlyter, Suzanne. 1993. The weaker language in bilingual Swedish-French children. In Kenneth Hyltenstam and Åke Viberg (eds.) *Progression and Regression in Language*. Cambridge: Cambridge University Press, pp. 289–308.

Schlyter, Suzanne and Gisela Håkansson. 1994. Word order in Swedish as the first language, second language and weaker language. In Kenneth Hyltenstam (ed.), *Scandinavian Working Papers on Bilingualism*. Stockholm University, Center for Research on Bilingualism, Stockholm, pp. 49–67.

Schmitt, Elena. 2000. Overt and covert code-switching in immigrant children from Russia. *International Journal of Bilingualism* 4: 9–28.

Scholz, Barbara C. and Geoffrey K. Pullum. 2002. Searching for arguments to support linguistic nativism. *The Linguistic Review* 19: 185–223.

Schulz, Barbara. 2005. Wh-scope marking in German-English and Japanese-English interlanguage grammars: an investigation of clustering syntactic properties. In Kamil Deen, Jun Nomura, Barbara Schulz & Bonnie Schwartz (eds.), *Proceedings of the Inaugural GALANA Conference*. Storrs: University of Connecticut Working Papers in Linguistics, pp. 309–320.

Schumann, John H. 1978. *The Pidginization Process: A Model for Second Language Acquisition*. Rowley, MA: Newbury House Publishers.

Schwartz, Bonnie. 1986. The epistemological status of second language acquisition. *Second Language Resesarch* 2: 120–159.

Schwartz, Bonnie and Rex Sprouse. 1996. L2 cognitive states and the Full Transfer/Full Access hypothesis. *Second Language Research* 12: 4–72.

Searchinger, Gene. 1995. Acquiring the human language: playing the language game. *The Human Language Series*, Program Two. New York, NY: Equinox Films/Ways of Knowing.

Sebba, Mark. 1997. *Contact Languages: Pidgins and Creoles*. New York: St. Martin's Press.

Seliger, Herbert W. and Robert M. Vago (eds.). 1991. *First Language Attrition*. Cambridge: Cambridge University Press.

Selinker, Larry. 1992. *Rediscovering Interlanguage*. London: Longman.

Sgall, Petr. 1995. Prague School Typology. In Masayoshi Shibatani and Theodora Bynon (eds.), *Approaches to Language Typology*. Oxford: Clarendon Press, pp. 49–84.

Shi, Dingxu. 1989. Topic chain as a syntactic category in Chinese. *Journal of Chinese Linguistics* 17: 223–262.

　　2000. Topic and topic-comment constructions in Mandarin Chinese. *Language* 76: 383–408.

Shin, Sarah. 2004. *Developing in Two Languages: Korean Children in America*. Clevedon: Multilingual Matters.

Siegel, Jeff. 2000. Substrate influence in Hawai'i Creole English. *Language in Society* 29: 197–236.

Silva-Corvalán, Carmen. 1994. *Language Contact and Change: Spanish in Los Angeles*. Oxford: Clarendon Press; New York: Oxford University Press.

Smith, Madorah E. 1931. A study of five bilingual children from the same family. *Child Development* 2: 184–187.

1935. A study of the speech of eight bilingual children of the same family. *Child Development* 6: 19–25.

Snow, Don. 2004. *Cantonese as Written Language: The Growth of a Written Chinese Vernacular*. Hong Kong: Hong Kong University Press.

Stern, Clara, and William Stern. 1907. *Die Kindersprache: Eine Psychologische und Sprach-theoretische Untersuchung*. Leipzig: Barth.

Stromswold, Karin. 1995. The acquisition of subject and object *wh*-questions. *Language Acquisition* 4: 5–48.

1996. Analyzing children's spontaneous speech. In Dana McDaniel, Cecile McKee, and Helen Smith Cairns (eds.), *Methods for Assessing Children's Syntax*. Cambridge, MA: MIT Press, pp. 23–53.

Swain, Merrill and Mari Wesche. 1975. Linguistic interaction: case study of a bilingual child. *Language Sciences* 37: 17–22.

Taeschner, Traute. 1983. *The Sun is Feminine: A study on Language Acquisition in Bilingual Children*. Berlin: Springer-Verlag.

Tager-Flusberg, Helen. 1989. Putting words together: later developments in the pre-school years. In Jean Berko-Gleason (ed.), *The Development of Language*, 2nd edition. Columbus, Ohio: Merrill, pp. 135–165.

Tai, James H-Y. 1975. On two functions of place adverbials in Mandarin Chinese. *Journal of Chinese Linguistics* 3: 154–179.

Tan, Hwee Hwee. 2001. *Mammon Inc*. Penguin.

Tan, Li-Hai and Charles Perfetti. 1998. Phonological codes as early sources of constraint in reading Chinese: A review of current discoveries and theoretical accounts. *Reading and Writing* (special issue on cognitive processing of the Chinese and the Japanese languages) 10: 165–220.

Tan, Li-Hai, Lin Chen, Alice Chan, Jing Yang, Virginia Yip, and Wai Ting Siok. To appear. Becoming a bilingual reader: activity levels in distinct brain regions predict how well native and second languages will be learned.

Tang, Sze-Wing. 1998. On the 'inverted' double object construction. In Stephen Matthews (ed.), *Studies in Cantonese Linguistics*. Linguistic Society of Hong Kong, pp. 35–52.

2000. Identity avoidance and constraint interaction: the case of Cantonese. *Linguistics* 38: 33–61.

2001. A complementation approach to Chinese passives and its consequences. *Linguistics* 39: 257–295.

Tang, Sze-Wing, Fan Kwok, Thomas Hun-Tak Lee, Caesar Lun, Kang Kwong Luke, Peter Tung and Kwan Hin Cheung. 2002. *Guide to LSHK Cantonese Romanization of Chinese Characters*. 2nd edition. Hong Kong: Linguistic Society of Hong Kong.

Tavakolian, Susan. 1981. The conjoined clause analysis of relative clauses. In Susan Tavakolian (ed.), *Language Acquisition and Linguistic Theory*. Cambridge, MA: MIT Press, pp. 167–187.

Thomason, Sarah Grey (ed.). 1996. *Contact Languages: A Wider Perspective.* Amsterdam: John Benjamins.

Thomason, Sarah Grey. 2001. *Language Contact: An Introduction.* Washington, DC: Georgetown University Press.

　2003. Social factors and linguistic processes in the emergence of stable mixed languages. In Yaron Matras and Peter Bakker (eds.), *The Mixed Language Debate: Theoretical and Empirical Advances.* Berlin: Mouton de Gruyter, pp. 21–40.

Thornton, Rosalind. 1990. Adventures in Wh-Movement. Doctoral dissertation, University of Connecticut, Storrs.

Thornton, Rosalind and Stephen Crain. 1994. Successful cyclic movement. In Teun Hoekstra and Bonnie Schwartz (eds.), *Language Acquisition Studies in Generative Grammar.* Amsterdam: John Benjamins, pp. 215–252.

Tomasello, Michael. 1998. The return of constructions. *Journal of Child Language* 25: 431–442.

　2003. *Constructing a Language: A Usage-based Theory of Child Language Acquisition.* Harvard University Press.

Tomasello, Michael and Daniel Stahl. 2004. Sampling children's spontaneous speech: How much is enough? *Journal of Child Language* 41: 101–121.

Toribio, Almeida J. 2004. Convergence as an optimization strategy in bilingual speech: evidence from code-switching. *Bilingualism: Language and Cognition* 2: 165–173.

Trask, R. L. 1996. *Historical Linguistics.* London and New York: Arnold.

Tsao, Feng-Fu. 1988. The Functions of Mandarin *gei* and Taiwanese *hou* in the Double Object and Passive Constructions. In Robert L. Cheng and Shuanfan Huang (eds.), *The Structure of Taiwanese: A Modern Synthesis.* Taipei: Crane Publishing Co., pp. 165–202.

Unsworth, Sharon. 2003. Testing Hulk & Müller (2000) on crosslinguistic influence: root infinitives in a bilingual German/English child. *Bilingualism: Language and Cognition* 6: 143–158.

Veenstra, Tonjes and Hans den Besten 1994. Fronting. In Jacques Arends, Pieter Muysken and Norval Smith (eds.), *Pidgins and Creoles: An Introduction.* Amsterdam/Philadelphia: Benjamins, pp. 303–315.

Vihman, Marilyn M. 1985. Language differentiation by the bilingual infant. *Journal of Child Language* 12: 297–324.

Vihman, Marilyn M., J. A. G. Lum, G. Thierry, S. Nakai and T. Keren-Portnoy. 2006. The onset of word form recognition in one language and in two. In Peggy McCardle and Erika Hoff (eds.), *Childhood Bilingualism: Research on Infancy through School Age.* Clevedon: Multilingual Matters, pp. 30–44.

Volterra, Virginia and Traute Taeschner. 1978. The acquisition of and development of language by bilingual children. *Journal of Child Language* 5: 311–326.

Waas, Margit. 1996. *Language Attrition Down under: German Speakers in Australia.* Frankfurt: Peter Lang.

Wang, Qi, Dianne Lillo-Martin, Catherine Best and Andrea Levitt. 1992. Null subject versus null object: some evidence from the acquisition of Chinese and English. *Language Acquisition* 2: 221–254.

Wee, Lionel and Umberto Ansaldo 2004. Nouns and noun phrases. In Lisa Lim (ed.), *Singapore English: A Grammatical Description*. Amsterdam: John Benjamins, pp. 57–74.

Weinreich, Uriel. 1953. *Languages in Contact: Findings and Problems*. New York: Linguistics Circle of New York.

Weissenborn, Jürgen and Barbara Höhle (eds.). 2001. *Approaches to Bootstrapping: Phonological, Lexical, Syntactic and Neurophysiological Aspects of Early Language Acquisition*. Vol. I and Vol. II. Amsterdam: John Benjamins.

Wekker, Herman (ed.). 1996. *Creole Languages and Language Acquisition*. Berlin: Mouton de Gruyter.

Werker, Janet, Whitney Weikum and Katherine Yoshida. 2006. Bilingual speech processing in Infants and Adults. In Peggy McCardle and Erika Hoff (eds.), *Childhood Bilingualism: Research on Infancy through School Age*. Clevedon: Multilingual Matters, pp. 1–18.

Wexler, Kenneth and Peter Culicover. 1980. *Formal Principles of Language Acquisition*. Cambridge, MA: MIT Press.

White, Lydia. 1989. *Universal Grammar and Second Language Acquisition*. Amsterdam: John Benjamins.

2003. *Second Language Acquisition and Universal Grammar*. Cambridge: Cambridge University Press.

Winford, Donald. 2003. *An Introduction to Contact Linguistics*. Oxford: Blackwell.

Wong, Kwok-Shing. 2003. The emergence of *bei2* 'give' constructions in Cantonese-speaking children. Unpublished PhD dissertation, University of Hong Kong.

2004. The acquisition of polysemous forms: the case of *bei2* 'give' in Cantonese. In Olga Fischer, Muriel Norde and Harry Perridon (eds.), *Up and Down the Cline: the Nature of Grammaticalization*. Amsterdam: John Benjamins, pp. 325–343.

Xu, Liejiong and Alain Peyraube. 1997. On the double object construction and the oblique construction in Cantonese. *Studies in Language* 21: 105–127.

Yap, Foong-Ha and Shoichi Iwasaki. 1998. 'Give' constructions in Malay, Thai and Mandarin Chinese: a polygrammaticalization perspective. In M. Catherine Gruber, Derrick Higins, Kenneth S. Olson, & Tamra Wysocki (eds.), CLS 34, Part I: Papers from the Main Session. Chicago: Chicago Linguistic Society, pp. 421–437.

2003. From causatives to passives: a passage in some East and Southeast Asian languages. In Eugene H. Casad and Gary B. Palmer (eds.), *Cognitive Linguistics and Non-Indo-European Languages*. Berlin: Mouton de Gruyter, pp. 419–445.

Yap, Foong-Ha, Stephen Matthews and Kaoru Horie. 2003. From pronominalizer to pragmatic marker: implications for unidirectionality from a crosslinguistic perspective. In Olga Fischer, Muriel Norde and Harry Perridon (eds.), *Up and Down the Cline: the Nature of Grammaticalization*. Amsterdam: John Benjamins, pp. 137–168.

Yip, Virginia. 1995. *Interlanguage and Learnability: From Chinese to English*. Amsterdam: John Benjamins.

2002. Early syntactic development in Cantonese-English bilingual children. Keynote speech delivered at the 9th International Symposium on Contemporary Linguistics in China, organized by the Institute of Linguistics, the Chinese Academy of Social Sciences and Beijing Foreign Studies University, PRC.

2004. Early syntactic development in Cantonese-English bilingual children. *Contemporary Linguistics* 6: 1–18 [in Chinese].

2006. Early bilingual acquisition in the Chinese context. In Li Ping, Li-Hai Tan, Elizabeth Bates and Ovid Tzeng (eds.), *Handbook of East Asian Psycholinguistics*. Vol. 1. Cambridge: Cambridge University Press, pp. 148–162.

Yip, Virginia and Stephen Matthews. 1995. I-interlanguage and typology: the case of topic-prominence. In Lynn Eubank, Larry Selinker and Mike Sharwood Smith (eds.), *The Current State of Interlanguage: Studies in Honor of William Rutherford*. Amsterdam: John Benjamins, pp. 17–30.

2000a. Syntactic transfer in a Cantonese-English bilingual child. *Bilingualism: Language and Cognition* 3: 193–208.

2000b. *Basic Cantonese: A Grammar and Workbook*. London: Routledge.

2001. *Intermediate Cantonese: A Grammar and Workbook*. London: Routledge.

2003. Phonological hyper-differentiation in Cantonese-English bilingual children. Paper presented at the Child Phonology Conference, University of British Columbia, Vancouver, Canada.

2005. Dual input and learnability: null objects in Cantonese – English bilingual children. In James Cohen, Kara McAlister, Kellie Rolstad and Jeff MacSwan (eds.), *Proceedings of the 4th International Symposium on Bilingualism*. Somerville, MA: Cascadilla Press, pp. 2421–2431.

2006. Assessing language dominance in bilingual acquisition: a case for Mean Length Utterance differentials. *Language Assessment Quarterly* 3: 97–116.

2007. Relative clauses in Cantonese-English bilingual children: typological challenges and processing motivations. *Studies in Second Language Acquisition* 29: 277–300.

Yip, Virginia, Stephen Matthews and Huang Yue-Yuan. 1996. Knowledge of binding in Hong Kong bilingual children. Paper presented at the Second Language Research Forum (SLRF), University of Arizona.

Yip, Virginia, Stephen Matthews and Ingrid Leung. 2001. Functional categories in the acquisition of Cantonese and English by bilingual children. Paper presented at the Pacific Second Language Research Forum, University of Hawaii, Manoa.

Yiu, Sze-Man Emily. 2005a. Asymmetrical language mixing in a Cantonese-English bilingual child. Paper presented at the 5th International Symposium on Bilingualism, Barcelona.

2005b. Language mixing and grammatical development in a Cantonese – English balanced bilingual child in Hong Kong. Unpublished MPhil. thesis, The University of Hong Kong.

Yuan, Boping. 1997. Asymmetry of null subjects and null objects in Chinese speakers' L2 English. *Studies in Second Language Acquisition* 19: 467–497.

Yue-Hashimoto, Anne. 1991. The Yue dialect. In William S-Y. Wang (ed.), *Languages and Dialects of China. Journal of Chinese Linguistics Monograph Series* 3: 294–324.

Zentella, Ana Celia. 1997. *Growing up Bilingual: Puerto Rican Children in New York*. Malden, MA: Blackwell.

Ziegeler, Debra. 1997. Retention in diachronic and ontogenetic grammaticalization. *Cognitive Linguistics* 8: 207–241.

Index

acceleration 31, 44, 107, 127, 259
Adam 118, 128 n. 7
adjectives 29, 48, 49, 176, 186 n. 4
adolescents 53
adopted children 3
Allison 220, 222
ambiguity
  of analysis 48, 259
  of evidence 48, 49, 179, 197–198, 208–209,
    223, 259, 261
  see also input ambiguity
animacy 214, 215
approximation 15
areal feature 16
argument structure 136
article 128 n. 10
aspect markers 75
  perfective 235–239
asymmetry in direction of transfer 121–122
asynchrony, developmental 2, 26, 42–44,
    107–108, 150, 175–176, 259
attributive clauses 159, 177–178
  and relative clauses 187 n. 4
audio/video recording 67, 68
auxiliary verb 118, 129 n. 17

Baba Malay 50, 252
babbling 34
balanced bilingual child 79, 81
balanced development 66
bidirectional influence, see influence
bilingual development, quantitative measures
  of 72–73
bilingual first language acquisition 14–15,
    26–27, 28, 31, 256, 259
bilingual instinct 5, 256
bilingual mode 143
bilingualism,
  cognitive advantages of 4, 60
  continuum of 29
  holistic view of 4
  universal 21 n. 9

birth order effects 65
Bislama 230–231
bootstrapping 42
  bilingual 16, 43, 57, 113, 126
bridging contexts 233, 252

calquing 242, 249, 251
Cantonese 63–71, 74–75
  characters 85 n. 6
  grammar 9
  monolingual development of 63
  monolingual corpus see Hong Kong
    Cantonese Child Language Corpus
  sound changes in 71, 224 n. 1
  typological characteristics of 174
  written 9
Cantonese Radio Corpus 197
caregivers 11, 65–66
case studies 7, 56–58
causative 240
Cebuano 65
Chaozhou (Chiu Chow, Teochew) dialect
    10–11, 20 n. 2, 64, 181–182, 232, 240,
    249, 254 n. 11
CHAT format 67, 85 n. 8
child-directed speech 197, 204, 209
Child Language Data Exchange System
    (CHILDES) 2, 61, 63, 215
child second language acquisition 4, 28–29,
    53, 82, 256, 259
Chinese characters 68
Chinese dialects 10, 19, 181, 186 n. 2
Chinese Pidgin English (CPE) 125–126
Chiu Chow, see Chaozhou
CLAN 68
classifier 159, 161, 165, 166, 167, 187 n. 9,
    251
code-mixing 8, 10, 17, 64, 68, 73, 76, 82–84,
    122, 211–212, 218, 264
  as instantiated in input 83
  direction of 83
code-switching 12, 14, 146, 193

cognitive development 4
comparability 74
  of MLUw across languages 76–77
competence 36, 38, 72, 84, 186 n. 3
competition 8
Competition Model 24
complementizer 173, 183, 188 n. 16, 228–229
computer simulations 53
conditional constructions 13, 17
congruence 16, 211, 253 n. 7
conjoined clause interpretation 180
Connectionism 24, 85 n. 2
conservative learning 151
Constituent Recognition Domain 157
Construction Grammar 24
contact-induced change 14–15, 16, 51–52, 199, 215
  see also grammaticalization, contact-induced
contact language 14, 50–52
contact linguistics 12
context, social 7
controls, monolingual 62
convergence 16, 17, 224
corpus 2, 260
  data 57
  dense 61–62, 163, 260
  Hong Kong Bilingual Child Language 2
coverbs 191
creoles 8, 14, 16, 17, 19, 50–53, 113, 252
creole grammars 33

Danish 82
dative alternation 201
dative constructions 16, 188 n. 12, 200–216, 246
  in typology 214, 215
delay 31
demonstrative 182–183
determiners 83
diary, diary data 6, 7, 56–57, 63, 72, 162–164, 260
  transcription of 7
differentiation 34–35, 257
  grammatical 33
  lexical 35
  perceptual 34
  phonological 35
  syntactic 55 n. 3
directionality 234
disambiguation 71
disorders, language 49, 264
divergence 234, 241
dominance, language dominance 2, 76–85, 120, 127, 175–176, 223

and transfer 80, 99
  shift of 123
dominant language 13, 26, 28, 39
double object construction 189
  in creoles 215
Dutch 147–148, 215

echo questions 89–90, 99–100, 121, 261
ecology 8, 14, 16, 20, 32, 152, 262
  as factor in child second language acquisition 21 n. 8
  external 8–9
  internal 8
Elvoo 236–237
embedded questions 116–117
emergentism 24
empty category 28, 135
epistemology 23–24
ethical issues 7
Eve 93, 96, 128 n. 7, 144, 220
evolution of languages 8
Ewe 214
existential verb 145
exposure 25–26, 27, 82

feature pool 8, 52, 253
finiteness 29, 34
first language 22–23, 28
first language attrition 27
free relatives 184, 188 n. 10
French 73, 147–148
frequency 15, 62, 72, 163
full access/full transfer 26

gender 54 n. 1
German 114, 147–148
grammaticalization 17–18, 227–233, 251
  apparent 18, 229, 230, 231
  contact-induced 19, 228–235, 248–250, 262
  definitions of 248
  ontogenetic 243–245
  pathways of 231, 232, 234, 240, 246–247
  principles of 233–234, 243, 251
  replica 231, 239–240, 249–251
Grammont's principle 6

Hakka dialect 13
Haitian Creole 51, 52
haplology 202–203
Hawaii 13
Hawaiian Creole English (HCE) 13–14, 51–53
Heavy NP Shift 204
helpers, domestic 11, 65, 66, 195
Hokkien 10–11, 19, 50, 125, 181–182, 235–236, 242, 249, 252

Hong Kong 9–12
  language policy of 9
Hong Kong Bilingual Child Language Corpus 63
Hong Kong Cantonese Child Language Corpus (Cancorp) 71–72, 193, 194–196, 202–203, 204, 205–209
Hong Kong Cantonese Adult Language Corpus 197

iconicity 192
identity 1
idiogrammaticization 229, 240
incomplete acquisition 29, 31
indeterminacy of input 32
indirect questions 116–117
inflectional morphology 74, 82
influence, bidirectional 4, 49, 213, 223
  cross-linguistic 2, 3, 6, 12, 37–43, 104, 119, 134
  directionality of 27
  systemic 38, 44
input 5–6, 7–8, 11–12, 25, 27, 30–33, 44–48, 62–63, 197–198, 208–211, 263
input ambiguity 2, 16, 26, 29, 39, 41, 45–49, 100, 120–121, 127, 147–149, 179–180, 193, 197–198, 209–210, 223, 259
interference 12, 15
interlanguage 11, 25, 27
interlingual identification 18, 39, 191, 229, 234, 238, 252
interpretation, rich 7
inversion, see subject – auxiliary inversion
isolating languages 74, 248
isomorphism 16
Italian 74, 147
Ivy Hypothesis 73, 82

Japanese 60
Jyut6 Ping3 romanization 68, 71

kindergartens 65, 66
Korean 4

Language Bioprogram Hypothesis 50, 53, 55 n. 7
language change 6, 13, 16, 19
language choice 27
language dominance 29, 34, 35–37, 40–42, 175–176, 258–259
  measures of 72–73
  shift in 214
language ecology 11
language evolution 19–20
language game 11

language instinct 5
language mixing 67
  direction of 73
language planning 15
language preference 73, 81
language shift 17
language transfer 18
language universals 191
layering 234
learnability 24, 31, 45, 91, 151
lexical borrowing 17
lexical gaps 83
lexical tones 17, 240
lexicon 17, 35
Linguistic Society of Hong Kong 68
literacy 4, 21 n. 11
localizers 224 n. 2
locative prepositional phrases, see prepositional phrases
logical problem of language acquisition 30–32
logical problem of bilingual acquisition 30, 54, 256
longitudinal data 63
longitudinal study 6, 7

Malay 181, 241
Mandarin 3, 9, 11, 12, 60, 159, 181, 201, 235–236
  as spoken in Taiwan 229
marriages, cross-cultural 1, 64
Mauritian Creole 33
Mean Length of Utterance (MLU) 40, 73–76
  differentials 76–81, 150
metalinguistic awareness 4, 230
methodological issues 260
methods
  diary 59–61, 260
  experimental 58, 62
Min dialects 10–11, 64, 183, 215
  Southern Min, Taiwanese 229
mixed households 52
mixed language 52
mixed utterances 43
morphological tier 71
morphological types 73
morphological typology 79
morphosyntactic development 27
Multi-Word or Multi-morpheme Utterances 73
multiple wh-questions, see wh-questions

negotiation 15
nominalizer 181–182
Noun Phrase Accessibility Hierarchy (NPAH) 156, 163, 171, 181, 186 n. 3
null arguments 10

null objects 16, 25, 28, 33, 36, 38, 75,
    133–153, 204, 210
  and language dominance 149–150
  in a monolingual child 139
  in adult Cantonese 134
  in verb particle construction 144
  rates of 143–144
null subjects 75, 152, 153, 153 n. 3,
    154 n. 6
null topics 36, 146, 148, 151, 152, 160

object fronting 15
Observer's Paradox 7
one as nominalizer 248–250
one parent – one language approach 6, 63–64,
    66, 258
ontogenetic grammaticalization 18
optional objects 136–139
over-generalization 191, 193
overlap, structural 39–40, 46–48, 121, 197,
    208, 218, 219, 261
  in surface structures 46–48

parameter settings 45, 63
parent-researcher 59, 72
parsing 157–158
passive 18–19, 232–233, 245
  give-passives 239–243, 245
passive familiarity, passive knowledge 10, 11,
    15, 64
permeability 12
permissive 18, 240, 243
persistence 234, 241, 253 n. 3
personality 65
Peter 220, 222
phonological reduction 240
phrasal verbs 145
pidgins 19
pidgin and creole linguistics 12
possessive noun phrases 111
postcode 68, 76
posture verbs 192, 193–194
poverty of the stimulus 31–32, 257
poverty of the dual stimulus 33, 256
prepositional phrases 16
  in bilingual children's Cantonese 190–199
  locative 191–192
prepositions 191, 247
present perfect 238
prestige 8, 11
processing 199, 261
  span 144
production data 59
proficiency 36
pronoun reversal 187 n. 9

prosody 66, 264
pseudo-passive 27

quantity of input 32, 37

reanalysis 241
register 158–159, 184
relative clauses 25, 155–185, 248–250, 261
  internally headed 160–161, 210
  postnominal 156, 170–174
  prenominal 7, 10, 155–159
  restrictive 163
relative pronouns 170, 183, 184
Relexification 12, 51, 233, 253 n. 1
resolution of non-target structures 150, 213
restructuring 8
resumptive pronouns 131 n. 34, 156, 167,
    170–174
right-dislocation 131 n. 28, 253 n. 7
root infinitives 39–40

sampling of child language 61–62
Sarah 128 n. 7
scope marker 110, 114, 116
second language 22–23
second language acquisition 12, 15, 18,
    23–24, 26–29, 51, 171, 189, 261
selection bias 61, 72
sentence final particles 75
sentence processing 24–25
serial verb constructions 14, 133, 191, 192,
    201–203, 212, 214, 246
siblings, source of input 65, 166
silent period 22, 81–82
simultaneous acquisition, simultaneous
  bilingual acquisition 25, 28, 60
Singapore 9, 10–11
Singapore Colloquial English 2, 9, 10, 13, 17,
    19, 50, 51–52, 123–125, 152, 181–183,
    235–236, 248–252, 262
  give-passives 243
sound change 8
Spanish 60
Specific Language Impairment (SLI) 49
Sranan 229
Sranan Tongo 53
stance 248–249
subject – auxiliary inversion
  in main clause 117–119
  in embedded clause 119
subjectivity 7
substrate features 17, 53, 124
substrate influence 17, 19, 51–52, 54, 113,
    123, 125–126, 181–183, 229, 252, 262
systemic 152, 235

substrate languages 13, 16
successive acquisition 25
Swedish 74, 83

Tagalog 11, 65
tagging 71
Taiwanese southern Min 229, 240
tense 129 n. 17, 227, 229, 238
Thai 214
third language 22
Tok Pisin 235
tone 66, 264
topic 27–28, 135, 149
topic chain construction 149
topic-prominence 135
topicalization 28, 121, 132 n. 35, 146, 204,
    210
transcription 68
transfer 3, 6, 8, 16, 26, 27–28, 37–44, 135,
    166, 258
  and language dominance 40
  bidirectional 189, 216–222
  conditions for 39–40
  direction(ality) of 2, 121–122, 185,
    189–190
  mechanisms of 19, 176
  of prenominal relative clauses 158,
    174–179
  syntactic 2, 17, 36, 40, 126, 146
transfer to somewhere 39
transferability 12
transparency, morphological 108, 113,
    259
typological characteristics
  of Cantonese 174
typological universals 186 n. 3
typology, areal 228

uneven development 58, 86 n. 13
Universal Grammar (UG) 5, 30, 186 n. 3, 215
unlearning 150–151
Upper Bound 73, 81
usage-based approaches 62

variables 58
variation, individual 245, 258
verb-particle constructions 25, 143–144,
    216–222
vulnerable domains 26, 49, 189–190, 210,
    216, 223, 258

weaker language 28–29, 73, 74, 83
wh-copying 115
wh-in-situ 9, 10, 13, 17, 87–88
  in bilingual children's English 94–104
  in Cantonese/Chinese 89
  in contact languages 123–126
  in English 90–92, 120–121
  in monolingual acquisition of English
    93–94, 96–98
  transfer of 119–122
wh-interrogatives 8, 87, 261
wh-movement 9, 87–89, 92, 103, 160
  and word order typology 122
  long-distance 58, 114, 131 n. 31
  optional 119, 124, 126
  partial 58, 114–116, 126
  transfer of 121, 122
wh-words, order of acquisition 104–106, 125
wh-questions 8, 25
  echo 121, 129 n. 16
  multiple 90, 113–114, 130 n. 27,
    131 n. 30
what questions, split 108–109
when questions 127 n. 2
where questions 109–111
whose questions 109, 111–112
why questions 112–113, 259
word divisions 74
word order 16, 29, 45, 189, 190
  canonical 181, 185
  changes in 200
  universals 199
word types 73

yes-no questions 11
Yue dialects 9

Author index

Aarts, Bas 136
Adone, Dany 33, 50, 215
Aikhenvald, Alexandra Y. 73, 190, 192, 234
Albom, Mitch 90
Alsagoff, Lubna 182, 248–249
Andersen, Roger W. 12, 39, 50
Ansaldo, Umberto 50, 228, 241, 248, 252
Aoun, Joseph 89
Ard, Josh 157, 171
Arends, Jacques 12, 18, 228
Artstein, Ron 90, 129 n.16

Backus, Ad 190
Baker, Carl Lee 30
Baker, Colin 36, 60
Bakker, Peter 52
Bao, Zhiming 13, 19, 136, 152, 235–236, 239, 242
Bates, Elizabeth 5, 23, 24
Bauer, Robert 9, 34
Bellugi, Ursula 118, 129 n.11
Benedict, Paul 34
Bernardini, Petra 28, 29, 49, 55 n.4, 58, 73–74, 76, 82, 86 n.13
Bever, Thomas G. 181
Bhatia, Tej K.
Bialystok, Ellen 4, 60
Bickerton, Derek 12, 50–51, 53, 55 n.7
Bley-Vroman, Robert 59
Bloom, Lois 63, 105, 145, 220, 222
Bloomfield, Leonard 5
Bosch, Laura 32, 34, 55 n.2
Bowerman, Melissa 30
Brandt, Silke 163, 169
Braunwald, Susan R. 59
Brislin, R. W. 59
Brown, Roger 63, 72, 93, 96–97, 128 n.5, 139, 220
Browning, Larry 201
Bruyn, Adrienne 18, 215, 229–230, 233–234

Cairns, Helen 62
Cenoz, Jasone 57
Chan, Angel Wing-Shan 202–204, 207, 209–210
Chan, Brian Hok-Shing 10, 83
Chan, Cecilia Yuet-Hung 160
Chang-Smith, Meiyun 3
Chao, Yuan-Ren 60, 201
Chappell, Hilary 186 n.2, 229
Chen, Ee-San 17
Cheng, Lisa L.S. 93
Cheng, Robert L. 229
Cheung, Hung-Nin Samuel 9
Cheung, Kwan Hin 9
Cheung Shuk-Yee Alice 105, 130 n.21, 130 n.22
Cheung Sik Lee 192
Chiat, Shula 43
Chiu, Bonnie 92, 115–116, 131 n.30
Chomsky, Noam 5, 30, 36
Clark, Eve 105
Clark, Herbert 105
Cole, Peter 93, 135, 169
Comrie, Bernard 156, 171, 176–178, 185
Corne, Chris 50, 252
Crago, Martha 264
Crain, Stephen 31, 58, 62, 109, 115, 131 n.32, 131 n.33, 155, 163
Crowther, Carrie 31
Culicover, Peter 24

Dahl, Östen 190, 228
Dasinger, Lisa 169
De Houwer, Annick 3, 7, 2–7, 34, 36–38, 57, 73, 258
de Villiers, Jill 91–92, 114
de Villiers, Peter 91
DeGraff, Michel 12, 50–51
Demuth, Katherine 127 n.1
den Besten, Hans 123
Denham, Kristen 93

Deuchar, Margaret 3, 7, 27, 36, 55 n.3, 57, 60–61, 72
Dier, John K. 126
Diessel, Holger 144, 163, 168–169, 220–221
Dixon, R. M. W. 73, 190
Döpke, Susanne 3, 37, 40, 73
Dryer, Matthew 157–158, 199

Elman, Jeffrey 24
Elster, Jon 13
Enfield, N. J. 228, 245, 252
Essegbey, James 214
Evans, Nicholas 233

Farkas, Igor 85 n.2
Fernald, Anne 55 n.2
Fernandez S.C. 35
Fillmore, Charles J. 137
Fodor, Janet Dean 31, 45–46, 48
Fodor, Jerry 32
Fong, Sandiway 181
Fong, Vivienne 124
Foster-Cohen, Susan, 29
Francis, Elaine 179, 191, 197
Fulmer, K. C. 4

Gass, Susan 157, 171
Gavruseva, Elena 109
Gawlitzek-Maiwald, Ira 16, 40, 42–43, 57, 113, 126
Gelman, Susan 91
Genesee, Fred 6, 28, 31–32, 34, 36–38, 42, 44, 57, 72, 175, 260, 264
Gibson, Edward 45, 181
Gil, David 182–183
Gisborne, Nikolas 184
Givón, Talmy 215
Gleitman, Lila R. 43
Goldberg, Adele 136–137
Goodz, Naomi 34
Gordon, Raymond G. 9
Grabois, Howard 4
Grammont, Maurice 21 n.7, 50
Greenberg, Joseph H. 118
Gries, Stefan Th. 220
Gropen, Jess 224 n.9
Grosjean, François 4, 29, 30, 143, 258, 264
Guéron, Jacqueline 128 n.3, 131 n.31
Gupta, Anthea Fraser 11, 13, 17, 118, 123–125, 181–182, 184, 252

Haegeman, Liliane 128 n.3, 131 n.31, 137
Håkansson Gisela 28
Hamburger, H. 155
Harrison, Godfrey 123–124
Haspelmath, Martin 215

Hawkins, John A. 122, 156–158, 171, 174, 185, 186 n.3, 188 n.13, 199, 226 n.21
Hawkins, Roger 160
Heine, Bernd 228, 230–236, 240–243, 248–249, 251–252, 253 n.2
Hermon, Gabriella 93, 135, 169
Ho Chee Lick 182, 248–249
Ho Mian-Lian 152, 235, 252
Ho, Samantha Shuk Kwan 145, 220, 222, 226 n.23
Hoff, Erika 55 n.2
Höhle, Barbara 43
Hoffman, Charlotte 3, 6
Holm, John 113
Hopper, Paul 233–234, 243, 253 n.3
Horie, Kaoru 248
Hornstein, Norbert 30
Hsiao, Franny 181
Huang, C.T. James 89, 131 n.28, 146, 153 n.1
Huang, Pai-Yuan Simon 86 n.11, 139–140, 153 n.3
Huang, Yue-Yuan 62
Hudelot, Christian 169
Hulk, Aafke 15, 37, 39–40, 46, 134, 147, 215, 218, 259
Hyams, Nina 151, 154 n.6
Hyltenstam, Kenneth 171

Ingham, Richard 138–139, 151, 154 n.5
Iwasaki, Shoichi 232, 241, 246

Jarvis, Scott 26
Jisa, Harriet 169

Keenan, Edward 156, 160, 171
Keesing, Roger M. 230
Kehoe, Margaret 35
Kern, Sophie 169
Killingley, Siew-Yue 215
Klee, Thomas 75, 85 n.10
Klima, Edward 118, 129 n.11
Kozinsky, Isaac 214
Krashen, Stephen D. 81
Kupisch, Tanja 40, 248
Kuteva, Tania 228, 230–236, 240–243, 251–252, 253 n.2
Kwan, Wing Man Stella 192, 197–198, 224 n.6
Kwan-Terry, Anna 11, 123, 127, 236–237

Labov, William 7
Lai, Regine Yee King 76, 83, 122, 143
Lakshmanan, Usha 36, 81
Lam, Victoria Yuk Ping 35
Lambrecht, Knud 169
Lanvers, Ursula 35

Lanza, Elizabeth 3, 7, 8, 21 n.7, 37, 57, 73, 82, 264
Lass, Roger 17
Lau, Elaine 181
Law, Sam Po 197, 209
Lee, Hun-Tak Thomas 63, 71, 105, 193, 195, 207, 209
Lee, Sherman 4, 10
Lefebvre, Claire 51–53, 233–234, 241, 253 n.1
Leopold, Werner 3, 6, 59
Leung, Ingrid Yan-Kit 95
Leung, Man Tak 197, 209
Leung, Shuk Ching Fiona 194, 196, 224 n.4
Li, Audrey Y. H. 89
Li, Charles 226 n.19
Li, David C. S. 10
Li, Michelle Kin-Ling 125
Li, Ping 9, 85 n.2
Li, Wei 4
Light, Timothy 60
Lightfoot, David 13, 30–32, 63
Lillo-Martin, Diane 163
Lim, Lisa 132 n.36
Lim, Soo Lin 123–124
Lin, Charles 181
Liu, Danqing 214
Lleó, Conxita 35
Lohse, Barbara 219
Lord, Carol 232, 246

MacWhinney, Brian 2, 5, 20 n.4, 24, 34, 63, 91, 220, 260–261
Major, Roy 27
Man, Yuk Hing Patricia 154 n.8
Maratsos, Michael 61
Marcus, Gary 31
Maslen, Robert 61, 163
Matthews, Stephen 8–9, 14, 34–35, 37, 40, 42, 44, 50, 62, 71–72, 74, 79, 86 n.11, 89, 94–95, 112, 120, 125, 128 n.9, 130 n.26, 131 n.28, 133–135, 140, 145, 147, 153 n.1, 156, 158–159, 161, 163, 170, 179–180, 183–184, 186 n.1, 186 n.3, 187 n.8, 190–191, 210, 214, 216, 224 n.1, 224 n.2, 225 n.10, 226 n.19, 232, 240–241, 246, 248, 252, 254 n.8
Maxfield, Thomas L. 92, 115–116, 131 n.30
McBride-Chang, Catherine 21 n.11
McCardle, Peggy 55
McCarthy, John 30
McDaniel, Dana 62, 92, 114–116, 131 n.30, 174
McKee, Cecile 62, 174
McLaughlin, Barry 25
McWhorter, John H. 33, 50
Meisel, Jürgen 3, 28, 34, 37, 43, 45,
Menn, Lise 62

Merkin, Susan 105
Mervis, Carolyn B. 59
Michaelis, Susanne 215
Montrul, Silvina 12
Mufwene, Salikoko S. 8, 16, 20, 50, 52–53, 229, 232, 240, 252
Müller, Natascha 16, 37–41, 46, 48–49, 58, 134, 147, 218, 259
Muntz, Rachel 36, 72
Muysken, Pieter 12, 18, 113, 215, 228

Nettle, Daniel 8, 19
Newbrook, Mark 184
Newmeyer, Frederick J. 253 n.4
Nicoladis, Elena 4, 28, 34, 36–37, 57, 72, 264
Noji, Junya 60, 260

O'Grady, William 24, 95, 105, 118, 121, 129 n.17
Oller, D.K. 35
Ozeki, Hiromi 60

Pacioni, Patricia 130 n.26
Packard, Jerome 73
Pallotti, Gabriele 21 n.8
Paradis, Johanne 6, 28, 31–32, 34–38, 42, 44, 57, 72, 175, 264
Pavlenko, Aneta 26
Pavlovitch, Ivan 3
Pearson, B. 35
Peng, Linda Ling-Ling 86 n.11, 95–97
Pérez-Leroux, Ana 157, 171
Perfetti, Charles 21 n.11
Peters, Stanley 30
Petersen, Jennifer 36, 82
Pietroski Paul 31
Pinker, Steven 5, 42, 201–202
Plag, Ingo 50, 229
Platt, David 57, 152, 235, 252
Platzack, Christer 49
Plunkett, Kim 24
Polinsky, Maria 214
Pollock, Karen 4
Poulin-Dubois, Dianne 34
Price, Johanna 4
Prys Jones, Sylvia 36
Pullum, Geoffrey K. 31

Quay, Suzanne 3, 7, 27, 55 n.3, 57, 60–61
Quirk, Randolph 90

Radford, Andrew 94, 128 n.5, 128 n.8, 129 n.11
Ratner, Nan B. 62
Reinecke, John E.13
Rispoli, Matthew 138, 154 n.4, 154 n.10

Roberts, Jenny 4
Roberts, Sarah Julianne 14, 53
Roeper, Thomas 21 n.9, 92, 151
Romaine, Suzanne 12–13, 19, 35–36, 52, 227
Ronjat, Jules 3, 6, 21 n.7
Rutherford, William 44

Sabbagh, Mark 91
Sánchez, Liliana 12
Satterfield, Teresa 53, 55 n.7
Saunders, George 40, 73
Sawyer, Joan 219, 226 n.22
Schlyter, Suzanne 28–29, 55 n.4, 58, 73–74,
   76, 83, 86 n.13
Schmitt, Elena 27
Scholz, Barbara C. 31
Schulz, Barbara 116
Schumann, John H. 12
Schwartz, Bonnie 23, 26
Searchinger, Gene 131 n.30
Sebastián-Gallés, Núria 32, 34
Sebba, Mark 19
Seliger, Herbert W. 27
Selinker, Larry 18, 81
Sgall, Petr 85 n.9
Shi, Dingxu 149
Shin, Sarah 4
Shirai, Yasuhiro 60
Siegel, Jeff 14
Silva-Corvalán, Carmen 16
Smith, Geoff P. 125
Smith, Madorah E. 3, 21 n.6, 59–60
Smith, Norval 12, 18, 228
Snedeker, Jesse 174
Snow, Don 9
Sprouse, Rex 26
Stahl, Daniel 61, 163, 260
Stern, Clara and William 59
Stromswold, Karin 59, 92, 94, 109, 118,
   128 n.3, 128 n.5,
Sung, Li May 135
Swain, Merrill 73

Taeschner, Traute 3, 33
Tager-Flusberg, Helen 177
Tai, James H.Y. 192
Tan, Hwee Hwee 249
Tan Li-Hai 21 n.11
Tang, Sze-Wing 68, 71, 201, 214, 224 n.8
Tavakolian, Susan 180
Terrell, Tracy D. 81
Thomason, Sarah Grey 14, 15, 16, 23, 50, 190,
   200, 228
Thompson, Sandra 226 n.19
Thornton, Rosalind 58, 62, 109, 115, 131
   n.32, 131 n.33, 156

Tjung, Yassir Nassanius 169
Tomasello, Michael 24, 61–62, 144, 163,
   168–169, 220–221, 260
Toupin, Cecile 169
Toribio, Almeida J. 12
Tracy, Rosemary 16, 40, 42–43, 57, 113, 126
Trask, Larry 228
Traugott, Elizabeth 234, 243
Tsao, Feng-Fu 240

Unsworth, Sharon 39–40

Vago, Robert M. 27
Vainikka, Anne 92
van der Linden, Elizabeth 15, 40, 215
Veenstra, Tonjes 11, 123
Verrips, Maaike 215
Vihman, Marilyn M. 3, 55 n.2
Volterra, Virginia 33

Waas, Margit 27
Wang, Qi 154 n.6
Wasow, Tom
Weber Heidi 152
Wee, Lionel 13, 19, 242, 248
Weikum, Whitney 32, 55 n.2
Weinreich, Uriel 12, 39, 229
Weissenborn, Jürgen 43
Wekker, Herman 50
Werker, Janet 32, 55 n.2
Wesche, M. 73
Wexler, Kenneth 24, 45, 154 n.6
Wilkins, David 233
Winford, Donald 51, 228
Wong, Colleen 71
Wong, Kwok-Shing 59, 245
Wootten, Janet 105

Xu, Huiling 232, 240–241

Yap, Foong-Ha 232, 241, 246, 248
Yeung, Louisa Y.Y. 158
Yip, Virginia 8–9, 25, 27, 30, 34–35, 37, 40,
   42, 44, 62, 71–72, 74, 79, 86 n.11, 89,
   94–95, 112, 120, 128 n.9, 131 n.28,
   133–135, 140, 145–147, 153, 153 n.1,
   156, 159, 161, 163, 170, 180, 183–184,
   186 n.1, 186 n.3, 187 n.8, 190, 210, 216,
   224 n.1, 224 n.2, 226 n.19, 232, 240–241
Yiu, Sze-Man Emily 81, 83
Yoshida Katherine 32, 55 n.2
Yuan, Boping 146, 153
Yue-Hashimoto, Anne 254 n.8

Zentella, Ana Celia 30
Ziegeler, Debra 245, 253 n.3